Introductory Readings in Government and Politics

Third Edition

Introductory Readings in Government and Politics

Third Edition

Mark O. Dickerson
Thomas Flanagan
Neil Nevitte
UNIVERSITY OF CALGARY

Nelson Canada

©Nelson Canada,
A Division of Thomson Canada Limited, 1991
1120 Birchmount Road
Scarborough, Ontario
M1K 5G4

Canadian Cataloguing in Publication Data

Introductory readings in government and politics

3rd ed.
Includes bibliographical references.
ISBN 0-17-603529-x

1. Comparative government.   2. Political science.
3. Canada — Politics and government.   I. Dickerson, M.O., 1934-
II. Flanagan, Thomas, 1944-   III. Nevitte, Neil.

JC131.I57   320.3   C91-093066-x

Publisher Ric Kitowski
Acquisitions Editor Dave Ward
Manager, Editorial Services Jean Lancee
Editor Nicole Gnutzman
Art Director Lorraine Tuson
Cover Design Janet Riopelle
Text Design Beth Haliburton

Printed and bound in Canada
   4 5 6   WC   94 93

The pages in this book open easily and lie flat, a result of the Otabind book-
binding process. Otabind combines advanced adhesive technology and a free-
floating cover to achieve books that last longer and are bound to stay open.

Contents

v

Preface

This reader is designed for use in introductory political science courses in Canada with the purpose of complementing general first-year political science texts. Often, introductory texts pass quickly over important ideas that can be a useful focus of discussion. This reader provides some illustrative material upon which those discussions may be based. It also addresses another concern. Canadian students confronting important political ideas for the first time typically find little reference or application to the Canadian context. As a result, the ideas may appear to be disembodied from Canadian politics, or students may be left to make the connections themselves. While this reader is in no measure a substitute for specific courses in Canadian politics, it does contain some selections which are explicitly relevant to Canadians.

The material is organized into four sections: *Basic Concepts, Ideology, Forms of Government*, and *The Political Process*. This mirrors the structure of Mark O. Dickerson and Thomas Flanagan's *An Introduction to Government and Politics*, third edition (Toronto: Nelson Canada, 1990), and instructors using that text may find this book especially useful.

Each of the four sections has a brief introduction that explains how the readings in that section are related to each other and to the overall topic. This introduction may aid instructors in deciding which readings to assign in their courses. Each selection also has a short introductory note to provide contextual information and to highlight the gist of the reading. Students may find these notes helpful in approaching unfamiliar texts. Full bibliographical information is provided in the acknowledgments section for those students who wish to consult the original source material.

Those who have used earlier editions of this book will recognize that we have added some new readings and cut some others more heavily than before. In teaching from the book, many instructors have found that students with limited background sometimes have difficulty in working their way through a richly illustrated argument. We hope that shortening some of these texts will make their central argument more evident to beginning students.

Several principles have guided our selection. None of the pieces demands technical background that cannot readily be explained to first-year students. However, some are more intellectually challenging than others, so instructors can choose from a spectrum of complexity. About a third of the material deals with Canada, enough to give a Canadian flavour to an introductory course without turning it into a study of Canadian politics. We have made a special effort to include selections from well-known authors whose names should become familiar to political science students (e.g., Hobbes, Madison, Renan, Morgenthau, Mill). The readings cover a broad range of topics within the discipline while not pretending to touch upon everything, which would be impossible even in a volume many times this size. By using several criteria for selection, we hope to have produced a flexible collection to serve multiple purposes at the introductory level.

This third edition of the reader drops eight selections from the second edition and adds twelve new ones. As the changes are distributed throughout the book, they do not greatly affect the overall configuration. This ongoing revision is partly a matter of keeping up with the march of world affairs and with developments in the discipline, and partly our continuing attempt to find important readings that "work" at the introductory level. As always, we would welcome any suggestions from the instructors and students who use this book in their courses.

Part I
Basic Concepts

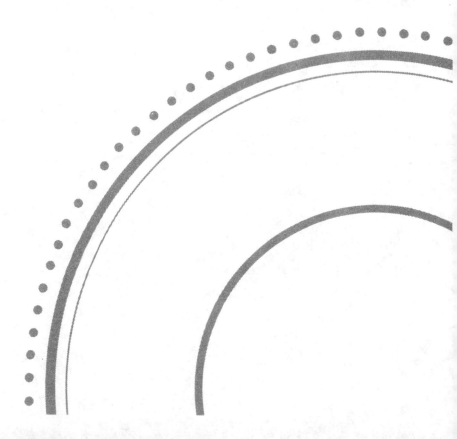

Introduction

Part I contains seven readings on some of the most fundamental problems of political science: politics, authority, sovereignty, state and nation, the rule of law, and the relationship between states in the international arena. Our working assumption is that students should "begin at the beginning," that is, come to grips with basic phenomena of politics that recur in political situations all over the world and throughout history.

We agree with Hans J. Morgenthau in Reading 7 that power is the currency of politics, and that there is a distinct science, political science, that specializes in the study of power. But power is not just simple domination; it also demands accommodation and conciliation, as Bernard Crick shows in Reading 1. And even if, following the teaching of Thomas Hobbes (Reading 3), power is centralized in sovereign authority, it can be bound by the rule of law as interpreted by impartial courts (Reading 6). Moreover, there must be some sort of community in which power is rooted, which in the modern world is most often the nation (Readings 4 and 5). As the example of Louis Riel shows (Reading 2), personal charisma is not an enduring source of either community or power. Thus, although these readings focus on different concepts, certain themes run through them: the inherent limitations of coercion, the necessity of legitimacy to sustain power, and the tension between reason and passion in the statesmanlike exercise of power.

1   Politics

One of the most famous quotations in political science is Aristotle's state-ment in the *Politics* that "man is by nature a political animal." As Aristotle took pains to point out, this means that human beings are a gregarious species like bees or monkeys. We not only live together socially; our capacity to reason expressed in speech allows, indeed compels, us to deliberate to-gether about the ends and means of this common existence. To be political is to participate in these discussions about collective action.

The British political scientist Bernard Crick further extends the implica-tions of the Aristotelian view of politics. Discussion and deliberation imply respect for differences between individuals and groups; otherwise there would be nothing to discuss. Politics as expounded by Crick in Reading 1 is intrinsically pluralistic. It is the art of accommodating different interests within the framework of a single community. It is an alternative to the monolithic enforcement by one group of its view or way of life upon other groups. It is, as Crick says, the recognition that a healthy community depends upon the "harmony" of many interests rather than an artificial or imposed "unity" that ignores the diversity of society. Crick's view of politics as the art of reconcil-ing opposed interests is admittedly narrower than many current definitions of politics, which emphasize conflict, not accommodation. But even if not all scholars want to adopt Crick's language, we include Reading 1 because it expresses a wide consensus about what politics can be at its best. That the best is not always achieved, and that the spirit of conciliation is sometimes replaced by unilateral dominance, does not make it any less worth striving for.

Bernard Crick is a professor of politics at the University of London. He has written numerous books on British and American politics, including a biography of George Orwell. Like Orwell, Crick is a social democrat who has strongly criticized the totalitarian aspects of some forms of socialism. This selection is from the second edition of his book *In Defence of Politics*.

● ● ● ● ● ● ● ● ● ●

Who has not often felt the distaste with democratic politics which Salazar expressed when he said that he "detested politics from the bottom of his heart; all those noisy and incoherent promises, the

impossible demands, the hotchpotch of unfounded ideas and imprac-
tical plans . . . opportunism that cares neither for truth nor justice, the
inglorious chase after unmerited fame, the unleashing of uncontrollable passions, the exploitation of the lowest instincts, the distortion of
facts . . . all that feverish and sterile fuss"?

From a leading article in
The Times, 16 November, 1961

Boredom with established truths is a great enemy of free men. So there is
some excuse in troubled times not to be clever and inventive in redefining
things, or to pretend to academic unconcern or scientific detachment, but
simply to try to make some old platitudes pregnant. This essay simply seeks
to help in the task of restoring confidence in the virtues of politics as a great
and civilising human activity. Politics, like Antaeus in the Greek myth, can
remain perpetually young, strong and lively so long as it can keep its feet
firmly on the ground of Mother Earth. We live in a human condition, so we
cannot through politics grasp for an absolute ideal, as Plato taught with
bewitching single-mindedness. But the surface of the earth varies greatly,
and being human we are restless and have many different ideals and are
forced to plan for the future as well as enjoy the fruits of the past, so equally
politics cannot be a "purely practical and immediate" activity, as those who
cannot see beyond the end of their own noses praise themselves by
claiming.

Politics is too often regarded as a poor relation, inherently dependent
and subsidiary; it is rarely praised as something with a life and character of
its own. Politics is not religion, ethics, law, science, history or economics; it
neither solves everything, nor is it present everywhere; and it is not any one
political doctrine, such as conservatism, liberalism, socialism, communism
or nationalism, though it can contain elements of most of these things.
Politics is politics, to be valued as itself, not because it is "like" or "really is"
something else more respectable or peculiar. Politics is politics. The person
who wishes not to be troubled by politics and to be left alone finds himself
the unwitting ally of those to whom politics is a troublesome obstacle to
their well-meant intentions to leave nothing alone.

To some this may seem very obvious. But then there will be no harm in
reminding them how few they are. All over the world there are men
aspiring to power and there are actual rulers who, however many different
names they go by, have in common a rejection of politics. Many Frenchmen
in 1958, warm defenders of the Republic, argued that General de Gaulle
was saving the French nation from the politicians; in 1961 an army rebellion
broke out in Algeria in which the same General was then accused of seeking
a "purely political solution" to the Algerian problem, and the rebel Gener-

als went on to deny that they themselves had any "political ambitions."
Fidel Castro tells a reporter: "We are not politicians. We made our revolution to get the politicians out. We are social people. This is a social revolution." In so many places the cry has gone up that *the* party or *the* leader is
defending *the* people against the politicians. "Politics, ill understood, have
been defined," wrote Isaac D'Israeli, "as 'the art of governing mankind by
deceiving them.' " Many people, of course, even in régimes which are
clearly political, think that they are not interested in politics, and even act as
if they are not; but they are probably few compared to the many who think
that politics is muddled, contradictory, self-defeatingly recurrent, un-pro-
gressive, un-patriotic, inefficient, mere compromise, or even a sham or
conspiracy by which political parties seek to preserve some particular and
peculiar social systems against the challenge of the inevitable future, etc.
The anti-political are very right to think that politics is an achievement far
more limited in time and place than politically-minded men, or men who
practise this odd thing politics, normally presume.

Many politicians, publicists and scholars in Western cultures are apt to
leap to the defence, or the propagandising, of words like "liberty," "democracy," "free-government," and then to be puzzled and distraught when,
even if their voices are heard at all elsewhere, they are only answered by
proud and sincere assurances that indeed all these good things exist and are
honoured in styles of government as different as my Soviet Union, my
China, my Spain, my Egypt, my Cuba, my Ghana, my Northern Ireland or
my South Africa. Even if precise meanings can be attached to these words,
they are too important as symbols of prestige to be readily conceded.
Publicists would perhaps do better simply to defend the activity of politics
itself. For it is a very much more precise thing than is commonly supposed;
it is essential to genuine freedom; it is unknown in any but advanced and
complex societies; and it has specific origins only found in European
experience. It is something to be valued almost as a pearl beyond price in
the history of the human condition, though, in fact, to overvalue it can be to
destroy it utterly.

Perhaps there is something to be said for writing in praise of an activity
which seems so general that few people can feel any great passion to
appropriate it, or to nationalise it, as the exclusive property of any one
group of men or of any particular programme of government.

It is Aristotle who first states what should be recognised as the fundamental, elementary proposition of any possible political science. He is, as it
were, the anthropologist who first characterises and distinguishes what still
appears to be a unique invention or discovery of the Greek world. At one
point in the second book of his *Politics*, where he examines and criticises
schemes for ideal states, he says that Plato in his *Republic* makes the

mistake of trying to reduce everything in the *polis* (or the political type of state) to a unity; rather it is the case that: "there is a point at which a *polis*, by advancing in unity, will cease to be a *polis*: there is another point, short of that, at which it may still remain a *polis*, but will none the less come near to losing its essence, and will thus be a worse *polis*. It is as if you were to turn harmony into mere unison, or to reduce a theme to a single beat. The truth is that the *polis* is an aggregate of many members." Politics arises then, according to great Aristotle, in organised states which recognise themselves to be an aggregate of many members, not a single tribe, religion, interest or tradition. Politics arises from accepting the fact of the simultaneous existence of different groups, hence different interests and different traditions, within a territorial unit under a common rule. It does not matter much how that unit came to be—by custom, conquest or geographical circumstance. What does matter is that its social structure, unlike some primitive societies, is sufficiently complex and divided to make politics a plausible response to the problem of governing it, the problem of maintaining order at all. But the establishing of political order is not just any order at all; it marks the birth, or the recognition, of freedom. For politics represents at least some tolerance of differing truths, some recognition that government is possible, indeed best conducted, amid the open canvassing of rival interests. Politics are the public actions of free men. Freedom is the privacy of men from public actions.

Common usage of the word might encourage one to think that politics is a real force in every organised state. But a moment's reflection should reveal that this common usage can be highly misleading. For politics, as Aristotle points out, is only one possible solution to the problem of order. It is by no means the most usual. Tyranny is the most obvious alternative—the rule of one strong man in his own interest; and oligarchy is the next most obvious alternative—the rule of one group in their own interest. The method of rule of the tyrant and the oligarch is quite simply to clobber, coerce or overawe all or most of these other groups in the interest of their own. The political method of rule is to listen to these other groups so as to conciliate them as far as possible, and to give them a legal position, a sense of security, some clear and reasonably safe means of articulation, by which these other groups can and will speak freely. Ideally politics draws all these groups into each other so that they each and together can make a positive contribution towards the general business of government, the maintaining of order. The different ways in which this can be done are obviously many, even in any one particular circumstance of competing social interests; and in view of the many different states and changes of circumstances there have been, are and will be, possible variations on the theme of political rule appear to be infinite. But, however imperfectly this process of deliberate conciliation works, it is nevertheless radically different from tyranny, oligarchy, kingship, dictatorship, despotism and—what is probably the only distinctively modern type of rule—totalitarianism.

Certainly it may sometimes seem odd, in light of common usage, to say that there is no politics in totalitarian or tyrannical régimes. To some it would be clearer to assert that while there is plainly some politics in all systems of government, yet some systems of government are themselves political systems: they function by or for politics. But usage does not destroy real distinctions. And this distinction has a great tradition behind it. When Chief Justice Fortescue in the mid-fifteenth century said that England was both *regimen politicum et regale*, he meant that while the King could declare law only by the consultation and consent of Parliament, yet he was absolute in power to enforce the law and to defend the realm. But a régime purely *regale* or royal would not be *politicum* at all. In the early modern period "polity" or "mixed government," that is the Aristotelian blending of the aristocratic with democratic principle, were terms commonly used in contrast both to tyranny or despotism and to "democracy"—even when democracy was just a speculative fear, or a theoretical extension of what might happen if all men acted like the Anabaptists or the Levellers. In the eighteenth century in England "politics" was commonly contrasted to the principle of "establishment." Politicians were people who challenged the established order of Crown, Court and Church; and they challenged it in a peculiar way, not by the Palace intrigues of despotism, but by trying to create clear issues of policy *and* by making them public. Politicians were people, whether high-minded like Pitt the Elder or low-minded like Jack Wilkes, who tried to assert the power of "the public" or "the people" (in reality, of course, always publics and peoples) against what Dr. Johnson called "the powers by law established." The term was pejorative. The Tory squires called the Whig magnates "politicians" because they enlisted the help of people like Wilkes; and the "big Whigs" themselves regarded people like Wilkes as politicians because he made use of "the mob," or rather the skilled urban workers. So being political in fact usually meant recognising a wider "constituency" than did the powers-that-be of the moment, a constituency which it was felt necessary to consult if government was to be effectively conducted, not in the past but in the present which was the emerging future.

So in trying to understand the many forms of government that there are, of which political rule is only one, it is particularly easy to mistake rhetoric for theory. To say that all governing involves politics is either rhetoric or muddle. Why call, for instance, a struggle for power "politics" when it is simply a struggle for power? Two or more factions within a single party; or the clients of two great men, struggle for a monopoly of power:

there may be no political or constitutional procedures whatever to contain this struggle, or powerful enough to do so, and the contestants will regard any compromise as a pure tactic or breathing-space on the way to the complete victory of one faction and the suppression of the other. Certainly there is a sense in which, even in a tyranny or totalitarian régime, politics exists up to the moment when the ruler finds himself free to act alone. While he is not free to act alone, while he is forced to consult other people whom he regards as his enemies, either through necessity or through a temporary ignorance of their real power, he is in some kind of a political relationship. But it is essentially fragile and unwanted. The ruler will not, nor may anyone else, regard it as normal, even if it could be shown that it is perennial. Politics is then regarded simply as an obstacle—and, in a sense, it is an obstacle, but it may not be an at all secure or effective one. Some politics may exist in un-free régimes, but it is unwanted—a measure to their rulers of inadequate progress towards unity; and every effort will be made to keep such disputes from the ruled, to prevent the formation of a "public." For Palace politics is private politics, almost a contradiction of terms. The unique character of political activity lies, quite literally, in its publicity.

There is no need, then, to deny that elements of politics can exist in tyrannical and other régimes—rather the contrary. Sophocles makes this point in the *Antigone*:

CREON   Then she is not breaking the law?
HAEMON   Your fellow-citizens would deny it, to a man.
CREON   And the *polis* proposes to teach me how to rule?
HAEMON   Ah. Who is it that's talking like a boy now?
CREON   Can any voice but mine give orders in this *polis*?
HAEMON   It is no *polis* if it takes orders from one voice.
CREON   But custom gives possession to the ruler.
HAEMON   You'd rule a desert beautifully alone.

Suppose I had made my point less strongly by rendering *polis* as simply "city"; we would still see a word being contested for by two different theories of government—call it "civil society" or "political society." Both claim that their theory is inherent in the concept—the primacy of autocracy or citizenship respectively. And which is the more realistic? The great hope for the political way of Haemon is that it is, in the long run, a more workable way of maintaining order than the one Creon chose or stuck to. Politics thus arises from a recognition of restraints. The character of this recognition may be moral, but more often it is simply prudential, a recognition of the power of social groups and interests, a product of being unable, without more violence and risk than one can stomach, to rule alone. (An anti-political moral heroine like Antigone may arouse the city, but it is the power of the city that counts. Creon is a bad man to refuse to let her bury her rebel brother, but he is a bad ruler because he does not allow for the power of the city on this issue.) It is, of course, often possible to rule alone. But it is always highly difficult and highly dangerous. "To make a desert and to call it peace" is not impossible, nor is it uncommon. But fortunately most ordinary politicians realise the incalculability of violence, and do not always need to wreck the State in learning this lesson.

Politics, then, can be simply defined as the activity by which differing interests within a given unit of rule are conciliated by giving them a share in power in proportion to their importance to the welfare and the survival of the whole community. And, to complete the formal definition, a political system is that type of government where politics proves successful in ensuring reasonable stability and order. Aristotle attempted to argue that these compromises of politics must in some sense be creative of future benefits—that each exists for a further purpose. But it is probably wiser to keep what we want to defend as simple as possible and simply to point out that no finality is implied in any act of conciliation or compromise. Each compromise has at least served some purpose, teleological or not, if at the time it is made it enables orderly government to be carried on at all. Orderly government is, after all, a civilised value compared to anarchy or arbitrary rule; and political government, other things being equal, clearly remains more acceptable to more people if they are ever given any chance or choice in the matter. Advocates of particular political doctrines—as will be seen—should beware of denying the context in which their doctrines can operate politically: their claims can never be exclusive. The political process is not tied to any particular doctrine. Genuine political doctrines, rather, are the attempt to find particular and workable solutions to this perpetual and shifty problem of conciliation. . . .

Politics, then, to Aristotle, was something natural, not of divine origin, simply the "master-science" among men. Politics was the master-science not in the sense that it includes or explains all other "sciences" (all skills, social activities and group interests), but in that it gives them some priority, some order in their rival claims on the always scarce resources of any given community. The way of establishing these priorities is by allowing the right institutions to develop by which the various "sciences" can demonstrate their actual importance in the common task of survival. Politics are, as it were, the market place and the price mechanism of all social demands— though there is no guarantee that a just price will be struck: and there is nothing spontaneous about politics—it depends on deliberate and continuous individual activity.

Now it is often thought that for this "master-science" to function, there must be already in existence some shared idea of a "common good," some "consensus" or *consensus juris*. But this common good is itself the process of practical reconciliation of the interests of the various "sciences," aggregates or groups which compose a state; it is not some external and intangible spiritual adhesive, or some allegedly objective "general will" or public interest. These are misleading and pretentious explanations of how a community holds together; worse, they can even be justifications for the sudden destruction of some elements in the community in favour of others—there is no right to obstruct the general will, it is said. But diverse groups hold together, firstly, because they have a common interest in sheer survival and, secondly, because they practise politics—not because they agree about "fundamentals," or some such concept too vague, too personal, or too divine ever to do the job of politics for it. The moral consensus of a free state is not something mysteriously prior to or above politics: it is the activity (the civilising activity) of politics itself.

Now, of course, our aspirations and actions will be sadly disembodied spirits if they cannot go beyond a mere appreciation of what politics is all about. We shall all want to do something with it. Those who sit tight and drift, murmuring incantations which did not wreck us yesterday, are apt to be cast away on hostile shores. Those who urge us to remember that our only clearly demonstrable task is simply to keep the ship afloat have a rather curious view of the purpose of ships. Even if there is no single predetermined port of destination, clearly all directions are still not equally preferable. "What politics is" does not destroy or exhaust the question "What do we want to get out of it?" But we may not go about trying to get what we want in a political manner at all.

For politics is to be seen neither as a set of fixed principles to be realised in the near future, nor yet as a set of traditional habits to be preserved, but as an activity, a sociological activity which has the anthropological function of preserving a community grown too complicated for either tradition alone or pure arbitrary rule to preserve it without the undue use of coercion. Burke's aphorism about the need to reform in order to preserve is a characterisation of the political method of rule far more profound than that of those conservatives who hold that politics is simply a communication received from tradition.

Politics is, then, an *activity*—and this platitude must be brought to life: it is not a thing, like a natural object or a work of art, which could exist if individuals did not continue to act upon it. And it is a *complex activity*: it is not simply the grasping for an ideal, for then the ideals of others may be threatened; but it is not pure self-interest either, simply because the more realistically one construes self-interest the more one is involved in relationships with others, and because, after all, some men in most part, most men in some part, have certain standards of conduct which do not always fit circumstances too exactly. The more one is involved in relationships with others, the more conflicts of interest, or of character and circumstance, will arise. These conflicts, when personal, create the activity we call "ethics" (or else that type of action, as arbitrary as it is irresponsible, called "selfish"); and such conflicts, when public, create political activity (or else some type of rule in the selfish interest of a single group).

Consider another human *activity*, almost as famous as politics—something which is again, neither an implementation of principles nor a matter of pure expediency: sexuality. They are both activities in which the tacit understanding of presuppositions often makes more formal propositions unnecessary; the sympathies that are a product of experience are better than the doctrines that are learnt from books. Sexuality, granted, is a more wide-spread activity than politics, but again the suspicion remains that the man who can live without either is either acting the beast or aping the god. Both have much the same character of necessity in essence and unpredictability in form. Both are activities which must be carried on if the community is to perpetuate itself at all, both serve this wider purpose, and yet both can become enjoyable ends in themselves for any one individual. Both activities can be repeated in an almost infinite variety of forms and different circumstances; and yet in both, the activity often becomes attached to a quite arbitrary or fortuitous individual instance, which we then proceed to treat as if that he or she, or Fatherland or Motherland, were the most perfect example ever found of the whole great enterprise. And both are activities in which the range of possible conduct is far greater than any conceivably desirable range of actual conduct. Both are activities in which the human group maintains itself amid the utmost variations in, for the actors involved, success and failure, tragedy and joy, passion and prudence, and in those dialectic syntheses more often domestic and familiar. Politics, then, like sexuality is an activity which must be carried on; one does not create it or decide to join in—one simply becomes more and more aware that one is involved in it as part of the human condition. One can only forsake, renounce or do without it by doing oneself (which can easily be done—and on the highest principles) unnatural injury. To renounce or destroy politics is to destroy the very thing which gives order to the pluralism and variety of civilised society, the thing which enables us to enjoy variety without suffering either anarchy or the tyranny of single truths, which become the desperate salvation from anarchy—just as misogamy and celibacy are forms of salvation for the overly passionate mind.

For political rule must be preceded by public order just as love must be preceded by social acquaintance and contained by social conventions. Politics and love are the only forms of constraint possible between free people. Rule or government preserve and often even create communities.

"Electoral representation," "liberty," "rights" and even, or especially—as we will see, "democracy," are specific and subsequent achievements of a civilisation which has already established order and constraint in a known territory. Those who glibly say that all government is based on consent, as if that settles anything, are being as passionately vague as those who say, for instance, that all love must be based on the absolute freedom of partners in love. If there were absolute freedom, there could be no love; if there is absolute consent, there could be no government. But people have every right to say that all government is based on consent, and there may be no harm in their saying so, so long as the small word "all" is taken seriously. For this shows us that the assertion can have little to do with any possible distinction between freedom and oppression—the most absolute tyrant must have his faithful dogs around him.

And equally the word "government" must be taken seriously and recognised for what it is: the organisation of a group of men in a given community for survival. Thomas Hobbes, after all, spent a great deal of time arguing the massively simple point that if one does not survive, there is no knowing whether one has made the right choice. But there are good grounds for thinking that politics is often a more effective way of ensuring survival than the absolute rule of Leviathan. Whether Leviathan is a monarch, a dictator, a party or a "nation in arms," he is apt to be a pretty clumsy fellow who has few reliable ways of knowing what is really going on (representative electoral institutions, for instance, seem a fairly good way by which a government can find out what people will do and what they will stand for). But this ignorance on the part of autocracy only arises because one part of survival is a continuous process of adaptation to complicated social changes, economic and technological; this need to consult cannot eliminate the other type of survival which is military, or at least militant, the capacity to act without compromise or normal consultation in a state of emergency, whether flood, famine, pestilence or war itself. Leviathan must be there already—he cannot be created in a hurry, but he is the guarantor of politics, neither the single leader nor the negation. His authority, like that of the two Dictators of Republican Rome, ceases with the ends of the emergency. *Quis custodiet custodes?* Who, indeed, shall guard the guardians? There is, perhaps it should be simply said, no possible general answer to this question. History is rich with experiment and examples, some relatively successful, some complete failures. Only the problem is clear enough. As Lincoln put it amid the agony of Civil War: "It has long been a grave question whether any government not too strong for the liberties of its people, can be strong enough to maintain its liberties in great emergencies." . . .

If the argument is, then, that politics is simply the activity by which government is made possible when differing interests in an area to be governed grow powerful enough to need to be conciliated, the obvious objection will be: "why do certain interests have to be conciliated?" And the answer is, of course, that they do not have to be. Other paths are always open. Politics is simply when they are conciliated—that solution to the problem of order which chooses conciliation rather than violence and coercion, and chooses it as an effective way by which varying interests can discover that level of compromise best suited to their common interest in survival. Politics allows various types of power within a community to find some reasonable level of mutual tolerance and support. Coercion (or secession or migration) need arise only when one group or interest feels that it has no common interest in survival with the rest. Put at its most obvious, most men would simply agree that coercion needs justification: conciliation justifies itself if it works. There may not be any absolute justification of politics. Let us be brazen and simply say, "We prefer politics." But such modesty had better be somewhat truculent. For it is, after all, too hard (indeed perverse) to respect the morality and wisdom of any who, when politics is possible, refuse to act politically.

Political rule, then, because it arises from the problem of diversity, and does not try to reduce all things to a single unity, necessarily creates or allows some freedom. Political freedom is a response to a need of government—it is not, as so many sentimentally think, an external impetus that somehow forces, or persuades, governments to act tolerantly. The freedom of a group will be established at the moment when its power or its existence cannot be denied and must be reckoned with in governing a country as it actually is. The American Revolution took place, for instance, not because people suddenly became super-sensitive to their rights, or—an even more unlikely theory—because they suddenly became nationalistic, but because the existing government broke down. The British Government had failed to recognise the peculiar interests and the peculiar character of the colonies which it suddenly tried to govern, with the Stamp Act of 1765, after a long century of what Burke had called "wise and salutary neglect." And it failed to recognise their interests because they were not represented. If they were "virtually represented" in Parliament, this was in numbers so few compared to their real power and commercial importance that they were not taken seriously until too late, until they had been driven into revolutionary violence. Political representation is, then, a device of government before ever it can be sensibly viewed as a "right" of the governed. If it is not made use of, a government may not be able to govern at all—unless it is willing to practise coercion and to suffer fear to the degree that it is ignorant of the interests of the governed. Almost any system of representation, however ramshackle, incomplete and at times even corrupt, is better than none; and is better than one that will represent only an alleged single interest of the governed. The English Reform Bills of 1832 and 1867 did not take place because old Whig gentlemen in Westminster suddenly became convinced, out of some movement in abstract ideas, that those Radical fellows were morally right, but because it became increasingly clear that government could not be carried on in an industrialised society unless the power and existence first of the entrepreneur and then of the skilled manual worker were recognised and represented.

"Politics," then, simply summarises an activity whose history is a mixture of accident and deliberate achievement, and whose social basis is to be found only in quite complicated societies. It is not as such motivated by principle, except in a dislike of coercion which can, in turn, be simply thought to be a matter of prudence. (To debate too hotly the rival integrity of different motives which lead to the same action is academic—either political folly or the luxury of an already established political order.) Political principles are, whatever they are, principles held within politics. Now the holding of political principles or doctrines, at some level, with some degree of consistency, seems quite inevitable for any but the beast or the god—and why not? There is a touch of doctrinaire absurdity in those conservatives who would argue that all political doctrines become doctrinaire. A political doctrine is only doctrinaire, firstly, if it refuses to recognise the power and existence of other forces and ideas within an established political order; or, secondly—and more obviously, when it seeks to argue that some of these groups must be eliminated urgently, illegally and unpolitically if other great benefits are to follow. Political doctrines must, in fact, be genuinely political (Marxism, for instance, as we shall see, is clearly an anti-political doctrine).

A political doctrine I take to be simply a coherently related set of proposals for the conciliation of actual social demands in relation to a scarcity of resources. As such, a political doctrine should make short shrift with the old and barren academic controversy over "fact" and "value"—for it is necessarily both evaluative and predictive. For a political doctrine always offers some generalisations about the nature of actual, or possible, political societies, but it always also offers some grounds, however disputable, for thinking some such possibilities desirable. By prediction I do not mean something that is necessarily measurable as in natural science, but merely something that guides our present actions according to our expectations of what will happen in the future (or, of course, of what we shall find in the past). And it is evaluative not merely because all thought is an act of selection from a potentially infinite range of relevant factors, but because we do in fact seek to justify some act of selection as in some way significant.

A political doctrine will state some purpose, but it will claim to be a realisable purpose; or it may state some sociological generalisation. But argument, if not analysis, will always reveal some ethical significance in wanting this relationship to be true, or to remain true. A political doctrine is thus just an attempt to strike a particular harmony in an actual political situation, one harmony out of many possible different (temporary) resolutions of the basic problem of unity and diversity in a society with complex and entrenched rival social interests. This problem is the germ of politics and freedom.

Some freedom, at least, must exist wherever there is political rule. For politics is a process of discussion, and discussion demands, in the original Greek sense, dialectic. For discussion to be genuine and fruitful when something is maintained, the opposite or some contrary case must be considered or—better—maintained by someone who believes it. The hallmark of free government everywhere, it is an old but clear enough test, is whether public criticism is allowed in a manner conceivably effective—in other words, whether opposition is tolerated. Politics needs men who will act freely, but men cannot act freely without politics. Politics is a way of ruling divided societies without undue violence—and most societies are divided, though some think that that is the very trouble. We can do much worse than honour "mere politics" so we must examine very carefully the claims of those who would do better.

2 Charismatic Authority

The recurrent utopian dream of a community without relations of command and subordination has never come to pass. To be effective, power requires foci of concentration in persons whose word is accepted by others. Max Weber has explained that the three pillars of authority are tradition, rational agreement expressed in law, and "charisma," which is a personal claim to rule based upon divine authorization or upon some quasi-religious equivalent, such as historical destiny. Reading 2 presents a Canadian example of charismatic authority in the life of Louis Riel. He initially became the leader of the Métis through the rational-legal means of election and representation; but he later came to see himself as a divinely inspired prophet with the mission of leading the Métis to unprecedented greatness in the North-West. The story of Riel is a poignant reminder of how politics, often so prosaic, concerned chiefly with things like the gross national product and the rate of inflation, can suddenly become a vehicle of intense spiritual expression.

This article is a revised version of Thomas Flanagan's "The Religion of Louis Riel," which appeared in volume 4 of the *Quarterly of Canadian Studies for the Secondary School*. Although the article is not footnoted, it is based on study of primary sources. Documentation can be found in the same author's *Louis 'David' Riel: 'Prophet of the New World'* (Toronto: University of Toronto Press, 1979). Flanagan is a professor of political science at the University of Calgary.

• • • • • • • • • •

The life of Louis Riel is an outstanding example of charismatic authority of the religious type, in which a political figure bases his claim to leadership on personal authorization from God. More precisely, Riel did not begin his career as a charismatic leader; he became one as reverses in the political field drove him ever further towards mystical experiences of consolation and inspiration. This article provides a biographical sketch of Riel's transformation into a revolutionary prophet, followed by an analysis of the charismatic bonds existing between him and his Métis followers.

Born in 1844 in the Red River Colony, in what is now Greater Winnipeg, Riel was a Métis, one-eighth Indian, seven-eighths white. His language was Canadian French, his religion Roman Catholic. He received the rudiments of an education at St. Boniface until, at the age of fourteen, he was sent to Montreal to study at the seminary of the Sulpician Priests. A.-A. Taché, Bishop of St. Boniface, had noticed the boy's keen mind and devout piety, and hoping he would return as a missionary priest, the bishop arranged for his education. Riel studied at the seminary for six and a half years, but did not quite complete his course. He wished to marry and become a lawyer, but when those plans did not work out, he left Montreal, eventually returning to Red River. He came back penniless, indeed in debt, knowing a good deal of Latin and Greek, but having no immediate prospects for a successful career.

The Rebellion of 1869-70 showed Riel that his natural profession was politics. Let us digress a moment to recall the main details of this rising. The Hudson's Bay Company, owner of Rupert's Land, which included Red River, sold the vast lands to Canada in 1869. The inhabitants of Red River, a majority of whom were French half-breeds, were uneasy about the sale. They were afraid that union with Canada might disturb their land titles and might threaten their French language and Catholic faith. In the autumn of 1869, they refused to allow officers of the Canadian government to enter until Ottawa had consulted the inhabitants of the North-West about the terms of the transfer.

Louis Riel did not create this popular movement, but he quickly became the acknowledged leader. He skilfully guided it to a more or less successful conclusion. Most of the Métis claims were granted in the Manitoba Act of 1870. But in the process Riel's hands were stained with blood. In a moment of poor judgment, he had a man from Ontario named Thomas Scott executed. Scott had participated in an uprising against Riel's Provisional Government, had been taken prisoner, and became very difficult to control in custody. Riel decided to make an example of him.

This action, more than any other, determined the future course of Riel's life. It meant that, even after Manitoba entered Confederation in the summer of 1870, Riel could not pursue a political career in Canada because of the Scott affair. In Ontario, Riel's name had become almost a synonym for villainy, and there was a warrant out for his arrest.

When Canada took possession of the North-West, Riel was forced to seek refuge south of the international line. From time to time he came back to Manitoba, but never without fears for his safety. He had been led to expect that the government would grant him an amnesty for the Scott case, but the pardon never came. Three times Riel was elected to Parliament, but he could not take his seat in Ottawa because of the Ontario warrant for his arrest over Scott's death. Finally in 1875 came the cruelest blow of all: Riel finally got his amnesty, but only on condition of five years banishment from Canada.

It was these prolonged misfortunes, following his brief moment of glory, which encouraged Riel to think more and more of religion. In 1869-70 he had been a purely political leader, asserting the claims of the Métis; he was involved in a religious cause only inasmuch as the Métis wished to defend their Catholic faith along with their land, religion, and culture. But after 1870 Riel turned more and more to God for consolation. He thought that Providence was the cause of his reverses. That is, God was making him suffer now to prepare him for a greater glory still to come. He felt that if he could only be steadfast during this period of testing, God would grant him a great triumph in the end. Riel began to compare himself to David as described in the Old Testament. By killing Goliath, David became a hero while still only a boy; but then King Saul turned against him and David was forced to flee for his life. However, he did not give up, and he remained faithful to God, and ultimately he was made king of the Jews. Riel took to signing his name "Louis 'David' Riel" to show his resemblance to the first David.

The longer he lived in these conditions, the more he thought along such lines, finally reaching the point where he believed that God had given him and the Métis a special mission to fulfill. He would be the prophet, and they the Chosen People of a new religion for the New World. God would use Riel and the Métis to renovate the spiritual life of humanity.

Toward the end of 1875, Riel found himself in Washington, D.C., unsuccessfully trying to get American support for an invasion of Western Canada. On December 8, the Feast of the Immaculate Conception, he had a mystical experience while attending Mass in St. Patrick's church. As he later described it:

> I suddenly felt in my heart a joy which took such possession of me that to hide from my neighbours the smile on my face I had to unfold my handkerchief and hold it with my hand over my mouth and cheeks. In spite of my precautions a young boy about ten years old, who was a little in front of me, saw my great joy.

Afterwards Riel always maintained that December 8, 1875, was the official inauguration of his mission. But to those around him it seemed more like the onset of madness. His friends restrained him, virtually keeping him under house arrest to prevent him from beginning to publicize his new religion. Naturally Riel resented their attitude; he, who had always been so polite and agreeable with his friends, now became difficult to live with. He was restless, insomniac, and aggressive about the need to tell the world he was God's prophet. This behaviour was in turn interpreted by his friends as a further symptom of his mental breakdown. Not being able to make him behave as they wished, they finally committed him to an insane asylum near Montreal, from where he was later transferred to another institution near Quebec City. Riel was hospitalized from March 6, 1876, to January 23, 1878 — not quite two years.

In this enforced leisure, he was able to work out the details of his religion. He accorded himself a central role in his new scheme of things. He was a prophet, i.e. the direct voice of God. He was also a priest, not by normal ordination but by a special act of God. But he was no ordinary priest; he was a priest-king. Like David of old, he was both a spiritual and temporal leader. Finally, he was the "infallible pontiff" of the church. He brought all these titles together into one grandiose signature: "Louis 'David' Riel: Prophet, Priest-King, Infallible Pontiff."

If he was blessed by God, so were his people. The Métis were the new Chosen People, God's instrument in the present age. The Métis had been produced by the mingling of two races, the French-Canadians and the Indians. Now the French-Canadians had always seen themselves as endowed with a special mission to civilize North America and bring the Catholic faith to the savages. A prominent French-Canadian bishop, a friend of Riel's, had written in 1866:

> The mission with which Providence entrusted French-Canadians is basically religious in nature: it is namely, to convert the unfortunate infidel local population to Catholicism, and to expand the Kingdom of God by developing a predominantly Catholic nationality.

In this enterprise, French-Canadians thought of themselves as carrying on the work of France, commonly called "the eldest daughter of the Church" because the Franks were the first Germanic tribe to be converted to Roman Christianity. Riel was only extending the idea one step farther, to apply it to the Métis, when he wrote:

> The French-Canadian nation has received from God the wonderful mission of continuing the great works of France on this side of the ocean. . . . When the French-Canadian nation will have done its work and will be afflicted with the infirmities of old age, its mission must pass to other hands. . . . We are working to make the French-Canadian Métis people sufficiently great to be worthy to receive the heritage of Lower Canada. . . .

And the Indians, according to Riel, were also noteworthy ancestors; for they were actually descended from ancient Hebrews who crossed the Atlantic around the time of Moses. The Métis were descended from the Jews; and Riel, through his Indian blood, was linked to King David. This fanciful pedigree gave the Métis genealogical credentials for playing the role of Chosen People in the present age.

This association with the Hebrews was a very serious matter for Riel. He wrote that his new church should revive some of the practices of the Law of Moses, that is, the very detailed set of regulations which governed the life of the ancient Israelites. Jesus, according to Riel (and he was correct in this) had been a Jew who had kept the Law; St. Paul was actually the first to clearly separate Christianity from Judaism. Now it was time to return to the original example of Jesus. Riel mentioned four particular aspects of the Mosaic Law which he wished to reintroduce. These were 1) male circumcision (then restricted to Jews, and not a standard medical practice as it is today); 2) celebration of the Lord's Day on Saturday rather than Sunday; 3) a married clergy (Jewish rabbis or teachers have never been prohibited from marriage); and 4) polygamy. Along the same line, but certainly not inspired by Judaism, Riel wished to permit marriage between brother and sister, in cases where the father of the family had died, leaving younger children to be raised. This incidentally, had been the position of Riel himself when his father's death in 1864 left him the oldest son with many younger brothers and sisters.

These innovations, startling as they were, were not, however, Riel's major change of doctrine. The centrepiece of his religion was a break with Rome. Riel declared that the Pope had become corrupt and that the Holy Spirit had left Rome to take up residence in the New World. For a time, the papacy would be located in Montreal, but eventually it would be moved to the village of St. Vital, Riel's home. Surprisingly, even though Riel liked to style himself "Infallible Pontiff," he wanted another man as actual pope. His choice was Ignace Bourget, Bishop of Montreal, who had befriended Riel with money and moral support.

Underlying all these teachings was the promise of a "millennium," that is, a period of happiness and peace brought to man by divine intervention. The word "millennium" comes from a prediction in the last book of the New Testament, known to Catholics as the Apocalypse and to Protestants as the Book of Revelation, that God will bind the devil for a thousand years when Jesus returns to found the Kingdom of Heaven on earth. *Mille* in Latin is "1000," *annus* means "year," hence a millennium is literally a period of a thousand years. Today the term is used to refer to any period of extraordinary happiness which men expect God to set up on the earth. The belief in the millennium is an important part of Christianity, as well as certain other religions. It is a great consolation to those who are oppressed to look forward to the day when God will intervene in the affairs of men to punish the wicked and reward the good. In essence, Riel's teaching was that the suffering of the Métis was only the prelude to the establishment of the Kingdom of God on earth, through the agency of his new religion. In comparison with such a great reward, the trials of the present moment were small and could be endured.

After his discharge from the asylum in January of 1878, Riel returned to the United States. Initially he hoped to settle down as a farmer in Nebraska and marry a friend's daughter with whom he had fallen in love. But because he could not raise the money to buy a farm and thereby to support a wife, these hopes did not work out. Frustrated in his private life, he turned once again to the thought of carrying out his mission. Now his ideas showed that they were not rigid but capable of growth and alteration to meet changing circumstances. Riel became interested in the notion of colonizing the open prairies of the Canadian West with immigrants from the Catholic nations of Europe like the Irish, Poles, Italians, *etc.* Riel proposed to bring them directly from the Old World, or else to encourage them to move from the cities of the Eastern United States, where so many immigrants then huddled in urban squalor. He went to St. Paul, Minnesota, to speak to Bishop John Ireland, who was operating just such a plan in the American West. But these talks led nowhere, and Riel moved again. In late summer of 1879 he went to Montana where a few hundred Métis, along with Indians of many tribes, were following the pitiful remnants of the buffalo. (The buffalo disappeared from the Canadian prairie after 1878, and a few retreated to the wilds of Montana, where they were exterminated by 1883.) On the way Riel made a detour to Canada to see Sitting Bull, who had taken refuge north of the line after destroying Custer's detachment at the battle of the Little Big Horn. Riel's plan was to mobilize Indians on both sides of the border for an invasion of Canada. After discussions with Sitting Bull, he went on to Montana to secure the allegiance of other tribes. The invasion was set for early summer 1880, but it was called off because both the North-West Mounted Police and the U.S. Army found out about it.

When this plan failed, Riel had no further political prospects. Within a few years he became an American citizen, married a young Métis girl, settled down as an obscure school teacher at St. Peter's mission in Montana, and started to raise a family. To all external appearances, he was entirely "normal." Yet his private papers show that he still nourished his beliefs that he was a prophet with a divinely appointed mission, that the Métis were a Chosen People, and that he would found a religion for the New World which would not be under Rome. In other words, his views were still those which had once been labelled insane, but now he had learned to manage them so as not to disturb his relations with his fellow man. For the most part, he confided his convictions only to those whom he expected to be sympathetic. This is important to note, for it shows the separability of belief and behaviour. Riel's mission was as much alive as ever, but it was, as it were, dormant, waiting for an opportunity to revive.

This chance came in June, 1884, when a delegation of four men rode up to Riel's tiny house. They had come from the district of St. Laurent on the South Saskatchewan River, about half-way between the towns of Saskatoon and Prince Albert. In that region there lived a large number of French half-breeds who, not liking the influx of white settlers into Manitoba, had moved further west. These Métis had a number of rather complicated grievances, mostly concerning title to land, which they had been presenting to the federal government for several years without obtaining any success. But turmoil was not restricted to only the Métis in the area. The West was very hard hit by the world-wide economic crash of 1883. The white farmers were in trouble because they could not sell their grain at a good price; the Indians' position was still more serious, even desperate, because the government had cut their beef rations as an economy measure. It was the Métis who first thought of asking Louis Riel to return to lead a popular movement of protest, but the Indians and many of the whites also approved the idea.

Thus when Riel returned he had widespread sympathy from several groups, all of whom had in common a dislike for the Western policies of Sir John A. Macdonald's government. Riel's task was to bring these different elements together to support a common petition of grievances to be sent to Ottawa. In the rest of 1884, he accomplished this with his old political skill. He pursued a moderate and statesmanlike course which won the adherence of many who were initially opposed to the return of this notorious rebel to Canada. He did not advocate any violent action, nor did he preach religious revolution. In December, the petition of grievances was signed and sent to the Department of the Interior.

Once again there commenced a period of waiting. The cabinet, it must be admitted, was extremely slow to reply, as it had always been. Sir John A. Macdonald's government, though it opened up the Canadian West, was not terribly responsive to the problems of those who lived there. But Riel was concerned with more than getting a response to the petition. He had also set in motion a train of secret negotiations to secure a sum of money from the government in return for his departure from Canada. This was, of course, blackmail; but before being morally outraged at Riel's dishonesty, we must recall that years before Sir John had in fact paid Riel to leave Canada. Sir John was not adverse to using money for such purposes, but having failed to buy off Riel permanently, he was not going to waste money a second time.

On February 4, 1885, a telegram came to Lt.-Governor Dewdney, asking him to inform the Métis that the government would appoint a commission to look into their land claims. This by no means satisfied the half-breeds, who also had a number of other grievances. More importantly, it did not satisfy Louis Riel's personal ambitions. It appeared that he would be left without anything for his efforts. From this point Riel became increasingly radical. It is said that when he heard about the telegram Riel cried out in anger: "In forty days Ottawa will have my answer!" It was almost exactly forty days to the outbreak of the North-West Rebellion.

The story of the Rebellion, which has been told many times, is too long to go into here. In what follows I will limit myself to the religious side of events. The Rebellion of 1885, in contrast to that of 1869-70, was as much a religious as a political movement. It was launched under sacred auspices. Riel declared his revolution on March 18, 1885, the eve of the feast of St. Joseph, whom Riel had always considered a special patron and who had recently been appointed by Bishop Grandin as the national saint of the Métis. Almost the first words that Riel spoke in the Rebellion were "*Rome est tombée*" ("Rome has fallen"). This makes perfect sense when we realize that he was now finally ready to reveal to the world the religion he had created ten years before. In his mind politics and religion were now indissolubly fused, and both in turn were merged with his personal destiny. The prophet and the Chosen People would rise or fall together.

Riel created a Provisional Government, as he had done in 1869-70, but this time it bore a religious name. Riel called it the "Exovedate," and its members "Exovedes," terms which he coined from the Latin words *ex* (of) and *ovile* (flock). He and his council were just "one of the flock," servants of God's will as expressed in the sacred people. The Exovedate proceeded to establish some of the main tenets of Riel's creed. Riel was officially declared a prophet. The fall of Rome was announced as well as the transfer of the papacy to Bishop Ignace Bourget in Montreal. The day of worship was changed from Sunday to Saturday. Needless to say, the Catholic missionaries in the area were not prepared to support such changes, so Riel put them under house arrest and took over certain priestly functions himself. With vague references to his plans for massive immigration, he promised the Métis that the Irish, Poles, Italians, Germans, *etc.* would come to their aid in the struggle against Canada. This was the religion which Riel had been nourishing in his heart, but it will be noted that some of the more extreme aspects were missing. As far as we know, Riel said nothing to his followers about polygamy or incest. Perhaps he judged that the time was not ripe for such innovations, or perhaps they were no longer important to him.

In 1869-70, Riel had been able to defy the Canadian government with success for two reasons: the North-West Territories were not yet officially part of Canada as long as the transaction with the Hudson's Bay Company was not complete; and more importantly, the absence of a transcontinental railway made it impossible for Ottawa to quickly field an army west of the Great Lakes. In 1885 neither condition still existed. The Canadian Pacific lacked only a few stretches to be complete, so soldiers could be rapidly put in the field. Riel never had more than a few hundred men fighting with him (the Indian bands who rose at the same time were partly inspired by Riel, but operated independently). The unequal struggle was concluded on May 12, and Riel surrendered three days later, although he could have escaped south of the international line, as did Gabriel Dumont and other prominent rebels.

Why did Riel voluntarily surrender? The answer to this question provides the key to comprehending his thinking in the last few months of his life. He surrendered because he thought his mission was not yet at an end. He expected to be tried for treason, but he also thought that the trial would provide him with a forum to advance his ideas. When he appeared in court at Regina, Riel's attorneys pleaded that he was not guilty by reason of insanity; but he himself scorned his defence and refused to co-operate with his lawyers in the insanity plea. When he finally had his chance to address the jury, he told them that he was "the prophet of the New World," and he explained his mission to them in considerable detail.

> It is true, gentlemen, I believed for years I had a mission. . . . God has maintained my view . . . he has maintained my health sufficiently to go through the world . . . and he has kept me from bullets, when bullets marked my hat. I am blessed by God. . . . As to religion, what is my belief? What is my insanity about that? My insanity, your Honors, gentlemen of the jury, is that I wish to leave Rome aside, inasmuch as it is the cause of division between Catholics and Protestants. . . . If it is any satisfaction to the doctors to know what insanity I have, if they are going to call my pretensions insanity, I say humbly, through the grace of God, I believe I am the prophet of the new world.

The jury did not think he was insane, but neither did they see him as a genuine prophet. The convicted him of high treason and he was sentenced to death, a verdict which was not changed on appeal to higher courts.

The shock of being sentenced to death caused Riel to sign a renunciation of his heresies so that he could rejoin the Catholic Church. He renounced his "false mission" and all the teachings which had followed from it. But his inner voice was irrepressible. Within a few days he was again receiving revelations, seeing visions and hearing voices. If he had doubted for a moment that he was a prophet, he quickly regained his confidence. Yet he also wished to remain part of the Catholic Church, now thinking that perhaps his religious reforms could be accomplished within the Church rather than by overthrowing it.

In the last weeks of his life he entered a new stage of his mission. Utterly powerless, he could no longer preach his gospel to the world. He was faced with the prospect of execution as a traitor. But now in his mind death became not the end of his mission but its continuation. Riel began to think of himself as dying, like Jesus, for the sins of men. And he would be rewarded like Christ! He too would rise from the dead! When on November 16, 1885, Riel walked to the scaffold, he was convinced that the power of God would restore him to life on the third day.

This apparently bizarre hope was logical in terms of the way Riel had always thought about his mission. His life was poised between the experience of suffering and the expectation of glory. It was his belief that if he was faithful to his calling, God would eventually give victory to him and the Métis. Faced with death, he extended his mission beyond the grave rather than think that it had been a delusion. Death was not the end but only another obstacle to be overcome. This type of thinking may seem strange, but it was a rather exact copy of the thought process which modern scholarship sees in the life of Christ. Every Christian is supposed to imitate the life of Christ; in the end Riel simply took this injunction more literally than most people.

CONCLUSION

Riel's claim to charismatic authority after December 8, 1875, was based on his prophetic mission. As the voice of God to a sinful world, he was authorized to exhort and even command men. He was not only a prophet but a priest and a king, a sacred king, like David of the Old Testament. Prior to the beginning of his religious mission, Riel claimed to speak for the Métis because of legal authorization; he was their elected representative in various capacities such as secretary and then president of the Métis committee of resistance, president of the Provisional Government, and Member of Parliament for Provencher. After December 8, 1875, these legal bases of authority paled into insignificance against the claim of direct, personal, divine authorization. Riel deliberately chose not to be elected to any office during the North-West Rebellion. He called himself Exovede and attended meetings of the Exovedate, but he was not strictly speaking a member. His authority now came from God, not the votes of men.

There was a strong personal aspect in all of this. Riel's religious star so obviously rose as his political star fell that it is tempting to interpret his mission as a self-created compensation for disappointment in politics. This is true, but it is only part of the truth and perhaps not the most important part. Riel's personal mission was closely correlated with the fate of the Métis. His prophetic role was to lead them to the greatness ordained in God's providential ordering of history. They would become the new Chosen People, living under a revived Mosaic Law and graced by the presence of a reformed papacy. Politically, they would be masters of the

North-West, assimilating new immigrants instead of being displaced by them. It was the coincidence between the personal crisis of Riel's career and the collective crisis of the Métis people which made him such a powerful symbol of their destiny.

This collective aspect of Riel's mission is essential to understanding his charisma, which was not an individual quality but a social relationship. When he first announced his mission in 1875/76 to his friends in the United States and Quebec, they saw only insanity. They dismissed his claims to spiritual and political authority and put him in a lunatic asylum "for his own good." Yet at Batoche in 1885 no one accused Riel of insanity, except a skeptical few who were not taken seriously. The Métis accepted Riel at face value. Each morning he communicated to them the revelations which he claimed to have received at night from the Holy Spirit. He also told the Métis that God would work through him a miracle to overcome the superior military force that Canada had sent against them. Riel's followers saw his behaviour as the external proof of his charismatic authority, just as the followers of Jesus saw his message validated in his life and works.

Separated from his followers after the Rebellion, Riel became anything but charismatic. To his defence attorneys he was a madman to be saved from the gallows by the plea of insanity. To the Crown prosecutors he was a criminal adventurer who had duped the gullible Métis by playing on their simple piety. To the priests at Regina he was an excommunicated heretic who had to sign a recantation of his errors before he could be readmitted to the sacraments of the Catholic Church. All were correct in a way. No one "is" anything apart from a social context; identity always results from a complex web of human relationships. Charisma belongs to the same category of terms as crime, lunacy or heresy; all designate a certain quality of relationship between an individual, upon whom attention is focused, and his human milieu. Riel "had" charisma, and the authority that goes with it, for a brief moment when he was intimately associated with the people to whom his message was directed. This intense community and Riel's charismatic authority were destroyed on the battlefield of Batoche.

3   Sovereignty

In the form of political community known as the "state," which has come to dominate the modern world, an organized structure of government rules a population living within fixed territorial boundaries. The existence of the state requires sovereignty, that is, a highest authority at the pinnacle of governmental organization. Sovereign authority may be distributed between levels of a federal system; it may be divided among a head of state, a ruling committee or parliament, or the people themselves; but it must exist somewhere.

Reading 3, a selection from Thomas Hobbes' *Leviathan*, is the classic liberal argument for the necessity of sovereignty. Hobbes argued in essence that human beings are naturally predatory upon one another. The only way to keep them in check is for them to agree to form "a common power, to keep them in awe." This common power Hobbes called "the sovereign," and he regarded sovereignty as indispensable to peaceful existence. Without it, life would be, in his memorable phrase, "solitary, poor, nasty, brutish and short."

Thomas Hobbes (1588-1679) is one of the giants of philosophy in general and political theory in particular. The *Leviathan* is still read carefully by all students of political thought. The selection printed here is from chapter 17 of the *Leviathan*, which appears in *The English Works of Thomas Hobbes*, edited by Sir William Molesworth. The orthography has been modernized following *Hobbes Selections*, edited by Frederick J.E. Woodbridge.

● ● ● ● ● ● ● ● ● ● ●

The final cause, end, or design of men, who naturally love liberty, and dominion over others, in the introduction of that restraint upon themselves, in which we see them live in commonwealths, is the foresight of their own preservation, and of a more contented life thereby; that is to say, of getting themselves out from that miserable condition of war, which is necessarily consequent, as hath been shown in chapter xiii, to the natural passions of men, when there is no visible power to keep them in awe, and tie them by fear of punishment to the performance of their covenants, and observation of those laws of nature set down in the fourteenth and fifteenth chapter.

For the laws of nature, as *justice, equity, modesty, mercy,* and, in sum, *doing to others, as we would de done to,* of themselves, without the terror of some power, to cause them to be observed, are contrary to our natural passions, that carry us to partiality, pride, revenge, and the like. And covenants, without the sword, are but words, and of no strength to secure a man at all. Therefore notwithstanding the laws of nature, which every one hath then kept, when he has the will to keep them, when he can do it safely, if there be no power erected, or not great enough for our security; every man will, and may lawfully rely on his own strength and art, for caution against all other men. And in all places, where men have lived by small families, to rob and spoil one another, has been a trade, and so far from being reputed against the law of nature, that the greater spoils they gained, the greater was their honour; and men observed no other laws therein, but the laws of honour; that is, to abstain from cruelty, leaving to men their lives, and instruments of husbandry. And as small families did then; so now do cities and kingdoms which are but greater families, for their own security, enlarge their dominions, upon all pretences of danger, and fear of invasion, or assistance that may be given to invaders, and endeavour as much as they can, to subdue, or weaken their neighbours, by open force, and secret arts, for want of other caution, justly; and are remembered for it in after ages with honour.

Nor is it the joining together of a small number of men, that gives them this security; because in small numbers, small additions on the one side or the other, make the advantage of strength so great, as is sufficient to carry the victory; and therefore gives encouragement to an invasion. The multitude sufficient to confide in for our own security, is not determined by any certain number, but by comparison with the enemy we fear; and is then sufficient, when the odds of the enemy is not of so visible and conspicuous moment, to determine the event of war, as to move him to attempt.

And be there never so great a multitude; yet if their actions be directed according to their particular judgments, and particular appetites, they can expect thereby no defence, nor protection, neither against a common enemy, nor against the injuries of one another. For being distracted in opinions concerning the best use and application of their strength, they do not help but hinder one another; and reduce their strength by mutual opposition to nothing: whereby they are easily, not only subdued by a very few that agree together; but also when there is no common enemy, they make war upon each other, for their particular interests. For if we could suppose a great multitude of men to consent in the observation of justice, and other laws of nature, without a common power to keep them all in awe; we might as well suppose all mankind to do the same; and then there neither would be, nor need to be any civil government, or commonwealth at all; because there would be peace without subjection.

Nor is it enough for the security, which men desire should last all the time of their life, that they be governed, and directed by one judgment, for a limited time; as in one battle, or one war. For though they obtain a victory by their unanimous endeavour against a foreign enemy; yet afterwards, when either they have no common enemy, or he that by one part is held for an enemy, is by another part held for a friend, they must needs by the difference of their interests dissolve, and fall again into a war amongst themselves.

It is true, that certain living creatures, as bees, and ants, live sociably one with another, which are therefore by Aristotle numbered amongst political creatures; and yet have no direction, than their particular judgments and appetites; nor speech, whereby one of them can signify to another, what he thinks expedient for the common benefit: and therefore some man may perhaps desire to know, why mankind cannot do the same. To which I answer,

First, that men are continually in competition for honour and dignity, which these creatures are not; and consequently amongst men there ariseth on that ground, envy and hatred, and finally war; but amongst these not so.

Secondly, that amongst these creatures, the common good differeth not from the private; and being by nature inclined to their private, they procure thereby the common benefit. But man, whose joy consisteth in comparing himself with other men, can relish nothing but what is eminent.

Thirdly, that these creatures, having not, as man, the use of reason, do not see, nor think they see any fault, in the administration of their common business; whereas amongst men, there are very many, that think themselves wiser, and able to govern the public, better than the rest; and these strive to reform and innovate, one this way, another that way; and thereby bring it into distraction and civil war.

Fourthly, that these creatures, though they have some use of voice, in making known to one another their desires, and other affections; yet they want that art of words, by which some men can represent to others, that which is good, in the likeliness of evil; and evil, in the likeness of good; and augment, or diminish the apparent greatness of good and evil; discontenting men, and troubling their peace at their pleasure.

Fifthly, irrational creatures cannot distinguish between *injury*, and *damage*; and therefore as long as they be at ease, they are not offended with their fellows: whereas man is then most troublesome, when he is most at ease: for then it is that he loves to shew his wisdom, and control the actions of them that govern the commonwealth.

Lastly, the agreement of these creatures is natural; that of men, is by covenant only, which is artificial: and therefore it is no wonder if there be somewhat else required, besides covenant, to make their agreement constant and lasting; which is a common power, to keep them in awe, and to direct their actions to the common benefit.

The only way to erect such a common power, as may be able to defend them from the invasion of foreigners, and the injuries of one another, and thereby to secure them in such sort, as that by their own industry, and by the fruits of the earth, they may nourish themselves and live contentedly; is, to confer all their power and strength upon one man, or upon one assembly of men, that may reduce all their wills, by plurality of voices, unto one will: which is as much as to say, to appoint one man, or assembly of men, to bear their person; and every one to own, and acknowledge himself to be author of whatsoever he that so beareth their person, shall act, or cause to be acted, in those things which concern the common peace and safety; and therein to submit their wills, every one to his will, and their judgments, to his judgment. This is more than consent, or concord; it is a real unity of them all, in one and the same person, made by covenant of every man with every man, in such manner, as if every man should say to every man, *I authorize and give up my right of governing myself, to this man, or to this assembly of men, on this condition, that thou give up thy right to him, and authorize all his actions in like manner.* This done, the multitude so united in one person, is called a COMMONWEALTH, in Latin CIVITAS. This is the generation of that great LEVIATHAN, to speak more reverently, of that *mortal god,* to which we owe under the *immortal God,* our peace and defence. For by this authority, given him by every particular man in the commonwealth, he hath the use of so much power and strength conferred on him, that by terror thereof, he is enabled to perform the wills of them all, to peace at home, and mutual aid against their enemies abroad. And in him consisteth the essence of the commonwealth; which, to define it, is *one person, of whose acts a great multitude, by mutual covenants one with another, have made themselves every one the author, to the end he may use the strength and means of them all, as he shall think expedient, for their peace and common defence.*

And he that carrieth this person, is called SOVEREIGN, and said to have *sovereign power;* and every one besides, his SUBJECT.

The attaining to this sovereign power, is by two ways. One, by natural force; as when a man maketh his children, to submit themselves, and their children, to his government, as being able to destroy them if they refuse; or by war subdueth his enemies to his will, giving them their lives on that condition. The other, is when men agree amongst themselves, to submit to some man, or assembly of men, voluntarily, on confidence to be protected by him against all others. This latter, may be called a political commonwealth, or commonwealth by *institution;* and the former, a commonwealth by *acquisition.* . . . .

4   What is a Nation?

The state as a structure of authority exists in tension with the social communities in which we live, of which the most important politically is the nation. As a community of psychological identification, what Ernest Renan in Reading 4 calls "a living soul, a spiritual principle," the nation does not depend upon sovereignty or territory. Renan's essay, one of the earliest and most influential attempts to specify the characteristics of the nation, shows how national identification arises from, but is not limited to, the ties of race, language, religion, and custom. There is a curious dialectic between the state and the nation. Renan's historical analysis shows that the national identities of Europe—English, French, German, Spanish, Italian—grew out of the territorial division of the Roman Empire by the Germanic invaders. It was "the fusion of the populations" in these successor states that produced what we now call nations. It appears that at some stage the existence of a state may help create a nation; but once national identification exists, it is no longer wedded to particular boundaries or a particular government. Thus Poland could emerge again as a state after World War I, after more than a century of partition among Germany, Austria-Hungary, and Russia.

Ernest Renan (1823-1890) was a leading French historian, who wrote widely on many subjects. This selection is an abridged version of "What is a Nation?" in *Poetry of the Celtic Races and Other Essays*, which is a translation of Renan's March 11, 1882 lecture at the Sorbonne, entitled "Qu'est-ce qu'une Nation?"

● ● ● ● ● ● ● ● ● ●

I propose to analyse with you an idea, simple in appearance, but capable of the most dangerous misunderstanding. The forms of human society are of the most varied types. Great conglomerations of people, as in the case of China, of Egypt, of ancient Babylon; the tribe, as in the case of the Hebrews and the Arabs; the city, as in the case of Athens and Sparta; unions of different countries, in the fashion of the Empire of Achaemenes, the Roman Empire, or the Carlovingian Empire; communities of no country, held together by the bond of religion, like the Israelites or the Parsees; nations like France, England, and the majority of modern European autonomies; confederations, as in the case of Switzerland and America; relationships similar to those which race and, in a greater degree, language establish between the different branches of the Teutonic family, the different branches of the Slavs; — these are modes of grouping which all exist, or at least have existed, and which cannot be confounded, the one with the other, without the most serious inconvenience. At the time of the French Revolution there was a belief that the institutions of small independent towns, such as Sparta and Rome, could be applied to our great nations of thirty or forty millions of souls. In our own day a still graver error is committed: the race is confounded with the nation, and to racial, or rather to linguistic groups, is attributed a sovereignty analogous to that of really existent peoples. Let us attempt to arrive at some precision in these difficult questions, where the least confusion in the sense of words, at the beginning of the discussion, may produce in the end the most fatal errors. . . .

I

Since the end of the Roman Empire, or rather since the disruption of the Empire of Charlemagne, Western Europe appears to us divided into nations, of which some, at certain epochs, have sought to exercise a supremacy over others, without any lasting success. What Charles V., Louis XIV., and Napoleon I. were unable to do in the past, is hardly likely to be achieved by any one in the future. The establishment of a new Roman Empire, or a new Carlovingian Empire, has become an impossibility. Europe is too deeply divided for an attempt at universal dominion not to provoke, and that quickly, a coalition which would force the ambitious nation to retire within its natural bounds. A species of equilibrium has long been in existence. France, England, Germany, Russia will still be, in centuries to come, and in spite of the vicissitudes they will have gone through, historic individualities, essential pieces of a chess-board, the squares of which vary unceasingly in importance and greatness, but are never altogether confused. . . .

What, then, is the characteristic feature of these different states? It consists in the fusion of the populations which compose them. In the countries that we have just enumerated, there is nothing analogous to what you will find in Turkey, where the Turk, the Slav, the Greek, the Armenian, the Arab, the Syrian, and the Kurd are as distinct now as on the day of their conquest. Two essential circumstances contributed to bring this result to pass. First of all is the fact, that the Teutonic tribes adopted Christianity as soon as they had had relations of some little duration with the Greek and Latin peoples. When conqueror and conquered are of the same religion, or rather when the conqueror adopts the religion of the conquered, the Turkish system, the absolute distinction of men according to their respective faiths, can no longer be possible. The second circumstance was the conquerors' forgetfulness of their own language. The grandsons of Clovis, of Alaric, of Gondebaud, of Alboin, and of Rollo were already speaking Romance. This fact was itself the consequence of another important peculiarity, namely, that the Franks, the Burgundians, the Goths, the Lombards, and the Normans had very few women of their own race with them. For several generations the chiefs espoused only Teutonic women; but their concubines were Latin, the nurses of their children were Latin; the whole tribe married Latin women. And so it was that the *Lingua Francica* and the *Lingua Gothica* had a very short existence, after the settlement of the Franks and the Goths in Roman territories. The same was not the case in England, for there can be no doubt that the Anglo-Saxon invaders had women with them; the ancient British population took to flight; and, moreover, Latin was no longer dominant in Britain, indeed it had never been so. Even if Gaulish had been generally spoken in Gaul in the fifth century, Clovis and his followers would not have abandoned Teutonic for it.

From this ensues the important fact, that in spite of the extreme violence of the manners of the Teutonic invaders, the mould that they imposed became, in the course of centuries, the very mould of the nation. France, very legitimately, came to be the name of a country into which only an imperceptible minority of Franks had entered. In the tenth century, in the earliest *Chansons de Geste*, which are such a perfect mirror of the spirit of the age, all the inhabitants of France are Frenchmen. The idea of a difference of races in the population of France, that is so apparent in Gregory of Tours, is not present to any extent in the French writers and poets, posterior to Hugh Capet. The difference between noble and serf is as accentuated as it well can be; but in no respect is the difference an ethnical one; it is a difference in courage, in habits, and in hereditarily transmitted education. The idea, that the beginning of it all may be a conquest, does not occur to anybody. The fictitious theories, according to which nobility owed its origin to a privilege, conferred by the king for great services rendered to the state, to such an extent that all nobility is an acquisition, were established as a dogma in the thirteenth century. The same thing was the sequel of nearly all the Norman conquests. At the end of one or two generations, the Norman invaders were no longer to be distinguished from the rest of the population. Their influence had not been the less profound; to the conquered land they had given a nobility, warlike habits, and a patriotism hitherto unexistent.

Forgetfulness, and I shall even say historical error, form an essential factor in the creation of a nation; and thus it is that the progress of historical studies may often be dangerous to the nationality. Historical research, in fact, brings back to light the deeds of violence that have taken place at the commencement of all political formations, even of those the consequences of which have been most beneficial. Unity is ever achieved by brutality. The union of Northern and Southern France was the result of an extermination, and of a reign of terror that lasted for nearly a hundred years. The king of France who was, if I may say so, the ideal type of a secular crystalliser, the king of France who made the most perfect national unity in existence, lost his prestige when seen at too close a distance. The nation that he had formed cursed him; and to-day the knowledge of what he was worth, and what he did, belongs only to the cultured.

It is by contrast that these great laws of the history of Western Europe become apparent. In the undertaking which the King of France, in part by his tyranny, in part by his justice, achieved so admirably, many countries came to disaster. Under the crown of St. Stephen, Magyars and Slavs have remained as distinct as they were eight hundred years ago. Far from combining the different elements in its dominions, the house of Hapsburg has held them apart, and often opposed to one another. In Bohemia the Czech element and the German element are superimposed like oil and water in a glass. The Turkish policy of separation of nationalities according to religion has had much graver results. It has brought about the ruin of the East. Take a town like Smyrna or Salonica; you will find there five or six communities, each with its own memories, and possessing among them scarcely anything in common. But the essence of a nation is, that all its individual members should have many things in common; and also, that all of them should hold many things in oblivion. No French citizen knows whether he is a Burgundian, an Alan, or a Visigoth; every French citizen ought to have forgotten St. Bartholomew, and the massacres of the South in the thirteenth century. There are not ten families in France able to furnish proof of a French origin; and yet, even if such a proof were given, it would be essentially defective, in consequence of a thousand unknown crosses, capable of deranging all genealogical systems.

The modern nation is then the historical result of a series of events, converging in the same direction. Sometimes unity had been achieved by a dynasty, as in the case of France; sometimes by the direct will of the provinces, as in the case of Holland, Switzerland, and Belguim; sometimes by a general feeling slowly vanquishing the caprices of feudality, as in the case of Italy and Germany. But a profound *raison d'être* has always governed these formations. The principles in such cases come to light in the most unexpected ways. In our own times we have seen Italy united by her defeats, and Turkey destroyed by her victories. Every defeat advanced the cause of Italy, every victory was a loss to Turkey; for Italy is a nation, Turkey, outside Asia Minor, is not. It is the glory of France to have proclaimed by the French Revolution that a nation exists by itself. We ought not to complain because we find ourselves imitated. Ours is the principle of nations. But what then is a nation? Why is Holland a nation, while Hanover or the Grand Duchy of Parma is not? How does France persist in being a nation, when the principle which created her has disappeared? How is Switzerland, with three languages, two religions, and three or four races, a nation, while Tuscany, for example, which is homogeneous, is not? Why is Austria a state and not a nation? In what respect does the principle of nationality differ from the principle of races? These are the points upon which a reflective mind must be fixed, if it is to find a satisfactory solution. . . .

II

In the opinion of certain political theorists a nation is, before all else, a dynasty representing an ancient conquest, a conquest first accepted and then forgotten by the mass of the people. According to the politicians of whom I speak, the grouping of provinces affected by a dynasty, by its wars, by its marriages, or by its treaties, comes to an end with the dynasty which has formed it. It is very true that the majority of modern nations owe their existence to a family of feudal origin, which contracted a marriage with the soil, and was in some measure a nucleus of centralisation. There was nothing natural or necessary about the boundaries of France in 1789. The large zone that the house of Capet added to the narrow limits of the Treaty of Verdun, was in every sense the personal acquisition of that house. At the time when the annexations were made, there was no idea of natural frontiers, or of the rights of nations, or of the will of the provinces. The union of England, Ireland, and Scotland was in like manner a dynastic act. The reason for Italy delaying so long in becoming a nation was that no one of her numerous reigning houses, before the present century, made itself the centre of unity. And it is a strange thing that it is from the obscure island of Sardinia, from territory scarcely Italian, that she has taken a royal title. Holland, which created herself by an act of heroic resolution, has nevertheless contracted a marriage with the house of Orange, and would run real dangers on the day of that union's being compromised.

But is such a law as this absolute? Certainly not. Switzerland and the United States, conglomerations formed by successive additions, have no dynastic base. I shall not discuss the question with regard to France. It would be necessary to have the secret of the future. Let us only say that the great royal house of France had been so highly national, that, on the morrow of its fall, the nation was able to stand without its support. And then the eighteenth century had changed everything. Man had returned, after centuries of abasement, to the old spirit, to self-respect, to the idea of his rights. The words "country" and "citizen" had resumed their significance. Thus it was that the boldest operation ever attempted in history was

accomplished—an operation which might be compared to what in phys-
iology would be the gift of life and its first identity, to a body from which
head and heart had been removed.

It must then be admitted that a nation can exist without a dynastic
principle; and even that nations formed by dynasties can separate themselves from them without, for that reason, ceasing to exist. The old principle
which held account of no right but that of princes, can no longer be
maintained; above the dynastic right there is the national right. On what
foundation shall we build up this national right, by what sign shall we
know it, from what tangible fact shall we derive it?

(I.) From race, say several with assurance. Artificial divisions resulting
from feudality, royal marriages, or diplomatic congresses, are unstable.
What does remain firm and fixed is the race of populations. That it is which
constitutes right and legitimacy. The Teutonic family, for example, according to this theory, has the right of reclaiming such of its members as are
beyond the pale of Teutonism—even when these members do not seek
reunion. The right of Teutonism over such a province is greater than the
right of the inhabitants of the province over themselves. Thus is created a
kind of primordial right, analogous to that of the divine right of kings; for
the principle of nations is substituted that of ethnography. This is a very
grave error, which, if it became dominant, would cause the ruin of European civilisation. So far as the national principle is just and legitimate, so far
is the primordial right of races narrow, and full of danger for true progress.
. . .

Racial considerations have then been for nothing in the constitution of
modern nations. France is Celtic, Iberian, Teutonic. Germany is Teutonic,
Celtic, and Slavonic. Italy is the country where ethnography is most confused. Gauls, Etruscans, Pelasgians, and Greeks, to say nothing of many
other elements, are crossed in an undecipherable medley. The British Isles,
as a whole, exhibit a mixture of Celtic and Teutonic blood, the relative
proportions of which it is singularly difficult to define.

The truth is that there is no pure race; and that making politics depend
upon ethnographical analysis, is allowing it to be borne upon a chimaera.
The most noble countries, England, France, Italy, are those where blood is
most mingled. Is Germany an exception to this rule? Is she purely Teutonic?
What an illusion is this! The whole of the South was once Gaulish. The
whole of the East beyond the Elbe is Slavonic. And what, in point of fact,
are the parts alleged to be really pure? . . .

Racial facts then, important as they are in the beginning, have a
constant tendency to lose their importance. Human history is essentially
different from zoology. Race is not everything, as it is in the case of rodents
and felines; and we have no right to go about the world feeling the heads of

people, then taking them by the throat, and saying, "You are of our blood; you belong to us!" Beyond anthropological characteristics there are reason, justice, truth, and beauty; and these are the same in all. Nay, this ethnographical politics is not even safe. You exploit it to-day on other people; some day you may see it turned against yourselves. Is it certain that the Germans, who have raised the flag of ethnography so high, will not see the Slavs coming to analyse in their turn the names of villages in Saxony and Lusatia, to seek for traces of the Wilzen or the Obotrites, and to ask account of the massacres and slavery which their ancestors suffered at the hands of the Othos? It is good for all to know how to forget. . . .

(II.) What we have been saying about race must also be said of language. Language invites re-union; it does not force it. The United States and England, Spanish America and Spain, speak the same languages, and do not form single nations. On the contrary, Switzerland, which owes her stability to the fact that she was founded by the assent of her several parts, counts three or four languages. In man there is something superior to language, — will. The will of Switzerland to be united, in spite of the variety of her languages, is a much more important fact than a similarity of language, often obtained by persecution.

It is an honourable fact for France, that she has never sought to procure unity of speech by measures of coercion. Can we not have the same feelings and thoughts, and love the same things in different languages? We were speaking just now of the inconvenience of making international politics depend on ethnography. There would not be less in making politics depend on comparative philology. Let us allow the fullest liberty of discussion to these interesting studies; do not let us mingle them with that which would affect their serenity. The political importance attached to languages results from the way in which they are regarded as signs of race. Nothing can be more incorrect. Prussia, where nothing but German is now spoken, spoke Slavonic a few centuries ago; Wales speaks English; Gaul and Spain speak the primitive idiom of Alba Longa; Egypt speaks Arabic; indeed, examples are innumerable. Even at the beginning similarity of speech did not imply similarity of race. Let us take the proto-Aryan or proto-Semitic tribe; there were to be found slaves accustomed to speak the same language as their masters; but nevertheless the slave was then very often of a different race from that of his master. Let us repeat it; these classifications of the Indo-European, Semitic, and other tongues, created with such admirable sagacity by comparative philology, do not coincide with the classifications of anthropology. Languages are historical formations, which give but little indication of the blood of those who speak them; and, in any case, cannot enchain human liberty, when there is a question of determining the family with which we unite ourselves for life and death. . . .

(III.) Nor can religion offer a sufficient basis for the establishment of a modern nationality. In the beginning religion was essential to the very existence of the social group. The social group was an extension of the family. Religious rites were family rites. The Athenian religion was the cult of Athens itself, of its mythical founders, of its laws and customs. It implied no dogmatic theology. This religion was in every sense of the term a State religion. If any one refused to practise it, he was no longer an Athenian. In reality it was the worship of the personified Acropolis. To swear on the altar of Agraulos was to take an oath to die for one's country. This religion was the equivalent of what drawing lots for military service, or the cult of the flag, is among us. To refuse to participate in such a worship was like a refusal of military service in our modern societies. It was a declaration that one was not an Athenian. From another point of view, it is clear that such a religion had no force for any one who was not an Athenian; and thus no proselytism was exercised to compel aliens to accept it. The slaves in Athens did not practise it. . . .

What was right at Sparta and Athens was already no longer so in the kingdoms that originated in Alexander's conquest; above all, was no longer right in the Roman Empire. The persecutions of Antiochus Epiphanes, for the purpose of forcing the worship of the Olympian Jupiter on the East, those of the Roman Empire for the purpose of keeping up a pseudo-State religion, were a mistake, a crime, a veritable absurdity. In our own days the position is perfectly clear. No longer are there masses of people professing a uniform belief. Every one believes and practises after his own fashion, what he can, as he pleases. The state-religion is a thing of the past. One can be a Frenchman, an Englishman, or a German; and at the same time be a Catholic, a Protestant, or a Jew, or else be of no creed at all. Religion has become a matter for the individual; it affects the individual's conscience alone. The division of nations into Catholic and Protestant no longer exists. Religion, which fifty-two years ago was so considerable an element in the formation of Belgium, retains all its importance in the spiritual jurisdiction of each man; but it has almost completely disappeared from the considerations that trace the limits of peoples.

(IV.) Community of interests is assuredly a powerful bond between men. But nevertheless can interests suffice to make a nation? I do not believe it. Community of interests makes commercial treaties. There is a sentimental side to nationality; it is at once body and soul; a *Zollverein* [customs union] is not a fatherland.

(V.) Geography, or what we may call natural frontiers, certainly plays a considerable part in the division of nations. Geography is one of the essential factors of history. Rivers have carried races forward; mountains have checked them. The former have favoured, the latter limited, historic movements. Can it be said, however, that, as certain persons believe, the boundaries of a nation are inscribed upon the map; and that this nation has a right to judge what is necessary, to round off certain contours, to reach some mountain or river, to which a species of *a priori* faculty of limitation is ascribed? I know of no doctrine more arbitrary, or more disastrous. By it all violence is justified. First, let us ask, do mountains or rivers constitute these so-called natural frontiers? It is incontestable that mountains separate; but, on the other hand, rivers unite. And then all mountains cannot cut off states. Which are those that separate, and those that do not separate? From Biarritz to the Tornea there is not a single river-estuary which, more than another, has the character of a boundary. Had history required it, the Loire, the Seine, the Meuse, the Elbe, and the Oder would have, to the same extent as the Rhine, that character of a natural frontier which has caused so many infractions of the fundamental right,—the will of men. Strategical considerations are mooted. Nothing is absolute; it is clear that many concessions must be made to necessity. But these concessions need not go too far. Otherwise the whole world would claim its military conveniences; and there would be war without end. No, it is no more the land than the race that makes a nation. The land provides the *substratum*, the field of battle and work; man provides the soul. Man is everything in the formation of that sacred thing which we call a people. Nothing of a material nature suffices for it. A nation is a spiritual principle, the result of profound historical complications, a spiritual family, not a group determined by the configuration of the soil. We have now seen what do not suffice for the creation of such a spiritual principle; race, language, interests, religious affinity, geography, military necessities. What more, then, is necessary?

III

A nation is a living soul, a spiritual principle. Two things, which in truth are but one, constitute this soul, this spiritual principle. One is in the past, the other in the present. One is the common possession of a rich heritage of memories; the other is the actual consent, the desire to live together, the will to preserve worthily the undivided inheritance which has been handed down. Man does not improvise. The nation, like the individual, is the outcome of a long past of efforts, and sacrifices, and devotion. Ancestor-worship is therefore all the more legitimate; for our ancestors have made us what we are. A heroic past, great men, glory—I mean glory of the genuine kind,—these form the social capital, upon which a national idea may be founded. To have common glories in the past, a common will in the present; to have done great things together, to will to do the like again,—such are the essential conditions for the making of a people. We love in proportion to the sacrifices we have consented to make, to the sufferings we have endured.

We love the house that we have built, and will hand down to our descendants. The Spartan hymn, "We are what you were; we shall be what you are," is in its simplicity the national anthem of every land.

In the past an inheritance of glory and regrets to be shared, in the future a like ideal to be realised; to have suffered, and rejoiced, and hoped together; all these things are worth more than custom-houses in common, and frontiers in accordance with strategical ideas; all these can be understood in spite of diversities of race and language. I said just now, "to have suffered together," for indeed suffering in common is a greater bond of union than joy. As regards national memories, mournings are worth more than triumphs; for they impose duties, they demand common effort.

A nation is then a great solidarity, constituted by the sentiment of the sacrifices that its citizens have made, and of those that they feel prepared to make once more. It implies a past; but it is summed up in the present by a tangible fact—consent, the clearly expressed desire to live a common life. A nation's existence is—if you will pardon the metaphor—a daily plebiscite, as the individual's existence is a perpetual affirmation of life. I know very well that this is less metaphysical than divine right, less brutal than pseudo-historic right. In the order of ideas that I submit to you, a nation has no more right than a king to say to a province, "Thou art mine; I take thee unto myself." For us, a province means its inhabitants; and if any one has a right to be consulted in such an affair, it is the inhabitants. A nation never favours its true interests when it annexes or retains a country, regardless of the latter's wishes. The will of nations is then the only legitimate criterion; and to it we must always return. . . .

The nations are not something eternal. They have had their beginnings, they shall have their end. A European confederation will probably take their place. But such is not the law of the age in which we live. At the present hour, the existence of nations is good, even necessary. Their existence is the guarantee of liberty, which would be lost if the world had but one law and one master.

By their diverse and often antagonistic faculties, the nations take part in the common work of civilisation; each brings a note to that great chorus of humanity, which in sum is the highest ideal reality to which we attain. Isolated, their parts are feeble. I often tell myself that an individual who should have the faults regarded by nations as good qualities, who should feed himself with vain glory, who should be in the same way jealous, egoistical, and quarrelsome, who should be able to bear nothing without drawing the sword, would be the most unsupportable of men. But all these discords of detail disappear in the mass. Poor humanity, how much thou hast suffered! How many trials await thee still! May the spirit of wisdom be thy guide, and preserve thee from the countless perils with which thy path is sown!

But to resume: man is neither enslaved by his race, nor by his language, nor by his religion, nor by the course of rivers, nor by the direction of mountain ranges. A great aggregation of men, sane of mind, and warm of heart, creates a moral consciousness, which is called a nation. So far as this moral consciousness proves its strength, through the sacrifices exacted by the individual's abdication for the good of the community, it is legitimate and has a right to exist. If doubts arise concerning frontiers, consult the populations in dispute. They have a very good right to have a voice in the matter. This no doubt will bring a smile to the transcendentalists of politics, those infallible beings who pass their lives in self-deception, and from the height of their superior principles look down in pity upon our modest views. "Consult the populations, indeed! What artlessness! These are the pitiful French ideas, which would replace diplomacy and war by an infantine simplicity." Let us wait; let us suffer the reign of the transcendentalists to pass away; let us know how to submit to the disdain of the strong. It may be that after much unfruitful groping the world will return to our modest empirical solutions. At certain times, the way to be right in the future consists in knowing how to resign ourselves to being out of the fashion in the present.

5   The Nation-State

"Nation," "state," and "nation-state" are notoriously slippery terms; although they are used sometimes as synonyms, important differences of meaning are often implied in the choice of word. In Reading 5, Leonard Tivey explores some nuances of the terms, and follows a consistent usage, in which the "state" is a structure of governmental authority based on sovereignty, not on personal identity; the "nation" is a community of identity in Renan's sense; and the "nation-state" is the political community that arises when the legal boundaries of the state coincide with the emotional boundaries of the nation. Tivey also puts the nation-state into perspective, showing that it is, like everything else in human history, a temporary formation. Nation-states were preceded by city-states and empires, and may one day be succeeded by some other form of organized political power. Yet for the time being, the nation-state remains the dominant paradigm of political community in the modern world, the standard against which all other possibilities are measured.

Leonard Tivey is Senior Lecturer in Political Science at the University of Birmingham in England. Reading 5 is taken from his edited book *The Nation-State: The Formation of Modern Politics*.

● ● ● ● ● ● ● ● ● ●

Swooping in from Mars, invaders of this planet would no doubt have many preconceptions. Whether they would guess that the earth's inhabitants were divided into a large number of separate groupings, very different in size, each claiming exclusive control of a patch of the earth's surface, is surely problematic. That this segmentation should seem to the inhabitants entirely normal and an inherent part of the order of things, would be an even less likely expectation.

However, such is the condition of mankind. . . . Though people have always associated in some sort of localized units, their congregation into nation-states is a modern development; indeed, in its fully fledged style it is essentially contemporary. . . .

STATES

The state is a specific type of political formation—that is, it is not *any* sort of polity or political system. For instance, there were in earlier times sets of social arrangements that relied so much on customary rules and on enforcement by social pressure that no real central authority existed within the community. Such rudimentary systems scarcely amounted to states. Again, in contemporary times the relations *among* states make up a political order but there is no supreme state. Whatever it is, the United Nations is not a state. Thirdly, there are within many institutions methods of rule, forms of government, types of political activity that clearly do not add up to a state. Some of these other institutional structures, such as churches, sporting organizations and multinational businesses transcend the frontiers of states. So politics is more than the state.

Though some of the earliest societies might not contain states, there certainly developed means of governing tribes or other human groups that might, in retrospect and with some generosity, be called states. This does not mean that such authorities were thought of in ways at all similar to the way in which modern people think of their states. Characteristically, the system of rule would be centred on a personal ruler, chief, king or emperor, and though there are many examples of other arrangements, they too were based on custom, religion, legend or magic. Only the Greeks managed to think about politics in its own terms. Detailed, rigid and autocratic administrative systems were built up by some rulers, such as the Pharaohs and the Incas, focussing of course on the supreme or god-king. But for most of the world and for most of the time, social and economic organization was a localized affair, with coercion applied mainly from outside and perhaps accepted as a necessary protection.

Three structures deserve special mention. The term *city-state* is applied to the cities of ancient Greece and Renaissance Italy, and to other similar political units. The title is deserved (retrospectively of course) since independent constitutional government was their essential attribute. Secondly, the largest political formation has been the great empire—overriding local rule by military force and leading to structures sometimes vast in extent, which in the greatest and more enduring examples, such as Rome, bring about the dissemination over wide areas of customs, law, culture and civilization. They may be called *empire-states* for convenience. The third structure, that of Western Europe in its middle ages, contained the Holy Roman Empire, founded by Charlemagne around 800, and numerous kingdoms, dukedoms, and lesser authorities, and the Roman Catholic Church claiming both independent control of religious matters and the right to judge the propriety of secular rule. The kingdoms of medieval Europe contained an apparatus of government that often aspired to statehood, but that was enmeshed in a system that did not allow it sovereign powers. What all three structures certainly lacked was the idea of the nation; whether or not they were states, they were not nation-states.

The word state came into its modern usage in Europe at the time of the Renaissance. From its Latin root it became *estat* in old French, and eventually *Staat* in German, *état* in French and *state* in English. The English word 'estate' has a similar derivation. The factor of land or territory is common to both terms, and both descend from a feudal system in which forms of landholding were fundamental to the political structure. However, Quentin Skinner notes in early usages the absence of 'the distinctively modern idea of the State as a form of public power separate from both the ruler and the ruled, and constituting the supreme political authority within a certain defined territory'.

The crucial element is that of an 'independent political apparatus' distinct from the ruler, and which indeed the ruler has a duty to maintain. This is the central conception of the modern state. There is ultimately an abstraction, capable of existing in perpetuity, but in practice it needs to be operated by an authoritative government, which can change.

This apparatus of continuing government embodies a system of law (at first derived from customary practices) backed by force. In Europe in the middle ages laws might be defined, and enforced, by civil authorities of various types (the emperor, kings or princes, feudal lords) or by the Church. The emergence of the modern state brought with it the idea of sovereignty—a single authority both for making laws and with force to sustain them—within a sharply defined and consolidated territory. The first part of the story of the rise of the nation-state is therefore the story of the rise of sovereignty. In Europe this meant the removal of entrenched rights and powers of lesser authorities—nobles, barons, local or regional autonomies, customary privileges—and the removal of the political jurisdiction of the Roman Catholic Church. The achievement of sovereignty involved long and confused struggles, and was nowhere a simple process. The sovereignty of the unified state was commonly brought about by the sovereignty of a particular state institution—in Europe's 'age of absolutism' that of monarchy (and hence that of the great dynasties, Romanoff, Hohenzollern, Bourbon and Habsburg) though eventually in Britain the legal sovereignty of Parliament was decisive. But such solutions were overtaken by a more fundamental political development—the basing of political legitimacy not on divine right nor on existing law, tradition or customs, but on contemporary choice: on the will of the people.

NATIONS

It is not appropriate to detail here the spread of democratic ideals or to examine the means for their fulfilment. The creation of the United States of America and the revolution in France were heralds of the new doctrine. The democratic revolutions, however, brought with them another new doctrine — nationalism. The famous opening words of the United States constitution of 1787 'We, the people of the United States . . .' (that is, not the states themselves, and not *any* people) are significant, and so is the retrospective interpretation by Abraham Lincoln: 'Fourscore and seven years ago, our fathers brought forth on this continent a new *nation* . . .' The revolution of 1789 proclaimed the Rights of Man, but it led to assertions of the sovereignty of the French people. In the aftermath, the people who should rule (or at least in whose name rule should be exercised) were conceptualized, delimited and moralized as 'the nation'.

The emergence of nationalism was of course another long process. Elie Kedourie confidently asserts that 'Nationalism is a doctrine invented in Europe at the beginning of the nineteenth century'. By that time, however, there were in existence countries that had long-established political and cultural unity, notably France and England. They may be taken as the prototypes. What was invented in the early nineteenth century was the ideology — the belief that nations were the natural and only true political units, the foundations on which states, governments and their policies should depend. Thus arrives the concept of the nation-state as an ideal. Its realization over the world did not take place until the twentieth century, when the great empires of Holland, Turkey, France and Britain collapsed. By that time the ideology had bitten very deeply indeed into people's political assumptions. By that time, too, serious problems were apparent.
. . .

What is 'a nation,' that it should have attracted such honour and respect? By derivation the word comes from the Latin root *nasci*, to be born, and so began with the idea of a people of common breed or place of origin. But an appeal to ethnicity begs many questions in view of invasions, migrations and racial mixtures in the same community. Nor does the social bond of common language provide an answer, for obviously some languages (English, Spanish, German) are used by many nations, and other nations even in Europe (the Swiss, the Belgians) have more than one language, while in Africa and Asia linguistic profusion continues. Perhaps the point to emphasize is that the state itself does not merely reflect the qualities of nations: it fashions them. By a state-enforced educational system, linguistic uniformity can be promoted. Moreover, by nationality laws the state registers an official membership of the nation, equating it with its own citizenship. Legal requirements for nationality look to parentage (as in Roman law) or to place of birth, or both. Acceptance of new-comers is described as 'naturalization.' In some countries, notably the United States, the quantity and variety of immigration made common citizenship a vital instrument of national consciousness and loyalty—not-withstanding the retention of other loyalties by sub-groups such as Irish Americans and African Americans. If American nationhood is one of the more remarkable achievements of the idea of nationality, the idea of a British nation was one of the boldest. For the creation of the state of Great Britain after 1707 (the United Kingdom of Great Britain and Ireland was established in 1805) led to a state-defined British nationality, still officially recognized in religion and some sports for example. The protean nature of nationality is not confined to its later-twentieth-century developments.

In order to avoid a description of the multiform complexities of actual nationalisms at this stage, and to avoid anticipating the essays themselves, a first understanding of 'the nation' may be achieved by noting the claims of its supporters, the nationalists.

(i) It is assumed, and if necessary vigorously asserted, that the nation is a natural unit of society: it is inherent and not imposed or artificial. Nor is it really something chosen or voluntary, for though it may admit some new recruits, they are assimilated to an existing body.

(ii) Members of a nation have a great deal in common: there is a form of homogeneity that (unlike citizenship) is not merely formal or legal. The foundations of this unity lie both in shared interests and in shared experiences, recounted in history and embodied in such things as literature, music, sport, cooking, customs and morality. Even religion may take on distinctive national forms.

(iii) Each nation needs its own polity, for otherwise it will not be able to realize the fruits of its character and culture—it will be oppressed. In practice the required polity is usually an independent sovereign state, though there are occasional examples where autonomy or home rule has sufficed.

(iv) All states, of course, control defined territories, but it is really the nation that has an inalienable right to its proper territory or home-land wherein to dwell.

(v) A nation should feel self-confident: it needs prestige and success, and to be respected by others. It needs to stand well in the world.

These claims of the nationalists represent an ideal. They are nowhere met in full. In some cases there is an approximation to the ideal, but in others there is bitter grievance over the absence of one requirement or another. Some-times nationalists urge their countrymen to stir themselves to greater efforts to achieve unity or prosperity or success or glory. They may sometimes urge emulation of other nations. They will certainly urge resistance, if necessary to the point of violence, against oppression or exploitation from another nation.

An important attribute of a nation, of course, is its own self-awareness. Many difficulties — such as lack of a common language, or a short history — may be overcome if people in a particular place become convinced of their own nationhood. The struggle to assert such nationhood may in fact generate the achievements (military or cultural) and fuse the unity that are necessary to establish the truth of the original assertion.

The general acceptance of nationalist beliefs is, paradoxically, shown by the terms used to describe counter-national arrangements. The most notable term is 'international,' which refers to relations or cooperation among nation-states. International bodies and internationalist beliefs do not reject nations or nationalism (though they may restrain excesses). They accept and endorse nations as the entities between which relations take place, and recognize states as their agents. The United Nations is in fact an organization of states, but its name asserts that it is bringing together existing nations, not miscellaneous peoples and groups. So too with terms like supranational, and multinational: they implicitly accept that what is being integrated or linked are states or associations or enterprises that belong to nations. There is a prior assumption of the reality of nations before the attempts to transcend them can be understood.

To get away from these assumptions is difficult. It is not easy even to find a vocabulary. 'Anarchy' implies a rejection of government by force, and is opposed to states in general rather than to particular forms. 'Individualism' is often used in senses that do not oppose nationalism — thus in contemporary politics many advocates of economic individualism and free markets are also strong believers in national prowess. 'Transnational' is sometimes used to imply that nations can be transcended, but it still hints that nations are real. The best available term seems to be 'cosmopolitan,' since it at least indicates that nationality as a political criterion might be rejected or ignored or relegated to a place of secondary concern. Cosmopolitanism as a distinctive political cause is very rarely made explicit. It can sometimes be discerned as an underlying attitude — in admirers of dynastic rule or of old conglomerate empires, in the managerial technocrats of some multinational businesses, in some high intellectual élites, in some schools of Marxists, and in some other revolutionaries. The cosmopolitan element is characteristically contingent on the rest of the outlook. Since most ideologies are capable of advantageous alliance with nationalism, there are few circumstances in which cosmopolitanism seems essential, and apart from the examples mentioned it attracts little support.

Thus it is now widely held not only that the nation-state is a universal phenomenon, but that nationalism is the common ideology of the world and is likely to remain so. . . . Yet there is point for the student of politics in understanding that nationalism *is* an ideology, that its origins and its forms can be explained, and that since there was a past without it, a future beyond it is not inconceivable. To acknowledge its present force or even to recommend its acceptance in preference to alternatives is not to suggest submergence in its values. In 1862 Lord Acton recognized the services of the idea of nationality:

> Although, therefore, the theory of nationality is more absurd and more criminal than the theory of socialism, it has an important mission in the world, and marks the final conflict, and therefore the end, of two forces which are the worst enemies of civil freedom—the absolute monarchy and the revolution.

Acton was a liberal and an optimist. Since he wrote, absolutisms, revolutions and nationalisms have abounded and the cosmopolitan individualism that he respected is not yet with us. Yet his message is significant. It is possible to recognize the role of nationalism, as Acton did, without being a nationalist. Certainly there are grounds on which its premises can be rejected and its morals questioned. It is not quite universal. Ernest Gellner in 1964 accepted that, in contemporary circumstances, nationality is a necessary condition and attribute of man, and a touchstone of the boundaries of political units. Thus nationhood, with statehood as its concomitant, is at present needed to satisfy certain ends. But Gellner also asks '. . . why should men have become particularly concerned about the ethnic rubric under which they survived? (Czechs who settled in Vienna, or Chicago, and in due course became Austrians or Americans, did not find this fate unbearable.)' The pragmatic case for the nation-state is not the same as the nationalist case for the nation-state.

ALTERNATIVES?

Is it possible to foresee a period after that of the nation-state? Can an alternative political formation be imagined? In previous eras, fragmentation was overborne by the raising of great empires. Is there a new way? Already there have been leagues, unions, communities, associations and organizations that try to establish something 'above' or 'among' states and that are intended to have a more or less enduring character. These arrangements begin by accepting existing states, and so have the virtue of practicality. The reasoning behind them has parallels with that behind those states that were created by process of 'unification'—that is, it is argued that the evils of hostility, rivalry and lack of coordination can be overcome by some sort of established rule or authority (albeit one dependent on wide consent) that will modify the absolute independence of states. Radical thinking on these lines looks towards actual federation as an even more effective step towards unity, perhaps ultimately hoping for a 'federation of the world' or some sort of 'world government' as the logical culmination — sometime in the future — of a widening span of effective political authority.

For others, these prospects seem daunting. A world-state is not only a distant possibility but if achieved would be for most people a very remote affair indeed. If it claimed sovereignty on the nation-state model, over the whole globe, it could develop into a system of universal oppression. Moreover, if its rule were to become acceptable it would need the underpinning of a common ideology. Could some version of 'humanism' serve the world as nationalism serves the state? Or, if a more precise set of common beliefs were necessary, would not such a universal dogma become in itself a form of intellectual and moral oppression?

So some look in other directions. In the early part of this century, a school of political writers attacked the sovereign pretentions of the state in favour of a version of pluralism, in which other associations (religious or economic) might attract similar loyalties. In the theory of international politics, David Mitrany argued that the functional requirements of modern society would result in the establishment of numerous overlapping organizations that would eventually limit the effectiveness of independent state action. In neither case was there an adequate explanation of what was to become of the basic role of the state in providing law backed by force, or of nationalist feelings. Nevertheless the growth of organizations that spread beyond the frontiers of states and the development of rapid communications are obvious contemporary phenomena. Theories of the breakdown of the effectiveness of sovereign independence therefore seem to have the merits of feasibility and of realism. They reflect things that are happening. The difficulty is that, for those who seek a way to human salvation, they are inadequate. The bonds on which they rely are not strong enough to restrain the legal authority and military coherence of states. . . .

6   The Rule of Law

An essential aspect of the political community is law—enforceable rules of conduct by which we can adjust our behaviour to the requirements of collective existence. Integrally related to Aristotle's understanding of politics as reasoned discussion is his notion of the supremacy of law:

> He who bids the law rule may be deemed to bid God and Reason alone rule, but he who bids man rule adds an element of the beast; for desire is a wild beast, and passion perverts the minds of rulers, even when they are the best of men.

The "rule of law" is the ordinary term used in Western political thought to describe this Aristotelian emphasis on reason over passion. The application of the rule of law to Canadian politics is illustrated by Reading 6, the opinion of Justice Rand in the case of *Roncarelli v. Duplessis*, decided by the Supreme Court of Canada in 1959. Maurice Duplessis, premier and attorney general of Quebec, had advised the manager of the Liquor Commission to cancel the liquor licence of Frank Roncarelli, who ran a restaurant in Montreal. The only reason given for the cancellation was that Roncarelli, a Jehovah's Witness, had repeatedly guaranteed bail for co-religionists charged with illegally selling pamphlets on the street.

No longer able to make a living as a restaurateur, Roncarelli sold his business. He later sued Premier Duplessis under a section of the Quebec Code of Civil Procedure which allowed citizens to recover damages caused by public officials acting outside their legal sphere of responsibility. Roncarelli won at the trial level and appealed to the Supreme Court of Canada after his initial victory had been reversed by the Quebec Court of Appeal. The Supreme Court then decided in his favour. Justice Rand held that the action of Duplessis was arbitrary because there was no rational connection between Roncarelli's legal activities as a Jehovah's Witness and his fitness to sell liquor.

Although the rule of law is now entrenched in the preamble to the Canadian Charter of Rights and Freedoms, it was not mentioned in any constitutional text at the time of *Roncarelli v. Duplessis*. But the Supreme Court held in effect that the rule of law was implicit in the Canadian constitution and could be used by the courts to justify review of executive action. In Aristotelian terms, it was a victory for reason over passion.

Reading 6 is the opinion of Justice Ivan Rand in *Roncarelli v. Duplessis.* Justice Rand, who sat on the Supreme Court from 1943 to 1959, is well known for his Supreme Court judgments in favour of civil liberties.

● ● ● ● ● ● ● ● ● ●

Rand, J.: — The material facts from which my conclusion is drawn are these. The appellant was the proprietor of a restaurant in a busy section of Montreal which in 1946 through its transmission to him from his father had been continuously licensed for the sale of liquor for approximately 34 years; he is of good education and repute and the restaurant was of a superior class. On December 4th of that year, while his application for annual renewal was before the Liquor Commission, the existing licence was cancelled and his application for renewal rejected, to which was added a declaration by the respondent that no future licence would ever issue to him. These primary facts took place in the following circumstances:

For some years the appellant had been an adherent of a rather militant Christian religious sect known as the Witnesses of Jehovah. Their ideology condemns the established church institutions and stresses the absolute and exclusive personal relation of the individual to the Deity without human intermediation or intervention.

The first impact of their proselytizing zeal upon the Roman Catholic church and community in Quebec, as might be expected, produced a violent reaction. Meetings were forcibly broken up, property damaged, individuals ordered out of communities, in one case out of the Province, and generally, within the cities and towns, bitter controversy aroused. The work of the Witnesses was carried on both by word of mouth and by the distribution of printed matter, the latter including two periodicals known as "The Watch Tower" and "Awake," sold at a small price.

In 1945 the provincial authorities began to take steps to bring an end to what was considered insulting and offensive to the religious beliefs and feelings of the Roman Catholic population. Large scale arrests were made of young men and women, by whom the publications mentioned were being held out for sale, under local by-laws requiring a licence for peddling any kind of wares. Altogether almost one thousand of such charges were laid. The penalty involved in Montreal, where most of the arrests took place, was a fine of $40, and as the Witnesses disputed liability, bail was in all cases resorted to.

The appellant, being a person of some means, was accepted by the Recorder's Court as bail without question, and up to November 12, 1946 he had gone security in about 380 cases, some of the accused being involved in repeated offences. Up to this time there had been no suggestion of impropriety; the security of the appellant was taken as so satisfactory that at times, to avoid delay when he was absent from the city, recognizances were signed by him in blank and kept ready for completion by the Court officials. The reason for the accumulation of charges was the doubt that they could be sustained in law. Apparently the legal officers of Montreal, acting in concert with those of the Province, had come to an agreement with the attorney for the Witnesses to have a test case proceeded with. Pending that, however, there was no stoppage of the sale of the tracts and this became the annoying circumstance that produced the volume of proceedings.

On or about November 12th it was decided to require bail in cash for Witnesses so arrested and the sum set ranged from $100 to $300. No such bail was furnished by the appellant; his connection with giving security ended with this change of practice; and in the result, all of the charges in relation to which he had become surety were dismissed.

At no time did he take any part in the distribution of the tracts: he was an adherent of the group but nothing more. It was shown that he had leased to another member premises in Sherbrooke which were used as a hall for carrying on religious meetings: but it is unnecessary to do more than mention that fact to reject it as having no bearing on the issues raised. Beyond the giving of bail and being an adherent, the appellant is free from any relation that could be tortured into a badge of character pertinent to his fitness or unfitness to hold a liquor licence.

The mounting resistance that stopped the surety bail sought other means of crushing the propagandist invasion and among the circumstances looked into was the situation of the appellant. Admittedly an adherent, he was enabling these protagonists to be at large to carry on their campaign of publishing what they believed to be the Christian truth as revealed by the Bible; he was also the holder of a liquor licence, a "privilege" granted by the Province, the profits from which, as it was seen by the authorities, he was using to promote the disturbance of settled beliefs and arouse community disaffection generally. Following discussions between the then Mr. Archambault, as the personality of the Liquor Commission, and the chief prosecuting officer in Montreal, the former, on or about November 21st, telephoned to the respondent, advised him of those facts, and queried what should be done. Mr. Duplessis answered that the matter was serious and that the identity of the person furnishing bail and the liquor licensee should be put beyond doubt. A few days later, that identity being established through a private investigator, Mr. Archambault again communicated with the respondent and, as a result of what passed between them, the licence, as of December 4, 1946, was revoked.

In the meantime, about November 25, 1946, a blasting answer had come from the Witnesses. In an issue of one of the periodicals, under the heading "Quebec's Burning Hate," was a searing denunciation of what was alleged to be the savage persecution of Christian believers. Immediately instructions were sent out from the Department of the Attorney-General ordering the confiscation of the issue and proceedings were taken against one Boucher charging him with publication of a seditious libel.

It is then wholly as a private citizen, an adherent of a religious group, holding a liquor licence and furnishing bail to arrested persons for no other purpose than to enable them to be released from detention pending the determination of the charges against them, and with no other relevant considerations to be taken into account, that he is involved in the issues of this controversy.

The complementary state of things is equally free from doubt. From the evidence of Mr. Duplessis and Mr. Archambault alone, it appears that the action taken by the latter as the General Manager and sole member of the Commission was dictated by Mr. Duplessis as Attorney-General and Prime Minister of the Province; that that step was taken as a means of bringing to a halt the activities of the Witnesses, to punish the appellant for the part he had played not only by revoking the existing licence but in declaring him barred from one "forever," and to warn others that they similarly would be stripped of provincial "privileges" if they persisted in any activity directly or indirectly related to the Witnesses and to the objectionable campaign. The respondent felt that action to be his duty, something which his conscience demanded of him; and as representing the Provincial Government his decision became automatically that of Mr. Archambault and the Commission. . . .

[Here are omitted lengthy excerpts from testimony proving the actions of the premier.]

In these circumstances, when the *de facto* power of the Executive over its appointees at will to such a statutory public function is exercised deliberately and intentionally to destroy the vital business interests of a citizen, is there legal redress by him against the person so acting? This calls for an examination of the statutory provisions governing the issue, renewal and revocation of liquor licences and the scope of authority entrusted by law to the Attorney-General and the Government in relation to the administration of the Act. . . .

The provisions of the statute, which may be supplemented by detailed Regulations, furnish a code for the complete administration of the sale and distribution of alcoholic liquors directed by the Commission as a public service, for all legitimate purposes of the populace. It recognizes the association of wines and liquors as embellishments of food and its ritual and as

an interest of the public. As put in Macbeth, the "sauce to meat is cere-
mony," and so we have restaurants, cafés, hotels and other places of
serving food, specifically provided for in that association.

At the same time the issue of permits has a complementary interest in
those so catering to the public. The continuance of the permit over the
years, as in this case, not only recognizes its virtual necessity to a superior
class restaurant but also its identification with the business carried on. The
provisions for assignments of the permit are to this most pertinent and they
were exemplified in the continuity of the business here. As its exercise
continues, the economic life of the holder becomes progressively more
deeply implicated with the privilege while at the same time his vocation
becomes correspondingly dependent on it.

The field of licensed occupations and businesses of this nature is
steadily becoming of greater concern to citizens generally. It is a matter of
vital importance that a public administration that can refuse to allow a
person to enter or continue a calling which, in the absence of regulation,
would be free and legitimate, should be conducted with complete impartiality and integrity; and that the grounds for refusing or cancelling a permit
should unquestionably be such and such only as are incompatible with the
purposes envisaged by the statute: the duty of a Commission is to serve
those purposes and those only. A decision to deny or cancel such a privilege
lies within the "discretion" of the Commission; but that means that decision is to be based upon a weighing of considerations pertinent to the object
of the administration.

In public regulation of this sort there is no such thing as absolute and
untrammelled "discretion," that is that action can be taken on any ground
of for any reason that can be suggested to the mind of the administrator; no
legislative Act can, without express language, be taken to contemplate an
unlimited arbitrary power, exercisable for any purpose, however capricious
or irrelevant, regardless of the nature or purpose of the statute. Fraud and
corruption in the Commission may not be mentioned in such statutes but
they are always implied as exceptions. "Discretion" necessarily implies
good faith in discharging public duty; there is always a perspective within
which a statute is intended to operate; and any clear departure from its lines
or objects is just as objectionable as fraud or corruption. Could an applicant
be refused a permit because he had been born in another Province, or
because of the colour of his hair? The ordinary language of the Legislature
cannot be so distorted.

To deny or revoke a permit because a citizen exercises an unchallengeable right totally irrelevant to the sale of liquor in a restaurant is equally
beyond the scope of the discretion conferred. There was here not only
revocation of the existing permit but a declaration of a future, definitive

disqualification of the appellant to obtain one: it was to be "forever." This purports to divest his citizenship status of its incident of membership in the class of those of the public to whom such a privilege could be extended. Under the statutory language here, that is not competent to the Commission and a *a fortiori* to the Government or the respondent: *McGillivray v. Kimber* (1915), 26 D.L.R. 164, 52 S.C.R. 146. There is here an administrative tribunal which, in certain respects, is to act in a judicial manner; and even on the view of the dissenting Justices in *McGillivray*, there is liability; what could be more malicious than to punish this licensee for having done what he had an absolute right to do in a matter utterly irrelevant to the *Alcoholic Liquor Act*? Malice in the proper sense is simply acting for a reason and purpose knowingly foreign to the administration, to which was added here the element of intentional punishment by what was virtually vocation outlawry.

It may be difficult if not impossible in cases generally to demonstrate a breach of this public duty in the illegal purpose served; there may be no means, even if proceedings against the Commission were permitted by the Attorney-General, as here they were refused, of compelling the Commission to justify a refusal or revocation or to give reasons for its action; on these questions I make no observation; but in the case before us that difficulty is not present: the reasons are openly avowed.

The act of the respondent through the instrumentality of the Commission brought about a breach of an implied public statutory duty toward the appellant; it was a gross abuse of legal power expressly intended to punish him for an act wholly irrelevant to the statute, a punishment which inflicted on him, as it was intended to do, the destruction of his economic life as a restaurant keeper within the Province. Whatever may be the immunity of the Commission or its member from an action for damages, there is none in the respondent. He was under no duty in relation to the appellant and his act was an intrusion upon the functions of a statutory body. The injury done by him was a fault engaging liability within the principles of the underlying public law of Quebec: *Mostyn v. Fabrigas* (1774), 1 Cowp. 161, 98 E.R. 1021, and under art. 1053 of the *Civil Code*. That, in the presence of expanding administrative regulation of economic activities, such a step and its consequences are to be suffered by the victim without recourse or remedy, that an administration according to law is to be superseded by action dictated by and according to the arbitrary likes, dislikes and irrelevant purposes of public officers acting beyond their duty, would signalize the beginning of disintegration of the rule of law as a fundamental postulate of our constitutional structure. An administration of licences on the highest level of fair and impartial treatment to all may be forced to follow the practice of "first come, first served," which makes the strictest observance of equal responsibility to all of even greater importance; at this stage of developing government it would be a danger of high consequence to tolerate such a departure from good faith in executing the legislative purpose. It should be added, however, that that principle is not, by this language, intended to be extended to ordinary governmental employment: with that we are not here concerned.

It was urged by Mr. Beaulieu that the respondent, as the incumbent of an office of state, so long as he was proceeding in "good faith," was free to act in a matter of this kind virtually as he pleased. The office of Attorney-General traditionally and by statute carries duties that relate to advising the Executive, including here, administrative bodies, enforcing the public law and directing the administration of justice. In any decision of the statutory body in this case, he had no part to play beyond giving advice on legal questions arising. In that role his action should have been limited to advice on the validity of a revocation for such a reason or purpose and what that advice should have been does not seem to me to admit of any doubt. To pass from this limited scope of action to that of bringing about a step by the Commission beyond the bounds prescribed by the Legislature for its exclusive action converted what was done into his personal act.

"Good faith" in this context, applicable both to the respondent and the General Manager, means carrying out the statute according to its intent and for its purpose; it means good faith in acting with a rational appreciation of that intent and purpose and not with an improper intent and for an alien purpose; it does not mean for the purposes of punishing a person for exercising an unchallengeable right; it does not mean arbitrarily and illegally attempting to divest a citizen of an incident of his civil status. . . .

A subsidiary defence was that notice of action had not been given as required by art. 88 *C.C.P.* This provides generally that, without such notice, no public officer or person fulfilling any public function or duty is liable in damages "by reason of any act done by him in the exercise of his functions." Was the act here, then, done by the respondent in the course of that exercise? The basis of the claim, as I have found it, is that the act was quite beyond the scope of any function or duty committed to him, so far so that it was done exclusively in a private capacity, however much in fact the influence of public office and power may have carried over into it. It would be only through an assumption of a general overriding power of executive direction in statutory administrative matters that any colour of propriety in the act could be found. But such an assumption would be in direct conflict with fundamental postulates of our Provincial as well as Dominion Government; and in the actual circumstances there is not a shadow of justification for it in the statutory language.

The damages suffered involved the vocation of the appellant within the Province. Any attempt at a precise computation or estimate must assume probabilities in an area of uncertainty and risk. The situation is one which the Court should approach as a jury would, in a view of its broad features; and in the best consideration I can give to them, the damages should be fixed at the sum of $25,000 plus that allowed by the trial Court.

I would therefore allow the appeals, set aside the judgment of the Court of Queen's Bench and restore the judgment at trial modified by increasing the damages to the sum of $33,123.53. The appellant should have his costs in the Court of Queen's Bench and in this Court.

7   Realism

Once states come into existence, the question arises as to how they will deal with one another. Broadly speaking, there are two schools of thought on this question in political science. The "realist" position holds that, in the absence of a supranational sovereign power to enforce international law, states will be guided by their own national interest, with self-preservation as their highest priority. Thus we cannot expect leaders of states to conduct foreign policy as if other states would always act morally. States must expect the worst and be prepared for it. Consequently, the highest virtue in international politics is prudence, and the test of morality is real-world consequences, not good intentions. In contrast, the "idealist" or "liberal" position holds that states can be bound by international law, and that morality can triumph over *Realpolitik*. Because history seems to offer greater support for realism, advocates of idealism usually postulate the necessity of some fundamental structural change, such as the creation of the League of Nations or the United Nations, as a precondition for more moral behaviour in the future. Without denying the value of such changes, realists note that it is not easy to alter the predatory aspects of human nature nor the logic of the state system, which pits states against one another in a Hobbesian "war of all against all."

Hans J. Morgenthau (1904-1980) was a German-Jewish refugee from fascism. For many years a professor of political science at the University of Chicago, he was a distinguished exponent of realism. He became an early opponent of American involvement in the Vietnam War, not because he shared the naive illusion that the Viet Cong were noncommunist agrarian reformers, but because he thought that Vietnam was too close to China for a Western power to be able to win the war. This selection is from chapter 1 of Morgenthau's well-known textbook of international relations, *Politics among Nations: The Struggle for Power and Peace.*

● ● ● ● ● ● ● ● ● ●

The history of modern political thought is the story of a contest between two schools that differ fundamentally in their conceptions of the nature of man, society, and politics. One believes that a rational and moral political order, derived from universally valid abstract principles, can be achieved here and now. It assumes the essential goodness and infinite malleability of human nature, and blames the failure of the social order to measure up to the rational standards on lack of knowledge and understanding, obsolescent social institutions, or the depravity of certain isolated individuals or groups. It trusts in education, reform, and the sporadic use of force to remedy these defects.

The other school believes that the world, imperfect as it is from the rational point of view, is the result of forces inherent in human nature. To improve the world one must work with these forces, not against them. This being inherently a world of opposing interests and of conflict among them, moral principles can never be fully realized, but must at best be approximated through the ever temporary balancing of interests and the ever precarious settlement of conflicts. This school, then, sees in a system of checks and balances a universal principle for all pluralist societies. It appeals to historic precedent rather than to abstract principles, and aims at the realization of the lesser evil rather than of the absolute good.

This theoretical concern with human nature as it actually is, and with the historic processes as they actually take place, has earned for the theory presented here the name of realism. What are the tenets of political realism? No systematic exposition of the philosophy of political realism can be attempted here; it will suffice to single out six fundamental princples, which have frequently been misunderstood.

SIX PRINCIPLES OF POLITICAL REALISM

1. Political realism believes that politics, like society in general, is governed by objective laws that have their roots in human nature. In order to improve society it is first necessary to understand the laws by which society lives. The operation of these laws being impervious to our preferences, men will challenge them only at the risk of failure.

Realism, believing as it does in the objectivity of the laws of politics, must also believe in the possibility of developing a rational theory that reflects, however imperfectly and one-sidedly, these objective laws. It believes also, then, in the possibility of distinguishing in politics between truth and opinion—between what is true objectivity and rationally, supported by evidence and illuminated by reason, and what is only a subjective judgment, divorced from the facts as they are and informed by prejudice and wishful thinking.

Human nature, in which laws of politics have their roots, has not changed since the classical philosophies of China, India, and Greece endeavored to discover these laws. Hence, novelty is not necessarily a virtue in political theory, nor is old age a defect. The fact that a theory of politics, if there be such a theory, has never been heard of before tends to create a presumption against, rather than in favor of, its soundness. Conversely, the fact that a theory of politics was developed hundreds or even thousands of years ago—as was the theory of the balance of power—does not create a presumption that it must be outmoded and obsolete. A theory of politics must be subjected to the dual test of reason and experience. To dismiss such a theory because it had its flowering in centuries past is to present not a rational argument but a modernistic prejudice that takes for granted the superiority of the present over the past. To dispose of the revival of such a theory as a "fashion" or "fad" is tantamount to assuming that in matters political we can have opinions but no truths. . . .

2. The main signpost that helps political realism to find its way through the landscape of international politics is the concept of interest defined in terms of power. This concept provides the link between reason trying to understand international politics and the facts to be understood. It sets politics as an autonomous sphere of action and understanding apart from other spheres, such as economics (understood in terms of interest defined as wealth), ethics, aesthetics, or religion. Without such a concept a theory of politics, international or domestic, would be altogether impossible, for without it we could not distinguish between political and nonpolitical facts, nor could we bring at least a measure of systematic order to the political sphere.

We assume that statesmen think and act in terms of interest defined as power, and the evidence of history bears that assumption out. That assumption allows us to retrace and anticipate, as it were, the steps a statesman—past, present, or future—has taken or will take on the political scene. We look over his shoulder when he writes his dispatches; we listen in on his conversation with other statesmen; we read and anticipate his very thoughts. Thinking in terms of interest defined as power, we think as he does, and as disinterested observers we understand his thoughts and actions perhaps better than he, the actor on the political scene, does himself.

The concept of interest defined as power imposes intellectual discipline upon the observer, infuses rational order into the subject matter of politics, and thus makes the theoretical understanding of politics possible. On the side of the actor, it provides for rational discipline in action and creates that astounding continuity in foreign policy which makes American, British, or Russian foreign policy appear as an intelligible, rational continuum, by and large consistent within itself, regardless of the different motives, preferences, and intellectual and moral qualities of successive statesmen. A realist theory of international politics, then, will guard against two popular fallacies: the concern with motives and the concern with ideological preferences.

To search for the clue to foreign policy exclusively in the motives of statesmen is both futile and deceptive. It is futile because motives are the most illusive of psychological data, distorted as they are, frequently beyond recognition, by the interests and emotions of actor and observer alike. Do we really know what our own motives are? And what do we know of the motives of others? . . .

We cannot conclude from the good intentions of a statesman that his foreign policies will be either morally praiseworthy or politically successful. Judging his motives, we can say that he will not intentionally pursue policies that are morally wrong, but we can say nothing about the probability of their success. If we want to know the moral and political qualities of his actions, we must know them, not his motives. How often have statesmen been motivated by the desire to improve the world, and ended by making it worse? And how often have they sought one goal, and ended by achieving something they neither expected nor desired?

Neville Chamberlain's politics of appeasement were, as far as we can judge, inspired by good motives; he was probably less motivated by considerations of personal power than were many other British prime ministers, and he sought to preserve peace and to assure the happiness of all concerned. Yet his policies helped to make the Second World War inevitable, and to bring untold miseries to millions of men. Sir Winston Churchill's motives, on the other hand, have been much less universal in scope and much more narrowly directed toward personal and national power, yet the foreign policies that sprang from these inferior motives were certainly superior in moral and political quality to those pursued by his predecessor. Judged by his motives, Robespierre was one of the most virtuous men who ever lived. Yet it was the utopian radicalism of that very virtue that made him kill those less virtuous than himself, brought him to the scaffold, and destroyed the revolution of which he was a leader.

A realist theory of international politics will also avoid the other popular fallacy of equating the foreign policies of a statesman with his philosophic or political sympathies, and of deducing the former from the latter. Statesmen, especially under contemporary conditions, may well make a habit of presenting their foreign policies in terms of their philosophic and political sympathies in order to gain popular support for them. Yet they will distinguish with Lincoln between their *"official* duty," which is to think and act in terms of the national interest, and their *"personal* wish," which is to see their own moral values and political principles realized throughout the world. Political realism does not require, nor does it condone, indifference to political ideals and moral principles, but it requires indeed a sharp distinction between the desirable and the possible—between what is desirable everywhere and at all times and what is possible under the concrete circumstances of time and place.

It stands to reason that not all foreign policies have always followed so rational, objective, and unemotional a course. The contingent elements of personality, prejudice, and subjective preference, and of all the weaknesses of intellect and will which flesh is heir to, are bound to deflect foreign policies from their rational course. Especially where foreign policy is conducted under the conditions of democratic control, the need to marshal popular emotions to the support of foreign policy cannot fail to impair the rationality of foreign policy itself. Yet a theory of foreign policy which aims at rationality must for the time being, as it were, abstract from these irrational elements and seek to paint a picture of foreign policy which presents the rational essence to be found in experience, without the contingent deviations from rationality which are also found in experience. . . .

3. Realism does not endow its key concept of interest defined as power with a meaning that is fixed once and for all. The idea of interest is indeed of the essence of politics and is unaffected by the circumstances of time and place. Thucydides' statement, born of the experiences of ancient Greece, that "identity of interests is the surest of bonds whether between states or individuals" was taken up in the nineteenth century by Lord Salisbury's remark that "the only bond of union that endures" among nations is "the absence of all clashing interests." It was erected into a general principle of government by George Washington:

A small knowledge of human nature will convince us, that, with far the greatest part of mankind, interest is the governing principle; and that almost every man is more or less, under its influence. Motives of public virtue may for a time, or in particular instances, actuate men to the observance of a conduct purely disinterested; but they are not of themselves sufficient to produce persevering conformity to the refined dictates and obligations of social duty. Few men are capable of making a continual sacrifice of all views of private interest, or advantage, to the common good. It is vain to exclaim against the depravity of human nature on this account; the fact is so, the experience of every age and nation has proved it and we must in a great measure, change the constitution of man, before we can make it otherwise. No institution, not built on the presumptive truth of these maxims can succeed. . . .

Yet the kind of interest determining political action in a particular period of history depends upon the political and cultural context within which foreign policy is formulated. The goals that might be pursued by nations in their foreign policy can run the whole gamut of objectives any nation has ever pursued or might possibly pursue. . . .

The realist parts company with other schools of thought before the all-important question of how the contemporary world is to be transformed. The realist is persuaded that this transformation can be achieved only through the workmanlike manipulation of the perennial forces that have shaped the past as they will the future. The realist cannot be persuaded that we can bring about that transformation by confronting a political reality that has its own laws with an abstract ideal that refuses to take those laws into account.

4. Political realism is aware of the moral significance of political action. It is also aware of the ineluctable tension between the moral command and the requirements of successful political action. And it is unwilling to gloss over and obliterate that tension and thus to obfuscate both the moral and the political issue by making it appear as though the stark facts of politics were morally more satisfying than they actually are, and the moral law less exacting that it actually is.

Realism maintains that universal moral principles cannot be applied to the actions of states in their abstract universal formulation, but that they must be filtered through the concrete circumstances of time and place. The individual may say for himself: "*Fiat justitia, pereat mundus* (Let justice be done, even if the world perish)," but the state has no right to say so in the name of those who are in its care. Both individual and state must judge political action by universal moral principles, such as that of liberty. Yet while the individual has a moral right to sacrifice himself in defense of such a moral principle, the state has no right to let its moral disapprobation of the infringement of liberty get in the way of successful political action, itself inspired by the moral principle of national survival. There can be no political morality without prudence; that is, without consideration of the political consequences of seemingly moral action. Realism, then, considers prudence—the weighing of the consequences of alternative political actions—to be the supreme virtue in politics. Ethics in the abstract judges action by its conformity with the moral law; political ethics judges action by its political consequences. Classical and medieval philosophy knew this, and so did Lincoln when he said:

> I do the very best I know how, the very best I can, and I mean to keep doing so until the end. If the end brings me out all right, what is said against me won't amount to anything. If the end brings me out wrong, ten angels swearing I was right would make no difference.

5. Political realism refuses to identify the moral aspirations of a particular nation with the moral laws that govern the universe. As it distinguishes

between truth and opinion, so it distinguishes between truth and idolatry. All nations are tempted—and few have been able to resist the temptation for long—to clothe their own particular aspirations and actions in the moral purposes of the universe. To know that nations are subject to the moral law is one thing, while to pretend to know with certainty what is good and evil in the relations among nations is quite another. There is a world of difference between the belief that all nations stand under the judgment of God, inscrutable to the human mind, and the blasphemous conviction that God is always on one's side and that what one wills oneself cannot fail to be willed by God also.

The lighthearted equation between a particular nationalism and the counsels of Providence is morally indefensible, for it is that very sin of pride against which the Greek tragedians and the Biblical prophets have warned rulers and ruled. That equation is also politically pernicious, for it is liable to engender the distortion in judgment which, in the blindness of crusading frenzy, destroys nations and civilizations—in the name of moral principle, ideal, or God himself.

On the other hand, it is exactly the concept of interest defined in terms of power that saves us from both that moral excess and that political folly. For if we look at all nations, our own included, as political entities pursuing their respective interests defined in terms of power, we are able to do justice to all of them. And we are able to do justice to all of them in a dual sense: We are able to judge other nations as we judge our own and, having judged them in this fashion, we are then capable of pursuing policies that respect the interests of other nations, while protecting and promoting those of our own. Moderation in policy cannot fail to reflect the moderation of moral judgment.

6. The difference, then, between political realism and other schools of thought is real, and it is profound. However much the theory of political realism may have been misunderstood and misinterpreted, there is no gainsaying its distinctive intellectual and moral attitude to matters political.

Intellectually, the political realist maintains the autonomy of the political sphere, as the economist, the lawyer, the moralist maintain theirs. He thinks in terms of interest defined as power, as the economist thinks in terms of interest defined as wealth; the lawyer, of the conformity of action with legal rules; the moralist, of the conformity of action with moral principles. The economist asks: "How does this policy affect the wealth of society, or a segment of it?" The lawyer asks: "Is this policy in accord with the rules of law?" The moralist asks: "Is this policy in accord with moral principles?" And the political realist asks: "How does this policy affect the power of the nation?" . . .

The political realist is not unaware of the existence and relevance of standards of thought other than political ones. As political realist, he cannot but subordinate these other standards to those of politics. And he parts company with other schools when they impose standards of thought appropriate to other spheres upon the political sphere. It is here that political realism takes issue with the "legalistic-moralistic approach" to international politics. That this issue is not, as has been contended, a mere figment of the imagination, but goes to the very core of the controversy, can be shown from many historical examples. Three will suffice to make the point.

In 1939 the Soviet Union attacked Finland. This action confronted France and Great Britain with two issues, one legal, the other political. Did that action violate the Covenant of the League of Nations and, if it did, what countermeasures should France and Great Britain take? The legal question could easily be answered in the affirmative, for obviously the Soviet Union had done what was prohibited by the Covenant. The answer to the political question depended, first, upon the manner in which the Russian action affected the interests of France and Great Britain; second, upon the existing distribution of power between France and Great Britain, on the one hand, and the Soviet Union on the other potentially hostile nations, especially Germany, on the other; and, third, upon the influence that the counter-measures were likely to have upon their interests of France and Great Britain and the future distribution of power. France and Great Britain, as the leading members of the League of Nations, saw to it that the Soviet Union was expelled from the League, and they were prevented from joining Finland in the war against the Soviet Union only by Sweden's refusal to allow their troops to pass through Swedish territory on their way to Finland. If this refusal by Sweden had not saved them, France and Great Britain would shortly have found themselves at war with the Soviet Union and Germany at the same time.

The policy of France and Great Britain was a classic example of legalism in that they allowed the answer to the legal question, legitimate within its sphere, to determine their political actions. Instead of asking both questions, that of law and that of power, they asked only the question of law; and the answer they received could have no bearing on the issue that their very existence might have depended upon.

The second example illustrates the "moralistic approach" to international politics. It concerns the international status of the Communist government of China. The rise of that government confronted the Western world with two issues, one moral, the other political. Were the nature and policies of that government in accord with the moral principles of the Western world? Should the Western world deal with such a government?

The answer to the first question could not fail to be in the negative. Yet it did not follow with necessity that the answer to the second question should also be in the negative. The standard of thought applied to the first—the moral—question was simply to test the nature and the policies of the Communist government of China by the principles of Western morality. On the other hand, the second—the political—question had to be subjected to the complicated test of the interests involved and the power available on either side, and of the bearing of one or the other course of action upon these interests and power. The application of this test could well have led to the conclusion that it would be wiser not to deal with the Communist government of China. To arrive at this conclusion by neglecting this test altogether and answering the political question in terms of the moral issue was indeed a classic example of the "moralistic approach" to international politics.

The third case illustrates strikingly the contrast between realism and the legalistic-moralistic approach to foreign policy. Great Britain, as one of the guarantors of the neutrality of Belgium, went to war with Germany in August 1914 because Germany had violated the neutrality of Belgium. The British action could be justified either in realistic or legalistic-moralistic terms. That is to say, one could argue realistically that for centuries it had been axiomatic for British foreign policy to prevent the control of the Low Countries by a hostile power. It was then not so much the violation of Belgium's neutrality per se as the hostile intentions of the violator which provided the rationale for British intervention. If the violator had been another nation but Germany, Great Britain might well have refrained from intervening. . . .

This realist defense of the autonomy of the political sphere against its subversion by other modes of thought does not imply disregard for the existence and importance of these other modes of thought. It rather implies that each should be assigned its proper sphere and function. Political realism is based upon a pluralistic conception of human nature. Real man is a composite of "economic man," "political man," "moral man," "religious man," etc. A man who was nothing but "political man" would be a beast, for he would be completely lacking in moral restraints. A man who was nothing but "moral man" would be a fool, for he would be completely lacking in prudence. A man who was nothing but "religious man" would be a saint, for he would be completely lacking in worldly desires. . . .

It is in the nature of things that a theory of politics which is based upon such principles will not meet with unanimous approval—nor does, for that matter, such a foreign policy. For theory and policy alike run counter to two trends in our culture which are not able to reconcile themselves to the assumptions and results of a rational, objective theory of politics. One of these trends disparages the role of power in society on grounds that stem from the experience and philosophy of the nineteenth century; we shall address ourselves to this tendency later in greater detail. The other trend, opposed to the realistic theory and practice of politics, stems from the very relationship that exists, and must exist, between the human mind and the political sphere. For reasons that we shall discuss later the human mind in its day-by-day operations cannot bear to look the truth of politics straight in the face. It must disguise, distort, belittle, and embellish the truth—the more so, the more the individual is actively involved in the processes of politics, and particularly in those of international politics. For only by deceiving himself about the nature of politics and the role he plays on the political scene is man able to live contentedly as a political animal with himself and his fellow men.

Thus it is inevitable that a theory which tries to understand international politics as it actually is and as it ought to be in view of its intrinsic nature, rather than as people would like to see it, must overcome a psychological resistance that most other branches of learning need not face. A book devoted to the theoretical understanding of international politics therefore requires a special explanation and justification.

Part II
Ideology

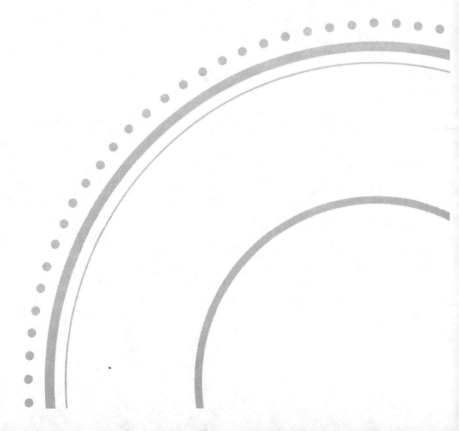

Introduction

That human beings are political animals in Aristotle's sense means that their participation in the life of the community is based upon reason and discussion. Their action and reaction upon one another is also "interaction" founded upon reflective consideration of common problems. Politics, therefore, always has intellectual and moral dimensions. As we reason and debate about which course of action to pursue, we make judgments of desirability based on concepts of right and wrong, on images of the sort of life that we do and should lead. Inevitably these reflections about the ends of political action and about the proper means to attain those ends do not remain mere random thoughts but cluster into patterns or systems of interrelated ideas.

"Ideology" is the term most commonly used today to designate such a system of ideas about the purpose and proper function of political institutions. In some ways the term is unfortunate because it is fraught with implications stemming from its history. It was coined in 1796 by the French writer Antoine Destutt de Tracy to mean the "science of the mind." Marx and Engels picked up the term after it had fallen into disuse and gave it quite another meaning. For them it did not imply a scientific study of ideas but referred to particular sets of ideas which they regarded as reflections of economic conditions or dominant economic forces.

Our use of the term "ideology" is not intended to carry with it any of these special implications. We merely follow the increasingly common tendency in the literature of social science to use "ideology" as a neutral label for sets of political ideas which are at least partially integrated, which have some mass acceptance, which place politics in a moral context, and which are not purely theoretical but provide guidance for practical action.

Part II of this book contains readings about the four most important ideologies of our age: liberalism, conservatism, socialism, and nationalism. Although these four "isms" do not exhaust the infinite variety of political thought, they have dominated political discussion in Western society since the French Revolution—and with the influence of the West over the rest of the world, they have now supplanted, if not wholly replaced, more traditional modes of thought in other societies. Anyone who becomes acquainted with the main tenets of these four ideologies will be able to follow most of the political debates of our time.

We also try to take into account the internal variety within ideological families. We thus present an example of classical liberalism—John Stuart

71

Mill in Reading 8—followed by an example of reform liberalism—T.H. Green in Reading 9. The two readings contrast strongly in their understanding of freedom, leading to rather different views about the role of government in society. Similarly, we present examples of the two major wings of socialism: Marx and Engels (Reading 11) as an instance of revolutionary socialism, and the Regina Manifesto (Reading 12) as an example of social democracy. Michael Oakeshott on conservatism (Reading 10) and Benito Mussolini on (an extreme form of) nationalism (Reading 13) complete the ideological tableau.

Finally, we offer some interpretive works on ideology in Canada. Gad Horowitz's famous essay (Reading 13), applying Hartzian fragment theory to Canada, is still the starting point of all discussion in this field. Reading 14 reports survey research by Roger Gibbins and Neil Nevitte which subjects the Hartz/Horowitz approach to empirical investigation using contemporary rather than historical data. Nevitte's discussion of the "new politics" in Reading 15 deals with recent ideological developments in Canada in the context of similar trends throughout the Western world. Drawing on the "post-materialism" thesis made famous by Ronald Inglehart, Nevitte shows how new ideologies such as environmentalism and feminism are becoming increasingly important in Canadian politics.

The post-materialist thesis holds that liberalism, conservatism, and socialism were ideologies of the industrial age, which was characterized by economic growth and struggles over distribution. Now that a high standard of material prosperity exists in Western nations, attention has increasingly shifted to "quality of life" issues such as the environment and the status of women. The older ideologies are being decisively reshaped, perhaps even rendered obsolete, by this profound social change. Such developments illustrate the fluid nature of ideologies and show how we are mistaken in thinking of them as rigid systems. They are tendencies of thought in constant flux, reflecting the ceaseless changes in our social milieu.

8   Classical Liberalism

The central concept of classical liberalism is freedom, understood as the absence of coercion. According to this view, we are free when no one uses force to interfere with our actions. Freedom, then, means acting according to our own will without encountering violence or threats of violence from others.

John Stuart Mill (1806-1873) worked out the implications of this view in his famous essay *On Liberty*, published in 1859. In particular, he addressed the question of what limits can justifiably be placed upon individual freedom. His answer was that we (or government acting on our behalf) are justified in using coercion only to protect our rights from invasion by others. We can coerce others to protect ourselves and our legitimate interests from those who would violate them, but we cannot coerce others in the name of *their* interests. Mill thus developed a liberal theory of the state as a protective device in contrast to the doctrine of paternalism, which would allow the state to look after the interests of individuals even against their own wishes.

Mill's version of classical liberalism requires a distinction to be drawn between "self-regarding" and "other-regarding" actions. Government has a legitimate right to regulate the latter, but not the former. Reading 8 illustrates Mill's attempt to draw this distinction. He was confident that he had succeeded in reducing the matter to "one very simple principle," but later generations have not found it so simple. Argument rages to this day over whether Mill's distinction between self-regarding and other-regarding behaviour tells us anything useful about the role of government in society. But regardless of where one stands in this argument, it is almost always conducted in the terms set by Mill.

The sections printed here are from the end of chapter 1 and the beginning of chapter 4 of *On Liberty*, as reprinted in *Utilitarianism and Other Writings*.

● ● ● ● ● ● ● ● ●

The object of this Essay is to assert one very simple principle, as entitled to govern absolutely the dealings of society with the individual in the way of compulsion and control, whether the means used be physical force in the form of legal penalties, or the moral coercion of public opinion. That principle is, that the sole end for which mankind are warranted, individually or collectively, in interfering with the liberty of action of any of their number, is self-protection. That the only purpose for which power can be rightfully exercised over any member of a civilised community, against his will, is to prevent harm to others. His own good, either physical or moral, is not a sufficient warrant. He cannot rightfully be compelled to do or forbear because it will be better for him to do so, because it will make him happier, because, in the opinions of others, to do so would be wise, or even right. These are good reasons for remonstrating with him, or reasoning with him, or persuading him, or entreating him, but not for compelling him, or visiting him with any evil in case he do otherwise. To justify that, the conduct from which it is desired to deter him must be calculated to produce evil to some one else. The only part of the conduct of any one, for which he is amenable to society, is that which concerns others. In the part which merely concerns himself, his independence is, of right, absolute. Over himself, over his own body and mind, the individual is sovereign.

It is, perhaps, hardly necessary to say that this doctrine is meant to apply only to human beings in the maturity of their faculties. We are not speaking of children, or of young persons below the age which the law may fix as that of manhood or womanhood. Those who are still in a state to require being taken care of by others, must be protected against their own actions as well as against external injury. For the same reason, we may leave out of consideration those backward states of society in which the race itself may be considered as in its nonage. The early difficulties in the way of spontaneous progress are so great, that there is seldom any choice of means for overcoming them; and a ruler full of the spirit of improvement is warranted in the use of any expedients that will attain an end, perhaps otherwise unattainable. Despotism is a legitimate mode of government in dealing with barbarians, provided the end be their improvement, and the means justified by actually effecting that end. Liberty, as a principle, has no application to any state of things anterior to the time when mankind have become capable of being improved by free and equal discussion. Until then, there is nothing for them but implicit obedience to an Akbar or a Charlemagne, if they are so fortunate as to find one. But as soon as mankind have attained the capacity of being guided to their own improvement by conviction or persuasion (a period long since reached in all nations with whom we need here concern ourselves), compulsion, either in the direct form or in that of pains and penalties for non-compliance, is no longer admissible as a means to their own good, and justifiable only for the security of others.

It is proper to state that I forego any advantage which could be derived to my argument from the idea of abstract right, as a thing independent of utility. I regard utility as the ultimate appeal on all ethical questions; but it must be utility in the largest sense, grounded on the permanent interests of a man as a progressive being. Those interests, I contend, authorise the subjection of individual spontaneity to external control, only in respect to those actions of each, which concern the interest of other people. If any one does an act hurtful to others, there is a *prima facie* case for punishing him, by law, or, where legal penalties are not safely applicable, by general disapprobation. There are also many positive acts for the benefit of others, which he may rightfully be compelled to perform; such as to give evidence in a court of justice; to bear his fair share in the common defence, or in any other joint work necessary to the interest of the society of which he enjoys the protection; and to perform certain acts of individual beneficence, such as saving a fellow-creature's life, or interposing to protect the defenceless against ill-usage, things which whenever it is obviously a man's duty to do, he may rightfully be made responsible to society for not doing. A person may cause evil to others not only by his actions but by his inaction, and in either case he is justly accountable to them for the injury. The latter case, it is true, requires a much more cautious exercise of compulsion than the former. To make any one answerable for doing evil to others is the rule; to make him answerable for not preventing evil is, comparatively speaking, the exception. Yet there are many cases clear enough and grave enough to justify that exception. In all things which regard the external relations of the individual, he is *de jure* amenable to those whose interests are concerned, and, if need be, to society as their protector. There are often good reasons for not holding him to the responsibility; but these reasons must arise from the special expediencies of the case: either because it is a kind of case in which he is on the whole likely to act better, when left to his own discretion, than when controlled in any way in which society have it in their power to control him; or because the attempt to exercise control would produce other evils, greater than those which it would prevent. When such reasons as these preclude the enforcement of responsibility, the conscience of the agent himself should step into the vacant judgment seat, and protect those interests of others which have no external protection; judging himself all the more rigidly, because the case does not admit of his being made accountable to the judgment of his fellow-creatures.

But there is a sphere of action in which society, as distinguished from the individual, has, if any, only an indirect interest; comprehending all that portion of a person's life and conduct which affects only himself, or if it also affects others, only with their free, voluntary, and undeceived consent and participation. When I say only himself, I mean directly, and in the first instance; for whatever affects himself, may affect others through himself; and the objection which may be grounded on this contingency, will receive consideration in the sequel. This, then, is the appropriate region of human liberty. It comprises, first, the inward domain of consciousness; demanding liberty of conscience in the most comprehensive sense; liberty of thought and feeling; absolute freedom of opinion and sentiment on all subjects practical or speculative, scientific, moral, or theological. The liberty of expressing and publishing opinions may seem to fall under a different principle, since it belongs to that part of the conduct of an individual which concerns other people; but, being almost of as much importance as the liberty of thought itself, and resting in great part on the same reasons, is practically inseparable from it. Secondly, the principle requires liberty of tastes and pursuits; of framing the plan of our life to suit our own character; of doing as we like, subject to such consequences as may follow: without impediment from our fellow-creatures, so long as what we do does not harm them, even though they should think our conduct foolish, perverse, or wrong. Thirdly, from this liberty of each individual, follows the liberty, within the same limits, of combination among individuals; freedom to unite, for any purpose not involving harm to others: the persons combining being supposed to be of full age, and not forced or deceived.

No society in which these liberties are not, on the whole, respected, is free, whatever may be its form of government; and none is completely free in which they do not exist absolute and unqualified. The only freedom which deserves the name, is that of pursuing our own good in our own way, so long as we do not attempt to deprive others of theirs, or impede their efforts to obtain it. Each is the proper guardian of his own health, whether bodily, *or* mental and spiritual. Mankind are greater gainers by suffering each other to live as seems good to themselves, than by compelling each to live as seems good to the rest. . . .

What, then, is the rightful limit to the sovereignty of the individual over himself? Where does the authority of society begin? How much of human life should be assigned to individuality, and how much to society?

Each will receive its proper share, if each has that which more particularly concerns it. To individuality should belong the part of life in which it is chiefly the individual that is interested; to society, the part which chiefly interests society.

Though society is not founded on a contract, and though no good purpose is answered by inventing a contract in order to deduce social obligations from it, every one who receives the protection of society owes a return for the benefit, and the fact of living in society renders it indispensable that each should be bound to observe a certain line of conduct towards the rest. This conduct consists, first, in not injuring the interests of one another; or rather certain interests, which, either by express legal provision or by tacit understanding, ought to be considered as rights; and secondly, in each person's bearing his share (to be fixed on some equitable principle) of the labours and sacrifices incurred for defending the society or its members

from injury and molestation. These conditions society is justified in enforcing, at all costs to those who endeavour to withhold fulfilment. Nor is this
all that society may do. The acts of an individual may be hurtful to others, or
wanting in due consideration for their welfare, without going to the length
of violating any of their constituted rights. The offender may then be justly
punished by opinion, though not by law. As soon as any part of a person's
conduct affects prejudicially the interests of others, society has jurisdiction
over it, and the question whether the general welfare will or will not be
promoted by interfering with it, becomes open to discussion. But there is no
room for entertaining any such question when a person's conduct affects
the interests of no persons besides himself, or needs not affect them unless
they like (all the persons concerned being of full age, and the ordinary
amount of understanding). In all such cases, there should be perfect freedom, legal and social, to do the action and stand the consequences.

It would be a great misunderstanding of this doctrine to suppose that it
is one of selfish indifference, which pretends that human beings have no
business with each other's conduct in life, and that they should not concern
themselves about the well-doing or well-being of one another, unless their
own interest is involved. Instead of any diminution, there is need of a great
increase of disinterested exertion to promote the good of others. But disinterested benevolence can find other instruments to persuade people to their
good than whips and scourges, either of the literal or the metaphorical sort.
I am the last person to undervalue the self-regarding virtues; they are only
second in importance, if even second, to the social. It is equally the business
of education to cultivate both. But even education works by conviction and
persuasion as well as by compulsion, and it is by the former only that, when
the period of education is passed, the self-regarding virtues should be
inculcated. Human beings owe to each other help to distinguish the better
from the worse, and encouragement to choose the former and avoid the
latter. They should be for ever stimulating each other to increased exercise
of their higher faculties, and increased direction of their feelings and aims
towards wise instead of foolish, elevating instead of degrading, objects and
contemplations. But neither one person, nor any number of persons, is
warranted in saying to another human creature of ripe years, that he shall
not do with his life for his own benefit what he chooses to do with it. He is
the person most interested in his own well-being: the interest which any
other person, except in cases of strong personal attachment, can have in it,
is trifling, compared with that which he himself has; the interest which
society has in him individually (except as to his conduct to others) is
fractional, and altogether indirect; while with respect to his own feelings
and circumstances, the most ordinary man or woman has means of knowledge immeasurably surpassing those that can be possessed by any one else.

The interference of society to overrule his judgment and purposes in what only regards himself must be grounded on general presumptions; which may be altogether wrong, and even if right, are as likely as not to be misapplied to individual cases, by persons no better acquainted with the circumstances of such cases than those are who look at them merely from without. In this department, therefore, of human affairs, Individuality has its proper field of action. In the conduct of human beings towards one another it is necessary that general rules should for the most part be observed, in order that people may know what they have to expect: but in each person's own concerns his individual spontaneity is entitled to free exercise. Considerations to aid his judgment, exhortations to strengthen his will, may be offered to him, even obtruded on him, by others: but he himself is the final judge. All errors which he is likely to commit against advice and warning are far outweighed by the evil of allowing others to constrain him to what they deem his good.

I do not mean that the feelings with which a person is regarded by others ought not to be in any way affected by his self-regarding qualities or deficiencies. This is neither possible nor desirable. If he is eminent in any of the qualities which conduce to his own good, he is, so far, a proper object of admiration. He is so much the nearer to the ideal perfection of human nature. If he is grossly deficient in those qualities, a sentiment the opposite of admiration will follow. . . .

9   Reform Liberalism

Classical liberalism's understanding of freedom as the absence of coercion led to a strictly limited view of the role of government in society. By the end of the nineteenth century, many thinkers who thought of themselves as liberals began to question this restrictive view of state action. They particularly believed that government intervention would be necessary to lift the industrial working class out of poverty and degradation.

Typical of this new generation of liberal writers was Thomas Hill Green (1836-1882), a professor of philosophy at Oxford and an active member of the Liberal Party of Great Britain. In seeking to justify an interventionist, reforming role for government, Green rethought the classical liberal definition of freedom, turning it into a much broader concept: "a positive power or capacity of doing or enjoying something worth doing or enjoying, and that, too, something that we do or enjoy in common with others." He saw this new understanding of freedom as justifying a much more activist use of government to help people fulfil their capacities.

A striking result of Green's revised liberalism was the demand to prohibit the sale of alcoholic beverages in the name of obtaining a higher freedom, which may in fact conflict with what people think they want. In comparison with the classical liberalism of John Stuart Mill, Green's reform liberalism contained a strong dose of paternalism, generating controversies that continue to reverberate in the modern welfare state.

Reading 9 is extracted from Green's "Lecture on Liberal Legislation and Freedom of Contract," delivered at Leicester in 1881 and subsequently published in *The Works of Thomas Hill Green*.

● ● ● ● ● ● ● ● ● ●

... [T]he most pressing political questions of our time are questions of which the settlement, I do not say necessarily involves an interference with freedom of contract, but is sure to be resisted in the sacred name of individual liberty, not only by all those who are interested in keeping things as they are, but by others to whom freedom is dear for its own sake, and who do not sufficiently consider the conditions of its maintenance in such a society as ours. In this respect there is a noticeable difference between the present position of political reformers and that in which they stood a generation ago. Then they fought the fight of reform in the name of individual freedom against class privilege. Their opponents could not with any plausibility invoke the same name against them. Now, in appearance—though, as I shall try to show, not in reality—the case is changed. The nature of the genuine political reformer is perhaps always the same. The passion for improving mankind, in its ultimate object, does not vary. But the immediate object of reformers, and the forms of persuasion by which they seek to advance them, vary much in different generations. To a hasty observer they might even seem contradictory, and to justify the notion that nothing better than a desire for change, selfish or perverse, is at the bottom of all reforming movements. Only those who will think a little longer about it can discern the same old cause of social good against class interests, for which, under altered names, liberals are fighting now as they were fifty years ago.

Our political history since the first reform act naturally falls into three divisions. The first, beginning with the reform of parliament, and extending to Sir R. Peel's administration, is marked by the struggle of free society against close privileged corporations. Its greatest achievement was the establishment of representative municipal governments in place of the close bodies which had previously administered the affairs of our cities and boroughs; a work which after an interval of nearly half a century we hope shortly to see extended to the rural districts. Another important work was the overhauling the immense charities of the country, and the placing them under something like adequate public control. And the natural complement of this was the removal of the grosser abuses in the administration of the church, the abolition of pluralities and sinecures, and the reform of cathedral chapters. In all this, while there was much that contributed to the freedom of our civil life, there was nothing that could possibly be construed as an interference with the rights of the individual. No one was disturbed in doing what he would with his own. Even those who had fattened on abuses had their vested interests duly respected, for the house of commons then as now had 'quite a passion for compensation.' With the ministry of Sir R. Peel began the struggle of society against monopolies; in other words, the liberation of trade. Some years later Mr. Gladstone, in his famous budgets, was able to complete the work which his master began, and it is now some twenty years since the last vestige of protection for any class of traders or producers disappeared. The taxes on knowledge, as they were called, followed the taxes on food, and since most of us grew up there has been no exchangeable commodity in England except land—no doubt a large exception—of which the exchange has not been perfectly free.

The realisation of complete freedom of contract was the special object of this reforming work. It was to set men at liberty to dispose of what they had made their own that the free-trader worked. He only interfered to prevent interference. He would put restraint on no man in doing anything that did not directly check the free dealing of some one in something else. But of late reforming legislation has taken, as I have pointed out, a seemingly different direction. It has not at any rate been so readily identifiable with the work of liberation. In certain respects it has put restraints on the individual in doing what he will with his own. And it is noticeable that this altered tendency begins, in the main, with the more democratic parliament of 1868. It is true that the earlier factory acts, limiting as they do by law the conditions under which certain kinds of labour may be bought and sold, had been passed some time before. The first approach to an effectual factory act dates as far back as the time of the first reform act, but it only applied to the cotton industry, and was very imperfectly put in force. It aimed at limiting the hours of labour for children and young persons. . . .

. . . [N]ow we have a system of law by which, in all our chief industries except the agricultural, the employment of children except as half-timers is effectually prevented, the employment of women and young persons is effectually restricted to ten hours a day, and in all places of employment health and bodily safety have all the protection which rules can give them.

If factory regulation had been attempted, though only in a piecemeal way, some time before we had a democratic house of commons, the same cannot be said of education law. It was the parliament elected by a more popular suffrage in 1868 that passed, as we know, the first great education act. That act introduced compulsory schooling. It left the compulsion, indeed, optional with local school-boards, but compulsion is the same in principle, is just as much compulsion by the state, whether exercised by the central government or delegated by that government to provincial authorities. . . .

The principle was established once for all that parents were not to be allowed to do as they willed with their children, if they willed either to set them to work or to let them run wild without elementary education. Freedom of contract in respect of all dealings with the labour of children was so far limited. . . .

The most mature man is prohibited by law from contracting to labour in factories, or pits, or workshops, unless certain rules for the protection of health and limb are complied with. In like manner he is prohibited from living in a house which the sanitary inspector pronounces unwholesome. The free sale or letting of a certain kind of commodity is thereby prevented. Here, then, is a great system of restriction, which yet hardly any impartial person wishes to see reversed; which many of us wish to see made more complete. Perhaps, however, we have never thoroughly considered the principles on which we approve it. It may be well, therefore, to spend a short time in ascertaining those principles. We shall then be on surer ground in approaching those more difficult questions of legislation which must shortly be dealt with, and of which the settlement is sure to be resisted in the name of individual liberty.

We shall probably all agree that freedom, rightly understood, is the greatest of blessings; that its attainment is the true end of all our effort as citizens. But when we thus speak of freedom, we should consider carefully what we mean by it. We do not mean merely freedom from restraint or compulsion. We do not mean merely freedom to do as we like irrespectively of what it is that we like. We do not mean a freedom that can be enjoyed by one man or one set of men at the cost of a loss of freedom to others. When we speak of freedom as something to be so highly prized, we mean a positive power or capacity of doing or enjoying something worth doing or enjoying, and that, too, something that we do or enjoy in common with others. We mean by it a power which each man exercises through the help or security given him by his fellow-men, and which he in turn helps to secure for them. When we measure the progress of a society by its growth in freedom, we measure it by the increasing development and exercise on the whole of those powers of contributing to social good with which we believe the members of the society to be endowed; in short, by the greater power on the part of the citizens as a body to make the most and best of themselves. Thus, though of course there can be no freedom among men who act not willingly but under compulsion, yet on the other hand the mere removal of compulsion, the mere enabling a man to do as he likes, is in itself no contribution to true freedom. In one sense no man is so well able to do as he likes as the wandering savage. He has no master. There is no one to say him nay. Yet we do not count him really free, because the freedom of savagery is not strength, but weakness. The actual powers of the noblest savage do not admit of comparison with those of the humblest citizen of a law-abiding state. He is not the slave of man, but he is the slave of nature. Of compulsion by natural necessity he has plenty of experience, though of restraint by society none at all. Nor can he deliver himself from that compulsion except by submitting to this restraint. So to submit is the first step in true freedom, because the first step towards the full exercise of the faculties with which man is endowed. But we rightly refuse to recognise the highest development on the part of an exceptional individual or exceptional class, as an advance towards the true freedom of man, if it is founded on a refusal of the same opportunity to other men. The powers of the human mind have probably never attained such force and keenness, the proof of what society can do for the individual has never been so strikingly exhibited, as among the small groups of men who possessed civil privileges in the small republics of antiquity. The whole framework of our political ideas, to say nothing of our philosophy, is derived from them. But in them this extraordinary efflorescence of the privileged class was accompanied by the slavery of the multitude. That slavery was the condition on which it depended, and for that reason it was doomed to decay. There is no clearer ordinance of that supreme reason, often dark to us, which governs the course of man's affairs, than that no body of men should in the long run be able to strengthen itself at the cost of others' weakness. The civilisation and freedom of the ancient world were shortlived because they were partial and exceptional. If the ideal of true freedom is the maximum of power for all members of human society alike to make the best of themselves, we are right in refusing to ascribe the glory of freedom to a state in which the apparent elevation of the few is founded on the degradation of the many, and in ranking modern society, founded as it is on free industry, with all its confusion and ignorant licence and waste of effort, above the most splendid of ancient republics.

If I have given a true account of that freedom which forms the goal of social effort, we shall see that freedom of contract, freedom in all the forms of doing what one will with one's own, is valuable only as a means to an end. That end is what I call freedom in the positive sense: in other words, the liberation of the powers of all men equally for contributions to a common good. No one has a right to do what he will with his own in such a way as to contravene this end. It is only through the guarantee which society gives him that he has property at all, or, strictly speaking, any right to his possessions. This guarantee is founded on a sense of common interest. Every one has an interest in securing to every one else the free use and enjoyment and disposal of his possessions, so long as that freedom on the part of one does not interfere with a like freedom on the part of others, because such freedom contributes to that equal development of the faculties of all which is the highest good for all. This is the true and the only justification of rights of property. Rights of property, however, have been and are claimed which cannot be thus justified. We are all now agreed that men cannot rightly be the property of men. The institution of property being only justifiable as a means to the free exercise of the social capabilities of all, there can be no true right to property of a kind which debars one class of men from such free exercise altogether. We condemn slavery no less when it arises out of a voluntary agreement on the part of the enslaved person. A contract by which any one agreed for a certain consideration to become the slave of another we should reckon a void contract. Here, then, is a limitation upon freedom of contract which we all recognise as rightful. No contract is valid in which human persons, willingly or unwillingly, are dealt with as commodities, because such contracts of necessity defeat the end for which alone society enforces contracts at all.

Are there no other contracts which, less obviously perhaps but really, are open to the same objection? In the first place, let us consider contracts affecting labour. Labour, the economist tells us, is a commodity exchangeable like other commodities. This is in a certain sense true, but it is a commodity which attaches in a peculiar manner to the person of man. Hence restrictions may need to be placed on the sale of this commodity which would be unnecessary in other cases, in order to prevent labour from being sold under conditions which make it impossible for the person selling it ever to become a free contributor to social good in any form. This is most plainly the case when a man bargains to work under conditions fatal to health, *e.g.* in an unventilated factory. Every injury to the health of the individual is, so far as it goes, a public injury. It is an impediment to the general freedom; so much deduction from our power, as members of society, to make the best of ourselves. Society is, therefore, plainly within its right when it limits freedom of contract for the sale of labour, so far as is done by our laws for the sanitary regulations of factories, workshops, and mines. It is equally within its right in prohibiting the labour of women and young persons beyond certain hours. If they work beyond those hours, the result is demonstrably physical deterioration; which, as demonstrably, carries with it a lowering of the moral forces of society. For the sake of that general freedom of its members to make the best of themselves, which it is the object of civil society to secure, a prohibition should be put by law, which is the deliberate voice of society, on all such contracts of service as in a general way yield such a result. The purchase or hire of unwholesome dwellings is properly forbidden on the same principle. Its application to compulsory education may not be quite so obvious, but it will appear on a little reflection. Without a command of certain elementary arts and knowledge, the individual in modern society is as effectually crippled as by the loss of a limb or a broken constitution. He is not free to develop his faculties. With a view to securing such freedom among its members it is as certainly within the province of the state to prevent children from growing up in that kind of ignorance which practically excludes them from a free career in life, as it is within its province to require the sort of building and drainage necessary for public health.

Our modern legislation, then with reference to labour, and education, and health, involving as it does manifold interference with freedom of contract, is justified on the ground that it is the business of the state, not indeed directly to promote moral goodness, for that, from the very nature of moral goodness, it cannot do, but to maintain the conditions without which a free exercise of the human faculties is impossible. . . .

Now, we shall probably all agree that a society in which the public health was duly protected, and necessary education duly provided for, by the spontaneous action of individuals, was in a higher condition than one in which the compulsion of law was needed to secure these ends. But we must take men as we find them. Until such a condition of society is reached, it is the business of the state to take the best security it can for the young citizens' growing up in such health and with so much knowledge as is necessary for their real freedom. In so doing it need not at all interfere with the independence and self-reliance of those whom it requires to do what they would otherwise do for themselves. The man who, of his own right feeling, saves his wife from overwork and sends his children to school, suffers no moral degradation from a law which, if he did not do this for himself, would seek to make him do it. Such a man does not feel the law as constraint at all. To him it is simply a powerful friend. It gives him security for that being done efficiently which, with the best wishes, he might have much trouble in getting done efficiently if left to himself. No doubt it relieves him from some of the responsibility which would otherwise fall to him as head of a family, but, if he is what we are supposing him to be, in proportion as he is relieved of responsibilities in one direction he will assume them in another. The security which the state gives him for the safe housing and sufficient schooling of his family will only make him the more careful for their well-being in other respects, which he is left to look after for himself. We need have no fear, then, of such legislation having an ill effect on those who, without the law, would have seen to that being done, though probably less efficiently, which the law requires to be done. But it was not their case that the laws we are considering were especially meant to meet. It was the overworked women, the ill-housed and untaught families, for whose benefit they were intended. And the question is whether without these laws the suffering classes could have been delivered quickly or slowly from the condition they were in. Could the enlightened self-interest or benevolence of individuals, working under a system of unlimited freedom of contract, have ever brought them into a state compatible with the free development of the human faculties? No one considering the facts can have any doubt as to the answer to this question. Left to itself, or to the operation of casual benevolence, a degraded population perpetuates and increases itself. Read any of the authorised accounts, given before royal or parliamentary commissions, of the state of the labourers, especially of the women and children, as they were in our great industries before the law was first brought to bear on them, and before freedom of contract was first interfered with in them. Ask yourself what chance there was of a generation, born and bred under such conditions, ever contracting itself out of them. Given a certain standard of moral and material well-being, people may be trusted not to sell their labour, or the labour of their children, on terms which would not allow that standard to be maintained. But with large masses of our population, until the laws we have been considering took effect, there was no such standard. There was nothing on their part, in the way either of self-respect or established demand for comforts, to prevent them from working and living, or from putting their children to work and live, in a way in which no one who is to be a healthy and free citizen can work and live. No doubt there were many high-minded employers who did their best for their workpeople before the days of state-interference, but they could not prevent less scrupulous hirers of labour from hiring it on the cheapest terms. It is true that cheap labour is in the long run dear labour, but it is so only in the long run, and eager traders do not think of the long run. If labour is to be had under conditions incompatible with the health or decent housing or education of the labourer, there will always be plenty of people to buy it under those conditions, careless of the burden in the shape of rates and taxes which they may be laying up for posterity. Either the standard of well-being on the part of the sellers of labour must prevent them from selling their labour under those conditions, or the law must prevent it. With a population such as ours was forty years ago, and still largely is, the law must prevent it and continue the prevention for some generations, before the sellers will be in a state to prevent it for themselves. . . .

I have left myself little time to speak of the principles on which some of us hold that, in the matter of intoxicating drinks, a further limitation of freedom of contract is needed in the interest of general freedom. . . .

We justify it on the simple ground of the recognised right on the part of society to prevent men from doing as they like, if, in the exercise of their peculiar tastes in doing as they like, they create a social nuisance. There is no right to freedom in the purchase and sale of a particular commodity, if the general result of allowing such freedom is to detract from freedom in the higher sense, from the general power of men to make the best of themselves. Now with anyone who looks calmly at the facts, there can be no doubt that the present habits of drinking in England do lay a heavy burden on the free development of man's powers for social good, a heavier burden probably than arises from all other preventible causes put together. It used to be the fashion to look on drunkenness as a vice which was the concern only of the person who fell into it, so long as it did not lead him to commit an assault on his neighbours. No thoughtful man any longer looks on it in this way. We know that, however decently carried on, the excessive drinking of one man means an injury to others in health, purse, and capability, to which no limits can be placed. Drunkenness in the head of a family means, as a rule, the impoverishment and degradation of all members of the family; and the presence of a drink-shop at the corner of a street means, as a rule, the drunkenness of a certain number of heads of families in that street. Remove the drink-shops, and, as the experience of many happy communities sufficiently shows, you almost, perhaps in time altogether, remove the drunkenness. Here, then, is a wide-spreading social evil, of which society may, if it will, by a restraining law, to a great extent, rid itself, to the infinite enhancement of the positive freedom enjoyed by its members. All that is required for the attainment of so blessed a result is so much effort and self-sacrifice on the part of the majority of citizens as is necessary for the enactment and enforcement of the restraining law. The majority of citizens may still be far from prepared for such an effort. That is a point on which I express no opinion. To attempt a restraining law in advance of the social sentiment necessary to give real effect to it, is always a mistake. But to argue that an effectual law in restraint of the drink-traffic would be a wrongful interference with individual liberty, is to ignore the essential condition under which alone every particular liberty can rightly be allowed to the individual, the condition, namely, that the allowance of that liberty is not, as a rule, and on the whole, an impediment to social good.

The more reasonable opponents of the restraint for which I plead, would probably argue not so much that it was necessarily wrong in principle, as that it was one of those short cuts to a good end which ultimately defeat their own object. They would take the same line that has been taken by the opponents of state-interference in all its forms. 'Leave the people to themselves,' they would say; 'as their standard of self-respect rises, as they become better housed and better educated, they will gradually shake off the evil habit. The cure so effected may not be so rapid as that brought by a repressive law, but it will be more lasting. Better that it should come more slowly through the spontaneous action of individuals, than more quickly through compulsion.'

But here again we reply that it is dangerous to wait. The slower remedy might be preferable if we were sure that it was a remedy at all, but we have no such assurance. There is strong reason to think the contrary. Every year that the evil is left to itself, it becomes greater. The vested interest in the encouragement of the vice becomes larger, and the persons affected by it more numerous. If any abatement of it has already taken place, we may fairly argue that this is because it has not been altogether left to itself; for the licensing law, as it is, is much more stringent and more stringently administered than it was ten years ago. A drunken population naturally perpetuates and increases itself. Many families, it is true, keep emerging from the conditions which render them specially liable to the evil habit, but on the other hand descent through drunkenness from respectability to squalor is constantly going on. The families of drunkards do not seem to be smaller than those of sober men, though they are shorter-lived; and that the children of a drunkard should escape from drunkenness is what we call almost a miracle. Better education, better housing, more healthy rules of labour, no doubt lessen the temptations to drink for those who have the benefit of these advantages, but meanwhile drunkenness is constantly recruiting the ranks of those who cannot be really educated, who will not be better housed, who make their employments dangerous and unhealthy. An effectual liquor law in short is the necessary complement of our factory acts, our education acts, our public health acts. Without it the full measure of their usefulness will never be attained. . . .

The danger of legislation, either in the interests of a privileged class or for the promotion of particular religious opinions, we may fairly assume to be over. The popular jealousy of law, once justifiable enough, is therefore out of date. The citizens of England now make its law. We ask them by law to put a restraint on themselves in the matter of strong drink. We ask them further to limit, or even altogether to give up, the not very precious liberty of buying and selling alcohol, in order that they may become more free to exercise the faculties and improve the talents which God has given them.

10   Conservatism

Although classical and reform liberalism differ greatly from each other, they share a certain rationalistic outlook. Each is marked by intellectual optimism about and confidence in a certain process: for classical liberals, the undirected process of free exchange; for reform liberals, the gradual process of government intervention. As Michael Oakeshott makes clear in Reading 10, conservatism differs fundamentally from liberalism in being less an articulated theory than a disposition or temperament. Conservatives through experience have come to appreciate the value of tradition. They recognize that changes are inevitable but wish them to come slowly enough for gradual accommodation. For conservatives, the purpose of government is not to impose upon society a rational plan, whether laissez-faire or reformist intervention. Its purpose is to protect the social order by minimizing and moderating the collisions between its members. This is a never-ending activity calling for the exercise of practical judgment, not the implementation of a theoretical scheme.

Michael Oakeshott was a professor of politics at the University of London. His reputation as a leading conservative thinker is derived as much from his unusual influence as a teacher as from his writings. The latter, while not particularly numerous, have been widely read. This section is from his essay "On Being Conservative," in *Rationalism in Politics*.

● ● ● ● ● ● ● ● ● ●

The common belief that it is impossible (or, if not impossible, then so unpromising as to be not worth while attempting) to elicit explanatory general principles from what is recognized to be conservative conduct is not one that I share. It may be true that conservative conduct does not readily provoke articulation in the idiom of general ideas, and that consequently there has been a certain reluctance to undertake this kind of elucidation; but it is not to be presumed that conservative conduct is less eligible than any other for this sort of interpretation, for what it is worth. Nevertheless, this is not the enterprise I propose to engage in here. My theme is not a creed or a doctrine, but a disposition. To be conservative is to be disposed to think and behave in certain manners; it is to prefer certain kinds of conduct and certain conditions of human circumstances to others; it is to be disposed to make certain kinds of choices. And my design here is to construe this disposition as it appears in contemporary character, rather than to transpose it into the idiom of general principles.

The general characteristics of this disposition are not difficult to discern, although they have often been mistaken. They centre upon a propensity to use and to enjoy what is available rather than to wish for or to look for something else; to delight in what is present rather than what was or what may be. Reflection may bring to light an appropriate gratefulness for what is available, and consequently the acknowledgment of a gift or an inheritance from the past; but there is no mere idolizing of what is past and gone. What is esteemed is the present; and it is esteemed not on account of its connections with a remote antiquity, nor because it is recognized to be more admirable than any possible alternative, but on account of its familiarity. . . .

If the present is arid, offering little or nothing to be used or enjoyed, then this inclination will be weak or absent; if the present is remarkably unsettled, it will display itself in a search for a firmer foothold and consequently in a recourse to and an exploration of the past; but it asserts itself characteristically when there is much to be enjoyed, and it will be strongest when this is combined with evident risk of loss. In short, it is a disposition appropriate to a man who is acutely aware of having something to lose which he has learned to care for; a man in some degree rich in opportunities for enjoyment, but not so rich that he can afford to be indifferent to loss. It will appear more naturally in the old than in the young, not because the old are more sensitive to loss but because they are apt to be more fully aware of the resources of their world and therefore less likely to find them inadequate. In some people this disposition is weak merely because they are ignorant of what their world has to offer them: the present appears to them only as a residue of inopportunities.

To be conservative, then, is to prefer the familiar to the unknown, to prefer the tried to the untried, fact to mystery, the actual to the possible, the limited to the unbounded, the near to the distant, the sufficient to the superabundant, the convenient to the perfect, present laughter to utopian bliss. Familar relationships and loyalties will be preferred to the allure of more profitable attachments; to acquire and to enlarge will be less important than to keep, to cultivate and to enjoy; the grief of loss will be more acute than the excitement of novelty or promise. It is to be equal to one's own fortune, to live at the level of one's own means, to be content with the want of greater perfection which belongs alike to oneself and one's circumstances. With some people this is itself a choice; in others it is a disposition which appears, frequently or less frequently, in their preferences and aversions, and is not itself chosen or specifically cultivated.

Now, all this is represented in a certain attitude towards change and innovation; change denoting alterations we have to suffer and innovation those we design and execute.

Changes are circumstances to which we have to accommodate ourselves, and the disposition to be conservative is both the emblem of our difficulty in doing so and our resort in the attempts we make to do so. Changes are without effect only upon those who notice nothing, who are ignorant of what they possess and apathetic to their circumstances; and they can be welcomed indiscriminately only by those who esteem nothing, whose attachments are fleeting and who are strangers to love and affection. The conservative disposition provokes neither of these conditions: the inclination to enjoy what is present and available is the opposite of ignorance and apathy and it breeds attachment and affection. Consequently, it is averse from change, which appears always, in the first place, as deprivation. A storm which sweeps away a copse and transforms a favourite view, the death of friends, the sleep of friendship, the desuetude of customs of behaviour, the retirement of a favourite clown, involuntary exile, reversals of fortune, the loss of abilities enjoyed and their replacement by others— these are changes, none perhaps without its compensations, which the man of conservative temperament unavoidably regrets. But he has difficulty in reconciling himself to them, not because what he has lost in them was intrinsically better than any alternative might have been or was incapable of improvement, nor because what takes its place is inherently incapable of being enjoyed, but because what he has lost was something he actually enjoyed and had learned how to enjoy and what takes its place is something to which he has acquired no attachment. Consequently, he will find small and slow changes more tolerable than large and sudden; and he will value highly every appearance of continuity. Some changes, indeed, will present no difficulty; but, again, this is not because they are manifest improvements but merely because they are easily assimilated: the changes of the seasons are mediated by their recurrence and the growing up of children by its continuousness. And, in general, he will accommodate himself more readily to changes which do not offend expectation than to the destruction of what seems to have no ground of dissolution within itself.

Moreover, to be conservative is not merely to be averse from change (which may be an idiosyncrasy); it is also a manner of accommodating ourselves to changes, in activity imposed upon all men. For, change is a threat to identity, and every change is an emblem of extinction. But a man's identity (or that of a community) is nothing more than an unbroken rehearsal of contingencies, each at the mercy of circumstance and each significant in proportion to its familiarity. It is not a fortress into which we may retire, and the only means we have of defending it (that is, ourselves) against the hostile forces of change is in the open field of our experience; by throwing our weight upon the foot which for the time being is most firmly placed, by cleaving to whatever familiarities are not immediately threatened and thus assimilating what is new without becoming unrecognizable to ourselves. The Masai, when they were moving from their old country to the present Masai reserve in Kenya, took with them the names of their hills and plains and rivers and gave them to the hills and plains and rivers of the new country. And it is by some such subterfuge of conservatism that every man or people compelled to suffer a notable change avoids the shame of extinction.

Changes, then, have to be suffered; and a man of conservative temperament (that is, one strongly disposed to preserve his identity) cannot be indifferent to them. In the main, he judges them by the disturbance they entail and, like everyone else, deploys his resources to meet them. The idea of innovation, on the other hand, is improvement. Nevertheless, a man of this temperament will not himself be an ardent innovator. In the first place, he is not inclined to think that nothing is happening unless great changes are afoot and therefore he is not worried by the absence of innovation: the use and enjoyment of things as they are occupies most of his attention. Further, he is aware that not all innovation is, in fact, improvement; and he will think that to innovate without improving is either designed or inadvertent folly. Moreover, even when an innovation commends itself as a convincing improvement, he will look twice at its claims before accepting them. From his point of view, because every improvement involves change, the disruption entailed has always to be set against the benefit anticipated. But when he has satisfied himself about this, there will be other considerations to be taken into the account. Innovating is always an equivocal enterprise, in which gain and loss (even excluding the loss of familiarity) are so closely interwoven that it is exceedingly difficult to forecast the final up-shot: there is no such thing as an unqualified improvement. For, innovating is an activity which generates not only the "improvement" sought, but a new and complex situation of which this is only one of the components. The total change is always more extensive than the change designed; and the whole of what is entailed can neither be foreseen nor circumscribed. Thus, whenever there is innovation there is the certainty that the change will be greater than was intended, that there will be loss as well as gain and that the loss and the gain will not be equally distributed among the people affected; there is the chance that the benefits derived will be greater than those which were designed; and there is the risk that they will be off-set by changes for the worse.

From all this the man of conservative temperament draws some appropriate conclusions. First, innovation entails certain loss and possible gain, therefore, the onus of proof, to show that the proposed change may be expected to be on the whole beneficial, rests with the would-be innovator. Secondly, he believes that the more closely an innovation resembles growth (that is, the more clearly it is intimated in and not merely imposed upon the situation) the less likely it is to result in a preponderance of loss. Thirdly, he thinks that an innovation which is a response to some specific defect, one designed to redress some specific disequilibrium, is more desirable than one which springs from a notion of a generally improved condition of human circumstances, and is far more desirable than one generated by a vision of perfection. Consequently, he prefers small and limited innovations to large and indefinite. Fourthly, he favours a slow rather than a rapid pace, and pauses to observe current consequences and make appropriate adjustments. And lastly, he believes the occasion to be important; and, other things being equal, he considers the most favourable occasion for innovation to be when the projected change is most likely to be limited to what is intended and least likely to be corrupted by undesired and unmanageable consequences.

The disposition to be conservative is, then, warm and positive in respect of enjoyment, and correspondingly cool and critical in respect of change and innovation: these two inclinations support and elucidate one another. The man of conservative temperament believes that a known good is not lightly to be surrendered for an unknown better. He is not in love with what is dangerous and difficult; he is unadventurous; he has no impulse to sail uncharted seas; for him there is no magic in being lost, bewildered or shipwrecked. If he is forced to navigate the unknown, he sees virtue in heaving the lead every inch of the way. What others plausibly identify as timidity, he recognizes in himself as rational prudence; what others interpret as inactivity, he recognizes as a disposition to enjoy rather than to exploit. He is cautious, and he is disposed to indicate his assent or dissent, not in absolute, but in graduated terms. He eyes the situation in terms of its propensity to disrupt the familiarity of the features of his world. . . .

How, then, are we to construe the disposition to be conservative in respect of politics? And in making this inquiry what I am interested in is not merely the intelligibililty of this disposition in any set of circumstances, but its intelligibility in our own contemporary circumstances.

Writers who have considered this question commonly direct our attention to beliefs about the world in general, about human beings in general, about associations in general and even about the universe; and they tell us that a conservative disposition in politics can be correctly construed only when we understand it as a reflection of certain beliefs of these kinds. It is said, for example, that conservatism in politics is the appropriate counter-part of a generally conservative disposition in respect of human conduct: to be reformist in business, in morals or in religion and to be conservative in politics is represented as being inconsistent. It is said that the conservative in politics is so by virtue of holding certain religious beliefs; a belief, for example, in a natural law to be gathered from human experience, and in a providential order reflecting a divine purpose in nature and in human history to which it is the duty of mankind to conform its conduct and departure from which spells injustice and calamity. Further, it is said that a disposition to be conservative in politics reflects what is called an "organic" theory of human society; that it is tied up with a belief in the absolute value of human personality, and with a belief in a primordial propensity of human beings to sin. And the "conservatism" of an Englishman has even been connected with Royalism and Anglicanism.

Now, setting aside the minor complaints one might be moved to make about this account of the situation, it seems to me to suffer from one large defect. It is true that many of these beliefs have been held by people disposed to be conservative in political activity, and it may be true that these people have also believed their disposition to be in some way con-firmed by them, or even to be founded upon them; but, as I understand it, a disposition to be conservative in politics does not entail either that we should hold these beliefs to be true or even that we should suppose them to be true. Indeed, I do not think it is necessarily connected with any particular beliefs about the universe, about the world in general or about human conduct in general. What it is tied to is certain beliefs about the activity of governing and the instruments of government, and it is in terms of beliefs on these topics, and not on others, that it can be made to appear intelligible. And, to state my view briefly before elaborating it, what makes a conser-vative disposition in politics intelligible is nothing to do with a natural law or a providential order, nothing to do with morals or religion; it is the observation of our current manner of living combined with the belief (which from our point of view need be regarded as no more than an hypothesis) that governing is a specific and limited activity, namely the provision and custody of general rules of conduct, which are understood, not as plans for imposing substantive activities, but as instruments enabling people to pursue the activities of their own choice with the minimum frustration, and therefore something which it is appropriate to be conser-vative about.

Let us begin at what I believe to be the proper starting-place; not in the empyrean, but with ourselves as we have come to be. I and my neighbours, my associates, my compatriots, my friends, my enemies and those who I am indifferent about, are people engaged in a great variety of activities. We are apt to entertain a multiplicity of opinions on every conceivable subject and are disposed to change these beliefs as we grow tired of them or as they prove unserviceable. Each of us is pursuing a course of his own; and there is no project so unlikely that somebody will not be found to engage in it, no enterprise so foolish that somebody will not undertake it. There are those who spend their lives trying to sell copies of the Anglican Catechism to the Jews. And one half of the world is engaged in trying to make the other half want what it has hitherto never felt the lack of. We are all inclined to be passionate about out own concerns, whether it is making things or selling them, whether it is business or sport, religion or learning, poetry, drink or drugs. Each of us has preferences of his own. For some, the opportunities of making choices (which are numerous) are invitations readily accepted; others welcome them less eagerly or even find them burdensome. Some dream dreams of new and better worlds: others are more inclined to move in familiar paths or even to be idle. Some are apt to deplore the rapidity of change, others delight in it; all recognize it. At times we grow tired and fall asleep: it is a blessed relief to gaze in a shop window and see nothing we want; we are grateful for ugliness merely because it repels attention. But, for the most part, we pursue happiness by seeking the satisfaction of desires which spring from one another inexhaustibly. We enter into relationships of interest and of emotion, of competition, partnership, guardianship, love, friendship, jealousy and hatred, some of which are more durable than others. We make agreements with one another; we have expectations about one another's conduct; we approve, we are indifferent and we disapprove. This multiplicity of activity and variety of opinion is apt to produce collisions: we pursue courses which cut across those of others, and we do not all approve the same sort of conduct. But, in the main, we get along with one another, sometimes by giving way, sometimes by standing fast, sometimes in a compromise. Our conduct consists of activity assimilated to that of others in small, and for the most part unconsidered and unobtrusive, adjustments. . . .

Surveying the scene, some people are provoked by the absence of order and coherence which appears to them to be its dominant feature; its wastefulness, its frustration, its dissipation of human energy, its lack not merely of a premeditated destination but even of any discernible direction of movement. It provides an excitement similar to that of a stock-car race; but it has none of the satisfaction of a well-conducted business enterprise. Such people are apt to exaggerate the current disorder; the absence of plan is so conspicuous that the small adjustments, and even the more massive arrangements, which restrain the chaos seem to them nugatory; they have no feeling for the warmth of untidiness but only for its inconvenience. But what is significant is not the limitations of their powers of observation, but the turn of their thoughts. They feel that there ought to be something that ought to be done to convert this so-called chaos into order, for this is no way for rational human beings to be spending their lives. Like Apollo when he saw Daphne with her hair hung carelessly about her neck, they sigh and say to themselves: "What if it were properly arranged." Moreover, they tell us that they have seen in a dream the glorious, collisionless manner of living proper to all mankind, and this dream they understand as their warrant for seeking to remove the diversities and occasions of conflict which distinguish our current manner of living. Of course, their dreams are not all exactly alike; but they have this in common: each is a vision of a condition of human circumstance from which the occasion of conflict has been removed, a vision of human activity co-ordinated and set going in a single direction and of every resource being used to the full. And such people appropriately understand the office of government to be the imposition upon its subjects of the condition of human circumstances of their dream. To govern is to turn a private dream into a public and compulsory manner of living. Thus, politics becomes an encounter of dreams and the activity in which government is held to this understanding of its office and provided with the appropriate instruments.

I do not propose to criticize this jump to glory style of politics in which governing is understood as a perpetual take-over bid for the purchase of the resources of human energy in order to concentrate them in a single direction; it is not at all unintelligible, and there is much in our circumstances to provoke it. My purpose is merely to point out that there is another quite different understanding of government, and that it is no less intelligible and in some respects perhaps more appropriate to our circumstances.

The spring of this other disposition in respect of governing and the instruments of government—a conservative disposition—is to be found in the acceptance of the current condition of human circumstances as I have described it: the propensity to make our own choices and to find happiness in doing so, the variety of enterprises each pursued with passion, the diversity of beliefs each held with the conviction of its exclusive truth; the inventiveness, the changefulness and the absence of any large design; the excess, the over-activity and the informal compromise. And the office of government is not to impose other beliefs and activities upon its subjects, not to tutor or to educate them, not to make them better or happier in another way, not to direct them, to galvanize them into action, to lead them or to co-ordinate their activities so that no occasion of conflict shall occur; the office of government is merely to rule. This is a specific and limited activity, easily corrupted when it is combined with any other, and, in the circumstances, indispensable. The image of the ruler as the umpire whose business is to administer the rules of the game, or the chairman who governs the debate according to known rules but does not himself participate in it.

Now people of this disposition commonly defend their belief that the proper attitude of government towards the current condition of human circumstance is one of acceptance by appealing to certain general ideas. They contend that there is absolute value in the free play of human choice, that private property (the emblem of choice) is a natural right, that it is only in the enjoyment of diversity of opinion and activity that true belief and good conduct can be expected to disclose themselves. But I do not think that this disposition requires these or any similar beliefs in order to make it intelligible. Something much smaller and less pretentious will do: the observation that this condition of human circumstance is, in fact, current, and that we have learned to enjoy it and how to manage it; that we are not children *in statu pupillari* but adults who do not consider themselves under any obligation to justify their preference for making their own choices; and that it is beyond human experience to suppose that those who rule are endowed with a superior wisdom which discloses to them a better range of beliefs and activities and which gives them authority to impose upon their subjects a quite different manner of life. In short, if the man of this disposition is asked: Why ought governments to accept the current diversity of opinion and activity in preference to imposing upon their subjects a dream of their own? It is enough for him to reply: Why not? Their dreams are no different from those of anyone else; and if it is boring to have to listen to dreams of others being recounted, it is insufferable to be forced to re-enact them. We tolerate monomaniacs, it is our habit to do so; but why should we be *ruled* by them? Is it not (the man of conservative disposition asks) an intelligible task for a government to protect its subjects against the nuisance of those who spend their energy and their wealth in the service of some pet indignation, endeavouring to impose it upon everybody, not by suppressing their activities in favour of others of a similar kind, but by setting a limit to the amount of noise anyone may emit?

Nevertheless, if this acceptance is the spring of the conservative's disposition in respect of government, he does not suppose that the office of government is to do nothing. As he understands it, there is work to be done which can be done only in virtue of a genuine acceptance of current beliefs simply because they are current and current activities simply because they are afoot. And, briefly, the office he attributes to government is to resolve some of the collisions which this variety of beliefs and activities generates; to preserve peace, not by placing an interdict upon choice and upon the diversity that springs from the exercise of preference, not by imposing substantive uniformity, but by enforcing general rules of procedure upon all subjects alike.

Government, then, as the conservative in this matter understands it, does not begin with a vision of another, different and better world, but with the observation of the self-government practised even by men of passion in the conduct of their enterprises; it begins in the informal adjustments of interests to one another which are designed to release those who are apt to collide from the mutual frustration of a collision. Sometimes these adjustments are no more than agreements between two parties to keep out of each other's way; sometimes they are of wider application and more durable character, such as the International Rules for the prevention of collisions at sea. In short, the intimations of government are to be found in ritual, not in religion or philosophy; in the enjoyment of orderly and peaceable behaviour, not in the search for truth or perfection.

But the self-government of men of passionate belief and enterprise is apt to break down when it is most needed. It often suffices to resolve minor collisions of interest, but beyond these it is not to be relied upon. A more precise and a less easily corrupted ritual is required to resolve the massive collisions which our manner of living is apt to generate and to release us from the massive frustrations in which we are apt to become locked. The custodian of this ritual is "the government," and the rules it imposes are "the law." One may imagine a government engaged in the activity of an arbiter in cases of collisions of interest but doing its business without the aid of laws, just as one may imagine a game without rules and an umpire who was appealed to in cases of dispute and who on each occasion merely used his judgment to devise *ad hoc* a way of releasing the disputants from their mutual frustration. But the diseconomy of such an arrangement is so obvious that it could only be expected to occur to those inclined to believe the ruler to be supernaturally inspired and to those disposed to attribute to him a quite different office—that of leader, or tutor, or manager. At all events the disposition to be conservative in respect of government is rooted in the belief that where government rests upon the acceptance of the current activities and beliefs of its subjects, the only appropriate manner of ruling is by making and enforcing rules of conduct. In short, to be conservative about government is a reflection of the conservatism we have recognized to be appropriate in respect of rules of conduct.

To govern, then, as the conservative understands it, is to provide a *vinculum juris* for those manners of conduct which, in the circumstances, are least likely to result in a frustrating collision of interests; to provide redress and means of compensation for those who suffer from others behaving in a contrary manner; sometimes to provide punishment for those who pursue their own interests regardless of the rules; and, of course, to provide a sufficient force to maintain the authority of an arbiter of this kind. Thus, governing is recognized as a specific and limited activity; not the management of an enterprise, but the rule of those engaged in a great diversity of self-chosen enterprises. It is not concerned with concrete persons, but with activities; and with activities only in respect of their propensity to collide with one another. It is not concerned with moral right and wrong, it is not designed to make men good or even better; it is not indispensable on account of "the natural depravity of mankind" but merely because of their current disposition to be extravagant; its business is to keep its subjects at peace with one another in the activities in which they have chosen to seek their happiness. And if there is any general idea entailed in this view, it is, perhaps, that a government which does not sustain the loyalty of its subjects is worthless; and that while one which (in the old puritan phrase) "commands for truth" is incapable of doing so (because some of its subjects will believe its "truth" to be error), one which is indifferent to "truth" and "error" alike, and merely pursues peace, presents no obstacle to the necessary loyalty.

Now, it is intelligible enough that any man who thinks in this manner about government should be averse from innovation: government is providing rules of conduct, and familiarity is a supremely important virtue in a rule. Nevertheless, he has room for other thoughts. The current condition of human circumstances is one in which new activities (often springing from new inventions) are constantly appearing and rapidly extend themselves, and in which beliefs are perpetually being modified or discarded; and for the rules to be inappropriate to the current activities and beliefs is as unprofitable as for them to be unfamiliar. For example, a variety of inventions and considerable changes in the conduct of business, seem now to have made the current law of copyright inadequate. And it may be thought that neither the newspaper nor the motor-car nor the aeroplane have yet received proper recognition in the law of England; they have all created nuisances that call out to be abated. Or again, at the end of the last century our governments engaged in an extensive codification of large parts of our law and in this manner both brought it into closer relationship with current beliefs and manners of activity and insulated it from the small adjustments to circumstances which are characteristic of the operation of our common law. But many of these Statutes are now hopelessly out of date. And there are older Acts of Parliament (such as the Merchant Shipping Act), governing large and important departments of activity, which are even more inappropriate to current circumstances. Innovation, then, is called for if the rules are to remain appropriate to the activities they govern. But, as the conservative understands it, modification of the rules should always reflect, and never impose, a change in the activities and beliefs of those who are subject to them, and should never on any occasion be so great as to destroy the *ensemble*. Consequently, the conservative will have nothing to do with innovations designed to meet merely hypothetical situations; he will prefer to enforce a rule he has got rather than invent a new one; he will think it appropriate to delay a modification of the rules until it is clear that the change of circumstance it is designed to reflect has come to stay for a while; he will be suspicious of proposals for change in excess of what the situation calls for, of rulers who demand extra-ordinary powers in order to make great changes and whose utterances are tied to generalities like "the public good" or "social justice," and of Saviours of Society who buckle on armour and seek dragons to slay; he will think it proper to consider the occasion of the innovation with care; in short, he will be disposed to regard politics as an activity in which a valuable set of tools is renovated from time to time and kept in trim rather than as an opportunity for perpetual re-equipment.

All this may help to make intelligible the disposition to be conservative in respect of government; and the detail might be elaborated to show, for example, how a man of this disposition understands the other great business of a government, the conduct of a foreign policy; to show why he places so high a value upon the complicated set of arrangements we call "the institution of private property"; to show the appropriateness of his rejection of the view that politics is a shadow thrown by economics; to show why he believes that the main (perhaps the only) specifically economic activity appropriate to government is the maintenance of a stable currency. But, on this occasion, I think there is something else to be said.

To some people, "government" appears as a vast reservoir of power which inspires them to dream of what use might be made of it. They have favourite projects, of various dimensions, which they sincerely believe are for the benefit of mankind, and to capture this source of power, if necessary to increase it, and to use it for imposing their favourite projects upon their fellows is what they understand as the adventure of governing men. They are, thus, disposed to recognize government as an instrument of passion; the art of politics is to inflame and direct desire. In short, governing is understood to be just like any other activity — making and selling a brand of soap, exploiting the resources of a locality, or developing a housing estate — only the power here is (for the most part) already mobilized, and the enterprise is remarkable only because it aims at monopoly and because of its promise of success once the source of power has been captured. Of course a private enterprise politician of this sort would get nowhere in these days unless there were people with wants so vague that they can be prompted to ask for what he has to offer, or with wants so servile that they prefer the promise of a provided abundance to the opportunity of choice and activity on their own account. And it is not all as plain sailing as it might appear: often a politician of this sort misjudges the situation; and then, briefly, even in democratic politics, we become aware of what the camel thinks of the camel driver.

Now, the disposition to be conservative in respect of politics reflects a quite different view of the activity of governing. The man of this disposition understands it to be the business of a government not to inflame passion and give it new objects to feed upon, but to inject into the activities of already too passionate men an ingredient of moderation; to restrain, to deflate, to pacify and to reconcile; not to stoke the fires of desire, but to damp them down. And all this not because passion is vice and moderation virtue, but because moderation is indispensable if passionate men are to escape being locked in an encounter of mutual frustration. A government of this sort does not need to be regarded as the agent of a benign providence, as the custodian of a moral law, or as the emblem of a divine order. What it provides is something that its subjects (if they are such people as we are) can easily recognize to be valuable; indeed, it is something that, to some extent, they do for themselves in the ordinary course of business or pleasure. They scarcely need to be reminded of its indispensability, as Sextus Empiricus tells us the ancient Persians were accustomed periodically to remind themselves by setting aside all laws for five hair-raising days on the death of a king. Generally speaking, they are not averse from paying the modest cost of this service; and they recognize that the appropriate attitude to a government of this sort is loyalty (sometimes a confident loyalty, at other perhaps the heavy-hearted loyalty of Sidney Godolphin), respect and some suspicion, not love or devotion or affection. Thus, governing is understood to be a secondary activity; but it is recognized also to be a specific activity, not easily to be combined with any other, because all other activities (except the mere contemplation of the scene) entail taking sides and the surrender of the indifference appropriate (on this view of things) not only to the judge but also to the legislator, who is understood to occupy a judicial office. The subjects of such a government require that it shall be strong, alert, resolute, economical and neither capricious nor over-active: they have no use for a referee who does not govern the game according to the rules, who takes sides, who plays a game of this own, or who is always blowing his whistle; after all, the game's the thing, and in playing the game we neither need to be, nor at present are disposed to be, conservative. . . .

11   Revolutionary Socialism

Karl Marx (1818-1883) and Friedrich Engels (1820-1895), the most important socialist writers of the nineteenth century, were ambiguous about the way in which socialism would come to power. At times, they spoke as if a violent revolution were the only way to attain power. Reading 11, an excerpt from the *Communist Manifesto*, sketches their famous theory of "historical materialism," which was supposed to make this revolution inevitable. According to Marx and Engels, history is the story of class struggle. Each era, each economic and social system, sees an internal contest between a ruling class that owns the means of production and an exploited class that languishes under its domination. But history is not endless cyclical recurrence; it is a progressive story with a happy ending. The last system — "capitalism" — destroys itself utterly through class warfare between bourgeoisie and proletariat. When the proletariat seizes power in a world revolution, it abolishes private property and uses the state to ratify the social changes that have already occurred. Society can become "classless" because other classes like the peasantry and middle classes, already reduced through relentless competition, lose their economic basis of private ownership. Once the numerically small bourgeoisie is dispossessed, there remains only the world proletariat. But a single-class society is essentially classless, for there is no longer a division based on wealth or power.

Reading 11 is excerpted from Karl Marx and Friedrich Engels' *Manifesto of the Communist Party*. Marx drafted most of this document with some help from Engels. Begun in 1847 as the programmatic statement of the Communist League, a rather shadowy revolutionary organization, it was first published in Germany early in 1848. It played no important role in the series of revolutions that swept across Europe in that year, but it later became a standard text of the socialist movement.

● ● ● ● ● ● ● ● ● ●

A spectre is haunting Europe — the spectre of Communism. All the Powers of old Europe have entered into a holy alliance to exorcize this spectre: Pope and Czar, Metternich and Guizot, French Radicals and German police spies.

Where is the party in opposition that has not been decried as Communistic by its opponents in power? Where the Opposition that has not hurled back the branding reproach of Communism, against the more advanced opposition parties, as well as against its reactionary adversaries?

Two things result from this fact:

I. Communism is already acknowledged by all European Powers to be itself a Power.

II. It is high time that Communists should openly, in the face of the whole world, publish their views, their aims, their tendencies, and meet this nursery tale of the Spectre of Communism with a Manifesto of the party itself.

To this end, Communists of various nationalities have assembled in London, and sketched the following Manifesto, to be published in the English, French, German, Italian, Flemish and Danish languages.

BOURGEOIS AND PROLETARIANS

The history of all hitherto existing society is the history of class struggles.

Freeman and slave, patrician and plebeian, lord and serf, guild-master and journeyman, in a word, oppressor and oppressed, stood in constant opposition to one another, carried on an uninterrupted, now hidden, now open fight, a fight that each time ended, either in revolutionary reconstitution of society at large, or in the common ruin of the contending classes.

In the earlier epochs of history, we find almost everywhere a complicated arrangement of society into various orders, a manifold gradation of social rank. In ancient Rome we have patricians, knights, plebeians, slaves; in the Middle Ages, feudal lords, vassals, guild-masters, journeymen, apprentices, serfs; in almost all of these classes, again, subordinate gradations.

The modern bourgeois society that has sprouted from the ruins of feudal society has not done away with class antagonisms. It has but established new classes, new conditions of oppression, new forms of struggle in place of the old ones.

Our epoch, the epoch of the bourgeoisie, possesses, however, this distinctive feature: it has simplified the class antagonisms. Society as a whole is more and more splitting up into two great hostile camps, into two great classes directly facing each other: Bourgeoisie and Proletariat.

From the serfs of the Middle Ages sprang the chartered burghers of the earliest towns. From these burgesses the first elements of the bourgeoisie were developed.

The discovery of America, the rounding of the Cape, opened up fresh ground for the rising bourgeoisie. The East-Indian and Chinese markets, the colonization of America, trade with the colonies, the increase in the means of exchange and in commodities generally, gave to commerce, to navigation, to industry, an impulse never before known, and thereby, to the revolutionary element in the tottering feudal society, a rapid development.

The feudal system of industry, under which industrial production was monopolized by closed guilds, now no longer sufficed for the growing wants of the new markets. The manufacturing system took its place. The guild-masters were pushed on one side by the manufacturing middle class; division of labour between the different corporate guilds vanished in the face of division of labour in each single workshop.

Meantime the markets kept ever growing, the demand ever rising. Even manufacture no longer sufficed. Thereupon, steam and machinery revolutionized industrial production. The place of manufacture was taken by the giant, Modern Industry, the place of the industrial middle class, by industrial millionaires, the leaders of the whole industrial armies, the modern bourgeois.

Modern industry has established the world market, for which the discovery of America paved the way. This market has given an immense development to commerce, to navigation, to communication by land. This development has, in its turn, reacted on the extension of industry; and in proportion as industry, commerce, navigation, railways extended, in the same proportion the bourgeoisie developed, increased its capital, and pushed into the background every class handed down from the Middle Ages.

We see, therefore, how the modern bourgeoisie is itself the product of a long course of development, of a series of revolutions in the modes of production and of exchange.

Each step in the development of the bourgeoisie was accompanied by a corresponding political advance of that class. An oppressed class under the sway of the feudal nobility, an armed and self-governing association in the medieval commune; here independent urban republic (as in Italy and Germany), there taxable "third estate" of the monarchy (as in France), afterwards, in the period of manufacture proper, serving either the semi-feudal or the absolute monarchy as a counterpoise against the nobility, and, in fact, corner-stone of the great monarchies in general, the bourgeoisie has at last, since the establishment of Modern Industry and of the world market, conquered for itself, in the modern representative State, exclusive political sway. The executive of the modern State is but a committee for managing the common affairs of the whole bourgeoisie.

The bourgeoisie, historically, has played a most revolutionary part.

The bourgeoisie, wherever it has got the upper hand, has put an end to all feudal, patriarchal, idyllic relations. It has pitilessly torn asunder the motley feudal ties that bound man to his "natural superiors," and has left remaining no other nexus between man and man than naked self-interest, than callous "cash payment." It has drowned the most heavenly ecstasies of religious fervour, of chivalrous enthusiasm, of philistine sentimentalism, in the icy water of egotistical calculation. It has resolved personal worth into exchange value, and in place of the numberless indefeasible chartered freedoms, has set up that single, unconscionable freedom—Free Trade. In one word, for exploitation, veiled by religious and political illusions, it has substituted naked, shameless, direct, brutal exploitation.

The bourgeoisie has stripped of its halo every occupation hitherto honoured and looked up to with reverent awe. It has converted the physician, the lawyer, the priest, the poet, the man of science, into its paid wage-labourers.

The bourgeoisie has torn away from the family its sentimental veil, and has reduced the family relation to a mere money relation.

The bourgeoisie has disclosed how it came to pass that the brutal display of vigour in the Middle Ages, which Reactionists so much admire, found its fitting complement in the most slothful indolence. It has been the first to show what man's activity can bring about. It has accomplished wonders far surpassing Egyptian pyramids, Roman aqueducts, and Gothic cathedrals; it has conducted expeditions that put in the shade all former Exoduses of nations and crusades.

The bourgeoisie cannot exist without constantly revolutionizing the instruments of production, and thereby the relations of production, and with them the whole relations of society. Conservation of the old modes of production in unaltered form, was, on the contrary, the first condition of existence for all earlier industrial classes. Constant revolutionizing of production, uninterrupted disturbance of all social conditions, everlasting uncertainty and agitation distinguish the bourgeois epoch from all earlier ones. All fixed, fast-frozen relations, with their train of ancient and venerable prejudices and opinions are swept away, all new-formed ones become antiquated before they can ossify. All that is solid melts into air, all that is holy is profaned, and man is at last compelled to face with sober senses, his real conditions of life, and his relations with his kind.

The need of a constantly expanding market for its products chases the bourgeoisie over the whole surface of the globe. It must nestle everywhere, settle everywhere, establish connexions everywhere.

The bourgeoisie has through its exploitation of the world market given a cosmopolitan character to production and consumption in every country. To the great chagrin of Reactionists, it has drawn from under the feet of industry the national ground on which it stood. All old-established national industries have been destroyed or are daily being destroyed. They are

dislodged by new industries, whose introduction becomes a life and death
question for all civilized nations, by industries that no longer work up
indigenous raw material, but raw material drawn from the remotest zones;
industries whose products are consumed, not only at home, but in every
quarter of the globe. In place of the old wants, satisfied by the productions
of the country, we find new wants, requiring for their satisfaction the
products of distant lands and climes. In place of the old local and national
seclusion and self-sufficiency, we have intercourse in every direction,
universal inter-dependence of nations. And as in material, so also in
intellectual production. The intellectual creations of individual nations
become common property. National one-sidedness and narrow-minded-
ness become more and more impossible, and from the numerous national
and local literatures, there arises a world literature.

The bourgeoisie, by the rapid improvement of all instruments of
production, by the immensely facilitated means of communication, draws
all, even the most barbarian, nations into civilization. The cheap prices of its
commodities are the heavy artillery with which it batters down all Chinese
walls, with which it forces the barbarians' intensely obstinate hatred of
foreigners to capitulate. It compels all nations, on pain of extinction, to
adopt the bourgeois mode of production; it compels them to introduce what
it calls civilization into their midst, i.e., to become bourgeois themselves. In
one word, it creates a world after its own image.

The bourgeoisie has subjected the country to the rule of the towns. It
has created enormous cities, has greatly increased the urban population as
compared with the rural, and has thus rescued a considerable part of the
population from the idiocy of rural life. Just as it has made the country
dependent on the towns, so it has made barbarian and semi-barbarian
countries dependent on the civilized ones, nations of peasants on nations of
bourgeois, the East on the West.

The bourgeoisie keeps more and more doing away with the scattered
state of the population, of the means of production, and of property. It has
agglomerated population, centralized means of production, and has concentrated property in a few hands. The necessary consequence of this was
political centralization. Independent, or but loosely connected, provinces
with separate interests, laws, governments and systems of taxation, became
lumped together into one nation, with one government, one code of laws,
one national class-interest, one frontier and one customs-tariff.

The bourgeoisie, during its rule of scarce one hundred years, has
created more massive and more colossal productive forces than have all
preceding generations together. Subjection of Nature's forces to man,
machinery, application of chemistry to industry and agriculture, steam-
navigation, railways, electric telegraphs, clearing of whole continents for

cultivation, canalization of rivers, whole populations conjured out of the ground—what earlier century had even a presentiment that such productive forces slumbered in the lap of social labour?

We see then: the means of production and of exchange, on whose foundation the bourgeoisie built itself up, were generated in feudal society. At a certain stage in the development of these means of production and of exchange, the conditions under which feudal society produced and exchanged, the feudal organization of agriculture and manufacturing industry, in one word, the feudal relations of property became no longer compatible with the already developed productive forces; they became so many fetters. They had to be burst asunder; they were burst asunder.

Into their place stepped free competition, accompanied by a social and political constitution adapted to it, and by the economical and political sway of the bourgeois class.

A similar movement is going on before our own eyes. Modern bourgeois society with its relations of production, of exchange and of property, a society that has conjured up such gigantic means of production and of exchange, is like the sorcerer, who is no longer able to control the powers of the nether world whom he has called up by his spells. For many a decade past the history of industry and commerce is but the history of the revolt of modern productive forces against modern conditions of production, against the property relations that are the conditions for the existence of the bourgeoisie and of its rule. It is enough to mention the commercial crises that by their periodical return put on its trial, each time more threateningly, the existence of the entire bourgeois society. In these crises a great part not only of the existing products, but also of the previously created productive forces, are periodically destroyed. In these crises there breaks out an epidemic that, in all earlier epochs, would have seemed an absurdity—the epidemic of over-production. Society suddenly finds itself put back into a state of momentary barbarism; it appears as if a famine, a universal war of devastation had cut off the supply of every means of subsistence; industry and commerce seem to be destroyed; and why? Because there is too much civilization, too much means of subsistence, too much industry, too much commerce. The productive forces at the disposal of society no longer tend to further the development of the conditions of bourgeois property; on the contrary, they have become too powerful for these conditions, by which they are fettered, and so soon as they overcome these fetters, they bring disorder into the whole of bourgeois society, endanger the existence of bourgeois property. The conditions off bourgeois society are too narrow to comprise the wealth created by them. And how does the bourgeoisie get over these crises? On the one hand by enforced destruction of a mass of productive forces; on the other, by the conquest of new markets, and by the more thorough exploitation of the old ones. That is to say, by paving the way for more extensive and more destructive crises, and by diminishing the means whereby crises are prevented.

The weapons with which the bourgeoisie felled feudalism to the ground are now turned against the bourgeoisie itself.

But not only has the bourgeoisie forged the weapons that bring death to itself; it has also called into existence the men who are to wield those weapons—the modern working class—the proletarians.

In proportion as the bourgeoisie, i.e., capital, is developed, in the same proportion is the proletariat, the modern working class, developed—a class of labourers, who live only so long as they find work, and who find work only so long as their labour increases capital. These labourers, who must sell themselves piecemeal, are a commodity, like every other article of commerce, and are consequently exposed to all the vicissitudes of competition, to all the fluctuations of the market.

Owing to the extensive use of machinery and to division of labour, the work of the proletarians has lost all individual character, and, consequently, all charm for the workman. He becomes an appendage of the machine, and it is only the most simple, most monotonous, and most easily acquired knack, that is required of him. Hence, the cost of production of a workman is restricted, almost entirely, to the means of subsistence that he requires for his maintenance, and for the propagation of his race. But the price of a commodity, and therefore also of labour, is equal to its cost of production. In proportion, therefore, as the repulsiveness of the work increases, the wage decreases. Nay more, in proportion as the use of machinery and division of labour increases, in the same proportion the burden of toil also increases, whether by prolongation of the working hours, by increase of the work exacted in a given time or by increased speed of the machinery, etc.

Modern industry has converted the little workshop of the patriarchal master into the great factory of the industrial capitalist. Masses of labourers, crowded into the factory, are organized like soldiers. As privates of the industrial army they are placed under the command of a perfect hierarchy of officers and sergeants. Not only are they slaves of the bourgeois class, and of the bourgeois State; they are daily and hourly enslaved by the machine, by the overlooker, and, above all, by the individual bourgeois manufacturer himself. The more openly this despotism proclaims gain to be its end and aim, the more petty, the more hateful and the more embittering it is.

The less the skill and exertion of strength implied in manual labour, in other words, the more modern industry becomes developed, the more is the labour of men superseded by that of women. Differences of age and sex have no longer any distinctive social validity for the working class. All are instruments of labour, more or less expensive to use, according to their age and sex.

No sooner is the exploitation of the labourer by the manufacturer, so far, at an end, that he receives his wages in cash, than he is set upon by the other portions of the bourgeoisie, the landlord, the shopkeeper, the pawn-broker, etc.

The lower strata of the middle class—the small tradespeople, shop-keepers, and retired tradesmen generally, the handicraftsmen and peas-ants—all these sink gradually into the proletariat, partly because their diminutive capital does not suffice for the scale on which Modern Industry is carried on, and is swamped in the competition with the large capitalists, partly because their specialized skill is rendered worthless by new methods of production. Thus the proletariat is recruited from all classes of the population.

The proletariat goes through various stages of development. With its birth begins its struggle with the bourgeoisie. At first the contest is carried on by individual labourers, then by the work-people of a factory, then by the operatives of one trade, in one locality, against the individual bourgeois who directly exploits them. They direct their attacks not against the bour-geois conditions of production, but against the instruments of production themselves; they destroy imported wares that compete with their labour, they smash to pieces machinery, they set factories ablaze, they seek to restore by force the vanished status of the workman of the Middle Ages.

At this stage the labourers still form an incoherent mass scattered over the whole country, and broken up by their mutual competition. If any-where they unite to form more compact bodies, this is not yet the conse-quence of their own active union, but of the union of the bourgeoisie, which class, in order to attain its own political ends, is compelled to set the whole proletariat in motion, and is moreover yet, for a time, able to do so. At this stage, therefore, the proletarians do not fight their enemies, but the enemies of their enemies, the remnants of absolute monarchy, the landowners, the non-industrial bourgeois, the petty bourgeoisie. Thus the whole historical movement is concentrated in the hands of the bourgeoisie; every victory so obtained is a victory for the bourgeoisie.

But with the development of industry the proletariat not only increases in number; it becomes concentrated in greater masses, its strength grows, and it feels that strength more. The various interests and conditions of life within the ranks of the proletariat are more and more equalized, in propor-tion as machinery obliterates all distinctions of labour, and nearly every-where reduces wages to the same low level. The growing competition among the bourgeois, and the resulting commercial crises, make the wages of the workers ever more fluctuating. The unceasing improvement of machinery, ever more rapidly developing, makes their livelihood more and more precarious; the collisions between individual workmen and individual bourgeois take more and more the character of collisions between two classes. Thereupon the workers begin to form combinations (Trades Unions) against the bourgeois; they club together in order to keep up the rate of wages; they found permanent associations in order to make provision beforehand for these occasional revolts. Here and there the contest breaks out into riots.

Now and then the workers are victorious, but only for a time. The real fruit of their battles lies, not in the immediate result, but in the ever-expanding union of the workers. This union is helped on by the improved means of communication that are created by modern industry and that place the workers of different localities in contact with one another. It was just this contact that was needed to centralize the numerous local struggles, all of the same character, into one national struggle between classes. But every class struggle is a political struggle. And that union, to attain which the burghers of the Middle Ages, with their miserable highways, required centuries, the modern proletarians, thanks to railways, achieve in a few years.

This organization of the proletarians into a class, and consequently into a political party, is continually being upset again by the competition between the workers themselves. But it ever rises up again, stronger, firmer, mightier. It compels legislative recognition of particular interests of the workers, by taking advantage of the divisions among the bourgeoisie itself. Thus the Ten Hours bill in England was carried.

Altogether collisions between the classes of the old society further, in many ways, the course of development of the proletariat. The bourgeoisie finds itself involved in a constant battle. At first with the aristocracy; later on, with those portions of the bourgeoisie itself, whose interests have become antagonistic to the progress of industry; at all times, with the bourgeoisie of foreign countries. In all these battles it sees itself compelled to appeal to the proletariat, to ask for its help, and thus, to drag it into the political arena. The bourgeoisie itself, therefore, supplies the proletariat with its own elements of political and general education, in other words, it furnishes the proletariat with weapons for fighting the bourgeoisie.

Further, as we have already seen, entire sections of the ruling classes are, by the advance of industry, precipitated into the proletariat, or are at least threatened in their conditions of existence. These also supply the proletariat with fresh elements of enlightenment and progress.

Finally, in times when the class struggle nears the decisive hour, the process of dissolution going on within the ruling class, in fact within the whole range of old society, assumes such a violent, glaring character, that a small section of the ruling class cuts itself adrift, and joins the revolutionary class, the class that holds the future in its hands. Just as, therefore, at an earlier period, a section of the nobility went over to the bourgeoisie, so now a portion of the bourgeoisie goes over to the proletariat, and in particular, a portion of the bourgeois ideologists, who have raised themselves to the level of comprehending theoretically the historical movement as a whole.

Of all the classes that stand face to face with the bourgeoisie today, the proletariat alone is a really revolutionary class. The other classes decay and finally disappear in the face of modern industry; the proletariat is its special and essential product.

The lower middle class, the small manufacturer, the shopkeeper, the artisan, the peasant, all these fight against the bourgeoisie, to save from extinction their existence as fractions of the middle class. They are therefore not revolutionary, but conservative. Nay more, they are reactionary, for they try to roll back the wheel of history. If by chance they are revolutionary, they are so only in view of their impending transfer into the proletariat, they thus defend not their present, but their future interests, they desert their own standpoint to place themselves at that of the proletariat.

The "dangerous class," the social scum, that passively rotting mass thrown off by the lowest layers of old society, may, here and there, be swept into the movement by a proletarian revolution; its conditions of life, however, prepare it far more for the part of a bribed tool of reactionary intrigue.

In the conditions of the proletariat, those of old society at large are already virtually swamped. The proletarian is without property; his relation to his wife and children has no longer anything in common with the bourgeois family relations; modern industrial labour, modern subjection to capital, the same in England as in France, in America as in Germany, has stripped him of every trace of national character. Law, morality, religion, are to him so many bourgeois prejudices, behind which lurk in ambush just as many bourgeois interests.

All the preceding classes that got the upper hand sought to fortify their already acquired status by subjecting society at large to their conditions of appropriation. The proletarians cannot become masters of the productive forces of society, except by abolishing their own previous mode of appropriation, and thereby also every other previous mode of appropriation. They have nothing of their own to secure and to fortify; their mission is to destroy all previous securities for, and insurances of, individual property.

All previous historical movements were movements of minorities, or in the interest of minorities. The proletarian movement is the self-conscious, independent movement of the immense majority, in the interest of the immense majority. The proletariat, the lowest stratum of our present society, cannot stir, cannot raise itself up, without the whole superincumbent strata of official society being sprung into the air.

Though not in substance, yet in form, the struggle of the proletariat with the bourgeoisie is at first a national struggle. The proletariat of each country must, of course, first of all settle matters with its own bourgeoisie.

In depicting the most general phases of the development of the proletariat, we traced the more or less veiled civil war, raging within existing society, up to the point where that war breaks out into open revolution, and where the violent overthrow of the bourgeoisie lays the foundation for the sway of the proletariat.

Hitherto, every form of society has been based, as we have already seen, on the antagonism of oppressing and oppressed classes. But in order to oppress a class, certain conditions must be assured to it under which it can, at least, continue its slavish existence. The serf, in the period of serfdom, raised himself to membership in the commune, just as the petty bourgeois, under the yoke of feudal absolutism, managed to develop into a bourgeois. The modern labourer, on the contrary, instead of rising with the progress of industry, sinks deeper and deeper below the conditions of existence of his own class. He becomes a pauper, and pauperism develops more rapidly than population and wealth. And here it becomes evident, that the bourgeoisie is unfit any longer to be the ruling class in society, and to impose its conditions of existence upon society as an overriding law. It is unfit to rule because it is incompetent to assure an existence to its slave within his slavery, because it cannot help letting him sink into such a state, that it has to feed him, instead of being fed by him. Society can no longer live under this bourgeoisie, in other words, its existence is no longer compatible with society.

The essential condition for the existence, and for the sway of the bourgeois class, is the formation and augmentation of capital; the condition for capital is wage labour. Wage labour rests exclusively on competition between the labourers. The advance of industry, whose involuntary promoter is the bourgeoisie, replaces the isolation of the labourers, due to competition, by their revolutionary combination, due to association. The development of Modern Industry, therefore, cuts from under its feet the very foundation on which the bourgeoisie produces and appropriates products. What the bourgeoisie, therefore, produces, above all, is its own gravediggers. Its fall and the victory of the proletariat are equally inevitable.

12   Social Democracy

Although an apocalyptic vision of world destruction and renewal pervades the *Communist Manifesto*, Marx and Engels spoke at other times in more sober tones of a gradual accession to political power through the democratic political systems that had come into being in Western Europe and North America. This gradualist strategy is the source of the less radical wing of socialism now known as social democracy or democratic socialism. Along with the idea of revolution, social democrats have abandoned the withering away of the state, the classless society, and other characteristic Marxian speculations.

Reading 12, the "Regina Manifesto," is an important Canadian example of social democracy. Adopted by the Co-operative Commonwealth Federation (CCF) in 1933 during the worst of the Depression, it was unremittingly hostile in tone to capitalism, calling for its eradication and replacement by a "full programme of socialized planning." Significantly, however, the Manifesto did not call for complete public ownership of the means of production; only certain key industries—finance, transportation, communications, utilities, and natural resources—were to be nationalized. Large areas of the economy, such as agriculture, manufacturing, wholesaling, retailing, and personal services, were to be left in private hands. Beyond this rather diluted program of socialization, the Manifesto's other proposals were similar in principle to reform liberalism: social security, protection of workers, socialized medicine, and redistribution through progressive taxation. All this was to be accomplished by constitutional means: "we do not believe in violence."

The Regina Manifesto was drafted in June 1933 by Frank Underhill, a history professor at the University of Toronto, and revised with the assistance of Eugene Forsey, F.R. Scott, and other colleagues in the League for Social Reconstruction, an association of socialist intellectuals modelled on the British Fabian Society and associated with the CCF. The Manifesto remained the CCF's major statement of principles until the party adopted a new declaration, much less openly socialist in tone, at the Winnipeg convention of 1956.

• • • • • • • • • •

The CCF is a federation of organizations whose purpose is the establishment in Canada of a Co-operative Commonwealth in which the principle regulating production, distribution and exchange will be the supplying of human needs and not the making of profits.

We aim to replace the present capitalist system, with its inherent injustice and inhumanity, by a social order from which the domination and exploitation of one class by another will be eliminated, in which economic planning will supersede unregulated private enterprise and competition, and in which genuine democratic self-government, based upon economic equality will be possible. The present order is marked by glaring inequalities of wealth and opportunity, by chaotic waste and instability; and in an age of plenty it condemns the great mass of the people to poverty and insecurity. Power has become more and more concentrated into the hands of a small irresponsible minority of financiers and industrialists and to their predatory interests the majority are habitually sacrificed. When private profit is the main stimulus to economic effort, our society oscillates between periods of feverish prosperity in which the main benefits go to speculators and profiteers, and of catastrophic depression, in which the common man's normal state of insecurity and hardship is accentuated. We believe that these evils can be removed only in a planned and socialized economy in which our natural resources and the principal means of production and distribution are owned, controlled and operated by the people.

The new social order at which we aim is not one in which individuality will be crushed out by a system of regimentation. Nor shall we interfere with cultural rights of racial or religious minorities. What we seek is a proper collective organization of our economic resources such as will make possible a much greater degree of leisure and a much richer individual life for every citizen.

This social and economic transformation can be brought about by political action, through the election of a government inspired by the ideal of a Co-operative Commonwealth and supported by a majority of the people. We do not believe in change by violence. We consider that both the old parties in Canada are the instruments of capitalist interests and cannot serve as agents of social reconstruction, and that whatever the superficial differences between them, they are bound to carry on government in accordance with the dictates of the big business interests who finance them. The CCF aims at political power in order to put an end to this capitalist domination of our political life. It is a democratic movement, a federation of farmer, labor and socialist organizations, financed by its own members and seeking to achieve its ends solely by constitutional methods. It appeals for support to all who believe that the time has come for a far-reaching reconstruction of our economic and political institutions and who are willing to work together for the carrying out of the following policies:

1. Planning

The establishment of a planned, socialized economic order, in order to make possible the most efficient development of the national resources and the most equitable distribution of the national income.

The first step in this direction will be setting up of a National Planning Commission consisting of a small body of economists, engineers and statisticians assisted by an appropriate technical staff.

The task of the commission will be to plan for the production, distribution and exchange of all goods and services necessary to the efficient functioning of the economy; to co-ordinate the activities of the socialized industries; to provide for a satisfactory balance between the producing and consuming power; and to carry on continuous research into all branches of the national economy in order to acquire the detailed information necessary to efficient planning.

The Commission will be responsible to the Cabinet and will work in co-operation with the Managing Boards of the Socialized Industries.

It is now certain that in every industrial country some form of planning will replace the disintegrating capitalist system. The CCF will provide that in Canada the planning shall be done, not by a small group of capitalist magnates in their own interests, but by public servants acting in the public interest and responsible to the people as a whole.

2. Socialization of Finance

Socialization of all financial machinery—banking, currency, credit, and insurance, to make possible the effective control of currency, credit and prices, and the supplying of new productive equipment for socially desirable purposes.

Planning by itself will be of little use if the public authority has not the power to carry its plans into effect. Such power will require the control of finance and of all those vital industries and services, which, if they remain in private hands, can be used to thwart or corrupt the will of the public authority. Control of finance is the first step in the control of the whole economy. The chartered banks must be socialized and removed from the control of private profit-seeking interests; and the national banking system thus established must have at its head a Central Bank to control the flow of credit and the general price level, and to regulate foreign exchange operations. A National Investment Board must also be set up, working in co-operation with the socialized banking system to mobilize and direct the unused surpluses of production for socially desired purposes as determined by the Planning Commission.

Insurance Companies, which provide one of the main channels for the investment of individual savings and which, under their present competitive organization, charge needlessly high premiums for the social services that they render, must also be socialized.

3. Social Ownership

Socialization (Dominion, Provincial or Municipal) of transportation, communications, electric power and all other industries and services essential to social planning, and their operation under the general direction of the Planning Commission by competent managements freed from day to day political interference.

Public utilities must be operated for the public benefit and not for the private profit of a small group of owners or financial manipulators. Our natural resources must be developed by the same methods. Such a programme means the continuance and extension of the public ownership enterprises in which most governments in Canada have already gone some distance. Only by such public ownership, operated on a planned economy, can our main industries be saved from the wasteful competition of the ruinous over-development and over-capitalization which are the inevitable outcome of capitalism. Only in a regime of public ownership and operation will the full benefits accruing from the centralized control and mass production be passed on to the consuming public.

Transportation, communications and electric power must come first in a list of industries to be socialized. Others, such as mining, pulp and paper and the distribution of milk, bread, coal and gasoline, in which exploitation, waste, or financial malpractices are particularly prominent must next be brought under social ownership and operation.

In restoring to the community its natural resources and in taking over industrial enterprises from private into public control we do not propose any policy of outright confiscation. What we desire is the most stable and equitable transition to the Co-operative Commonwealth. It is impossible to decide the policies to be followed in particular cases in an uncertain future, but we insist upon certain broad principles. The welfare of the community must take supremacy over the claims of private wealth. In times of war, human life has been conscripted. Should economic circumstances call for it, conscription of wealth would be more justifiable. We recognize the need for compensation in the case of individuals and institutions which must receive adequate maintenance during the transitional period before the planned economy becomes fully operative. But a CCF government will not play the role of rescuing bankrupt private concerns for the benefit of promoters and of stock and bond holders. It will not pile up a deadweight burden of unremunerative debt which represents claims upon the public treasury of a functionless owner class.

The management of publicly owned enterprises will be vested in boards who will be appointed for their competence in the industry and will conduct each particular enterprise on efficient economic lines. The machinery of management may well vary from industry to industry, but the rigidity of Civil Service rules should be avoided and likewise the evils of the patronage system as exemplified in so many departments of the Government today. Workers in these public industries must be free to organize in trade unions and must be given the right to participate in the management of the industry.

4. Agriculture

Security of tenure for the farmer upon his farm on conditions to be laid down by individual provinces; insurance against unavoidable crop failure; removal of the tariff burden from the operations of agriculture; encouragement of producers' and consumers' co-operatives; the restoration and maintenance of an equitable relationship between prices of agricultural products and those of other commodities and services; and improving the efficiency of export trade in farm products.

The security of tenure for the farmer upon his farm which is imperilled by the present disastrous situation of the whole industry, together with adequate social insurance, ought to be guaranteed under equitable conditions.

The prosperity of agriculture, the greatest Canadian industry, depends upon a rising volume of purchasing power of the masses in Canada for all farm goods consumed at home, and upon the maintenance of large scale exports of the stable commodities at satisfactory prices or equitable commodity exchange.

The intense depression in agriculture today is a consequence of the general world crisis caused by the normal workings of the capitalistic system resulting in: (1) Economic nationalism expressing itself in tariff barriers and other restrictions of world trade; (2) The decreased purchasing power of unemployed and under-employed workers and of the Canadian people in general; (3) The exploitation of both primary producers and consumers by monopolistic corporations who absorb a great proportion of the selling price of farm products. (This last is true, for example, of the distribution of milk and dairy products, the packing industry, and milling.)

The immediate cause of agricultural depression is the catastrophic fall in the world prices of foodstuffs as compared with other prices, this fall being due in large measure to the deflation of currency and credit. To counteract the worst effect of this, the internal price level should be raised so that the farmers' purchasing power may be restored.

We propose therefore:

(1) The improvement of the position of the farmer by the increase of purchasing power made possible by the social control of the financial system. This control must be directed towards the increase of employment as laid down elsewhere and towards raising the prices of farm commodities by appropriate credit and foreign policies.

(2) Whilst the family farm is the accepted basis for agricultural production in Canada the position of the farmer may be much improved by:

(a) The extension of consumers' co-operatives for the purchase of farm supplies and domestic requirements; and

(b) The extension of co-operative institutions for the processing and marketing of farm products.

Both of the foregoing to have suitable state encouragement and assistance.

(3) The adoption of a planned system of agricultural development based upon scientific soil surveys directed towards better land utilization, and a scientific policy of agricultural development for the whole of Canada.

(4) The substitution for the present system of foreign trade, of a system of import and export boards to improve the efficiency of overseas marketing, to control prices, and to integrate the foreign trade policy with the requirements of the national economic plan.

5. External Trade

The regulation in accordance with the National plan of external trade through import and export boards.

Canada is dependent on external sources of supply for many of her essential requirements of raw materials and manufactured products. These she can obtain only by large exports of the goods she is best fitted to produce. The strangling of our export trade by insane protectionist policies must be brought to an end. But the old controversies between free traders and protectionists are now largely obsolete. In a world of nationally organized economies Canada must organize the buying and selling of her main imports and exports under public boards, and take steps to regulate the flow of less important commodities by a system of licenses. By so doing she will be enabled to make the best trade agreements possible with foreign countries, put a stop to the exploitation of both primary producer and ultimate consumer, make possible the co-ordination of internal processing, transportation and marketing of farm products, and facilitate the establishment of stable prices for such export commodities.

6. Co-operative Institutions

The encouragement by the public authority of both producers' and consumers' co-operative institutions.

In agriculture, as already mentioned, the primary producer can receive a larger net revenue through co-operative organization of purchases and marketing. Similarly in retail distribution of staple commodities such as milk, there is room for development both of public municipal operation and of consumers' co-operatives, and such co-operative organization can be extended into wholesale distribution and into manufacturing. Co-operative enterprises should be assisted by the state through appropriate legislation and through the provision of adequate credit facilities.

7. Labour Code

A National Labour Code to secure for the worker maximum income and leisure, insurance covering illness, accident, old age, and unemployment, freedom of association and effective participation in the management of his industry or profession.

The spectre of poverty and insecurity which still haunts every worker, though technological developments have made possible a high standard of living for everyone, is a disgrace which must be removed from our civilization. The community must organize its resources to effect progressive reduction of the hours of work in accordance with technological development and to provide a constantly rising standard of life to everyone who is willing to work. A labor code must be developed which will include state regulation of all wages, equal reward and equal opportunity of advancement for equal services, irrespective of sex; measures to guarantee the right to work or the right to maintenance through stabilization of employment and through unemployment insurance; social insurance to protect workers and their families against the hazards of sickness, death, industrial accident and old age; limitation of hours of work and protection of health and safety in industry. Both wages and insurance benefits should be varied in accordance with family needs.

In addition workers must be guaranteed the undisputed right to freedom of association, and should be encouraged and assisted by the state to organize themselves in trade unions. By means of collective agreements and participation in works councils, the workers can achieve fair working rules and share in the control of industry and profession; and their organizations will be indispensable elements in a system of genuine industrial democracy.

The labor code should be uniform throughout the country. But the achievement of this end is difficult so long as jurisdiction over labor legislation under the BNA Act is mainly in the hands of the provinces. It is urgently necessary, therefore, that the BNA Act be amended to make such a national labor code possible.

8. Socialized Health Services
Publicly organized health, hospital and medical services.

With the advance of medical science the maintenance of a healthy population has become a function for which every civilized community should undertake responsibility. Health services should be made at least as freely available as are educational services today. But under a system which is still mainly one of private enterprise the costs of proper medical care, such as the wealthier members of society can easily afford, are at present prohibitive for great masses of the people. A properly organized system of public health services including medical and dental care, which would stress the prevention rather than the cure of illness should be extended to all our people in both rural and urban areas. This is an enterprise in which Dominion, Provincial and Municipal authorities, as well as the medical and dental professions, can co-operate.

9. BNA Act
The amendment of the Canadian Constitution, without infringing upon racial or religious minority rights or upon legitimate provincial claims to autonomy, so as to give the Dominion Government adequate powers to deal effectively with urgent economic problems which are essentially national in scope; the abolition of the Canadian Senate.

We propose that the necessary amendments to the BNA Act shall be obtained as speedily as required, safeguards being inserted to ensure that the existing rights of racial and religious minorities shall not be changed without their own consent. What is chiefly needed today is the placing in the hands of the national government of more power to control national economic development. In a rapidly changing economic environment our political constitution must be reasonably flexible. The present division of powers between Dominion and Provinces reflects the conditions of a pioneer, mainly agricultural, community in 1867. Our constitution must be brought into line with the increasing industrialization of the country and the consequent centralization of economic and financial power — which has taken place in the last two generations. The principle laid down in the Quebec Resolution of the Fathers of Confederation should be applied to the conditions of 1933, that "there be a general government charged with matters of common interest to the whole country and local governments for each of the provinces charged with the control of local matters in their respective sections."

The Canadian Senate, which was originally created to protect provincial rights, but has failed even in this function, has developed into a bulwark of capitalist interests, as is illustrated by the large number of company directorships held by its aged members. In its peculiar composition of a fixed number of members appointed for life it is one of the most reactionary assemblies in the civilized world. It is a standing obstacle to all progressive legislation, and the only permanently satisfactory method of dealing with the constitutional difficulties it creates is to abolish it.

10. External Relations
A Foreign Policy designed to obtain international economic co-operation and to promote disarmament and world peace.

Canada has a vital interest in world peace. We propose, therefore, to do everything in our power to advance the idea of international co-operation as represented by the League of Nations and the International Labor Organization. We would extend our diplomatic machinery for keeping in touch with the main centres of world interest. But we believe that genuine international co-operation is incompatible with the capitalist regime which is in force in most countries, and that strenuous efforts are needed to rescue the League from its present condition of being mainly a League of capitalist Great Powers. We stand resolutely against all participation in imperialist wars. With the British Commonwealth, Canada must maintain her autonomy as a completely self-governing nation. We must resist all attempts to build up a new economic British Empire in place of the old political one, since such attempts readily lend themselves to the purposes of capitalist exploitation and may easily lead to further world wars. Canada must refuse to be entangled in any more wars fought to make the world safe for capitalism.

11. Taxation and Public Finance
A new taxation policy designed not only to raise public revenues but also to lessen the glaring inequalities of income and to provide funds for social services and the socialization of industry; the cessation of the debt creating system of Public Finance.

In the type of economy that we envisage, the need for taxation, as we now understand it, will have largely disappeared. It will nevertheless be essential during the transition period, to use the taxing powers, along with the other methods proposed elsewhere, as a means of providing for the socialization of industry, and for extending the benefits of increased Social Services.

At the present time capitalist governments in Canada raise a large proportion of their revenues from such levies as customs duties and sales taxes, the main burden of which falls upon the masses. In place of such taxes upon articles of general consumption, we propose a drastic extension of income, corporation and inheritance taxes, steeply graduated according to ability to pay. Full publicity must be given to income tax payments and our tax collection system must be brought up to the English standard of efficiency.

We also believe in the necessity for an immediate revision of the basis of Dominion and Provincial sources of revenues, so as to produce a co-ordinated and equitable system of taxation throughout Canada.

An inevitable effect of the capitalist system is the debt creating character of public financing. All public debts have enormously increased, and the fixed interest charges paid thereon now amount to the largest single item of so-called uncontrollable public expenditures. The CCF proposes that in future no public financing shall be permitted which facilitates the perpetuation of the parasitic interest-receiving class; that capital shall be provided through the medium of the National Investment Board and free from perpetual interest charges.

We propose that all Public Works, as directed by the Planning Commission, shall be financed by the issuance of credit, as suggested, based upon the National Wealth of Canada.

12. Freedom

Freedom of speech and assembly for all; repeal of Section 98 of the Criminal Code; amendment of the Immigration Act to prevent the present inhuman policy of deportation; equal treatment before the law of all residents of Canada irrespective of race, nationality or religious or political beliefs.

In recent years, Canada has seen an alarming growth of Fascist tendencies among all governmental authorities. The most elementary rights of freedom of speech and assembly have been arbitrarily denied to workers and to all whose political and social views do not meet with the approval of those in power. The lawless and brutal conduct of the police in certain centres in preventing public meetings and in dealing with political prisoners must cease. Section 98 of the Criminal Code which has been used as a weapon of political oppression by a panic-stricken capitalist government, must be wiped off the statute book and those who have been imprisoned under it must be released. An end must be put to the inhuman practice of deporting immigrants who were brought to this country by immigration propaganda and now, through no fault of their own, find themselves victims of an executive department against whom there is no appeal to the courts of the land. We stand for full economic, political and religious liberty for all.

13. Social Justice

The establishment of a commission composed of psychiatrists, psychologists, socially minded jurists and social workers, to deal with all matters pertaining to crime and punishment and the general administration of law, in order to humanize the law and to bring it into harmony with the needs of the people.

While the removal of economic inequality will do much to overcome the most glaring injustices in the treatment of those who come into conflict with the law, our present archaic system must be changed and brought into accordance with a modern concept of human relationships. This new system must not be based as is the present one, upon vengeance and fear, but upon an understanding of human behaviour. For this reason its planning and control cannot be left in the hands of those steeped in the outworn legal tradition; and therefore it is proposed that there shall be established a national commission composed of psychiatrists, psychologists, socially minded jurists and social workers whose duty it shall be to devise a system of prevention and correction consistent with other features of the new social order.

14. An Emergency Programme

The assumption by the Dominion Government of direct responsibility for dealing with the present critical unemployment situation and for tendering suitable work or adequate maintenance; the adoption of measures to relieve the extremity of the crisis such as a programme of public spending on housing, and other enterprises that will increase the real wealth of Canada, to be financed by the issue of credit based on the national wealth.

The extent of unemployment and the widespread suffering which it has caused, creates a situation with which provincial and municipal governments have long been unable to cope and forces upon the Dominion government direct responsibility for dealing with the crisis as the only authority with financial resources adequate to meet the situation. Unemployed workers must be secured in the tenure of their homes, and the scale and methods of relief, at present altogether inadequate, must be such as to preserve decent human standards of living.

It is recognized that even after a Co-operative Commonwealth Federation Government has come into power, a certain period of time must elapse before the planned economy can be fully worked out. During this brief transitional period, we propose to provide work and purchasing power for those now unemployed by a far-reaching programme of public expenditure on housing, slum clearance, hospitals, libraries, schools, community halls, parks, recreational projects, reforestation, rural electrification, the elimination of grade crossing, and other similar projects in both town and country. This programme, which would be financed by the issuance of credit based on the national wealth, would serve the double purpose of creating employment and meeting recognized social needs. Any steps which the Government takes, under this emergency programme, which may assist private business, must include guarantees of adequate wages and reasonable hours of work, and must be designed to further the advance towards the complete Co-operative Commonwealth.

Emergency measures, however, are of only temporary value, for the present depression is a sign of the mortal sickness of the whole capitalist system, and this sickness cannot be cured by the application of salves. These leave untouched the cancer which is eating at the heart of our society, namely, the economic system in which our natural resources and our principal means of production and distribution are owned, controlled and operated for the private profit of a small proportion of our population.

No CCF Government will rest content until it has eradicated capitalism and put into operation the full programme of socialized planning which will lead to the establishment in Canada of the Co-operative Commonwealth.

13   Fascism

All varieties of liberalism, conservatism, and socialism have one thing in common: they are primarily concerned with the proper role of government in the political community. Nationalism, however, is more concerned with the boundaries of the political community: Who should be included and who should be excluded? There are as many varieties of nationalist ideology as there are communities because each nation generates its own mythology about the origin, history, and destiny of its people. This diversity means that nationalism is extraordinarily hard to characterize, and any single example is seriously misleading if taken as typical of all nationalist thought.

Reading 13 is Benito Mussolini's summmary of the ideology of fascism, which we consider to be an exaggerated form of nationalism. In Mussolini's doctrine, nation and state are fused into one totalitarian entity. He goes so far as to say that "the nation is created by the State," and further asserts that warfare of nation against nation is essential to fascism. Such militarism takes to an extreme the general nationalistic tendency to think of the nation as the community to which we owe our highest allegiance.

Benito Mussolini (1883-1945) was the founder of Italian fascism. He assumed leadership of the Italian government in 1922 through the famous "march on Rome." He had been a socialist until World War I brought his nationalism to the fore, and as a result his fascist ideology is a combination of nationalism and socialism with traditional conservative themes of order and hierarchy. The reading which follows is a translation of Mussolini's article on fascism from volume 14 of the *Enciclopedia Italiana* and appears in *Through Fascism to World Power: A History of the Revolution in Italy.*

● ● ● ● ● ● ● ● ● ●

FUNDAMENTAL IDEAS

Philosophic Conception.

1. Like every concrete political conception, Fascism is thought and action. It is action with an inherent doctrine which, arising out of a given system of historic forces, is inserted in it and works on it from within. It has therefore a form co-related to the contingencies of time and place; but it has at the same time an ideal content which elevates it into a formula of truth in the higher region of the history of thought.

There is no way of exercising a spiritual influence on the things of the world by means of a human will-power commanding the wills of others, without first having a clear conception of the particular and transient reality on which the will-power must act, and without also having a clear conception of the universal and permanent reality in which the particular and transient reality has its life and being. To know men we must have a knowledge of man; and to have a knowledge of man we must know the reality of things and their laws.

There can be no conception of a State which is not fundamentally a conception of Life. It is a philosophy or intuition, a system of ideas which evolves itself into a system of logical construction, or which concentrates itself in a vision or in a faith, but which is always, at least virtually, an organic conception of the world.

Spiritualised Conception.

2. Fascism would therefore not be understood in many of its manifestations (as, for example, in its organisations of the Party, its system of education, its discipline) were it not considered in the light of its general view of life. A spiritualised view.

To Fascism the world is not this material world which appears on the surface, in which man is an individual separated from all other men, standing by himself and subject to a natural law which instinctively impels him to lead a life of momentary and egoistic pleasure. In Fascism man is an individual who is the nation and the country. He is this by a moral law which embraces and binds together individuals and generations in an established tradition and mission, a moral law which suppresses the instinct to lead a life confined to a brief cycle of pleasure in order, instead, to replace it within the orbit of duty in a superior conception of life, free from the limits of time and space; a life in which the individual by self-abnegation and by the sacrifice of his particular interests, even by death, realises the entirely spiritual existence in which his value as a man consists.

Positive Conception of Life as a Struggle.

3. It is therefore a spiritualised conception, itself also a result of the general reaction of the Century against the languid and materialistic positivism of the Eighteenth Century. Anti-positivist, but positive: neither sceptical nor agnostic, neither pessimistic nor passively optimistic, as are in general the doctrines (all of them negative) which place the centre of life outside of man, who by his free will can and should create his own world for himself.

Fascism wants a man to be active and to be absorbed in action with all his energies: it wants him to have a manly consciousness of the difficulties that exist and to be ready to face them. It conceives life as a struggle, thinking that it is the duty of man to conquer that life which is really worthy of him: creating in the first place within himself the (physical, moral, intellectual) instrument with which to build it.

As for the individual, so for the nation, so for mankind. Hence the high value of culture in all its forms (art, religion, science) and the supreme importance of education. Hence also the essential value of labour, with which man conquers nature and creates the human world (economic, political, moral, intellectual).

Ethical Conception.

4. This positive conception of life is evidently an ethical conception. And it comprises the whole reality as well as the human activity which domineers it. No action is to be removed from the moral sense; nothing is to be in the world that is divested of the importance which belongs to it in respect of moral aims. Life, therefore, as the Fascist conceives it, is serious, austere, religious; entirely balanced in a world sustained by the moral and responsible forces of the spirit. The Fascist disdains the "easy" life.

Religious Conception.

5. Fascism is a religious conception in which man is considered to be in the powerful grip of a superior law, with an objective Will which transcends the particular individual and elevates him into a fully conscious member of a spiritual society. Anyone who has stopped short at the mere consideration of opportunism in the religious policy of the Fascist regime, has failed to understand that Fascism, besides being a system of government, is also a system of thought.

Historical and Realist Conception.

6. Fascism is an historic conception in which man could not be what he is without being a factor in the spiritual process to which he contributes, either in the family sphere or in the social sphere, in the nation or in history in general to which all nations contribute. Hence is derived the great importance of tradition in the records, language, customs and rules of human society. Man without a part in history is nothing.

For this reason Fascism is opposed to all the abstractions of an individualistic character based upon materialism typical of the Eighteenth Century; and it is opposed to all the Jacobin innovations and utopias. It does not believe in the possibility of "happiness" on earth as conceived by the literature of the economists of the Seventeenth Century; it therefore spurns all the teleological conceptions of final causes through which, at a given period of history, a final systematisation of the human race would take place. Such theories only mean placing oneself outside real history and life, which is a continual ebb and flow and process of realisations.

Politically speaking, Fascism aims at being a realistic doctrine; in its practice it aspires to solve only the problems which present themselves of their own accord in the process of history, and which of themselves find or suggest their own solution. To have the effect of action among men, it is necessary to enter into the process of reality and to master the forces actually at work.

The Individual and Liberty.

7. Anti-individualistic, the Fascist conception is for the State; it is for the individual only in so far as he coincides with the State, universal consciousness and will of man in his historic existence. It is opposed to the classic Liberalism which arose out of the need of reaction against absolutism, and which had accomplished its mission in history when the State itself had become transformed in the popular will and consciousness.

Liberalism denied the State in the interests of the particular individual; Fascism reaffirms the State as the only true expression of the individual.

And if liberty is to be the attribute of the real man, and not of the scarecrow invented by individualistic Liberalism, then Fascism is for liberty. It is for the only kind of liberty that is serious—the liberty of the State and of the individual in the State. Because, for the Fascist, all is comprised in the State and nothing spiritual or human exists—much less has any value—outside the State—the unification and synthesis of every value—interprets, develops and potentiates the whole life of the people.

Conception of a Corporative State.

8. No individuals nor groups (political parties, associations, labour unions, classes) outside the State. For this reason Fascism is opposed to Socialism, which clings rigidly to class war in the historic evolution and ignores the unity of the State which moulds the classes into a single, moral and economic reality. In the same way Fascism is opposed to the unions of the labouring classes. But within the orbit of the State with ordinative functions, the real needs, which gave rise to the Socialist movement and to the forming of labour unions, are emphatically recognised by Fascism and are given their full expression in the Corporative System, which conciliates every interest in the unity of the State.

Democracy.

9. Individuals form classes according to categories of interests. They are associated according to differentiated economical activities which have a common interest; but first and foremost they form the State. The State is

not merely either the numbers or the sum of individuals forming the majority of a people. Fascism for this reason is opposed to the democracy which identifies peoples with the greatest number of individuals and reduces them to a majority level. But if people are conceived, as they should be, qualitatively and not quantitatively, then Fascism is democracy in its purest form. The qualitative conception is the most coherent and truest form and is therefore the most moral, because it sees a people realised in the consciousness and will of the few or even of one only; an ideal which moves to its realisation in the consciousness and will of all. By "all" is meant all who derive their justification as a nation, ethnically speaking, from their nature and history, and who follow the same line of spiritual formation and development as one single will and consciousness—not as a race nor as a geographically determined region, but as a progeny that is rather the outcome of a history which perpetuates itself; a multitude unified by an idea embodied in the will to have power and to exist, conscious of itself and of its personality.

Conception of the State.

10. This higher personality is truly the nation, inasmuch as it is the State. The nation does not beget the State, according to the decrepit nationalistic concept which was used as a basis for the publicists of the national States in the Nineteenth Century. On the contrary, the nation is created by the State, which gives the people, conscious of their own moral unity, the will, and thereby an effective existence. The right of a nation to its independence is derived not from a literary and ideal consciousness of its own existence, much less from a *de facto* situation more or less inert and unconscious, but from an active consciousness, from an active political will disposed to demonstrate in its right; that is to say, a kind of State already in its pride (*in fieri*). The State, in fact, as a universal ethical will, is the creator of right.

Dynamic Reality.

11. The nation as a State is an ethical reality which exists and lives in measure as it develops. A standstill is its death. Therefore the State is not only the authority which governs and which gives the forms of law and the worth of the spiritual life to the individual wills, but it is also the power which gives effect to its will in foreign matters, causing it to be recognised and respected by demonstrating through facts the universality of all the manifestations necessary for its development. Hence it is organisation as well as expansion, and it may be thereby considered, at least virtually, equal to the very nature of the human will, which in its evolution recognises no barriers, and which realises itself by proving its infinity.

The Role of the State.

12. The Fascist State, the highest and the most powerful form of personality, is a force, but a spiritual one. It re-assumes all the forms of the moral and intellectual life of man. It cannot, therefore, be limited to a simple function of order and of safeguarding, as was contended by Liberalism. It is not a simple mechanism which limits the sphere of the presumed individual liberties. It is an internal form and rule, a discipline of the entire person: it penetrates the will as well as the intelligence. Its principle, a central inspiration of the living human personality in the civil community, descends into the depths and settles in the heart of the man of action as well as of the thinker, of the artist as well as of the scientist; the soul of our soul.

Discipline and Authority.

13. Fascism, in short, is not only a lawgiver and the founder of institutions, but an educator and a promoter of the spiritual life. It aims to rebuild not the forms of human life, but its content, the man, the character, the faith. And for this end it exacts discipline and an authority which descends into and dominates the interior of the spirit without opposition. Its emblem, therefore, is the lictorian *fasces*, symbol of unity, of force and of justice.

14   Conservatism, Liberalism, and Socialism in Canada

Although liberalism, conservatism, socialism, and nationalism are recognizably similar around the world, these ideologies interact with each other under the influence of political culture to form distinctive configurations within national boundaries. Reading 14 addresses this phenomenon. In showing how the unique factors of Canadian history have influenced political thought in this country, Gad Horowitz demonstrates that ideologies are not just abstract intellectual systems but rather are the ideas of living people in a specific setting. His interpretation is built on the "fragment theory" of the American writer Louis Hartz, who argued that the "new societies" of the modern age—Canada, the United States, Australia, South Africa—are ideological fragments of the more complex European matrix from which they arose. The founders of these colonial fragments carried with them a certain ideology that was important in its European mother country at the time of the founding—royal absolutism in the case of New France, Lockean liberalism in the case of the United States—but not dominant in Europe as a whole. Thus the key to understanding the political thought of a colonial new society is to understand the ideology that prevailed at the time of the founding. This is particularly challenging in the Canadian case, since there were several "foundings" widely separated in space and time. Horowitz attempts to unpack these complexities to produce a portrait of the abiding characteristics of Canadian political thought. His major conclusion is that in comparison to the United States, where liberalism has clearly dominated political thought for two centuries, Canada is more like Europe in its ideological variety.

Reading 14 is an abridged version of Gad Horowitz's article, "Conservatism, Liberalism and Socialism in Canada: An Interpretation," which appeared in volume 32 of the *Canadian Journal of Economics and Political Science*. The author is a professor of political science at the University of Toronto. Since it was published a quarter century ago, Horowitz's interpretation has been much debated and criticized, but it remains the starting point for the study of ideology in Canada.

● ● ● ● ● ● ● ● ● ●

INTRODUCTION: THE HARTZIAN APPROACH

In the United States, organized socialism is dead; in Canada socialism, though far from national power, is a significant political force. Why this striking difference in the fortunes of socialism in two very similar societies?

Any attempt to account for the difference must be grounded in a general comparative study of the English-Canadian and American societies. It will be shown that the relative strength of socialism in Canada is related to the relative strength of toryism, and to the different position and character of liberalism in the two countries.

In North America, Canada is unique. Yet there is a tendency in Canadian historical and political studies to explain Canadian phenomena not by contrasting them with American phenomena but by identifying them as variations on a basic North American theme. I grant that Canada and the United States are similar, and that the similarities should be pointed out. But the pan-North American approach, since it searches out and concentrates on similarities, cannot help us to understand Canadian uniqueness. When this approach is applied to the study of English-Canadian socialism, it discovers, first, that like the American variety it is weak, and second, that it is weak for much the same reasons. These discoveries perhaps explain why Canadian socialism is weak in comparison to European socialism; they do not explain why Canadian socialism is so much stronger than American socialism.

The explanatory technique used in this study is that developed by Louis Hartz in *The Liberal Tradition in America* and *The Founding of New Societies*. It is applied to Canada in a mildly pan-North American way by Kenneth McRae in "The Structure of Canadian History," a contribution to the latter book.

The Hartzian approach is to study the new societies founded by Europeans (the United States, English Canada, French Canada, Latin America, Dutch South Africa, Australia) as "fragments" thrown off from Europe. The key to the understanding of ideological development in a new society is its "point of departure" from Europe: the ideologies borne by the founders of the new society are not representative of the historic ideological spectrum of the mother country. The settlers represent only a fragment of that spectrum. The complete ideological spectrum ranges—in chronological order, and from right to left—from feudal or tory through liberal whig to liberal democrat to socialist. French Canada and Latin America are "feudal fragments." They were founded by bearers of the feudal or tory values of the organic, corporate, hierarchical community; their point of departure from Europe is before the liberal revolution. The United States, English Canada, and Dutch South Africa are "bourgeois fragments," founded by bearers of liberal individualism who have left the tory end of the spectrum behind them. Australia is the one "radical fragment," founded by bearers of the working class ideologies of mid-nineteenth-century Britain.

The significance of the fragmentation process is that the new society, having been thrown off from Europe, "loses the stimulus to change that the whole provides." The full ideological spectrum of Europe develops only out of the continued confrontation and interaction of its four elements; they are related to one another, not only as enemies, but as parents and children. A new society which leaves part of the past behind it cannot develop the future ideologies which need the continued presence of the past in order to come into being. In escaping the past, the fragment escapes the future, for "the very seeds of the later ideas are contained in the parts of the old world that have been left behind." The ideology of the founders is thus frozen, congealed at the point of origin.

Socialism is an ideology which combines the corporate-organic-collectivist ideas of toryism with the rationalist-egalitarian ideas of liberalism. Both the feudal and the bourgeois fragments escape socialism, but in different ways. A feudal fragment such as French Canada develops no whig (undemocratic) liberalism; therefore it does not develop the democratic liberalism which arises out of and as a reaction against whiggery; therefore it does not develop the socialism which arises out of and as a reaction against liberal democracy. The corporate-organic-collectivist component of socialism is present in the feudal fragment—it is part of the feudal ethos—but the radical rationalist-egalitarian component of socialism is missing. It can be provided only by whiggery and liberal democracy, and these have not come into being.

In the bourgeois fragment, the situation is the reverse: the radical rationalist-egalitarian component of socialism is present, but the corporate-organic-collectivist component is missing, because toryism has been left behind. In the bourgeois fragments "Marx dies because there is no sense of class, no yearning for the corporate past." The absence of socialism is related to the absence of toryism.

It is *because* socialists have a conception of society as more than an agglomeration of competing individuals—a conception close to the tory view of society as an organic community—that they find the liberal idea of equality (equality of opportunity) inadequate. Socialists disagree with liberals about the essential meaning of equality because socialists have a tory conception of society.

In a liberal bourgeois society which has never known toryism the demand for equality will express itself as left-wing or democratic liberalism as opposed to whiggery. The left will point out that all are not equal in the

competitive pursuit of individual happiness. The government will be required to assure greater equality of opportunity—in the nineteenth century,
by destroying monopolistic privileges; in the twentieth century by providing a welfare "floor" so that no one will fall out of the race for success, and
by regulating the economy so that the race can continue without periodic
crises.

In a society which thinks of itself as a community of classes rather than
an aggregation of individuals, the demand for equality will take a socialist
form: for equality of condition rather than mere equality of opportunity; for
co-operation rather than competition; for a community that does more than
provide a context within which individuals can pursue happiness in a
purely self-regarding way. At its most "extreme," socialism is a demand for
the *abolition* of classes so that the good of the community can truly be
realized. This is a demand which cannot be made by people who can hardly
see class and community: the individual fills their eyes.

THE APPLICATION TO CANADA

It is a simple matter to apply the Hartzian approach to English Canada in a
pan-North American way. English Canada can be viewed as a fragment of
the American liberal society, lacking a feudal or tory heritage and therefore
lacking the socialist ideology which grows out of it. Canadian domestic
struggles, from this point of view, are a northern version of the American
struggle between big-propertied liberals on the right and *petit bourgeois* and
working-class liberals on the left; the struggle goes on within a broad liberal
consensus, and the voice of the tory or the socialist is not heard in the land.
This pan-North American approach, with important qualifications, is
adopted by Hartz and McRae in *The Founding of New Societies*. English
Canada, like the United States, is a bourgeois fragment. No toryism in the
past; therefore no socialism in the present.

But Hartz notes that the liberal society of English Canada has a "tory
touch," that it is "etched with a tory streak coming out of the American
revolution." . . .

The most important un-American characteristics of English Canada,
all related to the presence of toryism, are: (*a*) the presence of tory ideology
in the founding of English Canada by the Loyalists, and its continuing
influence on English-Canadian political culture; (*b*) the persistent power of
whiggery or right-wing liberalism in Canada (the Family Compacts) as
contrasted with the rapid and easy victory of liberal democracy (Jefferson,
Jackson) in the United States; (*c*) the ambivalent centrist character of left-
wing liberalism in Canada as contrasted with the unambiguously leftist
position of left-wing liberalism in the United States; (*d*) the presence of an
influential and legitimate socialist movement in English Canada as con-

trasted with the illegitimacy and early death of American socialism; (*e*) the failure of English-Canadian liberalism to develop into the one true myth, the nationalist cult, and the parallel failure to exclude toryism and socialism as "un-Canadian"; in other words, the legitimacy of ideological diversity in English Canada.

From a world perspective, these imperfections in English Canada's bourgeois character may appear insignificant. From the point of view of one who is interested in understanding English Canada not merely as a bourgeois fragment, but as a unique bourgeois fragment, the imperfections are significant.

THE PRESENCE OF TORYISM AND ITS CONSEQUENCES

Many students have noted that English-Canadian society has been powerfully shaped by tory values that are "alien" to the American mind. The latest of these is Seymour Martin Lipset, who stresses the relative strength in Canada of the tory values of "ascription" and "elitism" (the tendency to defer to authority), and the relative weakness of the liberal values of "achievement" and "egalitarianism." He points to such well-known features of Canadian history as the absence of a lawless, individualistic-egalitarian American frontier, the preference for Britain rather than the United States as a social model, and generally, the weaker emphasis on social equality, the greater acceptance by individuals of the facts of economic inequality, social stratification, and hierarchy. One tory touch in English Canada which is not noted by Lipset, but has been noted by many others (including McRae), is the far greater willingness of English-Canadian political and business elites to use the power of the state for the purpose of developing and controlling the economy. . . .

. . . Let us put it this way: pre-revolutionary America was a liberal fragment with insignificant traces of toryism, extremely weak feudal survivals. But they were insignificant in the *American* setting; they were far over-shadowed by the liberalism of that setting. The Revolution did not have to struggle against them, it swept them away easily and painlessly, leaving no trace of them in the American memory. But these traces of toryism were expelled into a *new* setting, and in this setting they were no longer insignificant. In this new setting, where there was no pre-established overpowering liberalism to force them into insignificance, they played a large part in shaping a new political culture, significantly different from the American. As Nelson wrote in *The American Tory*, "the Tories' organic conservatism represented a current of thought that failed to reappear in America after the revolution. A substantial part of the whole spectrum of European . . . philosophy seemed to slip outside the American perspective." But it *reappeared* in Canada. Here the sway of liberalism has proved to be not total, but considerably mitigated by a tory presence initially and a socialist presence subsequently. . . .

The next step in tracing the development of the English-Canadian political culture must be to take account of the tremendous waves of British immigration which soon engulfed the original American Loyalist fragment. . . . The political culture of a new nation is not necessarily fixed at the point of origin or departure; the founding of a new nation can go on for generations. If the later waves of immigration arrived before the *point of congealment* of the political culture, they must have participated actively in the process of culture formation. If this be so, the picture of English Canada as an almost exactly American liberal society becomes very difficult to defend. For *even if* it be granted that the Loyalists were (almost exactly) American liberals, it is clear that later participants in the formation of the culture were not.

Between 1815 and 1850 almost one million Britons emigrated to Canada. The population of English Canada doubled in twenty years and quadrupled in forty. The population of Ontario increased tenfold in the same period—from about 95,000 in 1814 to about 950,000 in 1851. . . .

The difficulty in applying the Hartzian approach to English Canada is that although the point of departure is reasonably clear, it is difficult to put one's finger on the point of congealment. Perhaps it was the Loyalist period; perhaps it was close to the mid-century mark; there are grounds for arguing that it was in the more recent past. But the important point is this: no matter where the point of congealment is located in time, the tory streak is present before the solidification of the political culture, and it is strong *enough* to produce *significant* "imperfections," or non-liberal, un-American attributes to English-Canadian society.

My own opinion is that the point of congealment came later than the Loyalists. The United States broke from Britain early, and the break was complete. Adam Smith and Tom Paine were among the last Britons who were spiritual founding fathers of the United States. Anything British, if it is of later than eighteenth century vintage, is un-American. The American mind long ago cut its ties with Britain and began to develop on its own. When did Canada break from Britain? When did the Canadian mind begin to develop on its own? Not very long ago most Canadians described themselves as followers of the "British way of life," and many railed against egalitarian ideas from south of the border as "alien." Nineteenth-century British ideologists are among the spiritual founding fathers of Canada. In the United States they are alien, though we may make an exception for Herbert Spencer.

The indeterminate location of the point of congealment makes it difficult to account in any *precise* way for the presence of socialism in the

English-Canadian political culture mix, though the presence itself is indisputable. If the point of congealment came *before* the arrival of the first radical or socialist-minded immigrants, the presence of socialism must be ascribed primarily to the earlier presence of toryism. Since toryism is a significant part of the political culture, at least part of the leftist reaction against it will sooner or later be expressed in its own terms, that is, in terms of *class* interests and the good of the community as a corporate entity (socialism) rather than in terms of the individual and his vicissitudes in the competitive pursuit of happiness (liberalism). If the point of congealment is very early, socialism appears at a later point not primarily because it is imported by British immigrants, but because it is contained as a potential in the original political culture. The immigrants then find that they do not have to give it up—that it is not un-Canadian—because it "fits" to a certain extent with the tory ideas already present. If the point of congealment is very late, the presence of socialism must be explained as a result of *both* the presence of toryism and the introduction of socialism into the cultural mix before congealment. The immigrant retains his socialism not only because it "fits" but also because nothing really *has* to fit. He finds that his socialism is not un-Canadian partly because "Canadian" has not yet been defined.

Canadian liberals cannot be expected to wax enthusiastic about the non-liberal traits of their country. They are likely to condemn the tory touch as anachronistic, stifling, undemocratic, out of tune with the essentially American ("free," "classless") spirit of English Canada. They dismiss the socialist touch as an "old-fashioned" protest, no longer necessary (if it ever was) in this best (liberal) of all possible worlds in which the "end of ideology" has been achieved. The secret dream of the Canadian Liberal is the removal of English Canada's "imperfections"—in other words, the total assimilation of English Canada into the larger North American culture. But there is a flaw in this dream which might give pause even to the liberal. Hartz places special emphasis on one very unappetizing characteristic of the new societies—intolerance—which is strikingly absent in English Canada. Because the new societies other than Canada are unfamiliar with legitimate ideological diversity, they are unable to accept it and deal with it in a rational manner, either internally or on the level of international relations.

The European nation has an "identity which transcends any ideologist and a mechanism in which each plays only a part." Neither the tory, nor the liberal, nor the socialist, has a monopoly of the expression of the "spirit" of the nation. But the new societies, the fragments, contain only one of the ideologies of Europe; they are one-myth cultures. In the new setting, freed from its historic enemies past and future, ideology transforms itself into nationalism. It claims to be a moral absolute, "the great spirit of a nation."

In the United States, liberalism becomes "Americanism"; a political philosophy becomes a civil religion, a nationalist cult. The American attachment to Locke is "absolutist and irrational." Democratic capitalism is the American way of life; to oppose it is to be un-American.

To be an American is to be a bourgeois liberal. To be a French Canadian is to be a pre-Enlightenment Catholic; to be an Australian is to be a prisoner of the radical myth of "mateship"; to be a Boer is to be a pre-Enlightened bourgeois Calvinist. The fragments escape the need for philosophy, for thought about values, for "where perspectives shrink to a single value, and that value becomes the universe, how can value itself be considered?" The fragment demands solidarity. Ideologies which diverge from the national myth make no impact; they are not understood, and their proponents are not granted legitimacy. They are denounced as aliens, and treated as aliens, because they *are* aliens. The fragments cannot understand or deal with the fact that *all* men are *not* bourgeois Americans, or radical Australians, or Catholic French Canadians, or Calvinist South Africans. They cannot make peace with the loss of ideological certainty.

The specific weakness of the United States is its "inability to understand the appeal of socialism" to the third world. Because the United States has "buried" the memory of the organic medieval community "beneath new liberal absolutism and nationalisms" it cannot understand that the appeal of socialism to nations with a predominantly non-liberal past (including French Canada) consists precisely in the promise of "continuing the corporate ethos in the very process" of modernization. The American reacts with isolationism, messianism, and hysteria.

English Canada, because it is the most "imperfect" of the fragments, is not a one-myth culture. In English Canada ideological diversity has not been buried beneath an absolutist liberal nationalism. Here Locke is not the one true god; he must tolerate lesser tory and socialist deities at his side. The result is that English Canada does not direct an uncomprehending intolerance at heterodoxy, either within its borders or beyond them. (What a "backlash" Parti-Pris or PSQ-type separatists would be getting if Quebec were in the United States!) In English Canada it has been possible to consider values without arousing the all-silencing cry of treason. Hartz observes that "if history had chosen English Canada for the American role" of directing the Western response to the world revolution, "the international scene would probably have witnessed less McCarthyite hysteria, less Wilsonian messianism."

Americanizing liberals might consider that the Pearsonian rationality and calmness which Canada displays on the world stage—the "mediating" and "peace-keeping" role of which Canadians are so proud—is related to the un-American (tory and socialist) characteristics which they consider to be unnecessary imperfections in English-Canadian wholeness. The tolerance of English-Canadian domestic politics is also linked with the presence of these imperfections. If the price of Americanization is the surrender of legitimate ideological diversity, even the liberal might think twice before paying it.

. . . My argument is essentially that non-liberal British elements have entered into English-Canadian society *together* with American liberal elements at the foundations. The fact is that Canada has been greatly influenced by both the United States and Britain. This is not to deny that liberalism is the dominant element in the English-Canadian political culture; it is to stress that it is not the sole element, that it is accompanied by vital and legitimate streams of toryism and socialism which have as close a relation to English Canada's "essence" or "foundations" as does liberalism. English Canada's "essence" is both liberal and non-liberal. Neither the British nor the American elements can be explained away as "superstructural" excrescences.

UN-AMERICAN ASPECTS OF CANADIAN CONSERVATISM

So far, I have been discussing the presence of toryism in Canada without referring to the Conservative party. This party can be seen as a party of right-wing or business liberalism, but such an interpretation would be far from the whole truth; the Canadian Conservative party, like the British Conservative party and unlike the Republican party, is not monolithically liberal. If there is a touch of toryism in English Canada, its primary carrier has been the Conservative party. It would not be correct to say that toryism is *the* ideology of the party, or even that some Conservatives are tories. These statements would not be true even of the British Conservative party. The primary component of the ideology of business-oriented parties is liberalism; but there are powerful traces of the old pre-liberal outlook in the British Conservative party, and less powerful but still perceptible traces of it in the Canadian party. A Republican is always a liberal. A Conservative may be at one moment a liberal, at the next moment a tory, and is usually something of both.

If it is true that the Canadian Conservatives can be seen from some angles as right-wing liberals, it is also true that figures such as R.B. Bennett, Arthur Meighen, and George Drew cannot be understood simply as Canadian versions of William McKinley, Herbert Hoover, and Robert Taft. Canadian Conservatives have something British about them that American Republicans do not. It is not simply their emphasis on loyalty to the crown and to the British connection, but a touch of the authentic tory aura— traditionalism, elitism, the strong state, and so on. The Canadian Conservatives lack the American aura of rugged individualism. Theirs is not the characteristically American conservatism which conserves only *liberal* values.

It is possible to perceive in Canadian conservatism not only the elements of business liberalism and orthodox toryism, but also an element of "tory democracy"—the paternalistic concern for the "condition of the people," and the emphasis on the tory party as their champion—which, in Britain, was expressed by such figures as Disraeli and Lord Randolph Churchill. John A. Macdonald's approach to the emergent Canadian working class was in some respects similar to that of Disraeli. Later Conservatives acquired the image of arch reactionaries and arch enemies of the workers, but let us not forget that "Iron Heel" Bennett was also the Bennett of the Canadian New Deal.

The question arises: why is it that in Canada the *Conservative* leader proposes a New Deal? Why is it that the Canadian counterpart of Hoover apes *Roosevelt*? This phenomenon is usually interpreted as sheer historical accident, a product of Bennett's desperation and opportunism. But the answer may be that Bennett was not Hoover. Even in his "orthodox" days Bennett's views on the state's role in the economy were far from similar to Hoover's; Bennett's attitude was that of Canadian, not American, conservatism. Once this is recognized, it is possible to entertain the suggestion that Bennett's sudden radicalism, his sudden concern for the people, may not have been mere opportunism. It may have been a manifestation, a sudden activation under pressure, of a latent tory-democratic streak. Let it be noted also that the depression produced two Conservative splinter parties, both with "radical" welfare state programmes, and both led by former subordinates of Bennett: H.H. Stevens' Reconstruction party and W.D. Herridge's New Democracy.

The Bennett New Deal is only the most extreme instance of what is usually considered to be an accident or an aberration—the occasional manifestation of "radicalism" or "leftism" by otherwise orthodox Conservative leaders in the face of opposition from their "followers" in the business community. Meighen, for example, was constantly embroiled with the "Montreal interests" who objected to his railway policies. On one occasion he received a note of congratulation from William Irvine: "The man who dares to offend the Montreal interests is the sort of man that the people are going to vote for." This same Meighen expressed on certain occasions, particularly after his retirement, an antagonism to big government and creeping socialism that would have warmed the heart of Robert Taft; but he combined his business liberalism with gloomy musings about the evil of universal suffrage—musings which Taft would have rejected as un-American. Meighen is far easier to understand from a British than from an

American perspective, for he combined, in different proportions at different times, attitudes deriving from all three Conservative ideological streams: right-wing liberalism, orthodox toryism, and tory democracy.

The Western or agrarian Conservatives of the contemporary period, John Diefenbaker and Alvin Hamilton, who are usually dismissed as "prairie radicals" of the American type, might represent not only anti-Bay Street agrarianism but *also* the same type of tory democracy which was expressed before their time by orthodox business-sponsored Conservatives like Meighen and Bennett. The populism (anti-elitism) of Diefenbaker and Hamilton is a genuinely foreign element in Canadian conservatism, but their stress on the Tory party as champion of the people and their advocacy of welfare state policies are in the tory democratic tradition. Their attitudes to the monarchy, the British connection, and the danger of American domination are entirely orthodox Conservative attitudes. Diefenbaker Conservatism is therefore to be understood not simply as a Western populist phenomenon, but as an odd *combination* of traditional Conservative views with attitudes absorbed from the Western Progressive tradition.

Another aberration which may be worthy of investigation is the Canadian phenomenon of the red tory. At the simplest level, he is a Conservative who prefers the CCF-NDP to the Liberals, or a socialist who prefers the Conservatives to the Liberals, without really knowing why. At a higher level, he is a conscious ideological Conservative with some "odd" socialist notions (W.L. Morton) or a conscious ideological socialist with some "odd" tory notions (Eugene Forsey). The very suggestion that such affinities might exist between Republican and Socialists in the United States is ludicrous enough to make some kind of a point.

Red toryism is, of course, one of the results of the relationship between toryism and socialism which has already been elucidated. The tory and socialist minds have some crucial assumptions, orientations, and values in common, so that from certain angles they may appear not as enemies, but as two different expressions of the same basic ideological outlook. Thus, at the very highest level, the red tory is a philosopher who combines elements of socialism and toryism so thoroughly in a single integrated *Weltanschauung* that it is impossible to say that he is a proponent of either one as *against* the other. Such a red tory is George Grant, who has associations with both the Conservative party and the NDP, and who has recently published a book which defends Diefenbaker, laments the death of "true" British conservatism in Canada, attacks the Liberals as individualists and Americanizers, and defines socialism as a variant of conservatism (each "protects the public good against private freedom").

THE CHARACTER OF CANADIAN SOCIALISM

Canadian socialism is un-American in two distinct ways. It is un-American in the sense that it is a significant and legitimate political force in Canada, insignificant and alien in the United States. But Canadian socialism is also un-American in the sense that it does not speak the same language as American socialism. In Canada, socialism is British, non-Marxist,and worldly; in the United States it is German, Marxist, and other-worldly.

I have argued that the socialist ideas of British immigrants to Canada were not sloughed off because they "fit" with a political culture which already contained non-liberal components, and probably also because they were introduced into the political culture mix before the point of congealment. Thus socialism was not alien here. But it was not alien in yet another way; it was not borne by foreigners. The personnel and the ideology of the Canadian labour and socialist movements have been primarily British. Many of those who built these movements were British immigrants with past experience in the British labour movement; many others were Canadian-born children of such immigrants. And in British North America, Britons could not be treated as foreigners.

When socialism was brought to the United States, it found itself in an ideological environment in which it could not survive because Lockean individualism had long since achieved the status of a national religion; the political culture had already congealed, and socialism did not fit. American socialism was alien not only in this ideological sense, but in the ethnic sense as well; it was borne by foreigners from Germany and other continental European countries. These foreigners sloughed off their socialist ideas not simply because such ideas did not "fit" ideologically, but because as foreigners they were going through a general process of Americanization; socialism was only one of the many ethnically alien characteristics which had to be abandoned. The immigrant's ideological change was only one incident among many others in the general process of changing his entire way of life. According to David Saposs, "the factor that contributed most tellingly to the decline of the socialist movement was that its chief following, the immigrant workers, . . . had become Americanized.

A British socialist immigrant to Canada had a far different experience. The British immigrant was not an "alien" in British North America. The English-Canadian culture not only granted legitimacy to his political ideas and absorbed them into its wholeness; it absorbed him as a person into the English-Canadian community, with relatively little strain, without demanding that he change his entire way of life before being granted full citizenship. He was acceptable to begin with, by virtue of being British. It is impossible to understand the differences between American and Canadian socialism without taking into account this immense difference between the ethnic contexts of socialism in the two countries.

The ethnic handicap of American socialism consisted not only in the fact that its personnel was heavily European. Equally important was the fact that it was a *brand* of socialism—Marxism—which found survival difficult not only in the United States but in all English-speaking countries. Marx has not found the going easy in the United States; but neither has he found the going easy in Britain, Canada, Australia, or New Zealand. The socialism of the United States, the socialism of De Leon, Berger, Hillquit, and Debs, is predominantly Marxist and doctrinaire, because it is European. The socialism of English Canada, the socialism of Simpson, Woodsworth, and Coldwell, is predominantly Protestant, labourist, and Fabian, because it is British. . . .

The CCF has not been without its otherworldly tendencies; there have been doctrinal disagreements, and the party has always had a left wing interested more in "socialist education" than in practical political work. But this left wing has been a constantly declining minority. The party has expelled individuals and small groups—mostly Communists and Trotskyites—but it has never split. Its life has never been threatened by disagreement over doctrinal matters. It is no more preoccupied with theory than the British Labour party. It sees itself, and is seen by the public, not as a coterie of ideologists but as a party like the others, second to none in its avidity for office. If it has been attacked from the right for socialist "utopianism" and "impracticality," it has also been attacked from the right for abandoning the "true" socialist faith in an unprincipled drive for power. . . .

CANADIAN LIBERALISM: THE TRIUMPHANT CENTRE

Canadian Conservatives are not American Republicans; Canadian socialists are not American socialists; Canadian liberals are not American liberal Democrats.

The un-American elements in English Canada's political culture are most evident in Canadian conservatism and socialism. But Canadian liberalism has a British colour too. The liberalism of Canada's Liberal party should not be identified with the liberalism of the American Democratic party. In many respects they stand in sharp contrast to one another.

The three components of the English-Canadian political culture have not developed in isolation from one another; each has developed in interaction with the others. Our toryism and our socialism have been moderated by liberalism. But by the same token, our liberalism has been rendered "impure," in American terms, through its contacts with toryism and socialism. If English-Canadian liberalism is less individualistic, less ardently populistic-democratic, more inclined to state intervention in the economy, and more tolerant of "feudal survivals" such as monarchy, this is due to the uninterrupted influence of toryism upon liberalism, an influence wielded in and through the conflict between the two. If English-Canadian liberalism has tended since the depression to merge at its leftist edge with the democratic socialism of the CCF-NDP, this is due to the influence which socialism has exerted upon liberalism, in and through the conflict between them. The key to understanding the Liberal party in Canada is to see it as a *centre* party, with *influential* enemies on both right and left. . . .

King had to face the socialist challenge. He did so in the manner of European Liberal Reform. No need to worry about abandoning individualism; Locke was not Canada's national god; like European liberalism, Canadian liberalism had been revised. The similarity of socialism and Liberal Reform could be acknowledged; indeed it could be emphasized and used to attract the socialist vote. At the same time, King had to answer the arguments of socialism, and in doing so he had to spell out his liberalism. He had to stop short of socialism openly. Social reform, yes; extension of public ownership, yes; the welfare state, yes; increased state control of the economy, yes; but not too much. Not socialism. The result was that King, like the European liberals, could not go as far as Roosevelt. . . .

"In America, instead of being a champion of property, Roosevelt became the big antagonist of it; his liberalism was blocked by his radicalism." In Canada, since King had to worry not only about Bennett and Meighen and Drew, but also about Woodsworth and Coldwell and Douglas, King had to embark upon a defence of private property. *He* was no traitor to his class. Instead of becoming the antagonist of property, he became its champion; his radicalism was blocked by his liberalism.

An emphasis on the solidarity of the nation as against divisive "class parties" of right and left was "of the very essence of the Reformist Liberal position in Europe." "Who," asks Hartz, "would think of Roosevelt as a philosopher of class solidarity?" Yet that is precisely what Roosevelt would have been if he had had to respond to a socialist presence in the American political culture. And that is precisely what King was in fact in Canada. His party was "the party of national unity." One of the most repeated charges against the CCF was that it was a divisive "class party"; the purpose of the Liberal party, on the other hand, was to preserve the solidarity of the Canadian people—the solidarity of its classes as well as the solidarity of French and English.

Hartz sums up Roosevelt in these words: "What emerges then . . . is a liberal self that is lost from sight: a faith in property, a belief in class unity, a suspicion of too much state power, a hostility to the utopian mood, all of which were blacked out by the weakness of the socialist challenge." King's liberal self was not lost from sight, for the socialist challenge was stronger in Canada than in the United States.

The Liberal party has continued to speak the language of King: ambiguous and ambivalent, presenting first its radical face and then its conservative face, urging reform and warning against hasty, ill-considered change, calling for increased state responsibility but stopping short of socialism openly, speaking for the common people but preaching the solidarity of classes.

In the United States, the liberal Democrats are on the left. There is no doubt about that. In Canada, the Liberals are a party of the centre, appearing at times leftist and at times rightist. As such, they are much closer to European, especially British, Liberal Reform than to the American New Deal type of liberalism.

In the United States, the liberal Democrats are the party of organized labour. The new men of power, the labour leaders, have arrived politically; their vehicle is the Democratic party. In English Canada, if the labour leaders have arrived politically, they have done so in the CCF-NDP. They are nowhere to be found in the Liberal party. The rank and file, in the United States, are predominantly Democrats; in Canada at least a quarter are New Democrats, and the remainder show only a relatively slight, and by no means consistent, preference for the Liberals as against the Conservatives.

In the United States, left-wing "liberalism," as opposed to right-wing "liberalism," has always meant opposition to the domination of American life by big business, and has expressed itself in and through the Democratic party; the party of business is the Republican party. In Canada, business is close to both the Conservatives and the Liberals. The business community donates to the campaign funds of both and is represented in the leadership circles of both. . . .

The Liberal party in Canada does not represent the opposition of society to domination by organized business. It claims to be based on no particular groups, but on *all*. It is not against any particular group; it is for *all*. The idea that there is any real conflict between groups is dismissed, and the very terms "right" and "left" are rejected: "The terms 'right' and 'left' belong to those who regard politics as a class struggle. . . . The Liberal view is that true political progress is marked by . . . the reconciliation of classes, and the promotion of the general interest above all particular interests."

15　　　Left and Right in Canada and the United States

The Hartz/Horowitz approach to the study of ideology exemplified in Reading 14 is not only of historical significance. It also gives rise to predictions about the present that can be tested by using the methods of contemporary social science. In this spirit, Reading 15 by Roger Gibbins and Neil Nevitte compares ideological orientations among university students in English Canada, French Canada, and the United States. The authors' data and analysis show that the conventional left-right spectrum has more meaning and predictive power in the United States than in Canada, and more in English Canada than in French Canada. That is, there is more ideological polarization in the United States, at least among intellectual elites at the time of the study, than in Canada. This is contrary to what one might have expected on the basis of Horowitz. The tentative explanation proffered by Gibbins and Nevitte is that the importance of regional and territorial disputes in Canadian politics may have overlaid and blurred the normal lines of ideological demarcation.

　　Reading 15 is an abridged version of Roger Gibbins and Neil Nevitte's "Canadian Political Ideology: A Comparative Analysis, which appeared in volume 18 of the *Canadian Journal of Political Science*. The article makes use of statistical concepts, such as correlation and significance, that beginning students may not fully understand unless they are taking a concurrent course in statistics; but the analysis is clear enough if followed up by effort and intuition. The authors are professors of political science at the University of Calgary. The data reported here arise from a larger study of elite ideology in six countries, including the United Kingdom, France, Australia, and New Zealand. See Gibbins and Nevitte, *New Elites in Old States* (Toronto: Oxford University Press, 1990).

● ● ● ● ● ● ● ● ● ●

The comparison of political cultures of Canada and the United States has become an important cross-disciplinary scholarly tradition. In that large, and often contentious, literature, debate not only revolves around competing historical interpretations of the American revolutionary and the Canadian counter-revolutionary traditions — with primary attention being given to United Empire loyalism and Toryism, individualism and collectivism, elitism and egalitarianism — but it also extends to comparative evaluations of *contemporary* political values in the two countries. Given the broad and inexact conceptual scope of "political culture," and the sheer sweep of two centuries of historical references, it is not surprising that a consensus on Canada's uniqueness or the scope of Canadian-American similarities has been slow to develop.

A significant segment of the discourse on comparative political cultures is conceptualized in the language of political ideology. Differences in the traditions of Canada and the United States are not seen as mere historical curiosities, but are viewed as enduring features mirrored in the ideological landscape. The ideological aspect of the larger debate centres on questions of the degree of ideological spread in the two countries, and upon contrasting interpretations of the respective "lefts" and "rights." Gad Horowitz, for example, points to the existence of both "legitimate socialism" and a Tory right as decisively un-American characteristics and as evidence of Canada's greater ideological spread. S.M. Lipset, in contrast, disputes national differences in the ideological spread. He argues instead that the politically relevant aspects of English-Canadian social structure are similar to the American, that voting and other indicators point to fundamental similarities in the sociostructural conditions of both North American democracies, and that the United States has a comparable history of social democracy. He suggests differences in the constitutional and electoral rules of the game as causal factors which transform similar ideological landscapes into different political forms, thereby precluding viable third parties in the United States and channeling social democratic forces into the mainstream Democratic party.

Disagreements over the comparative degree of ideological spread spring from disputes about the character of both the ideological rights and ideological lefts in the two countries. With respect to the ideological right, Rod Preece suggests that the significance attached to Toryism in Canada has been overworked, while in contrast Horowitz characterizes the Canadian right as paternalistic, elitist, collectivist and lacking "the American aura of rugged individualism." George Grant, in a similar vein, sees self-styled American conservatives as old fashioned liberals, and views both the American left and right as "just different species of liberalism." As for the left, Horowitz characterizes Canadian socialism as "British, non-Marxist, and worldly," but American socialism as "German, Marxist, and otherworldly." And where Canadian left-wing liberalism is portrayed as "ambivalently centralist," its counterpart in the United States is "unambiguously left wing."

The literature on comparative Canadian-American political ideology thus reflects the basic areas of disagreement found in the broader analysis of comparative political culture. But it is also a literature which can be used as a source of working hypotheses. This article explores contemporary political ideologies in Canada and the United States using cross-national attitudinal survey data. . . .

DATA AND METHODOLOGY

The data employed are drawn from two surveys of senior undergraduates in Canada and the United States. The U.S. survey, administered in 1979, sampled senior undergraduates at ten regionally dispersed universities. The 364 completed and returned mailed questionnaires represent a 63 per cent response rate. The Canadian survey, conducted in early 1983, randomly sampled senior undergraduates at nine regional dispersed universities: Memorial, Dalhousie, Laval, University of Montreal, Queen's, Toronto, Wilfrid Laurier, Calgary and British Columbia. Taken together, the 558 completed and returned questionnaires from the 7 non-Quebec universities, and the 221 questionnaires from the 2 francophone universities, represented a 53 per cent response rate from the Canadian sample, a rate which is close to that expected through in-person survey techniques. In total, then, we have 1,143 respondents who replied to 118 questionnaire items common to both American and Canadian respondents. . . .

In the present analysis, survey data permit us to offer direct self-reported attitudinal evidence of ideological dispositions. Second, the sampling strategy specifically included a francophone Quebec component to enable us to extend the conventional two-way English Canadian-American comparison to a three-way comparison. Finally, survey analysis allows us to address important but relatively unexplored questions about the *comparative* structures of ideological beliefs in Canada and the United States, questions that cannot be addressed through more nonquantitative analytical techniques.

A substantial body of research stemming from Philip Converse's landmark study of belief systems in mass publics demonstrates that the political beliefs of most people are characterized by very little ideological or attitudinal constraint. Evidence drawn from cross-national research consistently points to the fact that the highest levels of ideological conceptualization and the clearest patterns of ideological coherence are found within relatively small segments of the general public, primarily those characterized by high levels of formal education. It is because the educated elite forms such a small portion of the general public that it has been difficult, generally, to study ideological patterns using survey data drawn from randomly sampled general populations. We cannot claim that the elite samples used here are representative of the Canadian and American populations. We argue instead that our samples are useful precisely because our research focus is upon ideological structures and coherence. It is by restricting our attention to those respondents who are most likely to bring order and structure to their outlooks on the political world that ideological patterns can be most clearly identified. . . .

ANALYSIS AND DISCUSSION

In essence, our study constitutes a straightforward quasi-experimental design. Taken together, our test group is sampled from that portion of a population which is most likely to demonstrate clear patterns of ideological coherence. The respondents are similar in that all are senior students attending North American universities. They have been randomly drawn, however, from three different contexts; 364 are found in American universities, 558 in English-Canadian universities, and 221 in French-language universities in Quebec. . . .

The three sets of respondents were asked to locate themselves on an identical, self-anchoring left-right scale, presented in Table 1. For the great majority of respondents, the question did not present any conceptual difficulty; the nonresponse rate was only 7.1 per cent for American respondents, climbing to 10.4 per cent and 12.0 per cent for French Quebeckers and English-Canadian respondents, respectively. As Table 1 indicates, however, there was a significant difference between anglophone Canadian respondents on the one hand, and French Quebeckers and American respondents on the other, in their mean location on the scale. English Canadians fell significantly farther to the ideological right ($p < .001$). The difference between the Quebec and U.S. respondents was statistically insignificant even though the Quebec sample was marked by the virtual absence of an ideological right.

The finding that the French Quebeckers locate themselves to the left of their English-Canadian counterparts is not surprising, given the ideological orientation of social democracy commonly associated with the onset of the Quiet Revolution. The lack of any significant difference between French Quebec and U.S. respondents, and the location of English-Canadian respondents to the right of their American counterparts, are more surprising. They certainly run counter to Lipset's observation that Canadian "have come to see their country as being to the left of the United States. That is, they think of Canada as less elitist, less capitalist, less reactionary, less stratified."

Here one could argue, of course, that the differences in Table 1 reflect the fact that the samples were collected at different times; that if the American respondents had not been frozen in 1979 they too would have been carried to the right by the wave of neo-conservatism that has swept across North America since the 1980 election of Ronald Reagan. The more recently interviewed Canadians, therefore, have simply been carried to the

TABLE 1
The Left-Right Scale

"In general, how would you describe your views on political matters?"

	English Canadians[a]		French Quebeckers[b]		Americans[c]	
	%	N	%	N	%	N
1. Far left	2.2	11	8.6	17	6.5	22
2. Very liberal	10.2	50	21.7	43	21.6	73
3. Somewhat liberal	29.1	143	28.3	56	37.6	127
4. Moderate	20.8	102	33.3	66	15.4	52
5. Somewhat conservative	26.7	131	5.6	11	15.7	53
6. Very conservative	9.2	45	1.0	2	3.0	10
7. Far right	1.8	9	1.5	3	0.3	1
Total	100.0%	491	100.0%	221	100.0%	338
Sample mean	3.94		3.15		3.22	

a Standard deviation = 1.30
b Standard deviation = 1.20
c Standard deviation = 1.24

right by those waves, passing in the process their inert counterparts in the American sample.

Yet it is this very line of argument that bedevils comparative research on political ideology. Taken to extreme, it implies that firm conclusions on national differences can only be drawn from identical questions administered to equivalent national samples drawn at the same time, conditions that are rarely met. On the other hand, and of considerable importance to our argument here, it may also demonstrate the frailty of national comparisons based upon comparison of samples along single dimensions. There are simply too many uncontrolled and idiosyncratic factors which can affect the location of national samples on any particular dimension. We need, then, a more powerful means of comparison than one which states that the citizens of country X are *more or less* liberal, conservative or authoritarian than are the citizens of country Y.

The following questions may provide a more fruitful basis for cross-national comparisons. Do these who locate themselves on the political right (or left) in different countries share a common ideological perspective on the world? Does the left-right scale itself organize political beliefs in a similar manner across national political cultures? Is there a greater degree of ideological constraint, coherence or polarization within some political cultures than in others?

To address such questions we drew four sets of dependent variables from the pool of questions common to both the American and Canadian surveys. The first two sets . . . measured respondent orientations towards *income redistribution* and the *size of government*. Not only are these issues of longstanding if not perennial ideological concern in Western states, but both have played a prominent role in attempts to differentiate the ideological landscapes of Canada and the United States. Grant, for example, points out that in general Canadians have been more willing than Americans to use government control over economic life to protect the public good against private freedom. That Canadian conservatives are distinguished from their American counterparts by their more activist use of the state, Horowitz suggests, is a part of the Tory democratic tradition, while on the left the demand for an activist state is seen as a demand for equality of result rather than equality of opportunity. In a similar vein, Lipset sees the American left as "anti-statist," notwithstanding the fact that welfare planning policies have been increasingly accepted since the 1930s. He cites Robert Presthus' findings as support for the general proposition that "Canadian conservatives as well as liberals, are much more favourable to using the state than are Americans comparably located on the political spectrum." . . .

The second two sets . . . measured respondent orientations towards *minority rights* and the *status of women*. To date, neither has played a significant role in attempts to differentiate the ideological landscape of Canada and the United States. However, as both have come to play a central role in the ideological debate *within* Canada and the United States, we suggest that they provide a useful basis for contemporary ideological comparisions between the two countries. . . .

The finding in Table 1, to the effect that the English-Canadian respondents locate themselves farther to the right than do the U.S. or French Quebec respondents, may mean little if the English-Canadian right (or left) is different in its ideological posture than the U.S. or French Quebec rights (or lefts). In Table 2, then, we look first at those respondents in each of the three samples who located themselves to the left of centre on the self-anchoring scale. . . .

Across the 18 dependent variables, significant English Canada/French Quebec differences are found on only three variables, with the Quebec respondents being more likely to agree that government should work to reduce the income gap, that people should earn about the same income, and that gender quotas should be used in job hiring. On balance, the appropriate conclusion to be drawn from the first panel of Table 2, is that

TABLE 2
T-Test Comparisons of the Three Political Lefts: English Canada, French Quebec, and the United States*

	English Canada/ French Quebec	English Canada/ United States	United States/ French Quebec
Income redistribution			
income limit		U.S. more likely to endorse income limits	
income gap	FQ more likely to favour closing gap	U.S. more likely to favour closing gap	FQ more likely to favour closing gap
income similarity	FQ more likely to favour all earning same	U.S. more likely to favour all earning same	
income tax		U.S. more likely to favour taxing rich	
Size of government			
deregulation		U.S. less likely to endorse deregulation	
private enterprise		U.S. less likely to say private enterprise is fair	
size of government		U.S. less likely to favour smaller government	
Minorities			
job treatment			
home sales			
media		U.S. less likely to perceive too much attention	

	English Canada/ French Quebec	English Canada/ United States	United States/ French Quebec
racial quotas		U.S. more likely to support racial quotas	U.S. more likely to support racial quotas
poverty		U.S. more likely to blame social conditions	U.S. more likely to blame social conditions
Status of women layoffs			
feminist leaders			
ERA		U.S. more supportive of ERA/more laws	U.S. more supportive of ERA/more laws
job discrimination		U.S. more likely to blame discrimination	U.S. more likely to blame discrimination
gender quotas	FQ more likely to support gender quotas	U.S. more likely to support gender quotas	
families			

* Differences indicated here are significant at the .01 level. Blank cells are ones in which the differences are not statistically significant.

the ideological postures of the English-Canadian and French Quebec lefts are essentially the same; to the extent that a difference is to be found, the English-Canadian left falls marginally to the right of the French Quebec left.

The second panel in Table 2 reveals a dramatic difference between the English-Canadian and U.S. lefts; significant differences emerged for 13 of the 18 dependent variables. The ideological direction of these differences, moreover, is consistent; simply put, the U.S. left is farther to the left than is the English-Canadian left. For example, American respondents who locate themselves to the left of centre on the self-anchoring scale were more likely to endorse the regulation of business, to support reducing the income gap, and to support taxing those with higher incomes to help the poor than were left-of-centre English-Canadian respondents.

In the third panel of Table 2, which compares American and French Quebec respondents, significant differences are found in only five cases. In four of those five, the French Quebec respondents fell to the right of the American respondents. It appears, then, that the Quebec left occupies an intermediate ideological position between the U.S. and English-Canadian lefts. More importantly, we find in Table 2 that the ideological difference between the English and French lefts in Canada is dwarfed by that between the English-Canadian and American left-of-centre respondents.

The same three-way comparison could not be conducted for the respondents locating themselves to the right of centre on the self-anchoring scale because there were too few (16) Quebec respondents.

However, when English-Canadian and American right-of-centre respondents were compared, there were no significant differences across 17 of the 18 dependent variables. The only difference to emerge was that American respondents were more likely than English-Canadian respondents to agree that "white people have a right to refuse to sell their homes to blacks/racial minorities." Overall, the English-Canadian and American rights were ideologically indistinguishable, offering no support for the belief that the Canadian right is distinguished by a "Tory streak." Contrary to what Lipset has argued, English-Canadian conservatives are not more likely than U.S. conservatives to favour an activist state. If anything, Table 2 suggests that left-of-centre English Canadians, and to a more modest degree left-of-centre French Quebeckers, are *less willing* to use the state than are their U.S. counterparts.

The findings discussed above suggest a greater degree of ideological polarization or spread among English-Canadian than among French Quebec respondents, and greater polarization among U.S. than among English-Canadian respondents. The first conclusion stems from Table 1, where we noted the virtual absence of Quebec respondents locating themselves to the right of centre on the left-right scale. While English-Canadian respondents ranged from the far right to the far left, French Quebec respondents ranged primarily from the moderate centre to the far left.

The second conclusion is not supported by Table 1, where we note that the English-Canadian standard deviation was greater than the U.S. standard deviation. Rather, it stems from the ideological *content* of the left and right in the two countries. While Table 2 illustrates that right-of-centre English-Canadian and American respondents were indistinguishable from one another in terms of policy preferences, this was not the case with respondents locating themselves to the left of centre on the left-right scale. In a policy or ideological sense, left-of-centre Americans were *farther to the left* than were left-of-centre English-Canadians. Americans on the left, for example, were more likely to endorse both income redistribution and a greater degree of government intervention in the economy. Thus if we move from the left-right scale itself to the policy preferences associated with the English-Canadian and American left and rights, we find a greater degree of ideological spread in the U.S. case. The difference, it should be

FIGURE 1
Mean Scores on Left-Right Scale by Partisan Identification of Respondent*

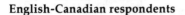

English-Canadian respondents

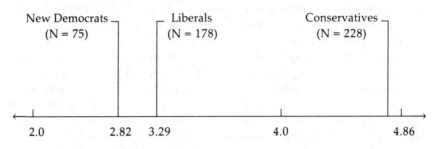

French Quebec respondents

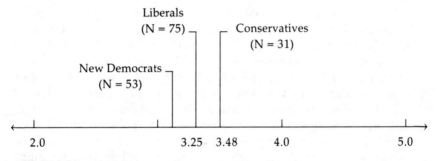

American respondents

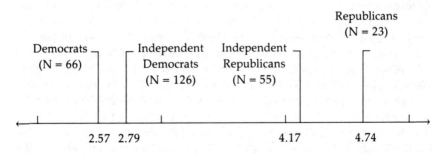

* 2.0 = very liberal; 3 = somewhat liberal; 4 = moderate; 5 = somewhat conservative

stressed, arises from differences between the English-Canadian and American lefts, and not from national differences on the right.

Parallel findings emerge when we compare the locations of partisan camps on the left-right scale. Figure 1 shows that, among English-Canadian respondents, the difference in scale location between Liberal and New Democratic respondents was relatively modest, whereas Progressive Conservative respondents placed themselves well to the right.

Among French Quebec respondents the partisan polarization was much less; while Quebec Liberals occupied the same position as their English-Canadian counterparts, Quebec New Democrats moved modestly to the right and Quebec Conservatives moved more dramatically to the left. As a consequence the ideological spread among the three partisan camps was negligible. The polarization was most pronounced in the American sample, not because Republicans were farther to the right than anglophone and francophone Canadian Conservatives but because Democrats were farther to the left than either the Liberals or New Democrats in both Canadian samples. Parenthetically, it should be noted that Liberals both inside and outside Quebec adopt, on average, virtually identical locations on the left-right scale whereas the two groups of Conservatives differ markedly.

Such differences in polarization suggest that the left-right scale should be of greater predictive value among American than among Canadian respondents, and among English-Canadian than among French Quebec respondents. Table 3 examines the predictive power of the left-right scale for the three samples by assessing the Pearson correlations between respondent location on the left-right scale and the ideological variables. . . .

Compared to the English-Canadian data, the correlations in the U.S. sample are very robust. Given a respondent's location on the left-right scale, one could predict a great deal about that person's outlook towards the size of government, minority rights, income redistribution or feminism. The correlations between the left-right scale and the four variables relating to income redistribution are particularly striking. When we turn to the English-Canadian respondents, the correlations are much less robust. While they are consistently in the same direction as the American correlations, their predictive power is, on average, only 36 per cent of that of the American correlations. Clearly, to know where an English-Canadian respondent locates himself or herself on the left-right scale tells us a great deal less about that person's ideological outlook than is the case for American respondents.

For the French Quebec respondents, the correlations in Table 3 are even weaker than in the English-Canadian case. Indeed, knowledge of a

TABLE 3

Pearson Product Moment Correlation Coefficients for Grouped Value Orientations With Left-Right Scale

	English-Canadian subsample r	French Quebec subsample r	American subsample r
Income redistribution			
income limit	.19	.13	.40
income gap	.29	.14	.55
income similarity	.33	.19	.53
income tax	.34	.08	.60
$\bar{x}_1 =$	.29	.135	.52
Size of government			
deregulation	−.38	−.14	−.41
private enterprise	−.41	−.21	−.54
size of government	−.34	−.04	−.45
$\bar{x}_1 =$	−.38	−.13	−.47
Minorities			
job treatment	.15	.13	.31
home sales	.18	−.05	.43
media	.24	.12	.53
racial quotas	.24	.04	.51
poverty	.24	.10	.47
$\bar{x}_1 =$	.21	.07	.45
Status of women			
layoffs	.10	.08	.21
feminist leaders	.20	−.11	.28
ERA	.13	.07	.39
job discrimination	.25	.15	.38
gender quotas	.23	.00	.53
families	.17	−.10	.31
$\bar{x}_1 =$	.18	.015	.35

respondent's location on the left-right scale tells us little about that person's predispositions towards minority rights and feminism, and very little about predispositions towards income redistribution and the size of government.

Bluntly put, the left-right scale is all but irrelevant for the ideological organization of political thought among French Quebec respondents. In part, this may be due to the absence of an ideological right; the foreshortened left-right scale displays less variance and thus, for statistical reasons alone, has less explanatory power. A less statistical interpretation might be that political life in Quebec is organized along a quite different dimension than is political life, and thus political thought, in English Canada and the United States. The principal organizer of political thought in Quebec may well be the stand one takes on the national question, on Quebec's relationship with the broader Canadian political community. This issue may have assumed such importance that it effectively precludes a more ideological, or left-right, organization of political thought.

The weakness of the left-right scale as an organizer of political thought among English-Canadian respondents, relative that is to U.S. respondents, may reflect the different political agendas of the two national communities. To the extent that regional and intergovernmental conflicts are more prevalent in Canada, they may well disrupt the more ideological organization of political thought in English Canada in a manner analogous to the "disruption" in Quebec with respect to the national question. Alternatively, it may be that political parties in Canada impose less ideological coherence upon the electorate than do parties in the United States.

In any event, Table 3 suggests that U.S. respondents are more ideologically constrained or coherent than are English-Canadian respondents and that both are more constrained than French Quebec respondents. This in turn suggests a more general conclusion. Ask an American to locate him or herself on the left-right scale, to declare whether one is liberal, somewhat conservative, or to the far right, and the interviewer may assume a great deal about that American's view of the political world. Given the same information for someone in English Canada, the interviewer may assume a good deal less, although some predictive power remains. Given the same information for a franchophone in Quebec, one can tell very little about that person's ideological outlook on the world. . . .

CONCLUSIONS

The results of this study suggest significant points of convergence and divergence among the political ideologies of anglophone Canada, francophone Quebec and the United States. First, and contrary to a general consensus in the literature, we found no support for a distinctive English-Canadian right; in an ideological sense, English-Canadian respondents who located themselves to the right of centre on the self-anchoring scale were indistinguishable from their counterparts in the United States, just as English-Canadian Progressive Conservatives were indistinguishable in their scale location from American Republicans. The French Quebec respondents, however, were set apart from both their English-Canadian and American counterparts by the virtual absence of an ideological right. Whereas English-Canadian and American respondents ranged across the left-right scale, French Quebec respondents ranged from the moderate middle to the far left.

When we examined respondents who located themselves on the political left, significant Canadian-American differences did emerge, while the English-Canadian and French-Quebec respondents tended to converge. With respect to policy content, the U.S. respondents on the left were, for example, more willing to endorse regulation of the private sector, more likely to support racial and gender quotas, more likely to blame the system than the poor for poverty, and more willing to endorse limits on incomes. As a consequence, the polarization between the English-Canadian left and right was less pronounced than the polarization between the U.S. left and right.

The difference in polarization was linked in turn to important differences in the ideological structure of the three political cultures. The American respondents displayed far greater attitudinal coherence, and stronger ideological linkages among sets of attitudes, than were found among English-Canadian respondents. French Quebec respondents diverged even more markedly from the American findings, being characterized by a general absence of attitudinal and ideological constraint.

It seems, then, that the political culture of the United States is more ideologically structured than that found in English Canada, and even more so than that found in francophone Quebec. There is, in other words, greater internal consistency and constraint, a more pronounced tendency to knit together political issues into coherent ideological packages. It could be, of course, that the American respondents were simply brighter and more logical, that they were characterized by greater clarity and consistency of thought than their more slow-witted Canadian counterparts. This explanation, however, seems both less interesting and less compelling than the argument that our student samples reflected fundamental national differences in the ideological structure of political cultures. In this sense, the relative lack of ideological coherence and structure in Canada could reflect a greater sense of moderation among Canadians, an ability to see many if not all sides of an issue, a wariness of ideological rigidity, and a willingness to tackle issues in isolation rather than as part of a larger ideological debate. Perhaps, then, Canadians are indeed more pragmatic and less dogmatic in their political life.

Alternatively, it may be the case that Canadian political life has been dominated by such issues as the constitution, federal-provincial relations,

the place of Quebec within the Canadian community, and western aliena-
tion, issues that are not easily or traditionally organized through the left-
right optic. . . . Thus there has been neither the need nor the opportunity for
Canadians to structure their political world along conventional ideological
lines.

16　　　　New Politics

To a considerable degree, the traditional ideologies of liberalism, conservatism, and socialism are preoccupied with the creation and distribution of wealth. Although they have differing views of the role of government in that process, they all address the same issues. According to Ronald Inglehart, a political scientist at the University of Michigan, there has been a decisive shift since World War II in the politics of industrial societies. The direction of change is toward what he calls "post-materialism"—heightened concern with individual expression and quality of life. Post-materialism gives rise to new issue complexes, such as multiculturalism, feminism, and environmentalism, that cut across the old lines of ideological division.

Reading 16, written by Neil Nevitte for this volume, applies Inglehart's thesis to Canada, using Canadian public opinion data in a comparative context. Readers looking for a more detailed and rigorous treatment of the same topic can consult "The Ideological Contours of 'New Politics' in Canada: Policy, Mobilization and Partisan Support" by Neil Nevitte, Herman Bakvis, and Roger Gibbins, in volume 17 of the *Canadian Journal of Political Science.*

● ● ● ● ● ● ● ● ●

Important changes seem to be sweeping across the western world. Citizens are more cynical about politics; trust in politicians has declined; confidence in government has eroded; and publics are less animated by the battles between the old left and the old right, the age-old conflicts between the haves and the have-nots. Traditional representative institutions are under stress and publics are harder to govern. These changes, some observers argue, are not haphazard. Rather, they signify the retreat of old politics and the emergence of new politics.

The central elements of the new politics thesis can be summarized fairly easily. The massive body of evidence pointing to the "decline of political parties," namely, the decomposition of longstanding electoral alignments, the weakening of citizen attachments to traditional political parties, and the increased electoral volatility among mass publics, indicate fundamental shifts in the value systems of the populations of modern states. The rise of new politics, it is suggested, has produced problems of governability for a combination of reasons. First, associated with the rise of new politics is the emergence of a new political agenda. That agenda gives prominence not to the class conflict that shaped political debate in the old industrial states, but to concerns about women, minorities, the environment, animal rights, gay rights, nuclear power, and peace. Central to the new agenda are those issues which are broadly defined as relevant to quality of life. Second, a substantial body of cross-national evidence shows that support for the new politics agenda is disproportionately concentrated within particular segments of the citizenry of advanced industrial states—a new class. That new class is younger, better educated, better informed about, and more interested in politics than its counterparts of preceding generations. New politics theorists argue that the emergence of this new class is a result of the structural changes associated with the late stages of industrialism, or post-industrialism. Members of the new class, mostly those born since the Second World War, are increasingly influential as they are now moving into the command posts of society. Because this new-class generation is only gradually displacing those generations that still cleave to old politics concerns, representative institutions are confronted with a dilemma, namely, how to satisfy a divided public, of which one part makes political demands based on a traditional agenda and the other part is driven by a new agenda.

Third, and perhaps of greatest significance, the rise of new politics is producing new patterns of political participation. Cross-national evidence drawn from a large number of advanced industrial states indicates that citizens holding new politics values are not just younger and better educated; they are also more knowledgeable about politics, more demanding of politicians and governments, and more "issue driven." In some ways, supporters of new politics exhibit precisely the qualities that make up the ideal citizen of the democratic polity: they are well-informed, articulate, sophisticated, and participatory. But they are also less deferential, more elite challenging, more critical of the status quo, and more dissatisfied with conventional hierarchically organized, representative institutions. The longstanding gap between the political skills of leaders and followers has narrowed. It is the combination of a new agenda and the redistribution of political skills that poses challenges to political parties, especially to those wedded to old assumptions about political leadership and representation. Thus, in West European countries in particular, the rise of new politics has not only reoriented and divided old political parties, it has also produced new ones and swelled the ranks of issue-driven social movements promoting the goals of the new agenda. New politics, in short, is boisterous politics.

e bwston; r

THE SHAPE OF NEW POLITICS

Most perspectives on new politics start with the observation that there are important qualitative differences between the early and late industrial experiences. First, advanced industrial, or post-industrial, states have crossed a number of thresholds. Typically, all have experienced sustained and increasing levels of affluence, their economies are driven by the service sector, the education level of their publics has risen, all have confronted the "information revolution" and a corresponding growth in communications-related technologies, all have extensive social welfare networks in place, and their populations have been subject to dramatic increases in social, geographic, and occupational mobility. Furthermore, these developments have taken place in a relatively short time span, in about the last twenty-five years.

Second, although new politics theorists argue that these structural transformations are linked to value change, they differ in the precise descriptions of the value changes. Some see the shift primarily in terms of the increased salience of inner-directedness. Others focus on the changing meaning attached to the idea of "success." Still others identify new attitudes towards authority, conformity, religiosity, and the work ethic as central. Regardless of differences in focus, there is substantial agreement that the traditional "old politics" goals which emphasized economic growth, public order, national security, and traditional lifestyles have been replaced by such new politics goals as individual freedom, social equality, participation, and the quality of life.

Third, there is also broad consensus about the consequences of structural and value change for political participation. We have already noted that the rise of a new agenda and the erosion of traditional patterns of political participation provide two indications of how conventional forms of political behaviour have been reshaped. New politics, however, is also related to vigorous new forms of unconventional political behaviour—direct action politics. Political protest is not new. Most western liberal democracies have had some historical experience with peasant revolts, food riots, and, later with industrial strife and protests from the disenfranchised and other marginalized groups. Working from traditional assumptions about the politics of industrialized societies, it would be reasonable to suppose that with an expanded franchise, with greater affluence, and with redistributive policies providing support for the vast majority of citizens, the incidence of protest would wane. The evidence, however, contradicts that expectation. Protest behaviour has increased in advanced industrial states. Furthermore, direct action politics is most frequently found in those societies that are most affluent. New politics protest differs from traditional forms of direct action in two significant respects. First, it is not the desperate weapon of last resort on the part of the disenfranchised; it is the strategy of choice from the politically astute middle class. Nor are new politics protests spontaneous; rather, they are a deliberate, planned tactic backed by both resources and sophisticated techniques—public awareness campaigns, organized demonstrations, and media opportunities—aimed at mobilizing public opinion and influencing policy makers.

EXPLAINING NEW POLITICS

There is general agreement about the essential elements of new politics and its consequences, but there are significant differences in the explanations of why new politics has emerged. One line of argument is that new politics is the result of inherent weaknesses in welfare states. Welfare states, it is suggested, have buckled under the structural stresses induced by late industrialism. Another line of reasoning is that new politics is nothing more or less than the politics of the new class. Some point out that new politics has simply filled an ideological vacuum caused by the erosion of sharp class conflicts. New politics has emerged, as it were, in the wake of receding traditional ideological polarities. Yet others argue that there has been no change in the ideological temperature; the polarities organizing debate and political life have simply shifted to work along different axes. Within this latter school of thought, Ronald Inglehart's post-materialism theory, elaborated in great detail in *The Silent Revolution*, provides one of the most comprehensive accounts of the origins, nature, and consequences of new politics value change. Inglehart identifies the rift between materialists and post-materialists as the primary value cleavage dividing publics in advanced industrial states. Like others, he links the origins of this value divide to the structural changes of late industrialism, and proceeds to demonstrate, with a vast body of cross-national evidence, how post-materialism has produced political changes.

The essential elements of post-materialist theory hinge on the combined effects of two hypotheses—the scarcity hypothesis and the socialization hypothesis. The scarcity hypothesis suggests, like the economic theory of diminishing returns, that individuals place value on those things that are in short supply. The socialization hypothesis stipulates that the basic values acquired by individuals are fundamentally shaped by the conditions that prevailed during their pre-adult years. Thus, those generations that experienced such first-hand traumas as the Second World War or the depression will give priority to materialist goals—economic security and safety needs—while those without direct experience of such traumas, those born for example since 1945 and who have been raised in an era of relative prosperity, will tend to take such goals as economic security for granted.

Instead, they will give priority to "higher-order" aesthetic, intellectual, and participatory needs for belonging and participating. Inglehart's post-materialist theory is elegant; it relies on only a few well-tested assumptions, and has been verified repeatedly in more than twenty countries over nearly two decades. The theory has attracted a great deal of interest as well as critical scrutiny, but its central findings and basic thesis remain intact.

NEW POLITICS IN CANADA
Given the vast accumulation of data indicating that new politics is now a feature of political life in most advanced industrial states, there is good reason to believe that it will also have an impact on Canadian politics. Indeed, it would be remarkable if that were not the case. By most standard measures, Canada certainly qualifies as a post-industrial state. It has enjoyed substantial increases in wealth in the course of the last twenty-five years, the service sector of the economy has grown, there has been a dramatic increase in educational opportunities, and the middle class has expanded. There is also qualitative evidence indicating that confidence in

FIGURE 1: Age Differences in Value Priorities

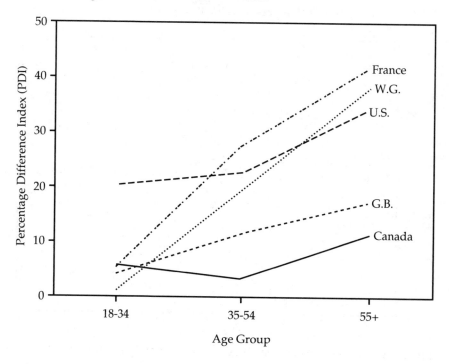

political institutions has declined while the political agenda now includes a host of new politics concerns—women's issues, environmentalism, minority rights—along with a wide range of other quality of life issues. But is there direct evidence of new politics value change? The short answer is yes. National attitudinal surveys conducted in 1981 and 1990 indicate that post-materialism, Inglehart's measure of new politics values, is on the rise. By 1990, one in four Canadians counted as post-materialists, up from one in six in 1981.

Detecting the presence of post-materialist values in Canada is one thing, but is the distribution of post-materialism in Canada typical of the distributions of new politics values in other advanced industrial states? The details of that story remain to be told, but available evidence suggests that they are. Figure 1, for example, illustrates the distribution of materialist/ post-materialist values across various age groups in Canada and in four other advanced industrial states.

The percentage difference index (PDI) is simply the percentage of materialists minus the percentage of post-materialists. Figure 1 illustrates two basic points. First it shows that compared to the other countries under

FIGURE 2: Education Differences in Value Priorities

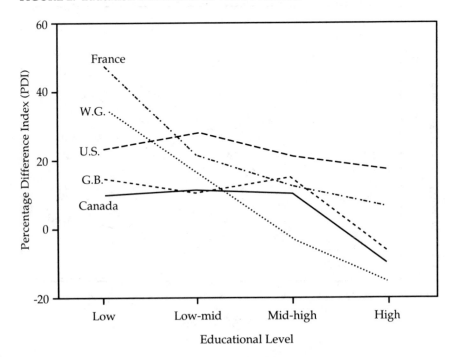

consideration, the level of post-materialism in Canada is relatively high. Those Canadians in the 18-34 age group exhibit levels of post-materialism that clearly are typical of those found in other states, and those in the older age groups exhibit levels that are somewhat higher than those found in comparable age groups elsewhere.

New politics theorists, Inglehart included, predict that post-materialist values are most likely concentrated among those with higher levels of formal education. Figure 2 provides unequivocal support for that prediction. Furthermore, these data show once more that the Canadian evidence conforms to patterns found elsewhere. With increased levels of education, there is a sharp decline in concern for materialist goals—economic growth and strong defense. With respect to both of these sociostructural indicators then, the Canadian evidence of the distribution of post-materialist/materialist values is consistent with evidence drawn from other post-industrial settings.

We have emphasized that a variety of theorists speculate that the rise of new politics is linked to a redistribution of political skills and that one

FIGURE 3: Political Interest by Value Priorities

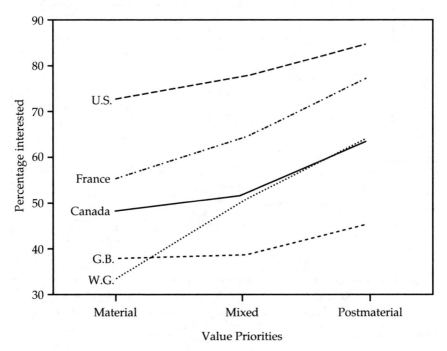

aspect of these skills is political interest. Consequently, we would expect to find relatively low levels of political interest on the part of materialists and relatively high levels among post-materialists. Figure 3 tracks the distribution of political interest among materialists, those respondents with a mix of materialist and post-materialist values, and those who qualify as pure post-materialists. Once again, these data show that Canadian respondents are entirely typical of the broader cross-national trend. Only American and French respondents are more interested in politics. But more important than the particular levels of political interest displayed in these data is the trend. Post-materialists, regardless of national setting, always report higher levels of political interest than do their materialist co-nationals.

Political interest, arguably, is a precondition for political action. We have indicated that new politics theorists expect post-materialists to be more likely than materialists to engage in unconventional forms of political participation. That, in the final analysis, is one main reason why countries with high levels of post-materialism are harder to govern. Canadians,

FIGURE 4: Protest Participation by Value Priorities

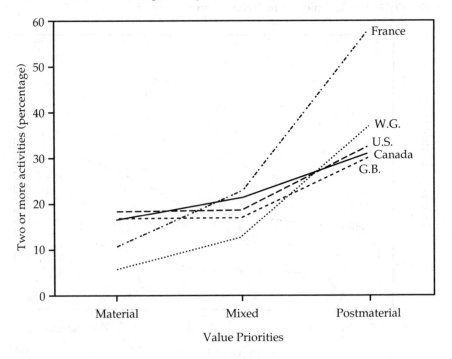

traditionally, have been depicted as deferential, counter-revolutionary, and supporters of "law and order." If that perspective has any contemporary validity, we would expect Canadians to be much less likely than their counterparts elsewhere, perhaps particularly their American counterparts, to engage in protest behaviour. Respondents surveyed in Britain, Canada, France, the United States, and West Germany were presented with an identical list of six "protest activites" ranging from "signing a petition" and "participating in a boycott" to "occupying a factory" and engaging in "physical violence." All were asked to report "which have you done?" The results of that rough measure of protest participation are presented in Figure 4 and the results are striking.

They show first that post-materialists are far more likely to have engaged in protest behaviour than are materialists. Second, they also show some dramatic cross-national differences and clustering across the post-materialist value types. French post-materialists, clearly, are far more likely to have participated in protest behaviour, a legacy perhaps of France's tradition of "hot politics." On the other hand, the similarities across the post-materialist value types in the other four countries are equally striking. There is no evidence, according to these data, of any historic residuals of the American Revolution or for that matter of Canada's counter-revolution. Indeed the differences between the American and Canadian data are so slight as to be insignificant.

CONCLUSIONS

We started this overview with the point that important changes seem to be sweeping across advanced industrial states. These changes, it was argued, have far-reaching implications for the distribution of political skills, the emergence of a new agenda, political participation, and for the kinds of demands that are placed upon political institutions. The speculation was that the forces that structured political debate and political conflict for a large part of the late nineteenth century and for about two thirds of the twentieth century seem to have run their course.

The new politics theories provide one perspective on the transformations that are taking place, and they offer a plausible account for why pressure groups promoting direct action strategies aimed at changing the status quo appear to have multiplied. By the same token, they may also help explain why institutions, political parties, and political leaders that are geared to conventional expectations about apathetic publics are surprised and under siege. According to the sketchy evidence presented here, there is no reason to suppose that Canada has escaped the winds of new politics. Indeed, Canadian politics appears to be buffeted by precisely the same forces that have reshaped political debate, political conflict, and political institutions in other states. The continued advance of new politics, however, is not guaranteed. With a sudden and deep economic downturn, for example, Inglehart predicts that the growth of post-materialism would halt or even temporarily reverse. But if economies in the western world continue to grow and if the political skills of citizens continue to expand, then the prospects for further advances of new politics and of even greater demands for citizen participation appear to be good. Precisely how the forces unleashed by new politics are played out, however, depends upon a variety of factors including how institutions and leaders respond to the new demands that are placed upon them, the electoral system, and the effectiveness of interest groups, factors that are unique to each national context.

Part III
Forms of Government

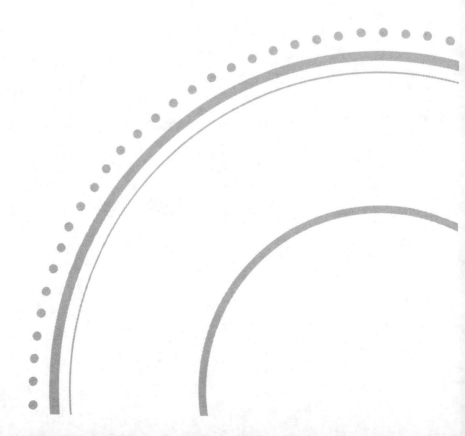

Introduction

Political ideologies provide useful summaries of the ideals shared in society; they also contain recommendations about how political power should be distributed. Government, it has been said, is the art of the possible, and one of the most fundamental challenges facing all societies is how to organize political authority so that governments can be both effective and can generate at least a minimal level of public support. The seven readings presented in Part III explore that theme from a variety of perspectives. The state-society relations perspective is examined in four readings. James Madison's Federalist No. 10 (Reading 17) remains a classic statement of the basic principles of pluralism; it is also an intellectual point of departure for more contemporary analyses of pluralism such as that of Bachrach and Baratz (Reading 18). The pluralist view that society should drive the state and that governments should play only a minimal role in the affairs of citizens stands in stark contrast to totalitarianism, whereby the state drives society. But can totalitarian regimes retain a firm grip on society in the face of sweeping global change? That question is intriguing and important, but the answer remains unclear. Stephen Cohen's article (Reading 19) provides a glimpse of how the forces of totalitarianism worked in one world power, the Soviet Union, and sheds light on how those forces can unravel. Many countries, however, fit neither the pluralist nor totalitarian models of state-society relations. Juan Linz, in Reading 20, argues that a third model, authoritarianism, deserves consideration.

The distribution of power not only depends upon the balance struck between state and society but also upon institutional arrangements. In Reading 21, Douglas Verney examines the division and coordination of political power in parliamentary and presidential systems. Garth Stevenson addresses the same broad issues of the division and coordination of powers from the standpoint of federalism in Reading 23. Social conditions clearly place very real constraints upon the effective organization of political power. Nonetheless, governments of societies that are deeply divided can be legitimate, effective, and stable through such institutional arrangements as consociationalism.

17   Pluralism

In this reading, James Madison (1751-1836), one of the principal framers of the Constitution of 1787 and the fourth president of the United States (1809-17), presents one of the most influential early statements of pluralism, or as he called it, "the factious spirit." The term pluralism has become an important part of social science vocabulary expressing the idea of diversity. Cultural pluralism refers to the diversity of cultures, social pluralism, the diversity of society. In political science, pluralism has come to mean the diversity of interests. Madison, like other liberals who assume that individuals are the best judge of their own interests, recognized that liberty feeds faction, and that the free play of faction could undermine the stability of governments. Rather than sacrificing liberty to achieve stable government, a cure worse than the disease, Madison searched for ways to structure government so as to control the worst effects of faction. The following reading, drawn from the famous Federalist No. 10, is an attempt by Madison to counter the arguments made by a landed minority which believed that a democratic republic would result in the oppression of that minority by the majority.

● ● ● ● ● ● ● ● ●

Among the numerous advantages promised by a well-constructed Union, none deserves to be more accurately developed than its tendency to break and control the violence of faction. The friend of popular governments never finds himself so much alarmed for their character and fate as when he contemplates their propensity to this dangerous vice. He will not fail, therefore, to set a due value on any plan which, without violating the principles to which he is attached, provides a proper cure for it. The instability, injustice, and confusion introduced into the public councils have, in truth, been the mortal diseases under which popular governments have everywhere perished, as they continue to be the favorite and fruitful topics from which the adversaries to liberty derive their most specious declamations. The valuable improvements made by the American constitutions on the popular models, both ancient and modern, cannot certainly be too much admired; but it would be an unwarranted partiality to contend that they have as effectually obviated the danger on this side, as was wished and expected. Complaints are everywhere heard from our most considerate and virtuous citizens, equally the friends of public and private faith and of public and personal liberty, that our governments are too unstable, that the public good is disregarded in the conflicts of rival parties, and that measures are too often decided, not according to the rules of justice and the rights of the minor party, but by the superior force of an interested and overbearing majority. However anxiously we may wish that these complaints had no foundation, the evidence of known facts will not permit us to deny that they are in some degree true. It will be found, indeed, on a candid review of our situation, that some of the distresses under which we labor have been erroneously charged on the operation of our governments; but it will be found, at the same time, that other causes will not alone account for many of our heaviest misfortunes; and, particularly, for that prevailing and increasing distrust of public engagements and alarm for private rights which are echoed from one end of the continent to the other. These must be chiefly, if not wholly, effects of the unsteadiness and injustice with which a factious spirit has tainted our public administration.

By a faction I understand a number of citizens, whether amounting to a majority or minority of the whole, who are united and actuated by some common impulse of passion, or of interest, adverse to the rights of other citizens, or to the permanent and aggregate interests of the community.

There are two methods of curing the mischiefs of faction: the one, by removing its causes; the other, by controlling its effects.

There are again two methods of removing the causes of faction: the one, by destroying the liberty which is essential to its existence; the other, by giving to every citizen the same opinions, the same passions, and the same interests.

It could never be more truly said than of the first remedy that it was worse than the disease. Liberty is to faction what air is to fire, an aliment without which it instantly expires. But it could not be a less folly to abolish liberty, which is essential to political life, because it nourishes faction than it would be to wish the annihilation of air, which is essential to animal life, because it imparts to fire its destructive agency.

The second expedient is as impracticable as the first would be unwise. As long as the reason of man continues fallible, and he is at liberty to exercise it, different opinions will be formed. As long as the connection subsists between his reason and his self-love, his opinions and his passions will have a reciprocal influence on each other; and the former will be objects to which the latter will attach themselves. The diversity in the faculties of men, from which the rights of property originate, is not less an insuperable obstacle to a uniformity of interests. The protection of these faculties is the first object of government. From the protection of different and unequal faculties of acquiring property, the possession of different degrees and kinds of property immediately results; and from the influence of these on the sentiments and views of the respective proprietors ensues a division of the society into different interests and parties.

The latent causes of faction are thus sown in the nature of man; and we see them everywhere brought into different degrees of activity, according to the different circumstances of civil society. A zeal for different opinions concerning religion, concerning government, and many other points, as well of speculation as of practice; an attachment to different leaders ambitiously contending for pre-eminence and power; or to persons of other descriptions whose fortunes have been interesting to the human passions, have, in turn, divided mankind into parties, inflamed them with mutual animosity, and rendered them much more disposed to vex and oppress each other than to co-operate for their common good. So strong is this propensity of mankind to fall into mutual animosities that where no substantial occasion presents itself the most frivolous and fanciful distinctions have been sufficient to kindle their unfriendly passions and excite their most violent conflicts. But the most common and durable source of factions has been the various and unequal distribution of property. Those who hold and those who are without property have ever formed distinct interests in society. Those who are creditors, and those who are debtors, fall under a like discrimination. A landed interest, a manufacturing interest, a mercantile interest, a moneyed interest, with many lesser interests, grow up of necessity in civilized nations, and divide them into different classes, actuated by different sentiments and views. The regulation of these various and interfering interests forms the principal task of modern legislation and involves the spirit of party and faction in the necessary and ordinary operations of government.

No man is allowed to be a judge in his own cause, because his interest would certainly bias his judgment, and, not improbably, corrupt his integrity. With equal, nay with greater reason, a body of men are unfit to be both judges and parties at the same time; yet what are many of the most important acts of legislation but so many judicial determinations, not indeed concerning the rights of single persons, but concerning the rights of large bodies of citizens? And what are the different classes of legislators but advocates and parties to the causes which they determine? Is a law proposed concerning private debts? It is a question to which the creditors are parties on one side and the debtors on the other. Justice ought to hold the balance between them. Yet the parties are, and must be, themselves the judges; and the most numerous party, or in other words, the most powerful faction must be expected to prevail. Shall domestic manufacturers be encouraged, and in what degree, by restrictions on foreign manufacturers? are questions which would be differently decided by the landed and the manufacturing classes, and probably by neither with a sole regard to justice and the public good. The apportionment of taxes on the various descriptions of property is an act which seems to require the most exact impartiality; yet there is, perhaps, no legislative act in which greater opportunity and temptation are given to a predominant party to trample on the rules of justice. Every shilling with which they overburden the inferior number is a shilling saved to their own pockets.

It is in vain to say that enlightened statesmen will be able to adjust these clashing interests and render them all subservient to the public good. Enlightened statesmen will not always be at the helm. Nor, in many cases, can such an adjustment be made at all without taking into view indirect and remote considerations, which will rarely prevail over the immediate interest which one party may find in disregarding the rights of another or the good of the whole.

The inference to which we are brought is that the *causes* of faction cannot be removed and that relief is only to be sought in the means of controlling its *effects*.

If a faction consists of less than a majority, relief is supplied by the republican principle, which enables the majority to defeat its sinister views by regular vote. It may clog the administration, it may convulse the society; but it will be unable to execute and mask its violence under the forms of the Constitution. When a majority is included in a faction, the form of popular government, on the other hand, enables it to sacrifice to its ruling passion or interest both the public good and the rights of other citizens. To secure the public good and private rights against the danger of such a faction, and at the same time to preserve the spirit and the form of popular government, is then the great object to which our inquiries are directed. Let me add that it is the great desideratum by which alone this form of government can be rescued from the opprobrium under which it has so long labored and be recommended to the esteem and adoption of mankind.

By what means is this object attainable? Evidently by one of two only. Either the existence of the same passion or interest in a majority at the same time must be prevented, or the majority, having such coexistent passion or interest, must be rendered, by their number and local situation, unable to concert and carry into effect schemes of oppression. If the impulse and the opportunity be suffered to coincide, we well know that neither moral nor religious motives can be relied on as an adequate control. They are not found to be such on the injustice and violence of individuals, and lose their efficacy in proportion to the number combined together, that is, in proportion as their efficacy becomes needful.

From this view of the subject it may be concluded that a pure democracy, by which I mean a society consisting of a small number of citizens, who assemble and administer the government in person, can admit of no cure for the mischiefs of faction. A common passion or interest will, in almost every case, be felt by a majority of the whole; a communication and concert results from the form of government itself; and there is nothing to check the inducements to sacrifice the weaker party or an obnoxious individual. Hence it is that such democracies have ever been spectacles of turbulence and contention; have ever been found incompatible with personal security or the rights of property; and have in general been as short in their lives as they have been violent in their deaths. Theoretic politicians, who have patronized this species of government, have erroneously supposed that by reducing mankind to a perfect equality in their political rights, they would at the same time be perfectly equalized and assimilated in their possessions, their opinions, and their passions.

A republic, by which I mean a government in which the scheme of representation takes place, opens a different prospect and promises the cure for which we are seeking. Let us examine the points in which it varies from pure democracy, and we shall comprehend both the nature of the cure and the efficacy which it must derive from the Union.

The two great points of difference between a democracy and a republic are: first, the delegation of the government, in the latter, to a small number of citizens elected by the rest; secondly, the greater number of citizens and greater sphere of country over which the latter may be extended.

The effect of the first difference is, on the one hand, to refine and enlarge the public views by passing them through the medium of a chosen body of citizens, whose wisdom may best discern the true interest of their country and whose patriotism and love of justice will be least likely to sacrifice it to temporary or partial considerations. Under such a regulation it may well happen that the public voice, pronounced by the representatives of the people, will be more consonant to the public good than if pronounced by the people themselves, convened for the purpose. On the other hand, the effect may be inverted. Men of factious tempers, of local prejudices, or of sinister designs, may, by intrigue, by corruption, or by other means, first obtain the suffrages, and then betray the interests of the people. The question resulting is, whether small or extensive republics are most favorable to the election of proper guardians of the public weal; and it is clearly decided in favor of the latter by two obvious considerations.

In the first place it is to be remarked that however small the republic may be the representatives must be raised to a certain number in order to guard against the cabals of a few; and that however large it may be they must be limited to a certain number in order to guard against the confusion of a multitude. Hence, the number of representatives in the two cases not being in proportion to that of the constituents, and being proportionally greatest in the small republic, it follows that if the proportion of fit characters be not less in the large than in the small republic, the former will present a greater option, and consequently a greater probability of a fit choice.

In the next place, as each representative will be chosen by a greater number of citizens in the large than in the small republic, it will be more difficult for unworthy candidates to practise with success the vicious arts by which elections are too often carried; and the suffrages of the people being more free, will be more likely to center on men who possess the most attractive merit and the most diffusive and established characters.

It must be confessed that in this, as in most other cases, there is a mean, on both sides of which inconveniences will be found to lie. By enlarging too much the number of electors, you render the representative too little acquainted with all their local circumstances and lesser interests; as by reducing it too much, you render him unduly attached to these, and too little fit to comprehend and pursue great and national objects. The federal Constitution forms a happy combination in this respect; the great and aggregate interests being referred to the national, the local and particular to the State legislatures.

The other point of difference is the greater number of citizens and extent of territory which may be brought within the compass of republican than of democratic government; and it is this circumstance principally which renders factious combinations less to be dreaded in the former than in the latter. The smaller the society, the fewer probably will be the distinct parties and interests composing it; the fewer the distinct parties and interests, the more frequently will a majority be found of the same party; and the smaller the number of individuals composing a majority, and the smaller the compass within which they are placed, the more easily will they concert and execute their plans of oppression. Extend the sphere and you take in a greater variety of parties and interests; you make it less probable that a majority of the whole will have a common motive to invade the rights of other citizens; or if such a common motive exists, it will be more difficult for all who feel it to discover their own strength and to act in unison with each other. Besides other impediments, it may be remarked that, where there is a consciousness of unjust or dishonorable purposes, communication is always checked by distrust in proportion to the number whose concurrence is necessary.

Hence, it clearly appears that the same advantage which a republic has over a democracy in controlling the effects of faction is enjoyed by a large over a small republic—is enjoyed by the Union over the States composing it. Does this advantage consist in the substitution of representatives whose enlightened views and virtuous sentiments render them superior to local prejudices and to schemes of injustice? It will not be denied that the representation of the Union will be most likely to possess these requisite endowments. Does it consist in the greater security afforded by a greater variety of parties, against the event of any one party being able to out-number and oppress the rest? In an equal degree does the increased variety of parties comprised within the Union increase this security. Does it, in fine, consist in the greater obstacles opposed to the concert and accomplishment of the secret wishes of an unjust and interested majority? Here again the extent of the Union gives it the most palpable advantage.

The influence of factious leaders may kindle a flame within their particular States but will be unable to spread a general conflagration through the other States. A religious sect may degenerate into a political faction in a part of the Confederacy; but the variety of sects dispersed over the entire face of it must secure the national councils against any danger from that source. A rage for paper money, for an abolition of debts, for an equal division of property, or for any other improper or wicked project, will be less apt to pervade the whole body of the Union than a particular member of it, in the same proportion as such a malady is more likely to taint a particular county or district than an entire State.

In the extent and proper structure of the Union, therefore, we behold a republican remedy for the diseases most incident to republican govern-ment. And according to the degree of pleasure and pride we feel in being republicans ought to be our zeal in cherishing the spirit and supporting the character of federalists. *Publius*

18   The Bias of Pluralism

Most pluralists reject the idea that there is a single common good or public interest and they see any attempt by governments to impose that idea on publics as a utopian recipe for disaster. Pluralists argue instead that the political agenda should emerge from the free competition of interests in society. Traditional pluralists did not assume that all of the people would be satisfied all of the time, but they did assume that most people would be satisfied in the long run. Contemporary pluralists, and some critics of pluralism, however, have challenged that idea. These "realists," as they are sometimes called, observe that the outcome of battles between different interests is typically decided in favour of those parts of society that command the most resources or power. Consequently, to understand the dynamics of pluralism it is also necessary to understand the dynamics of power in society.

For Bachrach and Baratz, the crucial question is: How does power really work? In probing that question, they argue that the dynamics of power, and consequently pluralism, are not one-dimensional. Rather, power often works in hidden ways, and the indirect expression of power and influence is just as important as the direct. Non-decisions are as important as decisions; and the status quo, far from being neutral, may reflect instead the uneven distribution of power and effective interests.

Bachrach and Baratz's article, "Two Faces of Power," appears in Henry S. Kariel's *Frontiers of Democratic Theory*, and was originally published in volume 56 of the *American Political Science Review*.

● ● ● ● ● ● ● ● ● ●

The concept of power remains elusive despite the recent and prolific outpourings of case studies on community power. Its elusiveness is dramatically demonstrated by the regularity of disagreement as to the locus of community power between the sociologists and the political scientists. Sociologically oriented researchers have consistently found that power is highly centralized, while scholars trained in political science have just as regularly concluded that in "their" communities power is widely diffused. Presumably, this explains why the latter group styles itself "pluralist," its counterpart "elitist."

There seems no room for doubt that the sharply divergent findings of the two groups are the product, not of sheer coincidence, but of fundamen-

tal differences in both their underlying assumptions and research methodology. The political scientists have contended that these differences in
findings can be explained by the faulty approach and presuppositions of
the sociologists. We contend in this paper that the pluralists themselves
have not grasped the whole truth of the matter; that while their criticisms of
the elitists are sound, they, like the elitists, utilize an approach and assumptions which predetermine their conclusions. Our argument is cast within
the frame of our central thesis: that there are two faces of power, neither of
which the sociologists see and only one of which the political scientists see.

I

Against the elitist approach to power several criticisms may be, and have
been leveled. One has to do with its basic premise that in every human
institution there is an ordered system of power, a "power structure" which
is an integral part and the mirror image of the organization's stratification.
This postulate the pluralists emphatically—and, to our mind, correctly—
reject, on the ground that

> nothing categorical can be assumed about power in any community.
> . . . If anything, there seems to be an unspoken notion among pluralist
> researchers that at bottom *nobody* dominates in a town, so that their
> first question is not likely to be, "Who runs this community?" but
> rather, "Does anyone at all run this community?" The first query is
> somewhat like, "Have you stopped beating your wife?" in that vir-
> tually any response short of total unwillingness to answer will supply
> the researchers with a "power elite" along the lines presupposed by
> the stratification theory.

Equally objectionable to the pluralists—and to us—is the sociologists'
hypothesis that the power structure tends to be stable over time.

> Pluralists hold that power may be tied to issues, and issues can be
> fleeting or persistent, provoking coalitions among interested groups
> and citizens, ranging in their duration from momentary to semi-per-
> manent. . . . To presume that the set of coalitions which exists in the
> community at any given time is a timelessly stable aspect of social
> structure is to introduce systematic inaccuracies into one's description
> of social reality.

A third criticism of the elitist model is that it wrongly equates reputed
with actual power:

> If a man's major life work is banking, the pluralist presumes he
> will spend his time at the bank, and not in manipulating community

decisions. This presumption holds until the banker's activities and participations indicate otherwise. . . . If we presume that the banker is "really" engaged in running the community, there is practically no way of disconfirming this notion, even if it is totally erroneous. On the other hand, it is easy to spot the banker who really *does* run community affairs when we presume he does not, because his activities will make this fact apparent.

This is not an exhaustive bill of particulars; there are flaws other than these in the sociological model and methodology—including some which the pluralists themselves have not noticed. But to go into this would not materially serve our current purposes. Suffice it simply to observe that whatever the merits of their own approach to power, the pluralists have effectively exposed the main weaknesses of the elitist model.

As the foregoing quotations make clear, the pluralists concentrate their attention, not upon the sources of power, but its exercise. Power to them means "participation in decision-making" and can be analyzed only after "careful examination of a series of concrete decisions." As a result, the pluralist researcher is uninterested in the reputedly powerful. His concerns instead are to (a) select for study a number of "key" as opposed to "routine" political decisions, (b) identify the people who took an active part in the decision-making process, (c) obtain a full account of their actual behaviour while the policy conflict was being resolved, and (d) determine and analyze the specific outcome of the conflict.

The advantages of this approach, relative to the elitist alternative, need no further exposition. The same may not be said, however, about its defects —two of which seem to us to be of fundamental importance. One is that the model takes no account of the fact that power may be, and often is, exercised by confining the scope of decision making to relatively "safe" issues. The other is that the model provides no *objective* criteria for distinguishing between "important" and "unimportant" issues arising in the political arena.

II

There is no gainsaying that an analysis grounded entirely upon what is specific and visible to the outside observer is more "scientific" than one based upon pure speculation. To put it another way:

If we can get our social life stated in terms of activity, and of nothing else, we have not indeed succeeded in measuring it, but we have at least reached a foundation upon which a coherent system of measurements can be built up. . . . We shall cease to be blocked by the intervention of unmeasurable elements, which claim to be themselves the real causes of all that is happening, and which by their spook-like arbitrariness make impossible any progress toward dependable knowledge.

The question is, however, how can one be certain in any given situation that the "unmeasurable elements" are inconsequential, are not of decisive importance? Cast in slightly different terms, can a sound concept of power be predicated on the assumption that power is totally embodied and fully reflected in "concrete decisions" or in activity bearing directly upon their making?

We think not. Of course power is exercised when A participates in the making of decisions that affect B. But power is also exercised when A devotes his energies to creating or reinforcing social and political values and institutional practices that limit the scope of the political process to public consideration of only those issues which are comparatively innocuous to A. To the extent that A succeeds in doing this, B is prevented, for all practical purposes, from bringing to the fore any issues that might in their resolution be seriously detrimental to A's set of preferences.

Situations of this kind are common. Consider, for example, the case— surely not unfamiliar to this audience—of the discontented faculty member in an academic institution headed by a tradition-bound executive. Aggrieved about a long-standing policy around which a strong vested interest has developed, the professor resolves in the privacy of his office to launch an attack upon the policy at the next faculty meeting. But, when the moment of truth is at hand, he sits frozen in silence. Why? Among the many possible reasons, one or more of these could have been of crucial importance: (a) the professor was fearful that his intended action would be interpreted as an expression of his disloyalty to the institution; or (b) he decided that, given the beliefs and attitudes of his colleagues on the faculty, he would almost certainly constitute on this issue a minority of one; or (c) he concluded that, given the nature of the law-making process in the institution, his proposed remedies would be pigeonholed permanently. But whatever the case, the central point to be made is the same: to the extent that a person or group—consciously or unconsciously—creates or reinforces barriers to the public airing of policy conflicts, that person or group has power. Or, as Professor Schattschneider has so admirably put it:

All forms of political organization have a bias in favor of the exploitation of some kinds of conflict and the suppression of others because *organization is the mobilization of bias*. Some issues are organized into politics while others are organized out.

Is such bias not relevant to the study of power? Should not the student be continuously alert to its possible existence in the human institution that he studies, and be ever prepared to examine the forces which brought it into being and sustain it? Can he safely ignore the possibility, for instance, that an individual or group in a community participates more vigorously in supporting the *non-decision-making* process than in participating in actual decisions within the process? Stated differently, can the researcher overlook the chance that some person or association could limit decision making to relatively noncontroversial matters, by influencing community values and political procedures and rituals, notwithstanding that there are in the community serious but latent power conflicts? To do so is, in our judgment, to overlook the less apparent but nonetheless extremely important, face of power.

III

In his critique of the "ruling-elite model," Professor Dahl argues that "the hypothesis of the existence of a ruling elite can be strictly tested only if . . . [t]here is a fair sample of cases involving key political decisions in which the preferences of the hypothetical ruling elite run counter to those of any other likely group that might be suggested. With this assertion we have two complaints. One we have already discussed, *viz.*, in erroneously assuming that power is solely reflected in concrete decisions, Dahl thereby excludes the possibility that in the community in question there is a group capable of preventing contests from arising on issues of importance to it. Beyond that, however, by ignoring the less apparent face of power Dahl and those who accept his pluralist approach are unable adequately to differentiate between a "key" and a "routine" political decision. . . .

Dahl's definition of "key political issues" in his essay on the ruling-elite model is open to the same criticism. He states that it is "a necessary although possibly not a sufficient condition that the [key] issue should involve actual disagreement in preferences among two or more groups. In our view, this is an inadequate characterization of a "key political issue," simply because groups can have disagreements in preferences on unimportant as well as on important issues. Elite preferences which border on the indifferent are certainly not significant in determining whether a monolithic or polylithic distribution of power prevails in a given community. Using Dahl's definition of "key political issues," the researcher would have little difficulty in finding such in practically any community; and it would not be surprising then if he ultimately concluded that power in the community was widely diffused.

The distinction between important and unimportant issues, we believe, cannot be made intelligently in the absence of an analysis of the "mobilization of bias" in the community; of the dominant values and the political myths, rituals, and institutions which tend to favor the vested interests of one or more groups, relative to others. Armed with this knowledge, one could conclude that any challenge to the predominant values or to the established "rules of the game" would constitute an "important" issue; all else, unimportant. To be sure, judgments of this kind cannot be entirely objective. But to avoid making them in a study of power is both to neglect a highly significant aspect of power and thereby to undermine the only sound basis for discriminating between "key" and "routine" decisions. In effect, we contend, the pluralists have made each of these mistakes; that is to say, . . . they have begun "their structure at the mezzanine without showing us a lobby or foundation," *i.e.*, they have begun by studying the issues rather than the values and biases that are built into the political system and that, for the student of power, give real meaning to those issues which do enter the political arena.

IV

There is no better fulcrum for our critique of the pluralist model than Dahl's recent study of power in New Haven.

At the outset it may be observed that Dahl does not attempt in this work to define his concept, "key political decision." In asking whether the "Notables" of New Haven are "influential overtly or covertly in the making of government decisions," he simply states that he will examine "three different 'issue-areas' in which important public decisions are made: nominations by the two political parties, urban redevelopment, and public education." These choices are justified on the grounds that "nominations determine which persons will hold public office. The New Haven redevelopment program measured by its cost—present and potential—is the largest in the country. Public eduation, aside from its intrinsic importance, is the costliest item in the city's budget." Therefore, Dahl concludes, "It is reasonable to expect . . . that the relative influence over public officials wielded by the . . . Notables would be revealed by an examination of their participation in these three areas of activity."

The difficulty with this latter statement is that it is evident from Dahl's own account that the Notables are in fact uninterested in two of the three "key" decisions he has chosen. In regard to the public school issue, for example, Dahl points out that many of the Notables live in the suburbs and that those who do live in New Haven choose in the main to send their children to private schools. "As a consequence," he writes, "their interest in the public schools is ordinarily rather slight." Nominations by the two political parties as an important "issue-area," is somewhat analogous to the public schools, in that the apparent lack of interest among the Notables in this issue is partially accounted for by their suburban residence—because of which they are disqualified from holding public office in New Haven.

Indeed, Dahl himself concedes that with respect to both these issues the Notables are largely indifferent: "Business leaders might ignore the public schools or the political parties without any sharp awareness that their indifference would hurt their pocketbooks. . . ." He goes on, however, to say that

> the prospect of profound changes [as a result of the urban-redevelopment program] in ownership, physical layout, and usage of property in the downtown area and the effects of these changes on the commercial and industrial prosperity of New Haven were all related in an obvious way to the daily concerns of businessmen.

Thus, if one believes—as Professor Dahl did when he wrote his critique of the ruling-elite model—that an issue, to be considered as important, "should involve actual disagreement in preferences among two or more groups," then clearly he has now for all practical purposes written off public education and party nominations as key "issue areas." But this point aside, it appears somewhat dubious at best that "the relative influence over public officials wielded by the Social Notables" can be revealed by an examination of their nonparticipation in areas in which they were not interested.

Furthermore, we would not rule out the possibility that even on those issues to which they appear indifferent, the Notables may have a significant degree of *indirect* influence. We would suggest, for example, that although they send their children to private schools, the Notables do recognize that public school expenditures have a direct bearing upon their own tax liabilities. This being so, and given their strong representation on the New Haven Board of Finance, the expectation must be that it is in their direct interest to play an active role in fiscal policy making, in the establishment of the educational budget in particular. But as to this, Dahl is silent: he inquires not at all into either the decisions made by the Board of Finance with respect to education nor into their impact upon the public schools. Let it be understood clearly that in making these points we are not attempting to refute Dahl's contention that the Notables lack power in New Haven. What we *are* saying, however, is that this conclusion is not adequately supported by his analysis of the "issue-areas" of public education and party nominations.

The same may not be said of redevelopment. This issue is by any reasonable standard important for purposes of determining whether New Haven is ruled by "the hidden hand of an economic elite." For the Economic Notables have taken an active interest in the program and, beyond that, the socioeconomic implications of it are not necessarily in harmony with the basic interests and values of businesses and businessmen.

In an effort to ensure that the redevelopment program would be acceptable to what he dubbed "the biggest muscles" in New Haven, Mayor Lee created the Citizens Action Commission (CAC) and appointed to it primarily representatives of the economic elite. It was given the function of overseeing the work of the mayor and other officials involved in redevelopment, and, as well, the responsibility for organizing and encouraging citizens' participation in the program through an extensive committee system.

In order to weigh the relative influence of the mayor, other key officials, and the members of the CAC, Dahl reconstructs "all the *important* decisions on redevelopment and renewal between 1950-58 . . . [to] determine which individuals most often initiated the proposals that were finally adopted or most often successfully vetoed the proposals of the others." The results of this test indicate that the mayor and his development administrator were by far the most influential, and that the "muscles" on the commission, excepting in a few trivial instances, "never directly initiated, opposed, vetoed, or altered any proposal brought before them. . . ."

This finding is, in our view, unreliable, not so much because Dahl was compelled to make a subjective selection of what constituted *important* decisions within what he felt to be an *important* "issue-area," as because the finding was based upon an excessively narrow test of influence. To measure relative influence solely in terms of the ability to initiate and veto proposals is to ignore the possible exercise of influence or power in limiting the scope of initiation. How, that is to say, can a judgment be made as to the relative influence of Mayor Lee and the CAC without knowing (through prior study of the political and social views of all concerned) the proposals that Lee did *not* make because he anticipated that they would provoke strenuous opposition and, perhaps, sanctions on the part of the CAC?

In sum, since he does not recognize *both* faces of power, Dahl is in no position to evaluate the relative influence of power of the initiator and decision maker, on the one hand, and of those persons, on the other, who may have been indirectly instrumental in preventing potentially dangerous issues from being raised. As a result, he unduly emphasizes the importance of initiating, deciding, and vetoing, and in the process casts the pluralist conclusions of his study into serious doubt.

V

We have contended in this paper that a fresh approach to the study of power is called for, an approach based upon a recognition of the two faces of power. Under this approach the researcher would begin—not, as does the sociologist who asks, "Who rules?" nor as does the pluralist who asks, "Does anyone have power?"—but by investigating the particular "mobilization of bias" in the institution under scrutiny. Then, having analyzed the dominant values, the myths, and the established political procedures and rules of the game, he would make a careful inquiry into which persons or groups, if any, gain from the existing bias and which, if any, are handicapped by it. Next, he would investigate the dynamics of *nondecision making*; that is, he would examine the extent to which and the manner in which the *status quo* oriented persons and groups influence those community values and those political institutions . . . which tend to limit the scope of actual decision making to "safe" issues. Finally, using his knowledge of the restrictive face of power as a foundation for analysis and as a standard for distinguishing between "key" and "routine" political decisions, the researcher would, after the manner of the pluralists, analyze participation in decision making of concrete issues.

We reject in advance as unimpressive the possible criticism that this approach to the study of power is likely to prove fruitless because it goes beyond an investigation of what is objectively measurable. In reacting against the subjective aspects of the sociological model of power, the pluralists have, we believe, made the mistake of discarding "unmeasurable elements" as unreal. It is ironical that, by so doing, they have exposed themselves to the same fundamental criticism they have so forcefully leveled against the elitists: their approach to and assumptions about power predetermine their findings and conclusions.

19   Totalitarianism

Extraordinary changes have been taking place in Eastern Europe since 1985. The Berlin Wall has been dismantled, nationalities within the Soviet Union are demanding the status of independent republics, and the leadership of the Communist Party of the Soviet Union is embarking on a reform program of historic significance. The scope and speed of these changes surprised experts, and there is substantial disagreement as to whether the changes signify decentralization, democratization, or disorder. The future directions that will result from the reforms also remain uncertain.

In this reading, Soviet specialist Stephen Cohen, professor of politics at Princeton University, traces the origins and scope of the transformations. He sketches the basic principles behind the program of reform, *perestroika*; identifies how bureaucratic and economic forces have been unleashed in the process; and points to the significant role played by rising public expectations regarding the outcomes. Although it is still too early to predict how the tensions surrounding the reforms will be played out, the portrait that is drawn is instructive. It illustrates how interests in a state-dominated society become embedded; it shows how civilian, military, and party bureaucracies achieved a measure of solidarity and thus continuity; and it also provides a picture of how, after generations of totalitarianism, the system that kept the state dominant over society is unravelling. The reading, "Gorbachev and the Soviet Reformation," appears in Stephen S. Cohen and Katrina Vanden Heuvel's *Voices of Glasnost: Interviews with Gorbachev's Reformers.*

● ● ● ● ● ● ● ● ● ●

A historic political drama has been unfolding in the Soviet Union since Mikhail Gorbachev became its leader in March 1985. In the face of large and deeply rooted obstacles, Gorbachev and his supporters are trying to carry out a full-scale political, economic, and social reformation, or what they call *perestroika*, in one of the world's largest, most authoritarian, and most conservative countries. Among other reforms, they are proposing to introduce a substantial degree of free market relations, private economic enterprise, rule of law, liberal political values, local self-government, and democratic procedures in a nation that has had virtually no experience with any of these practices and indeed has long regarded them as un-Soviet. All things considered, Gorbachev's proposed reformation is unprecedented in modern history. It is also, given the Soviet Union's superpower role in international affairs, probably the most fateful struggle underway in the world today.

The emergence of a Soviet leadership devoted to radical reform confounded most Western scholars and media commentators, who had long believed that the Soviet Communist system lacked any capacity for real change. Scholarly axioms and popular stereotypes can be tenacious. For two years, if not longer, many Western observers dismissed Gorbachev's policies as merely "technocratic" measures that would not affect the nature of the system, or even as deceitful propaganda. The torrent of remarkable changes inside the Soviet Union since 1985 has finally persuaded most serious observers that Gorbachev's program is both authentic and radical, but even those of us who study Soviet affairs still lack analytical concepts adequate to cope with the ongoing process of change. Unable to find new ways to think about the subject, some observers simply cling to their old convictions that the Soviet system is unreformable by prematurely concluding that perestroika will fail.

Three important questions have been obscured by the vexed Western reaction to the Soviet Union under Gorbachev. What is perestroika, how did it originate, and what has it achieved since 1985? Here too Western experiences and preconceptions can do little but mislead us. Gorbachev's reforms are not, for example, an effort to rid his country of socialism in favor of what we know as capitalism, but an epic quest for a new kind of Soviet socialism. The pursuit of technological modernization and economic efficiency are driving forces behind perestroika, but so too is the belief that genuine socialist values and practices, which are still associated at least loosely with the founding father Lenin, were lost during Stalin's despotic rule from 1929 to 1953. By any Western or modern-day Marxist criteria, Gorbachev's advocacy of a mixed economy and "socialist market" do not constitute a return to capitalism. Instead, for Gorbachev and his most fervent supporters, perestroika is a crusade for a "humane socialism." Many of them, including people in this book, even speak of "socialism with a human face," the aspiration identified with the Prague Spring crushed by Soviet tanks in 1968.

Those of us who are not socialists may find it difficult to sympathize with this kind of undertaking, or to believe that it is possible, but we should understand that successful reforms in any country must arise and evolve within the prevailing political culture. They must promise the nation a renewal of established values, not their repeal. As Aleksandr Bovin says below, a society cannot jump out of its own history. For the great majority of Soviet officials and ordinary citizens, who were born well after the Russian

Revolution of 1917, some kind of socialism, however ill-defined and un-satisfying over the years, remains the only legitimate and imaginable way of life. That is why we must take seriously Gorbachev's declarations that perestroika means a "renewal of socialism" and "more socialism." It also is why the final words spoken in Tengiz Abuladze's film *Repentance*, a powerful condemnation of Stalinism and a major political event when it opened in 1986, have become a refrain in so many Soviet criticisms of the existing system: "Of what use is a road if it doesn't lead to the Temple?"

The Russian word *perestroika* translates literally as "restructuring," but as conceived by the Gorbachev leadership it means the de-Stalinization of the Soviet system. If the major reforms already legislated since 1985 are actually implemented in the years ahead, they would greatly reduce and in some respects abolish the abolutist state controls Stalin imposed on society sixty years ago. Therein lies perestroika's potential as a historic reformation and recreation of Soviet socialism.

Gorbachev's reforms are a belated but direct response to the extraordi-nary history and size of the present-day Soviet state that is the enduring legacy of Stalinism. It took shape in Stalin's revolution from above of the 1930s—in the forcible collectivization of 25 million peasant households, the draconian drive for industrialization and urbanization, and mass depor-tations and police terror that eventually victimized tens of millions of people. In an all-out campaign to transform every area of Soviet life, from economic production and distribution to consumer services, culture, and politics, the Stalinist regime created a vast, nationwide system of state commands, control, and administration. Centered in enormous Moscow ministries, its countless republic, regional, and local branches, agents, procedures, and documents ensnared virtually every kind of enterprise, vocation, and citizen. Even the once dominant Communist Party, crushed by Stalin's terror in the late 1930s, was engulfed by the process of rampant statism, or what Soviet writers now call "bureaucratic statization."

The subsequent history of this statist system has been less traumatic but no less remarkable. The structure of its bureaucratic controls over society survived not only Stalin's death in 1953 but Nikita Khrushchev's de-Stalinization efforts of the 1950s and early 1960s. The Soviet state grew even larger during the long conservative reign of Leonid Brezhnev, from 1964 to 1982. Brezhnev's policies, which emphasized "stability of cadres" and shunned significant reform, further nurtured the myriad of ministerial bureaucracies at the center and across the country. By mid-1985, according to official figures that do not include collective farm administrators, the Ministry of Defense, the Ministry of Internal Affairs, or the KGB, the Soviet state employed 17.7 million functionaries. Through some 800,000 "organi-zational links," it administered—or to be precise, sought to administer—

several hundred thousand state-run industrial, agricultural, and trade enterprises and the prices of countless goods and services, while issuing millions of annual commands, instructions, and prohibitions in every area and at all levels of Soviet life. When Gorbachev's *perestroishchiki* talk about "liberating" society from this "thicket" of state controls and "banomania," they are not speaking metaphorically.

More specifically, what Gorbachev calls perestroika is based on five kinds of major reform, each of which would expand society's freedom of activity by diminishing the realm of the state. One is glasnost, or openness, which means a substantial reduction of state- and party-imposed bans and other forms of censorship in the mass media and in political, intellectual, and cultural life generally. The second is managerial decentralization, which seeks to free thousands of nationalized industrial and agricultural enterprises from the clutching directives of planning agencies and ministries in Moscow. The third reform is economic privatization, which would reduce the size of the state economy itself by turning over some portion of its functions to newly created cooperative and individually owned businesses. The fourth reform, economic marketization, follows from the previous two. It would compel many state enterprises to compete among themselves on the basis of efficiency and profitability, as well as with private firms. Finally, there is Gorbachev's "democratization" program, which would sharply reduce the number of party-state appointed officials by permitting multi-candidate elections to the new national parliament, the network of governmental soviets at every level across the country, at workplaces, and even inside the Communist Party.

As Gorbachev's supporters have written repeatedly, all of these reforms are designed to "destatize" the "Stalinist command-administrative system." When pressed to spell out the dimensions of their proposed "de-statization," they promise eventually to abolish fully half to two-thirds of all state bureaucratic positions. Like everyone who engages in politics in the Soviet Union, Gorbachev and his allies think and speak in the context and idiom of the Soviet historical experience. Therefore, for them perestroika as de-statization is synonymous with a "process of decisive de-Stalinization." That they have articulated this understanding of perestroika so candidly, persistently, and coherently should dispel notions that Gorbachev is some kind of centrist positioned between the party's radical and conservative factions and that his policies are makeshift measures without any overall conception. Like any successful national leader, Gorbachev understands, as he often says, that "politics is the art of the possible." But as his speeches and deeds since 1985 make clear, he is himself the visionary leader of the exceedingly radical reformation known as perestroika.

The advent of the Gorbachevian reformation still puzzles many Western experts whose conceptions of Soviet history and politics had excluded such a development. They did not believe, for example, that there was an anti-Stalinist tradition in the Soviet experience capable of inspiring an alternative to the existing order or that radical reformers, even if they existed at lower levels, could rise to high echelons of the Communist Party, much less emerge as its leadership. For these experts, the Gorbachev phenomenon remains a kind of inexplicable accident, an aberration without roots in the Soviet system and thus without any real prospects of success. A brief look at the origins of perestroika suggests a different way of thinking about its possibilities.

The basic ideas behind perestroika are not new, and the movement to translate them into official policy did not begin with Gorbachev. Their remote antecedents are to be found in Lenin's New Economic Policy (NEP), which in 1921 abandoned the party's extremist Civil War measures in favor of much more conciliatory ones. Until NEP was abolished by Stalin's revolution from above in 1929, it evolved into a whole series of related policies that anti-Stalinist reformers have long viewed as an embryonic model of socialism. Unlike the encompassing statist and terror-ridden Stalinist system that followed, NEP's characteristic features, though not democratic, strongly resembled those Gorbachev now ascribes to perestroika. They included a more limited and liberal form of one-party rule; official tolerance of considerable economic and social pluralism; a market economy composed of state, cooperative, and individual enterprises; intellectual and cultural activities relatively unrestricted by heavy-handed censorship; and broader parameters of debate and open conflict in sanctioned political institutions, including the Communist Party.

Perestroika is not and could not be simply a replication of the policies of the 1920s, when the Soviet Union was a predominantly backward, illiterate country of 125 million peasants. Nonetheless, NEP is perestroika's ancestral forerunner and the primary source of its ideological legitimacy. As Gorbachev and his reformers have made clear, the "lessons of NEP" are an essential part of their "renewal of socialism." Indeed, the lineage between NEP and perestroika is personified in the especially fulsome rehabilitation of the Bolshevik leader Nikolai Bukharin, who after Lenin's death in 1924 was the leading Politburo theorist and defender of NEP, first against the party's left opposition and then unsuccessfully against Stalin in 1928-29. Condemned as an "enemy of the people" at the notorious 1938 Moscow purge trial and executed on Stalin's orders, Bukharin was fully exonerated by the Gorbachev leadership in February 1988 and is now being honored as a forefather of perestroika.

The latter-day origins of perestroika lie, however, squarely in the first period of post-Stalin reform, from 1953 to 1964, led by Nikita Khrushchev. Because he was deposed by his Politburo colleagues and his role excised from official history for more than twenty years, many Western scholars have concluded that Khrushchev failed as a leader. They see in this only ominous signs for Gorbachev. But it makes little sense to evaluate a leader's record only by how his career ended. Khrushchev held office longer than has any American president except Franklin Roosevelt, and during those years he had many achievements as well as failures. His reform policies were limited and often ill prepared, and as a leader he was an erratic, conflicted figure—an anti-Stalinist shaped and constricted by his own Stalinist past, a man receptive to progressive ideas but frequently lurching back to retrograde ones, the patron of a new generation of which he was also wary. And yet, Khrushchev was a historic Soviet leader. Without the reforms he introduced, which changed the Soviet Union in fundamental and lasting ways, it is hard to imagine the rise of Gorbachev's full-scale reformation twenty years later.

Consider the most important ones. Under Khrushchev, Stalin's twenty-five-year mass terror was ended, millions of people freed from concentration camps and exile, the political police's Gulag empire radically curtailed, much of the truth told about the crimes of the past, and an irreparable blow dealt to the Stalin cult and its oppressive array of ideological and policy dogmas. As a result, personal despotism was ended and the Communist Party, with a form of collective leadership at its head, restored to primacy in the political system. Equally important, long-term investment was greatly increased in areas involving people's everyday needs—housing, consumer goods and services, and welfare—so that most Soviet citizens lived considerably better as a result of Khrushchev's years in power. No less ramifying, censorship was reduced sufficiently to produce the Khrushchev "thaw"—a first though lesser experiment with glasnost—which revived intellectual and cultural life, gave the intelligentsia a much larger role in political affairs, and marked the emergence of public opinion as a significant factor. Nor should we forget that having repudiated a number of Stalin's Cold War dogmas, Khrushchev was, along with President Dwight D. Eisenhower, the cofounder of what later became known as detente.

Great reforms anywhere are not a single event but a multi-chapter process that unfolds fitfully over decades, if only because they always encounter powerful opposition and widespread conservative resistance. Though the analogy is imperfect, Franklin Roosevelt's New Deal was a perestroika of American capitalism that began in the 1930s and continued, with major advances and setbacks, well into the 1960s, and whose last chapter may not yet have been written. Viewed in this way, the changes introduced by Khrushchev constituted the first chapter in the reformation of the Soviet Stalinist system—the beginning of perestroika, even though the word was not yet in use. However partial and though eventually stopped by his successors, Khrushchev's reforms created a precedent to inspire another chapter and a foundation upon which to build.

Still more, his struggle against neo-Stalinist elites and popular sentiments gave birth to an anti-Stalinist movement inside the modern-day Soviet Communist Party. Its inaugural event was the historic Twentieth Party Congress in February 1956, where Khrushchev delivered his stunning exposé of Stalin's mass crimes. The speech became the charter document of the anti-Stalinist movement. Though not published in the Soviet Union until March 1989, its contents became widely known at the time. In response to Khrushchev's leadership during the next eight years, anti-Stalinist reformers emerged in every area of the Soviet system, so much so that the movement grew much larger than its founding father and acquired a political life of its own, particularly in the realm of socialist ideology and programmatic thinking. With only a few exceptions, and despite his complaints about excessive bureaucracy, Khrushchev's policies did not seek to remove Stalinist state controls over society, but they inspired many ideas that proposed to do so and that survived his downfall. Suffice it to say that almost every ideological perspective and policy proposal now associated with Gorbachev's perestroika can be found, in one form or another, in discussions that began in newspapers, mass journals, and specialized publications under Khrushchev.

In short, the anti-Stalinist movement born under Khrushchev eventually grew, after many years of bitter political defeat and agony, into the perestroika movement led by Gorbachev in the 1980s. Its history is embodied in the first post-Stalin generation of young men and women who began their careers in the Khrushchev 1950s and early 1960s, becoming heirs to the reformist tradition he founded. A remarkable number of those people stand in the forefront of Gorbachev's reformation. They are, to use a Soviet expression, "the vanguard of perestroika." They include most of the people in this book, who characterize themselves as "children of the Twentieth Party Congress," which means, of course, Khrushchev's political offspring, as well as Mikhail Gorbachev, who began his career as a young party politician in 1955. Here, too, it can hardly be said that Khrushchev failed. Nor should it surprise us that by mid-1989 his official rehabilitation was well underway in Moscow.

To complete this interpretation of the origins of perestroika we must also call into question the Western view that overlooks or minimizes political diversity long existing inside the Soviet Communist Party. Political reactions to Khrushchev's reform policies were so diverse, and conflicts over them so great, that something akin to rival "parties" took shape inside the one-party Communist system. Precise language may be lacking here. They were not political parties in the Western sense. And because intra-party factions had been banned by Lenin and murderously eradicated by Stalin, nor were they formal entities. But they were more than merely inchoate tendencies. As time went on, each acquired distinctive ideas derived from Marxism-Leninism, a loose network of association and communication, institutional affiliation, and even publications. However we term these rival ideological and policy movements—crypto-parties, groupings, or "parties"—an awareness of their crimped, shadowy existence from the mid-1950s to the mid-1980s is necessary to understand Soviet political history from Khrushchev to Gorbachev.

At least three movements had formed inside the Communist Party by the time Khrushchev was overthrown in 1964: an anti-Stalinist "party" calling for a more far-reaching relaxation of state controls over society; a neo-Stalinist one charging that Khrushchev's policies had gravely weakened the state and demanding that it be rejuvenated; and a conservative "party" mainly devoted to preserving the existing post-Stalin status quo by opposing further major changes, whether forward or backward. During the next twenty years, these "multiparty" conflicts were waged in largely muted and subterranean ways. The conservative majority headed by Brezhnev ruled the Soviet Union, with some concessions to the neo-Stalinists, for almost two decades. The reform movement barely survived, but in 1985, along with Gorbachev, it came to power. Since that time, the polarizing conflicts engendered by perestroika, and the open polemics released by glasnost, leave no doubt that a de facto multiparty political situation is raging in the Soviet one-party system. In fact, by 1988 calls for a de jure multiparty system were being openly discussed in the Soviet press, including proposals that the Communist Party reconstitute itself into at least two parties to accommodate its own friends and foes of perestroika.

This is not the place for a detailed account of how anti-Stalinist reformers survived the long harsh winter of Soviet conservatism under Leonid Brezhnev. The great majority of those who did not abandon their convictions worked quietly, usually without promotion, at lower or middle levels in party, state, or soviet institutions. The fates of other reformers are represented by many of the people interviewed or discussed in this book. A few were sent into ambassadorial exile. Many more took refuge in academic institutes or cryptic journalism. Artists often had their best work banned until 1985. Some reformers became persecuted dissidents or emigrés. And a few, like the agricultural innovator Ivan Khudenko, died at the hands of local authorities. The full story of their saga remains to be told.

Nor can we explore here all the reasons why the party's reform movement headed by Gorbachev emerged victorious in the spring of 1985, though several important factors should be mentioned. By the late 1970s, the statist administrative system inherited from Stalin had brought the Soviet Union to what Gorbachev has described as a "precrisis." Among other indications, the economy had virtually stopped growing and technology lagged badly behind Western advances; consumer shortages, popular cynicism, alcoholism, workplace indifference, bureaucratic corruption, mafia-like crime, rural decay, ecological abuses, and social injustices had become widespread; and infants were dying in great numbers while adult life expectancy was declining. Censorship maintained public silence about most of these problems and their magnitude, but they were generally known to the ruling elites, including many high officials who were deeply concerned about their country's well-being at home and standing abroad. The growing welter of "precrisis" problems shook their confidence in longstanding Stalinist dogmas, particularly about the state-run economy, and made them more receptive to reformist solutions.

Meanwhile, a larger process that can be called de-Stalinization from below had been underway for many years. Far-reaching and autonomous social changes—among them, acclimation to city life and the spread of urban culture, the maturing of generations with much more education and exposure to the West, and the proliferation of professional groups and other middle-class strata—had made the Soviet Union profoundly unlike the "society of cogs in the Stalinist machine" of the 1930s, as Soviet writers now characterize that era. This inexorable process of de-Stalinization from below further exacerbated the inadequacies of the fifty-year-old Stalinist bureaucratic system. It could no longer effectively control an economy or society of such complexity. By the end of the 1970s, large segments of both had escaped the state's control, while the remainder responded with declining productivity. Despite the state's efforts to maintain a Red orthodoxy, as a Soviet scholar has aptly remarked, the economy developed its own "black market" and society its "black pluralism." Nor were party and state elites, with their greatly enhanced levels of education and professionalism, immune to all these social changes. This too gave the reform "party" a much larger constituency than it had had before.

By the early 1980s, the main obstacle to a new chapter of reform from above was the generation of aged officials who had begun their careers under Stalin in the 1930s. Now in their seventies, they had ruled the Soviet Union since Khrushchev's overthrow, with Brezhnev at their head. Having survived so many historical traumas, and identifying with the administrative system that had raised them so high and awarded them lifetime bureaucratic peerages, they were profoundly conservative. Brezhnev's death in November 1982 triggered the politics of leadership succession, but he was only one of scores of ailing septuagenarian influentials who passed from the scene in an inevitable procession. Thus the way was cleared for a reform movement swept along on a tide of generational change.

The choice of Yuri Andropov to succeed Brezhnev as general secretary marked the resurgence of the reform "party" in two important respects. Although already aged and ailing, he was known to be the most reform-minded senior member of Brezhnev's Politburo and a man with ties to younger reformers dating back to the 1960s. Andropov's selection showed that even the aged oligarchy, faced with growing problems and reformist sentiments, felt the need for at least some kind of limited change. It also enabled more radical reformers, with Andropov's help, to reenter or approach the center stage of Soviet politics. Andropov's death in February 1984, and the last stand of the Stalin generation under his seventy-two-year-old successor Konstantin Chernenko, who died in office thirteen months later, only slowed the resurgence of the reform movement. It was already gathered and waiting for Gorbachev, then the youngest member of the Politburo.

The man who has led the Soviet Union since 1985, is not, therefore, an aberration but the leader of a political movement, however embattled, with a long history in the Communist Party. One question cannot yet be answered with certainty. When did Gorbachev, who rose steadily in the conservative party apparatus over a period of almost thirty years, put himself at the head of the radical reform "party"? Many Western scholars believe that he recognized the need for a full-scale anti-Stalinist reformation only a year or more after becoming general secretary, when he discovered the full extent of the country's problems. Though not conclusive, there is evidence that points to a different interpretation of his political biography.

It suggests that even as a Moscow University student in the early 1950s, and then as a provincial party secretary in Stavropol, Gorbachev was already reform-minded. That soon after being promoted to Moscow in 1978 and appointed a Politburo member, he began to seek policy advice informally from well-known radical reformers. Certainly, by the early 1980s his speeches sometimes echoed their ideas, and when he took office in March 1985 representatives of the reform "party" soon appeared as his formal or informal advisers. Gorbachev no doubt learned much in office that altered his thinking, but it seems likely he was already committed to the de-Stalinization, or perestroika, of the Soviet system. If so, his cautious conduct during his first year or so in office is not baffling. A leader who wishes to introduce great reforms in a conservative country must also be a clever politician. As Gorbachev resumed the reformation begun by Khrushchev, surely he had learned that from the fate of his predecessor.

In 1989, a large number of articles appeared in the Western press commenting on the fourth anniversary of Gorbachev's rise to power. Focusing on the most serious shortcomings and disruptive consequences of his policies, many commentaries read like obituaries of perestroika. They left the impression that it had failed or soon would do so. "Perestroika isn't working," *Newsweek* reported. It seemed only a matter of time before Gorbachev's opponents would "topple him or eliminate his reforms."

As those articles pointed out, the Soviety economy remained in bad shape. The GNP had grown barely 1.5 percent in 1988, while food and other consumer shortages were even more acute in some areas than they had been in 1985. Too much disposable income chasing too few commodities had fueled inflation. And the state budget deficit had swollen due partly to an abortive campaign to curtail vodka sales and to the enormous costs of the 1986 Chernobyl nuclear disaster and 1988 Armenian earthquake. Meanwhile, Gorbachev's democratization and glasnost policies had spawned a multitude of raucous "informal" organizations challenging established political authority from the capital to provincial towns. Even more ominous, they had unleashed pent-up nationalist aspirations and ethnic hatreds in the vast multinational Soviet federation. Mass protests, some of them violent, erupted in several republics, from Estonia, Latvia, and Lithuania to Armenia, Azerbaijan, and Georgia. All this and more, including the possibility of greater unrest in Eastern Europe, convinced many observers that powerful Soviet elites and public opinion, already indifferent to perestroika, had turned against Gorbachev's reforms, frustrating the adoption of effective measures and thwarting ones already enacted.

None of those developments should be minimized, and still graver threats to perestroika may lie ahead. But they should not be taken as a full picture or basis for a reasoned analysis of Gorbachev's years in office. Given the epic dimensions of perestroika as a reformation—or, as the leadership proclaims, "a revolutionary political, economic, social, and psychological transformation"—its initial failures and traumas were predictable. A more balanced evaluation of them can be found in the interviews below and in the Soviet press, which openly acknowledges their gravity as the "unavoidable costs of change and democratization." Nor is there reason to think that Gorbachev expected his reforms to unfold quickly or painlessly. He has spoken candidly about the "risks" of perestroika and the enormous obstacles it faces, and about his own leadership mainly in terms of making a long process of change "irreversible," rather than of being able to see it through to the end.

In an economy as large, rigid, and problem-infested as the Soviet one, the transition to a new system will take years and involve serious dislocations. Moreover, many economic reformers insist that higher growth rates during the transition would be a negative indicator if there is to be a real shift from quantity to quality of production. As for the proliferation of unofficial political organizations, some of their behavior no doubt exceeds what Gorbachev would prefer, but they are largely the anticipated results of his own policies of "democratization" and "socialist pluralism." In any event, he has said little to discourage and much to encourage their activities. Nationalist unrest, with its potential to destabilize the Soviet Union, is a different matter, but here too it seems that only its intensity, not its existence, may have surprised Gorbachev and his advisers. And while demonstrations and ethnic conflicts in several republics have endangered his policies, thus far his leadership has contained them with remarkably little use of the coercion at its disposal.

Despite many generalizations in the Western press, no one knows exactly how the disappointments and disorders since 1985 have affected mass attitudes toward Gorbachev's perestroika, not even Soviet pollsters, who are now officially encouraged to study public opinion. The Soviet Union is an exceedingly diverse country, and the various reforms collectively known as perestroika mean different things to different segments of the populace. Clearly, in a nation whose citizens have long relied on a cradle-to-grave welfare state that may provide relatively meager benefits but demands little hard work or personal responsibility in return, there is widespread resistance to the kind of new social contract Gorbachev is proposing. Sixty years of deeply engrained Stalinist dogmas are also a major obstacle. Many people dislike cooperative and individual enterprises—some of them have been torched or looted—as well as other innovations that "betray our socialism." In addition, as the leadership admits, "people are fed up with shortages and with standing in lines." After more than four years, popular belief in the necessity or feasibility of perestroika will be hard to sustain if it does not soon begin to satisfy people's needs.

But it is a mistake to exaggerate the consumer demands of most Soviet citizens, whose living standards and expectations are far below those in the West, or to overlook the legions of enthusiastic perestroika supporters in every walk of life. They include many of the most entrepreneurial city and village dwellers, capable workers, peasants, managers, scientists, technicians, teachers, and artists, idealistic junior officials, and democratic-minded members of the party's rank and file. Crudely stated, Gorbachev is counting on his country's best and brightest citizens. To assume that the Soviet Union lacks such people in large numbers would be both unwise and contemptuous. All that can be said with certainty, as the Soviet press regularly reports, is that perestroika has "polarized" much of public opinion, while the rest remains undecided or apathetic.

Nor should powerful political opposition to perestroika be interpreted out of context. That it exists at middle and very high levels in the party and state apparatuses is evidenced by what has and has not happened since 1985—by Gorbachev's inability to alter the composition of either the Politburo or the Central Committee decisively in his favor; by compromises he has had to make in reform legislation; by bureaucratic "sabotaging" of policies already adopted; by frank admissions on the part of Gorbachev's supporters that publications such as the famous Nina Andreyeva letter published in a Central Committee newspaper in March 1988 are manifestos of "the anti-perestroika forces"; by similar speeches at the Nineteenth Party Conference in mid-1988; and by constant complaints about high-level efforts "to stop perestroika on the pretext of saving socialism." Indeed, at a Central Committee meeting on April 25, 1989, several provincial party bosses blamed perestroika, and thus by implication Gorbachev, for most of the country's problems, including social unrest, economic disorder, rising crime rates, disarray in the Communist Party, desecration of Soviet history, and a plague of "ideological AIDS."

And yet, if equally or more powerful pro-perestroika forces did not also exist in those same high places, Gorbachev could not have survived four years of radical changes, turmoil, and opposition. At that same Central Committee plenum where his policies were so sharply and openly assailed, for example, he nonetheless forced the retirement of a large number of its other members who had strong reasons to resent his leadership. As with most national leaders, Gorbachev's authority at home depends partly on his foreign policies, which have been unusually successful. Jettisoning longstanding Soviet national security dogmas for "new thinking," he managed to bring a Cold War American president to five summit meetings, including one in Moscow; negotiate a treaty abolishing a whole category of U.S.-Soviet missiles in Europe; end the disastrous nine-year Soviet war in Afghanistan and the twenty-five-year cold war with China; improve relations with Western Europe, Japan, and even Israel; and win for himself extraordinary international popularity. In the final analysis, however, Gorbachev has endured politically because he leads a reform movement at home, a "party" within the Communist Party, with a long historical tradition, a compelling program, and many official and rank-and-file followers in the "bloodless civil war," as Soviet writers have called it, raging over perestroika.

Above all, premature obituaries of perestroika dismiss or discount its remarkable accomplishments since 1985. In four years, the equivalent of one American presidential term, Gorbachev legislated virtually his entire program for a Soviet reformation. Additional laws, enabling acts, and probably constitutional changes will still be needed, but the general political, economic, social, and cultural features of perestroika, including their philosophy and stated goals, are now ratified in state and party documents. For the first time since 1929, the Soviet government is officially committed to creating a system and kind of socialism radically unlike Stalinism. Would any serious observer give low marks to a first-term American president with such a legislative record on the grounds that it had encountered problems and not yet been fully implemented?

Of perestroika's several components, Gorbachev's economic reforms have been the least successful not only because the structural problems are so large but because change must be implemented by recalcitrant ministerial and other bureaucracies—or at least with their acquiescence. Many forms of "sabotage" are underway in that conservative labyrinth stretching from the capital to the localities. Various agencies are simply ignoring new laws designed to free state enterprises from Moscow's tutelage, contriving new directives in the guise of reform, denying licenses to aspiring cooperative and individual firms or suffocating them with excessive taxation and regulations, devising technicalities to deprive peasants of their new right to lease land, and imposing more restrictions on local markets. For these and other reasons, including the leadership's fear of ending state subsidies and deregulating consumer prices, a flourishing market sector may be years in the making. Even so, fundamental economic reforms are underway in the Soviet Union for the first time since the 1930s. The formation of non-state property, particularly cooperative property, is on the rise with official backing. And increasing numbers of managers, workers, peasants, and small business people are exercising the rights given to them by Gorbachev's legislation.

Gorbachev's glasnost policies, on the other hand, have already been implemented with spectacular success since 1985, largely because they faced many fewer bureaucratic obstacles and had many more eager supporters. Soviet censorship continues to operate in formal and informal ways, but it has been dramatically reduced. Thousands of previously banned historical and contemporary subjects, forms of popular culture, ideas, authors, books, articles, and archive documents now flood the mass media. Moscow newspapers, journals, artistic unions, and theaters began the assault on "forbidden zones" and taboo subjects, but national television and radio programs have caught up and are carrying glasnost to the provinces, where bureaucratic opposition is more entrenched. Despite important limits on free speech, there is an ongoing explosion of public information and opinion. The decades-long coverup of everything from

Stalin's genocidal policies and current abuses of power to economic, social, and ecological calamities is over. As a result, Soviet political, intellectual, and cultural life has become extraordinarily rich and interesting. It is said, "People can't eat glasnost," but glasnost is an essential component of Gorbachev's perestroika, and many Soviet citizens consider it one of his greatest achievements.

The ongoing public trial of Stalinism is an especially important part of glasnost. Brezhnev's conservative restoration stopped partial revelations about the past initiated by Khrushchev and rehabilitated the Stalinist period as a "heroic and positive" era. Under Gorbachev, the whole criminal history of Stalin's twenty-five-year rule is being told in the mass media, from the murderous assault on the peasantry during collectivization to the massive political terror that continued until the despot's death. The Soviet press now confirms that tens of millions of innocent men, women, and children perished in the holocaust caused by Stalinism. An authoritative account published in 1989 revealed for the first time, for example, that "almost 20 million people" were arrested just from January 1, 1935, to the German invasion on June 22, 1941; 7 million were shot and the rest dispatched to forced labor camps, where most of them died. All this is being related with graphic details of famine, deportations, torture, executions, slow death in the camps, and orphaned children. Killing fields and mass graves used fifty years ago by Stalin's police, the NKVD, are even being uncovered near many cities. Nor has the Gorbachev leadership avoided its official responsibility. It has rehabilitated the original Communist elite slaughtered by Stalin. And faced with millions of other fraudulent cases against ordinary citizens, it has simply declared them to have been "falsified," exonerating most of the victims *en masse* and setting up special commissions to help surviving relatives.

Without truth-telling and historical justice of this magnitude, Gorbachev's proposed reformation stands no chance. Only a full national process of moral reckoning can free the Soviet socialist idea from the Stalinist past and its "barracks socialism." As the nation is being told by the mass media, "Stalinism lives on today" not only in the system's institutions and administrative controls over society but in widespread popular dogmas and habitual submission to bureaucratic authority. Unless those legacies are exorcized, the leadership's call for perestroika "from below" will fall on too many hostile or fearful ears. Gorbachev's anti-Stalinist campaign unfolded cautiously until 1987, but since then it has grown into a fervent crusade. Clearly, he and his supporters are determined, as one remarked, "to drive a stake through this vampire's heart once and for all." Little now remains of the once glorious official history of the Stalinist 1930s and 1940s, which are being portrayed as a "catastrophic tragedy" imposed by an illegitimate regime that treated people like "cogs in a bureaucratic machine." Until Gorbachev became leader, such criticisms were routinely punished as political crimes. Now they are guiding tenets in the leadership's program, ideology, and dialogue with the nation. In the context of Gorbachev's proposed reformation, that too is a historic achievement.

Finally, there are the large-scale political reforms that Gorbachev terms "democratization." Legislation adopted since 1985 promises in effect to create a new kind of Soviet political system featuring "a state based on the rule of law." These reforms call for turning the former rubber-stamp Supreme Soviet into a real national parliament; transferring governmental power from party and state bureaucracies across the country to the thousands of local soviets whose deputies are to be chosen in multi-candidate elections; forming a more just and humane legal and penal system that also would protect civil liberties against bureaucratic caprice and other abuses of power; and giving considerably more sovereignty to the fifteen national republics that make up the Soviet Union.

Most of these ambitious democratic reforms still are only on paper, but not all of them. Since 1985, along with the spread of glasnost, a far-reaching process of liberalization has taken place in the Soviet Union. Hundreds of political prisoners have been released, the criminal code partly depoliticized, and the KGB and regular police force exposed to some public scrutiny. Restrictions on religious worship and foreign travel have been considerably reduced, and a number of once persecuted dissidents have become active in sanctioned politics. Encouraged by Gorbachev's endorsement of "socialist pluralism," thousands of unofficial fronts, associations, and clubs have emerged around the country to compete with the Communist Party and other established organizations, thereby ending the one-party state's sixty-year monopoly on political life. With them have come, at national and grass-roots levels, a multitude of new political activists and leaders. Insurgent groups demanding democratization have formed even inside the 20 million-member Communist Party and its 36 million-member junior counterpart, the Young Communist League, or Komsomol. Indeed, political glasnost has begun to penetrate the party's Central Committee, whose voting and uncensored proceedings were made public in 1989 for the first time since the 1920s.

Above all, perhaps, the country has held its first national multi-candidate election since 1917. In a complex process lasting from March to May 1989, the nation elected a new 2,250-member Congress of People's Deputies. Leaving aside 750 members from various public organizations, approximately 75 per cent of the deputies were chosen in multi-candidate district elections preceded by hotly contested and widely publicized campaigns. Among the losing candidates were many powerful state officials, party bosses, and other dignitaries. Among the winners were many unorthodox political figures, including young grassroots activists, radical intellectuals, the maverick party politician Boris Yeltsin, and the former dissidents Andrei Sakharov and Roy Medvedev.

The Soviet system is still far from being democratic, but Gorbachev's policies have moved farther and faster in that direction than almost anyone imagined possible. Some Western observers interpreted the defeat of so many party and state officials in the 1989 elections as a defeat for Gorbachev's leadership. That was not the case. As with "democratization" more generally, the introduction of multi-candidate elections was his reform. And as he and his allies rightly claimed, the results were a popular referendum in favor of perestroika and a major blow against its opponents. Here too there is hardly any reason to conclude that Gorbachev's reformation has already failed.

My effort to give a more balanced evaluation of Gorbachev's reforms since 1985 should not be taken as an argument that perestroika is certain to succeed. Despite what has already been accomplished, the process of change still could be stopped and even reversed. To do so at this stage would probably require considerable repression, but in a country with a long despotic tradition, that too is conceivable. No one can foresee the future of a full-scale reformation that has just begun, that faces so many enormous obstacles, and that will need so many years to unfold—not even the people interviewed below, participants in these historic events. As for those of us in the West who study the Soviet Union, we have barely begun to find ways to think about all the dimensions and complexities of perestroika, or even the language to describe them. At best, only a few generalizations and unanswerable questions about the future are possible.

Just as revolutions always bring forth counterrevolution, reformations are always opposed by powerful forces of counterreformation. The struggle over perestroika is being waged at every level of the Soviet system and in every area of Soviet life—not just between the ruling officialdom and the people but within those party and state bureaucracies and society itself. Given the vast dimensions of perestroika and all the vested interests it threatens, there is no reason to expect this "civil war" to diminish or be decided conclusively in the foreseeable future. Moreover, even if perestroika is largely implemented over a long historical period, its opponents are likely to win some major battles along the way, as happened during the decades-long history of the New Deal. All that can be said with any confidence is that the struggle will go on, and many of us will not live long enough to witness the eventual outcome.

That is also why constant Western speculation about Gorbachev's own position, which fluctuates between announcing his "consolidation of power" and predicting his downfall, is pointless. No one can know what lies ahead, not even Gorbachev; too many unpredictable and incalculable developments, manmade and otherwise, are possible. It is enough to understand, as Machiavelli put it, that a great reformer is always an endangered prince. Even as his reforms begin to succeed, deepen, and become more radical, supporters often grow less staunch, conservative enemies more numerous, and the risks he must take still greater. Nor should we overlook the fact that, for the first time since Lenin, a Soviet leader is relying more on the force of his ideas and program than on the power of an *apparat*. Thus far, Gorbachev's high-level opponents have tried to emasculate his radical policies rather than to remove him, perhaps because they lack a credible leader of their own. But even in the best of political circumstances, so long as he stands at the head of a Soviet reformation, Gorbachev will always be an embattled leader.

Indeed, programmatic alternatives challenging his radical reforms have already appeared in the official Soviet press. Not surprisingly, they come from the other longstanding "parties" inside the Communist Party. One demands conservative solutions to the country's problems instead of a reformation—for the most part, limited economic changes without the Gorbachevian "excesses" (as they are derisively called by his opponents) of glasnost, anti-Stalinism, and democratization. The other anti-Gorbachev challenge comes from the party's neo-Stalinist, openly counterreformist wing, which clamors for a revival of despotic state power, reimposition of social order and ideological orthodoxy, and restoration of Cold War policies toward the outside world. Considering the enormity of the Soviet Union's problems and the fact that glasnost has made them known to virtually every citizen, it seems unlikely that the conservative center, or a muddle-through leadership, could now govern the country effectively or for any length of time. The real choice, as a pro-Gorbachev editorial in *Izvestia* emphatically declared in April 1989, is either "a Stalinist kind of 'order' or democracy with its inevitable costs."

Whatever the balance of forces, the struggle over perestroika will be fought not only in Moscow—over the actual power of the new national "parliament," for example—but also on crucial battlefields in the provinces. One pits the fledgling cooperative economic movement against hostile local authorities and popular suspicions of even this "socialist" form of private enterprise. The number of registered cooperatives grew dramatically between January 1988 and January 1989, from 13,921 firms employing 155,880 people to 77,548 with 1.4 million employees, but they remain a tiny fraction of the economy. In the more congenial environment of Moscow, for example, in April 1989 they provided only 2.2 percent of the city's consumer goods and services. Unless the cooperative movement, including small manufacturing enterprises and banks, can overcome the array of barriers in the provinces, where most citizens live, there will be no flourishing Soviet marketplace, substantial nonstate property, or economic reformation.

The same is true of Gorbachev's political reforms, which are closely related. As in the West, the lives of Soviet citizens are most directly affected by local government—in their case, local Communist Party secretaries and soviet executive committees. But it is there that official opposition to all of Gorbachev's reforms is most broadly and deeply entrenched. Unlike Peter the Great and Stalin, with whom he is mistakenly compared, Gorbachev cannot root it out with centralized state power. Even if he had the capacity to do so, which he does not, it would undermine his own program to de-Stalinize the Soviet system by reducing the reach of the state. That is why he is counting on perestroika "from below."

Gorbachev is hoping that "democratization," and particularly the broadening process of multi-candidate elections, will eventually oust or overwhelm local soviet and party conservatives. The results of the 1989 national election may have confirmed his assumption that a majority of ordinary citizens, party members and nonmembers alike, will rally behind perestroika if they are given a democratic opportunity to fight its bureaucratic opponents. More than 87 percent of the winning candidates, including those who defeated powerful party bosses, were Communist Party members. But provincial soviet and party elections, which are only beginning, are a different battleground. If nothing else, local authorities will find many more ways to manipulate the electoral process, and insurgent candidates and voters much less glasnost to protect them. If Gorbachev's supporters are right in speaking of an ongoing civil war, even fiercer battles will have to be fought in the provinces.

In the final analysis, however, the largest obstacle confronting Gorbachev's proposed reformation is not any specific elite or group. It is Russia's long tradition of bureaucratic state power over society that began centuries before the Revolution and reached a new apotheosis in the Stalinist system. Has the grip of that powerful statist tradition been considerably weakened by social and political developments in recent decades? Has a Soviet civil society matured sufficiently to take on the self-governing and other initiatives from below necessary if Gorbachev's perestroika is to succeed? Those crucial questions are being passionately debated in the Soviet press. But as readers will see from the interviews that follow, no one really knows the answers.

20   Authoritarianism

While pluralism is often characterized as the domination of the state by society, totalitarianism can be viewed as the reverse—the domination of society by the state. In the following reading, Juan Linz, a professor of political sociology at Yale University, argues that the political experiences of many countries do not fit easily into either of these categories. In these countries, which Linz classifies as authoritarian, the state penetrates society but does not dominate it. Drawing upon the example of Spanish politics during the era of Francisco Franco's dictatorship, Linz outlines the distinctive characteristics of authoritarian regimes and explores the balance of forces that can make authoritarian systems stable. Typically, authoritarian regimes exercise limited control over society; some interests are shaped by the state, but others enjoy a measure of autonomy. Mass participation is discouraged because it is viewed as a potential threat to order, yet the power of authoritarian leaders is constrained by, and exercised through, an often uneasy coalition of elites representing military, economic, clerical, and other traditional as well as civilian bureaucratic interests. In the absence of a single ideal or coherent ideology justifying the legitimacy of the state, authoritarian regimes claim the role of guarantors of traditional values. Linz's article, "An Authoritarian Regime: Spain," appears in *Mass Politics: Studies in Political Sociology.*

● ● ● ● ● ● ● ● ● ●

TYPES OF POLITICAL SYSTEMS
This paper attempts to conceptualize some differences between political systems, taking the present Spanish regime as example and point of departure. In the decades since World War II, the distinction elaborated by political scientists between democratic governments and totalitarian societies has proven useful scientifically and even more polemically. The terms democratic and totalitarian have come to be used as dichotomous or as least as a continuum. An effort is made to fit various regimes into one or the other type, often basing the decision on nonscientific criteria. While the classification has been useful, it is increasingly necessary to go beyond it. From the beginning social scientists have felt uneasy about placing countries like Spain, and even Fascist Italy or pre-1945 Japan, into the total-

itarian category. The uneasiness has grown as they came to deal with the "progressive" one-party regimes of the underdeveloped areas and the "modernizing" military dictatorships. So for example A. Inkeles remarks on

> ... a mode of analysis which can encompass totalitarian systems as divergent in their concrete institutional structure as the Communist and Nazi systems, which most closely approximate the ideal type; Fascist Italy, which only imperfectly approximated it; and Franco Spain which only imperfectly fits the model in a few crucial respects.

Even a correspondent like Herbert Matthews, far from friendly to the Spanish regime, writes:

> The power [of Franco] is almost unlimited. This does not make Spain a totalitarian country in either the Communist or the Fascist sense. It is an authoritarian country. The authority is exercised by keeping all parts of the regime weak or in conflict with each other. Order is kept essentially because the Spanish people want it, and through the Army and police. This makes Franco's power supreme when he wants to exercise it. Since, like all modern dictators, he does not allow any single man or group to become strong and threaten his power, there is no alternative to Francisco Franco, at least no visible alternative. As long as his position is not attacked and the nation's affairs function smoothly, he keeps hands off.

Raymond Aron faced the same problem after characterizing the constitutional pluralist regimes and the regimes *de parti monopoliste*, when he wrote about a "third class of regime where there is no single party nor multiple parties, not based on electoral legitimacy nor on revolutionary legitimacy," giving as examples Portugal, Spain and the first phase of Vichy.

Gabriel Almond, in his important article on comparative political systems, has formulated most clearly some main characteristics of this type of regime which we shall call authoritarian; the term is used by many in this connection, even by spokesmen of such regimes. Almond writes:

> [The totalitarian political structure] is anti-pluralistic in intent and method if not in accomplishment. ... Recent developments in the Soviet Union seem to be directed toward providing some explicit structural bases for policy discussion and conflict. ... But what has so far been attained ... is far from the structural pluralism which is so typical for authoritarian regimes. If one takes such a system as that of Spain it is evident that religious bodies, organized interests, status

groups, bureaucratic agencies, as well as the Falange party are "acknowledged" elements in a pluralistic political structure. Interest conflict is built into the system, and is not merely latent and spasmodic as in the totalitarian pattern.

The structures of the two systems differ in a second significant respect. The totalitarian system tends to be highly mobilized, tense and expansive internally and externally. The authoritiarian tends to be more stable, more relaxed, athough these are differences in degree.

It could be argued that there is no need for a new type—the authoritarian—since regimes so described are really imperfect forms of either totalitarian or democratic polities, tending ultimately in one or the other direction and close, at least in their ideals, to one or the other pole. Failure to reach the totalitarian stage might be due to administrative inefficiency, economic underdevelopment, or external influences and pressures. In regimes approving in principle a Western "progressive" conception of democracy—like the Mexican or Turkish leadership after their national revolutions—failure might be attributed to economic backwardness and religious traditionalism. To formulate it as sociologists, we might say that when certain functional prerequisites for a stable democracy are absent, some form of authoritarianism is established, in order—presumably—to prepare the country for it; or in other cases a premature transition to democracy leads to a setback in the form of an authoritarian regime. From another angle, we might say that certain characteristics of the social structure make it impossible for those in power to move toward true totalitarianism without endangering their own position. This hypothesis assumes that those in power are deliberately pursuing a totalitarian social order, which strictly speaking may not be the case even for some stages in a transition which actually results in a totalitarian society.

We prefer for purposes of analysis to reject the idea of a continuum from democracy to totalitarianism and to stress the distinctive nature of authoritarian regimes. Unless we examine the features unique to them, the conditions under which they emerge, the conceptions of power held by those who shape them, regimes which are not clearly either democratic or totalitarian will be treated merely as deviations from these ideal types and will not be studied systematically and comparatively.

Like any ideal type, the notion of the authoritarian regime is an abstraction which underlines certain characteristics and ignores, at least for the time being, the fluidity of reality, differences in degree, and contradictory tendencies present in the real world. In any of the European regimes of the inter-war years that we would call authoritarian, Fascist elements played a role and significant minorities were striving for a totalitarian state;

the Hungary of Horthy, the colonels' regime in Poland, the Rumanian and Yugoslav royal dictatorships, the Portuguese Estado Novo, the Austrian corporative Dollfuss regime, Vichy, are examples. Today the model of the Soviet Union operates similarly in many underdeveloped areas. Such regimes exist under many formal garments and their lack of an elaborate and consistent ideology makes them particularly susceptible to mimicry.

The external forms of the thirties and forties, the uniforms and ceremonies and terminology, and the appeals of today to democratic or socialist values, are more easily assimilated than the institutional realities they represent. We may be seriously misled if we study such regimes through constitutions, laws, speeches, the writing of unknown and unrewarded "ideologists," without inquiring how these are actually translated into social reality. The laws may say, for example, that everyone has to be a member of certain organizations, but later almost nobody is; the law gives the corporative system a monopoly of interest representation, but a study of businessmen shows that they belong to literally hundreds of autonomous interest groups which existed before the regime came to power; a political indoctrination course is provided for in the universities but it turns out to be a course in labour and welfare institutions, and everyone is allowed to pass.

The utility of treating authoritarian regimes as a distinct type will lie in helping us understand the distinctive ways in which they resolve problems common to all political systems: maintaining control and gaining legitimacy, recruiting elites, articulating interests and aggregating them, making decisions and relating to various institutional spheres like the armed forces, religious bodies, the intelligentsia, the economy, etc. If we can find that they handle such problems differently from both democratic and totalitarian regimes, and furthermore if quite different regimes, classified as authoritarian, handle them in ways that turn out to be similar, the distinction will have been justified. Later we will explore in some detail a few examples along these lines. . . .

DEFINITION OF AN AUTHORITARIAN REGIME

Authoritarian regimes are political systems with limited, not responsible, political pluralism: without elaborate and guiding ideology (but with distinctive mentalities); without intensive nor extensive political mobilization (except at some points in their development); and in which a leader (or occasionally a small group) exercises power within formally ill-defined limits but actually quite predictable ones.

To avoid any confusion we want to make it clear that personal leadership is a frequent characteristic but not a necessary one, since a junta arrangement can exist and the leader's personality might not be the decisive factor. Furthermore, the leader does not need to have charismatic qualities, at least not for large segments of the population nor at all stages of development of the system. In fact he may combine elements of charismatic, legal and traditional authority in varying degrees, often at different points in time—though the charismatic element often tends to be more important than the legal authority, at least for some sectors of the population.

PLURALISM

We speak of regime, rather than government, to indicate the relatively low specificity of the political institutions: they often penetrate the life of the society, preventing, even forcibly, the political expression of certain group interests (as religion in Turkey and Mexico, labor in Spain) or shaping them by interventionist economic policies. But in contrast to some of the analysts of totalitarianism, such as Inkeles, we speak of regimes rather than societies because the distinction between state and society is not obliterated. The pluralistic element is the most distinctive feature of these regimes, but let us emphasize that in contrast to democracies with their almost unlimited pluralism, we deal here with *limited* pluralism. The limitation may be legal or de facto, serious or less so, confined to strictly political groups or extended to interest groups, as long as there remain groups not created by nor dependent on the state which influence the political process one way or another. Some regimes even institutionalize the political participation of a limited number of independently existing groups or institutions, and actually encourage their emergence. To take an example, when Primo de Rivera created his National Assembly he provided for the representation of the church, cultural institutions, the nobility, the army and the business community, as well as the newly created party; at the same time he encouraged the creation of economic interest groups that have been the pressure groups of Spanish business ever since. Another example is the institutionalization of a complex pluralism in the officially dominant Partido Revolucionario Institucional of Mexico, that prompts V. Padgett to write: "An 'official' party need not necessarily be an instrument of imposition. It may be a device for bridging the gap between authoritarianism and representative democracy." With such a limited but relatively autonomous pluralism, there is likely to be some competition for power, more or less informal, despite open declarations of monopoly. It is quite characteristic in this respect that the Falange, after entering the Franco coalition, dropped Point 27, which read:

> We shall work to triumph in the struggle with only the forces subject to our discipline. We shall make very few pacts. Only in the final push for the conquest of the state will the command arrange for the necessary collaborations, always provided that our predominance be assured.

This pluralism contrasts with the strong domination, if not the monopoly, imposed by the totalitarian party after conquering power; its penetration, through the process the Nazis called Gleichschaltung (synchronization), of all kinds of groups and organizations; the creation of functional organizations serving as transmission belts and auxiliaries for the party, politicizing even areas remote from politics, like sports and leisure.

Serrano Suñer, the once powerful brother-in-law of Franco, head of the Junta Politica, minister of interior and foreign affairs and master engineer of the decree founding the unified party, writes quite accurately and with awareness of the alternatives, as follows:

> In truth, be it an advantage or disadvantage, it is time to say that in Spain there has never been anything that would really look like a totalitarian state, since for this it seems to be a necessary condition that the single party should exist in strength and be really the sole basis of support for the regime—the only instrument and in a sense the only holder of power . . . the complex of forces participating in the Uprising—the army, traditional elements, parties, etc.—has never disappeared, thanks to a policy of equilibrium and through the persistence of the unified elements without ever fusing and without deciding in favor of a total pre-eminence of the official party.
>
> To give each his due: this regime has not been totalitarian as it has not been democratic or liberal. What it would have been without the world war only God knows. What it will finally be is still to be seen.

The difference between authoritarian and democratic pluralism is that the latter is in principle almost unlimited; it is not only tolerated but legitimate; and its open participation in the competition for power, through political parties, is institutionalized. In a democracy political forces not only reflect social forces, but represent them and to some extent commit them to the support of government policies once these are arrived at; political forces are dependent on the support of constituencies. The "iron law of oligarchy" may make this relative, but the formal principle is upheld.

In authoritarian regimes the men who come to power reflecting the views of various groups and institutions do not derive their position from the support of these groups alone, but from the trust placed in them by the leader, monarch or "junta," who certainly takes into account their prestige and influence. They have a kind of constituency, we might call it a potential constituency, but this is not solely or even principally the source of their power.

The co-optation of leaders is a constant process by which different sectors or institutions become participants in the system. In the consolidated totalitarian system this process takes place between bureaucracies or organizations that are part of the political structure created by the system, generally dependent on the party or an outgrowth of it; in the authoritarian regime pre-existent or newly emergent elements of the society can be represented by this means. The authoritarian regime may go very far toward suppressing existing groups or institutions inimical to the social order; this process of control may affect others, and the threat of control is always present; but due to a number of circumstances the control process is arrested. The strength of ideological commitments; the size, integration, quality of the group wishing a monopoly of power; the strength and legitimacy of existing institutions, and their international ties; the degree of economic autarchy possible; all are factors which may limit maximum suppression of dissidence. Ultimately the conception of power held by the authoritarian leader may make the decisive difference.

MENTALITY VERSUS IDEOLOGY

Styles of leadership, and different ways of conceiving the relation between state power and society, must be examined if we are to analyze the authoritarian regime in its various forms.

We will purposely use the term mentality rather than "ideology." The German sociologist Theodor Geiger has formulated a useful distinction between *ideologies*, which are systems of thought more or less intellectually elaborated and organized, often in written form, by intellectuals, pseudo-intellectuals, or with their assistance; and *mentalities*, which are ways of thinking and feeling, more emotional than rational, that provide non-codified ways of reacting to situations. Ideologies have a strong utopian element; mentalities are closer to the present or the past. Totalitarian systems have ideologies, a point emphasized by all students of such systems, while authoritarian regimes are based more on distinctive mentalities which are difficult to define. The more traditional an authoritarian regime is, the greater the role of the military and civil servants, the more important "mentalities" become in understanding the system, and the more a focus on ideologies, even those loudly proclaimed by the regime, may be misleading. . . .

APATHY VERSUS MOBILIZATION

Stabilized authoritarian regimes are characterized by lack of extensive and intensive political mobilization of the population. Membership participation is low in political and para-political organizations and participation in the single party or similar bodies, whether coerced, manipulated or voluntary, is infrequent and limited. The common citizen expresses little enthusiastic support for the regime in elections, referenda, and rallies. Rather than enthusiasm or support, the regime often expects — even from office holders and civil servants—passive acceptance, or at least they refrain from public anti-government activity. Let us stress this depolitization is characteristic of stabilized authoritarian regimes, but would not be necessarily true for their formative stages, particularly since their emergence in a crisis would involve considerable and often very intensive popular participation. We would like to argue that this participation is not likely to be maintained over a long period of time, unless the regime moves into a totalitarian or a more formally democratic direction. However, the degrees of mobilization might be the most useful criteria on which to distinguish subtypes of authoritarian regimes.

On the one side we have those that Raymond Aron has characterized as "regimes without parties" which "require a kind of depoliticization of the governed" and others we could call "populistic" in which there is a more continuous effort of mobilization, without reaching the pervasiveness and intensity of the totalitarian model. Recognizing the importance of such a distinction, we would like to suggest that often the difference might be more that of stages in the development of nondemocratic regimes than a substantive difference. It would be to misunderstand contemporary Spain to ignore the high level of participation in party activities, youth groups, politically oriented welfare activities—not to mention rallies, parades, etc.—during the years of the Civil War in Nationalistic Spain; and the intensity of involvement, ideological and emotional, of people in all sectors of the population must be stressed. No one can deny that this disappeared during the years after the victory. This was not only because, first, the leadership lacked interest in maintaining it, but also because the social structure of a semideveloped country, and the social, institutional and ideological pluralism, made such levels of participation untenable without either channeling them through organized parties or substituting that pluralism with a hierarchical, disciplined and ideologically committed single party. In the contest of the early forties, the first possibility was excluded and the will to impose a truly totalitarian system, destructive of the coalition character of the forces Franco led to victory, was absent from an army (including its leaders) which had no single well-defined ideology. I would like to leave the question open if in the future some of the more "populistic" one-party regimes in Africa and the Moslem countries will not undergo a similar process, transforming the parties and connected organizations into adjuncts of the state apparatus (the bureaucracy) and/or patronage organizations, with little genuine participation, even of a manipulative type. . . .

It would take too long to analyze here all the causes of low mobilization or our doubts about the capacity of such regimes to sustain a significant degree of mobilization for any length of time (without considerable changes in other respects—limitation of pluralism and emphasis on an ideology—in a totalitarian direction), but we may list at least some factors. In the absence of a modern revolutionary ideology, reformism, particularly bureaucratic and technocratic reformism, does not provide a chiliastic vision for action, and the structure of underdeveloped countries does not motivate sustained, regular day-to-day activity. . . . With social and economic change come the growth of private interests and the struggle to improve one's living standard. Only in a society where the government is the principal employer, or controls the economy as through co-operatives, can it offer financial rewards to the citizens who participate, but this does not insure that participation will be political; it may come to resemble participation in interest groups like those characterizing democratic society. Economic development and industrialization seem to be a precondition for a lively associational life under any system. Limited literacy and low incomes are such obstacles that only the diversion of considerable resources can assure participation for any length of time.

Undoubtedly such social and structural factors may be overcome if the leadership is really committed to the idea of a mobilized society, as the Communist and, even to a minor extent, the Italian Fascist experiences show. The very different attitude of one typical authoritarian leader is well described in these comments of Macartney writing about a Hungarian political leader in the 20's:

> He did not mean opposition ever to be in a position to seriously challenge his own will. But he did not think it any part of the duty of government to pry into and regiment each detail of the subject's conduct, much less his thoughts. For this he was too large-minded, or too cynical, too little a perfectionist. . . .

In authoritarian regimes, intermediate systems are frequent: membership may be obligatory but involve nothing more than paying dues, or strictly voluntary without creating any advantages. Presumably political goals take primacy in totalitarian organizations while specific interests predominate in democratic organizations. . . .

The depoliticization of officially created associations has certainly not been unique to Spain; with the "end of ideology," the politicization of interest and leisure groups characteristic of European democratic parties from the turn of the century to World War II has also receded. In fact it could be argued that authoritarianism provided a welcome relief from over-politicization in democratic societies which had not developed apolitical voluntary associations in proportion to the number of fiercely conflicting political groups. An Italian metal worker in his fifties expressed this when he said of his working class neighborhood in Genoa:

I was born here. Then everyone used to know each other, we used to get together, loved each other. After the war came politics. Now we all hate each other. You are a Communist, I am a Socialist, he is a Demo-Christian. And so we avoid each other as much as possible. . . .

THE AUTHORITARIAN PARTY

According to the legal texts of many authoritarian regimes, their single parties occupy a similarly dominant position: to the totalitarian party monopolizing power, recruiting the elite, transmitting both the aspirations of the people and the directives of the leadership. In fact, however, some regimes that in reality approach the totalitarian model legally have multi-party systems, while in others which are legally single party monopolies, the party plays a comparatively limited role. Therefore it is imperative to examine the authoritarian party in its sociological reality.

First and foremost, the authoritarian party is not a well-organized ideological organization which monopolizes all access to power. As we will see later, a considerable part of the elite has no connection with the party and does not identify with it. Party membership creates few visible advantages and imposes few, if any, duties. Ideological indoctrination is often minimal, the conformity and loyalty required may be slight, and expulsions and purges are not frequent and do not represent an important mechanism of social control. The party is often ideologically and socially hetero-geneous. Far from branching out into many functional organizations, in an effort to control the state apparatus and penetrate other spheres of life as the Nazi party did, it is a skelton organization of second-rate bureaucrats. The party becomes only one more element in the power plualism; one more group pressing for particular interests, one more channel through which divergent interests try to find access to power; one more recruiting ground for elite members. Since tight discipline lacks widespread ideological legit-imacy, various functional groups that might have been transmission belts for the leadership's directives, become apolitical interest groups, or autono-mous nuclei where a few activists, even those emerging from the grass roots, may follow independent policies.

The importance of the party has many indicators: the number of high officials that were active in the party before entering the elite; the mem-bership figures; the degree of activity indicated by the party budget; agit-prop activity; the prestige of power accorded to party officials; the presence of party cells or representatives in other institutions; the importance of training centers; the attention paid to party organs and publications; the vigor of ideological polemics within the party factions. By all these criteria the Spanish party has never been too strong and today is obviously weak. A look at the party's provincial headquarters, in contrast to other government offices of the Sindicatos (a functional organization theoretically dependent on the party) should convince anyone of the party's second-rate role in Spain.

The different roles of the authoritarian and totalitarian parties may be explained by differences in their origin. Most single parties in authoritarian countries have been created after accession to power rather than before. They have been created by fusing a variety of groups with different ideolological traditions and varying social bases, not by completely subordinating some elements to one dominant force. Where politicians of other groupings, including the minor Fascist parties, have been co-opted, no disciplined, integrated organization emerged. In other cases, when the military dictator has tried to create a patriotic national unity organization, the effort was carried out by officers and bureaucrats, who typically do not have the demagogic skills needed to create a lively organization. They are further hampered because they continue devoting most of their attention to government or army offices, where real power, and not merely the promise of it, lies. The old politicians, rallying to organizations like the Imperial Rule Assistance Association or the ex-CEDA (conservative-demochristian deputies in the Republic) leaders in the Falange, are not able to adopt the new style that a totalitarian party requires. Since the party is not tested in a struggle for power, it attracts more than its share of office seekers and opportunists, few idealists, true believers, real revolutionaries. Since its ideology is not defined, indoctrination of the numerous newcomers, entering en masse, is likely to be scanty, and the facts of life soon disillusion the more utopian. Since the primary staff need is to staff the state apparatus, the premium will be on recruiting professionals and bureaucrats, and not the armed intellectuals or bohemians, the marginal men that give the totalitarian movement its peculiar style.

The prominence of the army or civil service in the regime before the party was created, and the solidarity of these groups against newcomers when it comes to making key appointments, makes the rewards of party activity less appealing than membership in the NSDAP or, later, the SS. In underdeveloped countries the army is particularly important, since it does not like the rise of rivals and will seek to prevent the creation of anything like party militias or workers' guards. Any attempt to build up the party beyond a certain point, particularly after the German experience, is likely to encounter the open opposition of the army, as Perón soon discovered. . . . A comment by Serrano Suñer, former chairman of the Junta Politica of the party, describes the relation between army and political groups in many such regimes: "In the last analysis the center of gravity, the true support of the regime (despite all the appearances which we foolishly try to exaggerate) was and would continue to be the army; the nationalist army—an army that was not politically defined." . . .

FORMS OF SOCIAL CONTROL

Similarities between authoritarian regimes and the totalitarians can perhaps go furthest in the control of mass media, particularly in countries in the process of modernization where the technological and capital requirements for setting up the media make such control very easy. Media may vary greatly in autonomy, even under the same regime, but limited pluralism readily creates some islands of exemption; in Spain, for example, church publications are free from government censorship.

The small size of the elite and the persistence within the regime of ties created prior to it, allow for considerable free communication, unless the regime is willing to use a good deal of coercion. The same may be said of contacts with other countries, particularly by the elite. While the monopoly of mass media may be as great as that in totalitarian societies, the impact of this monopoly is less because it is not enhanced by intensive personal propagandizing through agitators and other informal leaders. Even when the freedom of the press is curtailed, truly totalitarian control is not present if there is freedom of travel and, at least, freedom of conversation. (As long as one does not make more than five copies of one's opinions, one cannot be prosecuted for illegal propaganda in Spain.) It may well be that the excesses of control to which a Stalin or Hitler went are really unnecessary. . . .

THE POSITION OF THE MILITARY

All political systems face the problem of subordinating the military to political authority, and once military dictators start devoting their energies to political problems, they face the same issue. Methods of controlling the military differ in democracies, totalitarian systems, and authoritarian regimes; the equilibrium established between political and military authority will differ as well. In most authoritarian regimes the limited popular consensus, which made such forms of rule necessary or possible in the first place, means there is more need for potential force; this gives the army a privileged position. Normally military affairs are left to military men and not to civilians. The absence of a mass party, and in some countries of a trustworthy and specialized bureaucracy, often leads to the use of military men in political appointments, patronage positions and the administration. The technical branches provide experts for public service or nationalizaed industries. Nationalism as a simple ideology, easily shared by all classes, makes for an emphasis on the army as a bearer of national prestige. If the break with the past was made by a military coup, the position of the army is likely to be even more enhanced. . . .

In such regimes emerging from a military action, the army may enjoy a privileged position and hold on to key positions, but it soon co-opts politicians, civil servants and technicians who increasingly make most decisions. The more a regime becomes consolidated, the fewer purely military men staff the government, except when there are no alternative sources of elites. In this sense it may be misleading to speak of a military dictatorship, even when the head of state is an army man. In fact he is likely to carry out a careful policy of depoliticization and professionalization of the army, while he maintains close ties with the officer corps to hold its loyalty.

The military background of key men in authoritarian regimes, and their usual lack of ideological sophistication, make it particularly important to understand the military mentality in relation to internal politics, to styles of political life, conceptions of authority, ideas about cost versus results, legitimate forms for expressing grievances, and so on. The few studies on the role of the military in politics have only raised the issue; real data are still to be assembled.

AUTHORITARIAN REGIMES AND WEBER'S TYPES OF LEGITIMACY

Due to the prominent role of the leader in authoritarian regimes, there is some temptation to identify them with charismatic rule. However we would like to argue that Max Weber's categories can and should be used independently of the distinction between democracy, authoritarianism, and totalitarianism. Within each of these systems the legitimacy of the ruler, for the population or his staff, can be based on one or another of these types of belief.

Undoubtedly charisma has played an important role for masses and staff under Hitler and Lenin; totalitarian regimes have also made demands on their civil service, based on legal authority; and democratic prime ministers have enjoyed charisma. Authoritarian regimes may also have a charismatic element, since they often come into being during serious crisis situations, and control of the mass media facilitates the creation of an "image" of the unique leader. Genuine belief in charisma is likely to be limited, however, since the man assuming leadership was often unknown before, and to his fellow officers is often a primus inter pares, who owes his position often simply to rank. With notable exceptions — Perón or Nasser — the modern army as a rational institution does not breed the irrational leadership type, full of passion, demagogic, convinced of his mission. He is not likely to have, at least for his fellow officers and collaborators, the same appeal that a Lenin or a Hitler could have for those who initiated with him, as marginal men, the long hard struggle for power.

At the same time limited pluralism and the lack of ideological self-righteousness allow more room for the development of general rules institutionalizing the exercise of power, and there is thus a trend toward the secularization of whatever charisma was acquired during crisis. This transition to legal authority has been emphasized in the case of the Spanish regime by one of its leading political theorists, and is even reflected in legal texts. Staffing the system with officers and civil servants, rather than the "old shirts" of street fighting days, contributes to the growth of legalism.

Authoritarian regimes may come to power as de facto authorities with little legitimacy, and develop some charismatic appeal; but they end in a mixture of legal, charismatic and traditional authority. The low level of mobilization may often mean that large parts of the population remain in the position of subjects, recognizing agents of power without questioning their legitimacy; for them habit and self-interest may be more important, and belief unnecessary for effective control.

TRADITIONAL AND AUTHORITARIAN REGIMES

One question some of our readers may raise is: Aren't many such regimes really only a form of autocratic and conservative rule like we find in preconstitutional and traditional monarchies? It would be foolish to deny that the distinctions are fluid, that a number of authoritarian regimes have emerged out of such political forms, and that the formal constitutional framework may still be a monarchical one. However, we want to stress that we would not want to include in our concept any political system which would strictly fit under the concept of traditional authority in Weber's sense and where rule is based on historical continuity, impersonal familial or institutionalized charisma or various mixtures of patrimonial or feudal rule ... using these terms in a somewhat technical sense. To make it clear, neither Abyssinia, nor Yemen before the recent revolution, nor Tibet, Afghanistan, nor some of the other political entities along the Himalayan border fit our concept, to mention contemporary systems. Nor would the prerevolutionary European absolute monarchies of the past. Authoritarian regimes are a likely outcome of the breakdown of such traditional forms of legitimacy. This results from a partial social and political mobilization and a questioning of the traditional principles of legitimacy (largely due to their secularization) by significant segments of the society. Authoritarian systems—even those we might call reactionary—are modernizing in the sense that they represent a discontinuity with tradition, introducing criteria of efficiency and rationality, personal achievement and populistic appeals. . . . The attempts of the present Spanish regime to find its constitutional and legitimacy form as a traditional monarchy certainly suggest the difficulties encountered when moving from an authoritarian regime to a traditional one. There can be no doubt that many of those who are willing to recognize the claims to legitimate rule of Franco would not transfer their allegiance to a traditional monarchy. In our times authoritarian rule almost inevitably leads to questioning traditional authority, if for no other reason than by making the people aware of the importance of the effective head of the government and its secular character. Authoritarian rule might be an intermediate stage in or after the breakdown of traditional authority, but not the route toward its restoration. To specify further the differences would take us at this time too far from the Spanish case.

This might be the place to stress a very important characteristic of many, if not most, authoritarian regimes: the coexistence in them of different legitimizing formulae. The actual pluralism of such regimes and the lack of effective legitimate institutionalization of that pluralism within a single legitimate political formula allowing competition of the pluralistic elements for power, almost inevitably lead to the coexistence of competing legitimacy formulae. So in the case of Spain the traditionalist monarchy desired by the Carlists, a restoration of the pre-1931 monarchy, some form of Catholic corporativism like the present regime under monarchical (or even republican) form, a more dynamic totalitarian vision along fascist lines, even a transition to a democratic republic under christian democratic leadership, are all different formulas open to the supporters of the regime. These supporters give their support in the hope that the regime will satisfy their aspirations and they withdraw their support in so far as they realize that the regime is not doing so, or unable to do so. If we had more space we could develop some of the parallels with Binder's description of the Iranian situation.

Fortunately for many such systems, the great mass of the population in semi- or underdeveloped societies is not concerned with the legitimizing formulae. Instead the population obeys out of a mixture of habit and self-interest, either characterizing the political culture of passive subjects or the parochial (to use the terminology of Almond and Verba). The confusion concerning the sources of legitimacy inherent in many such regimes contributes much of the confusion and pessimism of those most likely to be politically involved. Because of this often the more privileged and those close to the centers of power may appear more alienated from the regime than they really are (at least for all practical purposes). This can help to explain the relative stability of many such systems despite the freedom with which criticism is expressed. The identification with such regimes may not be found in their political formulas, but in the identification with the basic values of the society, its stratification system, and many nonpolitical institutions, which are their infra-structure.

21 Parliamentary and Presidential Systems of Government

State-society relations indicate a great deal about the performance of political systems. But a more complete picture emerges when we understand how political authority is institutionally organized. The vast majority of contemporary political systems work from parliamentary or presidential principles of the distribution of power. In this reading, Douglas Verney, a professor of political science at York University, Toronto, sets out the main features of parliamentary and presidential government. In tracing the historical origins of both types of government, Verney identifies important common ground: both aim to limit abuses of power. In comparing these systems it is tempting to resort to such catch phrases as "separation of powers," "checks and balances," and "balance of powers" to capture the differences. Verney, however, provides an important antidote to this formalistic perspective. He shows that, in parliamentary systems, the possible abuse of power can be checked without separating institutions and that, in presidential systems, effective government can only be achieved through the coordination of separate executive, legislative, and judicial functions. This historical perspective also underscores the important fluctuations in the relative balance of power between the executive, the legislative, and the judiciary in presidential systems and the shifting locus of influence within parliamentary systems. The reading was excerpted from Douglas Verney's book *Analysis of Political Systems*.

● ● ● ● ● ● ● ● ●

PARLIAMENTARY GOVERNMENT

Parliamentarism is the most widely adopted system of government, and it seems appropriate to refer to British parliamentary experience in particular because it is the British system which has provided an example for a great many other countries. Nowadays when it is fashionable to speak of political systems and theories as "not for export" it is worth bearing in mind the success with which a system adopted piecemeal to suit British constitutional developments has proved feasible in different situations abroad. This is not to imply that the British parliamentary system should be taken as the model and that others are, as it were, deviations from the norm, although generations of Englishmen have been tempted to make this assumption.
. . .

Indeed an examination of parliamentarism in various countries indicates that there are two main types of parliamentary procedure, the British and the Continental. In British parliamentary procedure, as adopted in the Commonwealth and Ireland, legislation is initiated in the full Assembly and not in committees. Private members speak only from their places, not from a tribune. Continental procedure is sometimes called "French" but seems to have parallel origins in Sweden and Norway. Moreover according to Hawgood in practice "it was Belgium, and not Britain, France, Sweden or Norway, that became the pattern and prototype for constitutional monarchies everywhere during the century following 1831"—the year in which the Belgian Constitution came into force.

This analysis of parliamentarism is concerned less with distinguishing the various forms of parliamentarism than with establishing the highest common factors in different parliamentary systems. It is not therefore necessary to account for all the political institutions existing in parliamentary countries, still less to describe devices such as federalism which are common to all three types of government, presidential and conventional as well as parliamentary. It may surprise those who have tended to regard British government as the model as well as the Mother of Parliaments to know that the United Kingdom could abolish the Monarchy, adopt a single code of constitutional laws on the pattern of the French or American Constitutions, transform the House of Lords into a Senate (or even do away with it), introduce a multi-party system based on proportional representation, institute a number of parliamentary committees to deal with specific topics such as finance and foreign affairs, and still possess a parliamentary system.

There would seem to be a number of basic principles applicable to both of the chief varieties of parliamentary government. These can be analysed and later used for purposes of comparison with presidential and convention government.

The Assembly Becomes a Parliament
Where parliamentary government has evolved rather than been the product of revolution there have often been three phases, though the transition from one to the other has not always been perceptible at the time. First there has been government by a Monarch who has been responsible for the whole political system. Then there has arisen an Assembly of members who have challenged the hegemony of the King. Finally the Assembly has taken over responsibility for government, acting as a Parliament, the Monarch being deprived of most of his traditional powers.

This has certainly been the pattern in Britain. As late as the seventeenth century King James I could still preach the doctrine of the Divine

Right of Kings. Addressing the Houses of Parliament in 1609 he said, "For Kings are not only God's Lieutenants upon earth, and sit upon God's throne, but even by God Himself they are called Gods." In France the Charter of 1814, framed on the restoration of the French Monarchy during Napoleon's exile to Elba, assumed the divine right of the Bourbons to the throne. During this first phase, if such it may be called, the "Government" consisted of Secretaries who helped the King in his administration. If there was a "Parliament" it was partly because a high court of justice was necessary and partly because the Monarch wanted a sounding-board of public opinion and needed support, especially of a financial nature, for his foreign policies. Between 1302 and 1614 the French States-General met as a whole in less than forty-two years. Even in England the Houses of Parliament met in only 198 of the years between 1295 and 1614—though whereas the English Parliament was about to assert its real authority by the end of the period the States-General was to meet for the last time until 1789. The foundations of the English Parliament's strength were maintained and strengthened in the Tudor period and it required considerable finesse on the part of the Monarch to manage the two Houses. But there was as yet no question of challenging the supreme position of the Monarch as Executive. . . .

However, by establishing their power over the purse, Assemblies were ultimately able to claim their own area of jurisdiction. Henceforth the Monarch's role was increasingly that of an Executive dependent ultimately on the goodwill of the Legislature. Constitutional development entered a second phase in which the term "legislative power" was given to Assemblies to distinguish them from the "executive power" of the King. The English Civil War and the 1688 Revolution did not establish parliamentarism in England but made explicit this division of executive and legislative power between the King and the two Houses. No doubt, as we can now see, the ultimate supremacy of the Houses of Parliament could never be challenged again, but John Locke was quite right to say, as he did in his *Second Treatise of Civil Government*, that both authorities could in a sense claim to be supreme. During the eighteenth century division of responsibility became generally acknowledged and thanks to the writings of Montesquieu and Blackstone this device of government became widely celebrated as the "separation of powers." Whereas on the Continent of Europe despotic governments were the rule there was in Britain a division of power between the King and the Houses of Parliament which Englishmen considered to be the "guardian of their liberties and a bulwark against tyranny." . . .

But even as the theory of the separation of powers was coming into vogue the transition to the third and present phase was under way in

Britain. In the eighteenth century the King was already losing his executive power to Ministers who came to regard the Assembly, not the Monarch, as the sovereign to whom they were really responsible. Ministers were increasingly chosen from among members of the Assembly and resigned when the Assembly withdrew its confidence from them. The change was slow and it was not until the reign of Queen Victoria that parliamentary government as we know it today was fully established. As late as 1867 Bagehot could still feel it necessary to deny that the executive and legislative powers were separated in Britain, and to argue that in the British political system there was a "fusion of powers." By this time parliamentary government was already formalized in the Belgian Constitution. In Sweden, where the separation of powers had only recently been established, the introduction of parliamentarism had to wait until the formation of Liberal Governments in the first two decades of the twentieth century.

In parliamentary monarchies such as Britain, Belgium and Sweden, the Monarch has ceased in practice (though not in form) to exercise even the executive power. Government has passed to "his" Ministers who are responsible to the Legislature. Parliamentary government implies a certain fusion of the executive and legislative functions, the body which has been merely an Assembly of representatives being transformed into a Parliament.

In short, the first phase ended in Britain about the time of the death of Elizabeth I, the last of the Tudors. The following century (1603-1714), known as the Stuart period, saw the rise of Parliament and the recognition of its distinct sphere of influence and power. But the gradual transition to the third and present phase of parliamentary government, which began with the appointment of Walpole as First Minister in 1721, was not completed until the reign of Victoria (1837-1901) since when parliamentary government has been in operation.

It is somewhat confusing, however, to find the term "Parliament" commonly used to describe the Assembly throughout all three phases. Clearly the English Parliament of the sixteenth century was a very different body from the British Parliament of today. For the sake of clarity, the term "Assembly" or "Houses of Parliament" is used in this study to describe the British Parliament as it was before the introduction of parliamentary government, that is to say before the Government came to consist of members of Parliament responsible to that body rather than to the Monarch.

Equally confusing is the use of the term "Parliament" at the present time in two different senses. The statement "Parliament is supreme" refers to Parliament as a whole, members of the Government included, and is correct usage. On the other hand the phrase "The Government is responsible to Parliament" presumably means that the Government is dependent upon the support of *other* members of the Legislature, the Government excluded. In the one instance "Parliament" is used broadly, to include both members of the Government and "private members" as they are often called in Britain, and in the other it connotes these private members only. Unfortunately there is no generic term to describe the private members, either in Britain or abroad. (The term "private member"—and still less "back-bencher"—hardly does justice to the eminent office of Her Majesty's Leader of the Opposition, or even to his colleagues on the Opposition Front Bench.) This fact alone demonstrates the fusion of powers which has taken place, and for all practical purposes the Assembly as such has ceased to exist. Indeed, it is arguable that to insist upon the drawing of a distinction is to encourage a misunderstanding of the nature of parliamentary government, which has so successfully obliterated it.

It is true that for the most part the use of the term "Parliament" at one time to include the Government and at others to exclude it seems to cause little difficulty, provided some knowledge of the parliamentary system is assumed. In a comparative study of political systems, however, such ambiguity presents certain problems if like is to be compared with like. It therefore becomes necessary to insist on a more precise usage. "Parliament" will at all times signify a body which includes the Government. When it is necessary to refer to the Legislature excluding members of the Government the term "Assembly" will be used. . . .

Not all parliamentary systems are monarchical, and in those countries which are republics another personage, usually called the President, takes the place of the constitutional monarch as Head of State. A noteworthy feature of several republics is that at one time they too were monarchies, but during revolutions the monarchy was swept away. The process of constitutional development was often crowded into a very short period, some republics passing straight from a state of monarchical despotism to a form of parliamentarism. . . .

The first characteristic of parliamentarism may now be summarized. It is a political system where the Executive, once separate, has been challenged by the Assembly which is then transformed into a Parliament comprising both Government and Assembly.

The Executive Is Divided into Two Parts
One important consequence of the transformation of the Assembly into a Parliament is that the Executive is now split in two, a Prime Minister or Chancellor becoming head of the Government and the Monarch or President acting as Head of State. Usually the Monarch occupies his throne by hereditary title (though elected monarchies, e.g. in Malaya, are not unknown), while a President is elected by Parliament. It does not follow that

the Head of State fills a purely formal or decorative office. Constitutional monarchs still have important prerogatives and even if those which they do not (or dare not) use are left out of consideration there remains a considerable field in which their powers are politically significant.

In principle there should be no objection to, and perhaps much to be said for, a clear statement of the respective functions of Head of State and Government. But the British view appears to be that the relationship of the two parts of the Executive is better left to the operation of flexible convention than written into the law of the Constitution. In several European monarchies there has been a similar transfer of power from Monarch to Ministry, but without a re-statement of their respective functions. Thus Article 4 of the Swedish Constitution still reads: "The King alone shall govern the realm." Part of Article 30 of the Norwegian Constitution reads:

> Everyone who holds a seat in the Council is in duty bound to express fearlessly his opinions, to which the King is bound to listen. But it remains with the King to take a resolution according to his own judgment.

The Governments of these countries are thus shielded by the Constitution when they claim freedom of action on the part of the Crown whose powers they wield.

Where the Head of State is a President there is less reticence about making the duties of the divided Executive explicit, presumably because the President is elected by Parliament. In constitutional monarchies experience has shown that if the Monarch does not have his duties constitutionally defined and protected greater flexibility is possible. (In other words, the King can be deprived of more and more of his prerogative powers.) There is an important exception to this rule in Japan. Fear that the Emperor might not accept the role of a constitutional Monarch has led to the explicit withdrawal of all governmental functions from him in the new constitution. Executive power is vested expressly in the Cabinet. In parliamentary republics there is a fairly general apprehension lest the President engross the powers which pertain to the Government. The Constitution of the French Fourth Republic accordingly stated what powers the President of the Republic (Articles 29-44) and the President of the Council of Ministers (45-54) might wield.

On the other hand Presidents are sometimes allowed a greater authority than Monarchs because their status is achieved, not ascribed as a result of inherited title. The French President, for example, had a temporary veto over legislation which Monarchs might possess in theory but certainly do not exercise in practice. But where, as in the Fifth Republic and in Finland, the President has special rights comparable with or superior to those of the Ministry, the system ceases at this point to be truly parliamentary.

It is a characteristic of hereditary monarchies that the King cannot be held personally responsible and so his Ministers must bear responsibility for him. No such inhibition seems to affect republics, where the President is elected. Consequently when the President oversteps his position he is subject to impeachment, for high treason in France, for unconstitutional activity in the Federal German Republic, and for both in Italy.

The second characteristic of parliamentarism may now be summarized. The Executive is divided into a Head of State and a Government whose relationship with the Head of State may or may not be precisely formulated.

The Head of State Appoints the Head of Government
The value of a divided Executive in constitutional monarchies is fairly obvious. For one thing, the proper business of State can be carried on by a government responsible to the Legislature while the mystique of Monarchy is preserved. There seems no apparent reason, at first glance, for dividing it in Republics. Admittedly it is useful to have someone above the day-to-day political warfare to receive ambassadors and to decorate ceremonial occasions, but this hardly seems to justify the expense of such an office. After all, the President of the United States, who as head of the American government bears the greatest responsibilities of any stateman in the world, manages to combine with his high and lonely eminence the even higher office of Head of State.

However, it is in the very nature of the parliamentary system that there shall be two distinct offices, and that the head of the Government shall be appointed by the Head of State. Were the electorate itself to perform this task, directly or through a special College of electors as in the United States or Finland, the system would become, in this respect at least, presidential in character. For Parliament to elect the head of the Government would be to adopt the procedure which is characteristic of the convention system. The different methods of selecting the head of the Government distinguish as clearly as anything else the three theories of governmental organization.

Nor is the duty of appointing the head of the Government a mere formality. It is true that the Head of State is bound by the results of parliamentary elections and must appoint the head of the party which is clearly the victor. But this is the situation only where one party or stable coalition has obtained an absolute majority of seats, which is called appropriately in Scandinavia "Majority-parliamentarism." But in many parliamentary systems, especially multi-party systems, no party has an absolute majority and "minority-parliamentarism" prevails. In selecting the Prime

Minister who can best obtain a working majority the Head of State may have to use his personal discretion. The last occasion on which such a situation arose in Britain was in 1931, and the role of the Monarch during this crisis is still disputed. Even where there is majority-parliamentarism problems may occur. The Prime Minister may resign for personal reasons, as Sir Anthony Eden did in 1957, without leaving an obvious successor, and then the Monarch has to make a very important personal decision. The Conservative Party was criticised on this occasion for not appointing a leader before this situation arose, and no doubt the Queen's selection would have been merely a formality had this been done. But it is quite possible that on some future occasion, for example when a party is divided about a new leader, the Head of State may once again be compelled to use his or her discretion. It may be desirable that where the Head of State is a Monarch the selection of the head of the Government shall be a formality but this can by no means be guaranteed in a parliamentary system.

Some parliamentary republics, notably Western Germany and the French Fourth Republic, have escaped from this dilemma by the introduction of an element of convention theory whereby selection of a Prime Minister has three stages. The President nominates a candidate, the Assembly shows its approval by electing him (in Germany) or by giving him a vote of confidence (in France) and then the President appoints him as Prime Minister.

Parliamentarism, therefore, implies some balance of power even though the separation of institutions still characteristic of presidential government has given way to fusion. Unlike convention government it is not government by Assembly, nor is it the absorption of the Executive by the Assembly. It is the creation of a completely new institution in the political system, a Parliament, in which the Assembly and the Government are somehow miraculously blended. The duty of the Head of State to appoint the head of the Government—the third characteristic of parliamentarism—is as necessary to preserve that balance as the popular election of both President and Assembly is to preserving the balance in presidential systems.

The Head of the Government Appoints the Ministry

An interesting feature of parliamentarism is the distinction made between the Prime Minister and other Ministers. The former is appointed by the Head of State; the latter are nominated by the Prime Minister after his appointment. Usually the selection of various Ministers allows a certain amount of personal choice to a head of Government, which cannot usually be said of the appointment of a Prime Minister by the Head of State. Ministers are formally appointed by the Head of State, who may often no doubt exert an informal influence upon appointments—but so may the state on party alignments and factions in the Assembly. It remains a cardinal principle that the Prime Minister alone is responsible for the composition of the Ministry. Where, as in Australia, Ministers are sometimes elected by their party this is a departure from the parliamentary principle in the direction of convention government.

The Ministry (or Government) Is a Collective Body
The transfer from the monarchical Executive to a Council of Ministers has meant that a single person has been replaced by a collective body. Whereas under *anciens régimes* it was the King's pleasure (*le Roi le veult*), under parliamentarism the Prime Minister is merely first among equals (*primus inter pares*), though no doubt some Prime Ministers are more forceful than others. . . . In the United States, of course, the President is sole Executive, but it is a hallmark of the parliamentary system that the Government shall be collective.

Ministers Are Usually Members of Parliament
Members of the Government have a double role to play in the parliamentary system. They are not only Ministers but are at the same time members of Parliament, elected (unless they are members of the British House of Lords) like the members of the Assembly and equally dependent upon the goodwill of their constituents. The problem of distinguishing between Parliament and Assembly is most acute when this role is analysed. In Britain there is no law that Ministers must be members of one of the Houses of Parliament (though it is required that at least three members of the Cabinet must be drawn from the House of Lords) but there is a convention that they are in fact always members of one or other. Thus when Mr. Bevin became Minister of Labour in 1940 a seat was found for him in the House of Commons. When Sir Percy Mills joined Mr. Macmillan's Government in 1957 he was made a peer. The Constitution of the French Fourth Republic specifically stated that Ministers are collectively and individually responsible to the National Assembly and there is an implication that they should be members of that body.

Since, according to the usage adopted in this chapter, Parliament comprises both Government and Assembly, a member of the Government is *ipso facto* a member of Parliament, but by definition he cannot be a member of the Assembly. In full parliamentary countries such as the United Kingdom where Ministers are members of Parliament it is difficult to make the distinction between Government, Parliament and Assembly clear. Indeed the attempt to make one seems artificial.

However, not all parliamentary countries have accepted the necessity for Ministers to be members of one of the Houses of Parliament. In Sweden up to a third of the Ministry of fifteen members have on occasion in recent years not been Members of Parliament. In the Netherlands, Norway and Luxembourg, Ministers are actually forbidden to be Members of Parliament after their appointment. Here there is a relic of the old doctrine of the separation of powers when Ministers were responsible to the Monarch. (Traces of the doctrine may be found elsewhere, for example, in the traditional French rule that Ministers may not be members of parliamentary committees.)

Generally speaking, nevertheless, it is usual for most if not all Ministers to be Members of Parliament. Where they are not, the system may still be said to be of the parliamentary type if they can take part in parliamentary debates and are truly responsible to the Assembly for the conduct of the Executive. In Norway, Sweden, the Netherlands and Luxembourg, all parliamentary monarchies, these conditions are fulfilled. In the French Fifth Republic, where the government is not responsible to Parliament for the conduct of the President, they are not.

The Government Is Politically Responsible to the Assembly

In parliamentary systems the Government is responsible to the Assembly which may, if it thinks that the Government is acting unwisely or unconstitutionally, refuse to give it support. By a formal vote of censure or by simply not assenting to an important Government proposal the Assembly can force the Government to resign and cause the Head of State to appoint a new Government.

In the *anciens régimes* of Europe Ministers were responsible not to the Assembly but to the King, as in Nepal today. They were truly Ministers of the Crown. The question "To whom is the Monarch responsible?" was not one which a constitutional lawyer or a political scientist would care to answer, though a moral philosopher would probably say that he was governed by the moral law or the spirit of the constitution. There was no institution charged with the enforcement of his responsibility and no definition of what constituted responsible and irresponsible action. Legally as "God's Lieutenant," though not morally, the King could do no wrong. Hobbes went so far as to assert in the mid-seventeenth century that there should be no limits to the Sovereign's power and that in practice an absolute sovereign power was better than the alternative—anarchy. To this day Monarchs as a rule cannot be held constitutionally responsible for their actions.

An escape from this dilemma was first provided by the introduction of a rule that Ministers could be held responsible by the Assembly for the advice which they rendered. Thus although Article 30 of the Norwegian Constitution stressed the right of the King to act according to his own judgement, Article 5 stated: "The King's person shall be sacred; he cannot be blamed or accused. The responsibility shall rest upon his Council." During the period of what may be termed "limited monarchy" or the "separation of powers" before parliamentarism was established the Assembly was supposed to hold Ministers responsible by this device.

In comparison with the present-day procedure of an adverse vote the method adopted was complicated and not altogether successful. Ministers were required to countersign all documents issued by the King-in-Council before they became law. A committee of the Assembly examined these documents and held the countersigning Minister responsible for their contents. In certain countries, such as Sweden, a distinction was drawn between advice which was unwise and proposals which were unconstitutional. Where the committee of the Assembly decided that due regard had not been paid to the welfare of the State it could advise the Assembly to request the Monarch to dismiss the offending Minister. But no action could be taken to ensure that this request was acceded to. Where Ministers were deemed to have acted unconstitutionally they could be impeached before a special court. Neither means of checking the Government proved effective in Sweden in the nineteenth century and today these provisions of the Constitution are a dead letter. Yet some Swedish authorities have been reluctant to accept the notion that day-to-day political pressure in the Assembly has replaced them, partly, no doubt, because Sweden has only recently (1917) emerged from a century of limited monarchy. It is particularly difficult for constitutional lawyers to recognize conventions which run counter to the letter of the Constitution.

Countersignature still has its uses in republics as a last resort to prevent the Head of State from acting unconstitutionally. A President elected by the Assembly is more likely in a time of crisis to claim to represent the real public interest. Unless he can obtain a countersignature for his actions he leaves himself open to criticism and can, if necessary, be impeached. Although a dead letter in the constitutions of parliamentary monarchies, the requirement of a countersignature has been written into several recent constitutions in parliamentary republics.

The Head of Government May Advise the Head of State to Dissolve Parliament

In the pre-parliamentary monarchies of Europe the Monarch could, if dissatisfied with his Assembly, dissolve one or more Houses in the hope of securing a more amenable selection of representatives after a new election. Today, when the Executive is divided, it is still the Head of State who dissolves Parliament, but he does so on the request, and only on the request, of the head of Government. In Denmark the Constitution actually states that either the King or the Prime Minister may dissolve Parliament. But where the Head of State acts independently, as President Macmahon did in France in 1877, parliamentarism is not being practised.

For parliamentary dissolution is very different from the earlier form of dissolution. In the old days a challenge by the Assembly to the Executive did not lead to a change of Executive but to a change (or attempted change) of the Assembly. Nowadays a defeat of the Government by the Assembly causes the Prime Minister either to resign or to request a dissolution. But the dissolution is not of the Assembly but of Parliament, that is to say of the Government as well—although the Government (in Britain at least) stays in power until the new Parliament assembles. The conflict between the two parts of Parliament is left to the electorate to resolve.

The power of the Government to request a dissolution is a distinctive characteristic of parliamentarism. Some British writers consider that the threat of dissolution is essential in order that the Ministry may secure the loyal support of its party, but other parliamentary systems survive without Whips who whisper hints of dissolution to recalcitrant back-benchers.

Nevertheless, dissolution must remain the ultimate sanction. . . .

Certain states generally regarded as parliamentary severely restrict the right of the Executive to dissolve the Assembly. In Norway the *Storting* dissolves itself, the Head of State being allowed to dissolve only special sessions, but this is a departure from parliamentarism inspired by the convention theory of the French Revolution. In France, where the right of the Government of the Fourth Republic to request a dissolution of Parliament was restricted by the Constitution, the political system also exhibited certain convention characteristics.

Parliament as a Whole Is Supreme Over Its Constituent Parts, Government and Assembly, Neither of Which May Dominate the Other

The notion of the supremacy of Parliament as a whole over its parts is a distinctive characteristic of parliamentary systems. This may seem a glimpse of the obvious to those accustomed to parliamentary government, but it is in fact an important principle, all too often forgotten, that neither of the constituent elements of Parliament may completely dominate the other. The Government depends upon the support of the Assembly if it is to continue in office, but the Assembly is not supreme because the Government can, if it chooses, dissolve Parliament and appeal to the electorate at the polls. Many parliamentary systems have failed because one or other of them has claimed supremacy, and Parliament as a whole has not been supreme over both Government and Assembly.

In practice the nature of parliamentary supremacy varies from country to country. In the United Kingdom and Scandinavia the emphasis is on the Government's role in Parliament and in Britain the system is actually called "Cabinet Government." In others, notably the French Third and Fourth Republics, the dominant role in Parliament was played by the Assembly. Generally speaking, where there is majority-parliamentarism the Government has a sense of security, subject only to the sudden onset of a crisis. No Government has been defeated on a motion of confidence in the House of Commons for about thirty years, though it took merely a drop in his customarily large majority to cause Mr. Chamberlain to resign as Prime Minister in 1940. Governments lacking the support of an absolute majority of members are in a much more exposed position, and in France for example, changes of Government following loss of confidence by the Chamber of Deputies or National Assembly were fairly frequent.

Many countries appear in practice to depart from the parliamentary ideal of a balance between the Government and the Assembly. On the one hand there are states like France where the capacity of the Assembly to change Governments at will has been an indication not, as is sometimes thought, of an interesting variation of the parliamentary principle, but of a departure from it in the direction of Assembly government. On the other there are countries like the United Kingdom where the increasing tendency for the Government to dominate parliamentary business may be a departure from the parliamentary principle in the opposite direction. . . .

It would be more in keeping with parliamentarism as it is defined in this study to deny the right of either Government or Assembly such absolute authority. Parliamentarism implies co-operation between the executive and legislative branches, neither dominating the other and both recognizing the supremacy of the larger institution, Parliament as a whole.

The notion of parliamentary supremacy described in this section is not to be confused with the legal notion of parliamentary sovereignty. Whereas the former explains the relation of Parliament to its component parts, the latter is concerned with its external relations. All Parliaments are supreme over the Governments and Assemblies which compose them. But not all are sovereign, that is to say legally unrestricted in their powers. In Britain Parliament is sovereign in the sense that the Queen-in-Parliament is not limited legally by the Constitution. In other parliamentary states, however, the power of Parliament and the Head of State is limited by the terms of written constitutions. It need hardly be emphasized therefore that parliamentary sovereignty, which plays so large a part in British politics, is by no means a characteristic of parliamentary systems generally.

And of course parliamentary supremacy or sovereignty is strictly a governmental notion affecting relations between the branches of government. It is compatible with the belief that in a very real sense it is the electorate which is ultimately supreme: hence the notion of popular sovereignty, taken for granted in the United States and assumed in the United Kingdom by those who believe that government should act in accordance with a mandate from the people.

The Government as a Whole Is Only Indirectly Responsible to the Electorate

A parliamentary Government, though directly responsible to the Assembly, is only indirectly responsible to the electorate. The Government as a whole is not directly elected by the voters but is appointed indirectly from amongst the representatives whom they elect to the Assembly. The earlier direct relationship of Monarch and people whereby persons could petition their Sovereign disappeared as parliamentarism was introduced. Today the route to the Government lies through elected representatives though in Britain, for example, one may still formally petition the Monarch. It is true that members of the Government, like other members of Parliament, must (unless they are peers) stand before their constituents for election. However, they do so not as members of the Government but as candidates for the Assembly in the ordinary way. The responsibility for transforming them, once elected, into Ministers rests with the Prime Minister alone (and of course with the Monarch in the case of the Prime Minister).

As late as the nineteenth century in Britain it was thought to be bad form for a member of the Government, including the Prime Minister, to appeal to the electorate in general as well as to his constituents during an election. Not until after the second Reform Bill of 1867 was there a departure from this tradition. Today elections are fought on a national basis, Government and Opposition appealing as national parties to a national electorate. There has also grown up an important channel of direct communication between Ministries and the public, and even Prime Ministers have their public relations advisers. Nevertheless, this growth in direct communication has not been accompanied by a feeling of direct responsibility to the electorate. A Prime Minister returning from an important international conference does not usually address the public either by Press or television until he has first reported to Parliament.

It may still be argued that in reality, if not in constitutional theory, there is an exception to this principle of indirect responsibility, at least in two-party states. Are not, it may be asked, the people at election time presented in fact with two alternative Governments for one of which they vote? In a broad sense this is no doubt true, but there is a world of difference between, say, the election of the American President by the American people and the appointment of a British Government. The individual

British voter, unlike his American counterpart, elects only a member of the Assembly. He may even, if he is a Liberal, Independent or Communist, vote for a particular candidate or party with full knowledge that he cannot have anything to do with the formation of a Government, at least in the immediate future. Should the voter elect a Labour Member of Parliament and then discover that the Labour Party is to form the new Government, his responsibility is indirect, as is that of all Labour voters. The people have not directly elected a Government: what they have done is to elect a party whose leader is called upon by the Monarch to form a Government of *his* own choosing.

This point is not always well taken. In a recent book, *The British Political System*, a French writer, André Mathiot, describes the British Cabinet under the heading "A Government Chosen by the People." He rightly points to the plebiscitary element in British elections as a result of the two-party system. It is true that "The electorate actually votes for members of Parliament, but they are really choosing the government by deciding which party is to have a majority in the House of Commons." But Mathiot slurs over the fact that *members* of the Government are selected neither by the people nor by the victorious party. It is a misleading oversimplification to state that "the Prime Minister and the Cabinet are appointed by the Queen but really chosen by the people." Ministers are in fact chosen by the Prime Minister, and as for the premiership itself this has been transferred on many occasions without any consultation of the people. There were no general elections preceding the appointments of Lloyd George in 1916, Stanley Baldwin in 1923, Winston Churchill in 1940 or Harold Macmillan in 1957.

Where there is a multi-party system in which no party has a majority the relation of Government and voters is much more indirect. Of course nobody knows which parties will increase their representation, but even if this can be guessed the nature of the coalition Government may be unknown. The task of forming a Government falls to party leaders and the Head of State after the results are announced, and is hardly the direct result of the election. In such circumstances the electors clearly are responsible directly only for candidates and parties, the Government being the responsibility of those leaders who are successful in the election.

Parliament Is the Focus of Power in the Political System

The fusion of the executive and legislative powers in Parliament is responsible for the overriding ascendancy of Parliament in the political order. It is the stage on which the drama of politics is played out; it is the forum of the nation's ideas; and it is the school where future political leaders are trained. For parliamentarism to succeed, the Government must not fret at the constant challenge which the Assembly offers to its programme, nor wince at the criticism made of its administration. The Assembly in turn must resist the temptation to usurp the functions of Government. Here is a delicate balance of powers which check each other without the benefit of separate institutions.

Above all, politicians, party militants and voters have to accept the parliamentary spirit of give and take. They must be loyal to Parliament as well as to their party, not doubting the good faith of those with whom they disagree. Where this confidence is lacking or is betrayed, parliamentarism falls into disrepute and the system may become unworkable. The weakness of parliamentarism in France has been due in large measure to the unwillingness of large numbers of Frenchmen to give their Parliament this trust and loyalty. Many party militants on the Right have wanted to abolish Parliament and replace it with a separated Executive and Assembly as in presidential theory. Many on the Left would have preferred to see power transferred to the Assembly as in the brief days of the Convention and the Commune. In all parties, within and without the National Assembly, there were those who could not be true parliamentarians because they doubted the suitability of parliamentary government for France. In such circumstances parliamentarism cannot flourish. It must be, if it is to succeed, the focal point of the nation's political interest, the centre of the political system. . . .

PRESIDENTIAL GOVERNMENT

Presidential government is often associated with the theory of the separation of powers which was popular in the eighteenth century when the American Constitution was framed. Two writers in particular drew attention to this notion. John Locke, writing at the end of the seventeenth century, suggested that the long conflict between the British Monarch and the Houses of Parliament would best be resolved by the separation of the King as Executive from the two Houses as Legislature, each body having its own sphere. In the mid-eighteenth century a French observer of the British political scene, Montesquieu, pronounced himself in favour of the British system of government as one which embodied, in contrast to the despotism of the Bourbons, the separation of the executive, legislative and judicial powers. Historically the theory as expounded by Locke and more especially Montesquieu is important for an understanding of the climate of opinion in which the American Constitution was framed.

However, it is one thing to study this celebrated theory for historical purposes but quite another to trace its contemporary significance for an understanding of presidential government. It was, after all, based on the assumption that a Monarch would act as Executive and an Assembly as

Legislature. The theory was considered to be an improvement on the absolute monarchies of the Continent, which it undoubtedly was, and was praised with them in mind. There was as yet no experience of parliamentarism. Today such constitutional monarchies as still survive are based on the parliamentary principle.

Another offspring and successor of the theory is presidential government, but the substitution of an elected President for a hereditary Monarch has, as we have seen, created a system hardly comparable with pre-parliamentary limited monarchies. If presidential government is regarded simply as a direct form of expression of the eighteenth century doctrine of the separation of powers then (as indeed many people have thought) the Americans may, by adopting their rigid Constitution, have artificially prevented their political system from developing into parliamentarism. But if, as it is argued here, the system is a successor to that doctrine then it is not like limited monarchy, the precursor of parliamentary government, but one of its two offsprings, the other being parliamentarism.

Indeed the use of the term "separation of powers" to describe the presidential system is something of a misnomer, as is its counterpart the "fusion of powers" of parliamentarism. In theory it is possible to conceive of complete separation of the executive, legislative and judicial functions, but there is no evidence of its practical feasibility. If government is to be carried on the powers must be co-ordinated and must overlap. Thus in the United States the President (the Executive) wields legislative power when he signs or vetoes bills sent to him by Congress. Congress (the legislative branch) shares in the Executive's authority when it ratifies treaties and confirms appointments. The Supreme Court (the Judiciary) may use its power to interpret the Constitution so as to encroach on both the executive and legislative spheres. In parliamentary theory, despite the fusion of powers implied by parliamentary supremacy, an important distinction is drawn between the three branches, and textbooks on constitutional law begin with an account of the separation of powers. It is still considered everywhere to be one of the bulwarks against tyranny and dictatorship— except perhaps in the Vatican. (Article I of the Fundamental Law of the City of the Vatican states: "The Sovereign Pontiff, sovereign of the City of the Vatican, has full legislative, executive and judicial powers.") If the powers are not really separated in presidential systems, neither are they altogether fused in parliamentary states.

Where presidential and parliamentary governments *do* differ is over the separation not of powers but of institutions and persons. In the parliamentary system there is a single institution called Parliament which combines two other institutions and their personnel—the Government and the Assembly. It may, as in the United Kingdom, combine part of the judiciary as well (the House of Lords being the highest court of appeal) and thus Parliament may seem to wield executive, legislative and judicial power. There is no such combination of functions in presidential systems, the Executive being quite separate from the Assembly as an institution. Moreover the personnel of the two institutions, and of the Judiciary, are different.

The term "separation of powers" is therefore an inadequate and misleading description of the theory underlying presidential government. It is inadequate because as stated by Montesquieu and Blackstone it applied to a monarchical Executive which has since been generally replaced by parliamentarism, and because it does not explain the theory of presidential government. It is misleading because the powers are separated in both presidential and parliamentary theory. These are distinguished partly by the degree of separation of powers but more particularly by the separation of institutions and persons which is so marked a characteristic of presidential but not parliamentary theory.

In parliamentary government, where the legislative and executive powers have to a marked degree been fused, it is sometimes difficult to draw a distinction between the Government and the Assembly which together form Parliament. In presidential government, on the other hand, a clear distinction *is* drawn between these two branches of the political system. The President is the Executive, being both Head of State and head of Government, and is quite separate from the Assembly. Indeed the use of the terms "Government" and "Ministry" employed in parliamentarism to distinguish the repository of real political power from the Head of State is inappropriate in the presidential context. Americans tend to use the expression "Administration" to describe the President and his aides. The term "Parliament" is never used because in presidential systems there is no place for an institution which combines the executive and legislative powers.

The term *presidential* has been chosen because in this system the offices of head of Government and Head of State are combined in a President. The term is as expressive as *parliamentary* was to describe the system where the Government and Assembly are fused in a Parliament.

It seemed appropriate to begin an analysis of parliamentary government by reference to British political institutions. It is equally valuable to study presidentialism by first examining the American political system. The United States was the first important country to break with the European monarchical tradition and to shake off colonial rule. The break occurred in the eighteenth century when Britain was still a limited monarchy and the theory of the separation of powers was in vogue. The American Constitution bears witness to these influences and to the colonial government of Governor and Legislature, an elected President replacing the King or Governor as the Executive power. A number of countries—all twenty American republics, Liberia, the Philippines, South Korea and South Vietnam—have followed the example of the United States, though rarely with comparable success. The American political system is therefore the model and prototype of presidential government. Yet the United States, like the United Kingdom, could abolish or transform many of its institutions and remain based on the same theory of government. For example, the framers of the 1787 Constitution could have proposed an elective Monarch instead of a President, a House of Lords rather than a Senate, and a unitary political system instead of a federal union of states without destroying the presidential principle—though the name "presidential" would hardly be suitable for a system where the Executive was an elective Monarch. Presidential, like parliamentary, theory has certain basic characteristics irrespective of any particular political system.

The nature of presidential theory can best be understood by re-stating the eleven propositions of Chapter II [of *Analysis of Political Systems* . . .] as they apply to presidential government.

The Assembly Remains an Assembly Only

Parliamentary theory implies that the second phase of constitutional development, in which the Assembly and Judiciary claim their own areas of jurisdiction alongside the Executive, shall give way to a third in which Assembly and Government are fused in a Parliament. Presidential theory on the other hand requires the Assembly to remain separate as in the second phase. The American Revolution led to a transfer from colonial rule to the second stage of separate jurisdiction, and there have been some observers who have thought that the rigid Constitution has prevented the "natural" development of the American political system towards parliamentarism. This is not so. By abolishing the Monarchy and substituting a President for the King and his Government, the Americans showed themselves to be truly revolutionary in outlook. The presidential system as established in the U.S.A. made parliamentarism both unnecessary and impracticable in that country. The Assembly (Congress in the United States) remains an Assembly.

The Executive Is Not Divided but Is a President Elected by the People for a Definite Term at the Time of Assembly Elections

The retention of a separate Executive in the United States was made feasible because the Executive remained undivided. It was not, of course, the same institution as the pre-parliamentary monarchical Executive. Such a Monarch governed by virtue of an ancient tradition into which he was born, and with all the strength and potential weaknesses that this implied.

The presidential Executive is elected by the people. In an era when Governments have had to rely not on some mystique but on popular support the Americans have found a solution which has enabled their separate single Executive to withstand criticism. The suggestions that the United States should adopt parliamentarism have proved abortive largely because it cannot be said of the Presidency, as it could of hereditary Monarchy, that the institution lacked democratic roots.

An undivided Executive obviously requires no delineation of the respective functions of Head of State and the Government. The powers of the Executive are defined vis-à-vis the Assembly and the Judiciary and each checks the others to ensure that the balance of power is not unduly disturbed. Yet this has not prevented a change in their status and role. In the United States as late as 1884 Woodrow Wilson (then a professor of political science, not President of the United States) could regard the Senate and House of Representatives as the pivot of the system and could call his book on American politics *Congressional Government*. Today, as the title of this chapter ["Presidential Government"] indicates, the influence of the President has appreciably extended. In other presidential systems the President usually wields very considerable powers. If there is any trend it is away from parliamentarism, not towards it.

The President is elected for a definite term of office. This prevents the Assembly from forcing his resignation (except by impeachment for a serious misdemeanour) and at the same time requires the President to stand for re-election if he wishes to continue in office. It seems desirable that the chief Executive's tenure should be limited to a certain number of terms. For a long time there was a convention in the United States that no President should run for a third term. . . . President Roosevelt swept the convention aside in 1940—but some of his most loyal friends refused to support his candidacy. After his re-election for the fourth time in 1944 there was a movement to make it unconstitutional to run more than twice. An amendment to the Constitution to this effect was passed by Congress in 1947 and adopted by the necessary three-quarters of the States by 1951.

Equally important for the proper operation of the presidential system is the election of the President at the time of the Assembly elections. This associates the two branches of government, encourages party unity and clarifies the issues. Admittedly in the United States simultaneous elections do not prevent the return of a Republican President and a Democratic Congress, but the tensions would be even greater if the President was elected for a seven-year term as in France. General de Gaulle was elected as President in 1958 about the time of the Assembly elections, but the opportunity to make this coincidence permanent was not seized. However, since the de Gaulle Constitution allows for dissolution of Parliament as well as the resignation of the Government (but not the President) serious difficulty may be avoided.

The Head of the Government Is Head of State
Whereas in pre-parliamentary Monarchies the Head of State was also the head of the Government, in the presidential system it is the head of the Government who becomes at the same time Head of State. This is an important distinction because it draws attention to the limited pomp and circumstance surrounding the presidential office. The President is of little consequence until he is elected as political head by the electorate and he ceases to have any powers once his term of office has expired. The ceremonial aspect of his position is but a reflection of his political prestige.

Presidential theory, if it is to be successfully applied, demands a certain sophistication of the electorate. In parliamentary states, as Sir Winston Churchill once noted, war victories are celebrated by a cheer for the Head of State; defeats by a change of Government. In presidential systems a voter who may oppose the President as head of the Government has nevertheless to be loyal to the President as Head of State.

In the appointment of a political Executive it is a characteristic of parliamentary systems that the head of Government shall be appointed by the Head of State. The absence of any distinction between the two offices in presidential systems makes such an appointment unnecessary. Nor is the Executive elected by the Assembly since this would be contrary to the doctrine of the separation of powers. It is the mark of presidential government that both Executive and Assembly should be selected by the electorate.

The President Appoints Heads of Departments
Who Are His Subordinates
In parliamentarism the Prime Minister appoints his colleagues who together with him form the Government. In presidential systems the President appoints Secretaries (sometimes called Ministers) who are heads of his Executive Departments. Formally, owing to the rule whereby appointments are subject to the confirmation of the Assembly or one of its organs (in the United States the Senate, in the Philippines the commission on appointments) his choice may be restricted to persons of whom that body approves. In practice the President has a very wide choice. Whereas in parliamentary systems Ministers are usually selected from those who have served a political apprenticeship in the Assembly, it is by no means customary in presidential systems for heads of Departments (or for that matter the President himself) to have had experience in the legislative branch of government.

The President Is Sole Executive

In contrast to parliamentary government, which is collective, the Prime Minister being first among equals, presidential government tends to be individual. Admittedly the term "Cabinet" is used in the United States to describe the meetings of the President with his Secretaries, but it is not a Cabinet or Ministry in the parliamentary sense. There is a famous story of Abraham Lincoln meeting with his Cabinet. He put a proposal to them and then took a vote in which he alone supported his suggestion. He then remarked: "Noes 7, Ayes 1. The Ayes have it." In this respect the "loneliest office in the world" bears some resemblance to pre-parliamentary Monarchies where the King alone wielded executive power. President Truman made the point even more succinctly as President by placing a notice on his desk: *The buck stops here.* Such being the nature of the presidential Executive it would seem inappropriate to use the term "Cabinet" at all. . . .

Members of the Assembly Are Not Eligible for Office in the Administration and Vice-Versa

Instead of the parliamentary convention or law whereby the same persons may be part of both the executive and legislative branches of government, it is customary in presidential states for the personnel to be separate. Neither the President nor his aides may sit in the U.S. Congress. Few of the other American republics have copied the complete separation practised in the United States. While Ministers may not be members of the Assembly (except in Cuba and Peru) they are usually entitled to attend and take part in debates. This appears to accord with the practice of some pre-parliamentary Monarchies where, despite a strict rule that the Monarch should not attend debates, Ministers were often allowed to be present whether members or not. In a few countries (Costa Rica, Bolivia, El Salvador and Panama) Ministers give up their seats to alternates (*suplente*) for the period they hold office.

The Executive is Responsible to the Constitution

The President is not, like parliamentary Governments, responsible to the Assembly. Instead he is, like pre-parliamentary Monarchs, responsible to the Constitution. But whereas in the *anciens régimes* this was but a vague notion, in presidential systems it is usually laid down with some precision in a constitutional document. Acts of the President may, as in the United States, be declared unconstitutional by the Supreme Court, though as Chief Justice Marshall discovered when attempting to protect the rights of the Cherokee Indians, it is one thing to hand down a decision and another to enforce it. However, should a President persist in acting unconstitutionally the Assembly can take action itself and impeach him or his aides. (The term "civil officer" is used to describe them in the United States.)

Impeachment in pre-parliamentary Monarchies was confined to Ministers who were held responsible for the King's actions through an elaborate system of counter-signature. The Monarch himself could only be dealt with by drastic action for which there was no constitutional procedure. He could be forced to abdicate without any right of self-defence, as happened to James II of England, Gustav IV of Sweden, Kaiser Wilhelm II of Germany, and Napoleon I, Charles X, Louis Philippe and Napoleon III of France. If he appeared to stand in the way of important political and social changes he might even be executed like Charles I of England or Louis XVI of France. In presidential systems, however, both Ministers and Presidents may be impeached. Where, as in Honduras and Paraguay, there is no provision for impeachment the system is not, in this important respect, presidential. In several South American Constitutions there are provisions which compel the President to dismiss his Ministers through political pressure as well as after impeachment. Thus in Peru ministers must resign after a vote of no-confidence.

It is usually the Assembly which holds the President ultimately responsible to the Constitution by the impeachment process. This does not imply that he is responsible to that body in the parliamentary sense of depending on its confidence in any political capacity. Impeachment enforces *juridical* compliance with the (constitutional) letter of the law and is quite different from the exercise of political control over the President's ordinary conduct of his office. Political responsibility implies a day-to-day relationship between Government and Assembly; impeachment is the grave and ultimate penalty (only one American President, Andrew Johnson was impeached, unsuccessfully) necessary where ordinarily the Executive and Assembly are not mutually dependent.

The President may not be dependent on the Assembly for his political survival but he is very dependent on its goodwill for the furtherance of his policies. The Budget, foreign programmes, senior appointments all require its acquiescence. If there is no agreement the Assembly may decide to take no action. It cannot however replace the President.

The President Cannot Dissolve or Coerce the Assembly
The Assembly, as we have just seen, cannot dismiss the President. Likewise the President may not dissolve the Assembly. Neither, therefore, is in a position to coerce the other, and it is not surprising that this system is, par excellence, one of checks and balances. In countless ways almost incomprehensible to those accustomed to parliamentarism the presidential system exhibits this mutual independence of the executive and legislative

branches of government. In the United States, President Eisenhower declined for some time to take issue in 1954 with Senator McCarthy on the grounds that a Senator's conduct was primarily the responsibility of the U.S. Senate, not the Executive. In 1957, after the suicide of the Canadian Ambassador to Egypt, the President was unable to assure the Canadian people that congressional committees would in future exercise more discretion since he was not responsible for the behaviour of the Senate. Conversely, the Senate, whose Southern members had blocked civil rights legislation for over half a century, did nothing in 1948 when President Truman abolished racial segregation in the armed forces—even in the South. For as President Mr. Truman was Commander-in-Chief and could act without reference to Congress.

The position of a President is very different from that of a pre-parliamentary Monarch who could dissolve his Assembly if he felt that this was desirable. A President may call a special session of the Assembly if he fails to obtain his demands at the ordinary session and he may, if the Houses disagree, adjourn their meetings (though no American President has attempted the latter). But he may not appeal to the electorate to think again about its choice of a legislative branch of government by dissolving the Assembly. Where the President does have the constitutional authority of dissolution, as in Haiti and Paraguay, the system does not conform to the presidential pattern.

The Assembly Is Ultimately Supreme Over the Other Branches of Government and There Is No Fusion of the Executive and Legislative Branches as in a Parliament

It was remarked of parliamentary systems that neither the Government nor the Assembly is supreme because both are subordinate parts of the parliamentary institution. In presidential systems such fusion of the executive and legislative powers is replaced by separation, each having its own sphere. As we have just observed, constitutionally the Executive cannot interfere in the proceedings of the Assembly, still less dissolve it, and the Assembly for its part cannot invade the province of the Executive.

In practice the relation of the two, at least in the United States, is much more subtle than the theory of the separation of powers and checks and balances would indicate. The President is head of the Government and leader of his party. He controls an immense amount of patronage. He is responsible for the preparation of major legislation (even if technically it is introduced by members of the Assembly) and for securing its successful passage through the Assembly. Certainly Franklin D. Roosevelt effectively dominated the United States Congress in the famous "Hundred Days" of 1933. Conversely, to say that Congress cannot invade the province of the

Executive does not mean that it cannot obstruct his policies, or, if it so chooses, refuse the appropriations which are usually necessary for their implementation. If the United States Congress refused to grant the President the funds he required he would have to go without. In practice a compromise is nearly always reached, and the President is left to mind his own Executive business. In certain Latin American countries the President can automatically decree the budget if the Legislature fails to vote it. There is also a provision to this effect in the constitution of the French Fifth Republic.

Since there is no Parliament there can be no parliamentary supremacy. Where, then, does supreme power lie in the event of a serious controversy? It has been demonstrated that the Assembly cannot force the resignation of the President any more than he can dissolve the Assembly. Moreover, both branches of government may find that their actions are declared unconstitutional by yet a third power, the Judiciary. In a sense the Constitution is supreme. The short answer is that it is intended in presidential government that the different branches shall check and balance one another and that none shall predominate.

Yet in a very real sense it is the Assembly which is ultimately supreme. The President may have considerable authority allocated to him in the Constitution but he may be powerless unless the Assembly grants him the necessary appropriations. If he acts unconstitutionally the Assembly may impeach him. In the event of a serious conflict even the Judiciary must bow to the will of the Assembly because this body has the right to amend the Constitution. The American Constitution is not, as is sometimes asserted, simply "what the judges say it is."

It may be suggested that the position does not appear to be altogether different from that in parliamentary states where ultimately the legislature may amend the Constitution. This is not so. In parliamentary states the Constitution has to be amended by both Government and Assembly acting as Parliament, whereas in presidential systems the Assembly may amend the constitution without regard to the President. For example, the American Congress has limited the presidential tenure of office to two terms.

It is true that this authority of the Assembly is sometimes qualified. In the United States three-quarters of the State legislatures or conventions must ratify amendments to the constitution. In states which possess unitary constitutions it is often thought desirable that amendments shall be passed only if there is a two-thirds majority in favour or if, following a general election, a new Assembly gives further approval. The "sovereign people" themselves are thus consulted. But in each instance it is an Assembly, not the Executive or Judiciary, which has the power to change the constitution: it is the legislative branch which is supreme.

The Executive Is Directly Responsible to the Electorate

Governments in parliamentary countries are appointed by the Head of State; they are not elected. By contrast the presidential Executive is dependent on a popular vote and the President alone (and Vice-President if there is one), of all the persons in the political system, is elected by the whole body of electors. Whereas the pre-parliamentary Monarchies could not in the end withstand the pressure of the people's representatives upon their control of government a President can say to members of the Assembly: "You represent your constituency: I represent the whole people." There is no reply to this argument, and it is perhaps not surprising that in many South American countries and in France at various times the President has been able to go one step further and to assert that he *alone* represented the people.

Admittedly in form the President of the United States is still indirectly elected by an Electoral College, but so long as there are two main parties and one candidate who obtains at least fifty per cent of the vote in the College the result is a foregone conclusion after the national elections. The growth of political parties and the realities of political life have in practice placed the nomination of candidates for the Presidency in the hands of the parties, and elections in those of the electorate. If one of the various proposals to abolish the College were adopted, it might alter the balance of power among the States but it would make no difference to the fundamentally direct relationship of President and people. In other presidential countries, without exception, election is direct.

It is a distinctive feature of the system that the President should owe his position not, as in parliamentary government, to appointment, nor, as in convention theory, to selection by the Assembly, but to the electorate at election time. Between elections the President speaks to the voters directly, not indirectly through an Assembly. He cannot, except on special occasions, deliver a speech to the Assembly and unlike Prime Ministers in parliamentary states he may not use it as a forum. Hence in the United States has grown up the fireside chat, the television appearance, and above all the weekly press conference where the President is the host.

The electorate in presidential countries therefore bears a double burden. The voters elect representatives from their own districts to the Assembly, but instead of leaving the selection of the Government to the Assembly and Head of State they also elect a President as Executive. In their wisdom they may prefer a President who belongs to a party which has only minority status in the Assembly. They will, nevertheless, at least in the United States, expect the two branches of government to reach a workable compromise.

There Is No Focus of Power in the Political System
The political activities of parliamentary systems have their focal point in Parliament. Heads of State, Governments, elected representatives, political parties, interest groups and electorates all acknowledge its supremacy.

It is tempting to assume that there must be a similar focal point in presidential systems. This is not so. Instead of concentration there is division; instead of unity, fragmentation. In the design of Washington, D.C., the President's home, the White House, is at the opposite end of Pennsylvania Ave. to the capital where Congress meets. Geographical dispersion symbolizes their political separation.

Nor is it accurate to say that the difference is simply one of degree of fusion: that instead of one focus there are several. It would hardly be less apposite to say that the difference between a political system in which there is only one political party and others in which there are two or more lies simply in the number of parties. In both instances there is a difference in kind more fundamental than the obvious one of degree.

In parliamentary systems, for example, there cannot for long be profound differences of opinion between Government and Assembly. Where a division appears it is in the nature of parliamentarism either for the Government to resign or for an election to take place. The differences must be resolved in order that mutual confidence between Government and Assembly, essential to the operation of the system, be restored. Differences are confined to political parties, which exist to express the various opinions in the matter.

In presidential systems there are also differences between parties and where there is federalism there may be important differences between regions as well. But in addition there is a gulf between the President and the Assembly (to say nothing of possible differences between members of his Administration, bound together by no ties of collective responsibility). Moreover, these differences, especially those between the President and Assembly, are part of the system, friction and discord being an indication not of imminent chaos but of its proper operation. In the late spring of every year the *New York Times* remarks on the unwillingness of Congress to enact the President's programme and tries to forecast the probability of his most important measures passing into Law. Later in the summer as Congress recesses it lists those which have been successful. In 1957 they amounted to barely half of President Eisenhower's 155 bills.

Parliamentarians often find it incredible that the Executive in a presidential system should at times have so little control over legislation. "What is the use," they ask, "of a Government which does not govern?" But of course in a presidential system there is no Government. There is no recognized centre of the political system on which people and politicians focus their interests and aspirations. Unlike parliamentarism, which ensures the co-ordination of the various branches of the political system, the presidential system assumes that the executive and legislative branches shall be constantly checking and balancing each others' activities. It may therefore prevent action from being taken unless there is wide agreement and considerable pressure (hence the role of pressure groups in the United States).

Those who admire efficient government may be inclined towards the Cabinet government form of parliamentarism. Those who prefer more limited government may turn towards presidentialism. It should not be assumed, however, that the presidential form, because it is divided, is necessarily one of weak government. Admittedly, where presidential leadership is lacking the system may even appear to be on the verge of breaking down. But where there is a vigorous Executive he may in fact dominate the Assembly, as several American Presidents (notably Franklin D. Roosevelt) have succeeded in doing.

Miraculously, in the United States this domination has never gone too far. In much of Central and South America, where there is the form of presidential government but not the substance, the presidential system has been distorted by dictatorship.

It is difficult to explain the failure of presidential government in so many parts of South America and it is perilous to confine such explanation to purely political factors. Historically and culturally South and Central America are utterly different from the United States. However, there are a number of particular political features of these countries' systems which deserve note, not least of which is the multi-party system which characterises several of them. Where a President is elected by what is in effect a minority vote instead of by the clear majority customary in the United States he lacks that sense of being the people's representative which is so marked a feature of the American presidency. At the very least it adds a complicating factor to the relations of President, Assembly and people, and in all probability contributes to political instability.

Where there is a multi-party system there is the temptation to add to the President's status and independence by giving him a longer term of office than the Assembly. Not surprisingly the French Fifth Republic's constitution gives the President a term of seven years compared to the Assembly's four. Such a long term, while of small moment in a parliamentary system, may make a President in a non-parliamentary system a powerful figure.

22   Federalism

Political systems can also be examined from the perspective of how political power is spatially distributed. The spatial dimension, typically, is understood as a continuum. At one pole, in unitary systems, political power is formally concentrated in the hands of central governments. In practice, most unitary political systems allow local governments to exercise some authority, but that authority, in the final analysis, is only exercised at the will of central governments. In federal systems, powers are shared by central and constituent governments, which each have a share of sovereignty. At the other pole, in confederal systems, constituent governments retain sovereignty except when they specifically delegate functions to the central government.

In the following reading, Garth Stevenson, a professor of political science at Brock University, traces the roots of federal and confederal political systems and contrasts both with unitary systems. He argues that traditional legal definitions of federalism are not quite sufficient because they obscure the dynamic qualities of federalism. Stevenson suggests that because federalism rests on the division of jurisdictions between at least two levels of government, and because no one level of government can abolish the jurisdiction of the other, federalism entails a continual process of bargaining. In exploring a variety of cross-national examples of the origins and workings of federal systems, Stevenson places Canadian federalism in a larger context. The reading is drawn from Stevenson's book *Unfulfilled Union: Canadian Federalism and National Unity*.

● ● ● ● ● ● ● ● ● ●

During Canada's centennial celebrations in 1967, a national magazine invited its readers to participate in selecting the most typically Canadian joke. The winning entry proved to be a local version of the ancient elephant joke, which recounts how persons of various nationalities responded in different ways to the task of writing an essay on some aspect of the elephant. While the German wrote on the elephant as a military weapon, the Frenchman on the elephant's love life, and so forth, the Canadian essayist's title was "The elephant: Does it fall under federal or provincial jurisdiction?"

Not only the outcome but the occasion of this contest testifies to the pervasiveness of federalism in Canadian life. The centennial which we celebrated in 1967, after all, was not really the centennial of Canada, not even the centennial of the Canadian state (which was founded in 1841), but only the centennial of Canadian federalism. In geo-political terms it was also the centennial of the date at which New Brunswick and Nova Scotia became part of Canada, but that event was not the first, the last, nor even the most important step in Canada's territorial expansion, although it may have paved the way for the greater expansion that followed.

Federalism, clearly, is for most Canadians inseparable from their image of their country, and this has probably never been more true than it is at present. Except among separatists, belief in the desirability of some kind of federalism, however defined, seems to be virtually universal. Indeed even some separatists in western Canada favour a federation, although one that would be confined to the four western provinces. If political science students observed by the author over several years are in any way representative, it appears that Canadians are completely unable to imagine their country as being other than federal, or as having any existence apart from federalism. If pressed to consider alternatives, they invariably assume that this must mean the dissolution of the federal tie and independence for each of the ten provinces.

While unusual and perhaps even unique by world standards, this obsession with federalism is by no means misguided. Federalism is undoubtedly, for better or for worse, a fundamental attribute of the way in which Canada conducts its public business. Interest groups and political parties are structured along federal lines, corresponding with the structures of government itself, as are educational institutions, the professions, and even the private sector of the economy. Statistical data are collected and organized in such a way as to highlight the boundaries between the provinces. Intergovernmental conferences have become a basic part of the political process, arguably more important than Parliament or the provincial legislatures.

These facts are not in dispute, nor can they be explained away, even by those who agree with John Porter that the obsession with federalism is an obstacle to creative politics and who dismiss the reputed sociocultural differences between the various provinces as "hallowed nonsense." Porter's point, however, is well taken when he argues that the attention given to federalism distracts attention from other issues, and may even be deliberately designed to do so. If politics is about who gets what, when, and how, Canadians are subtly but constantly encouraged to view these fundamental questions in jurisdictional or interprovincial terms. What does Quebec want? What does Alberta stand to lose? What is "Ottawa" taking from "the provinces" and what will they seek in return? Are we becoming more centralized or more decentralized?

A few lonely critics, like Porter, have argued that these are completely meaningless questions, designed only to mystify the masses. In contrast, politicians, the media, and an increasing number of academics often go to the other extreme and give the impression that these are the only significant questions in Canadian political life. The reality lies somewhere between the two extremes. Questions about federalism are real and important, even if they may sometimes be posed in mystifying lanugage, but they are not the only questions in our political life. So pervasive is federalism to Canadians, however, that the more fundamental questions to which Porter and others have drawn attention cannot easily be considered or resolved outside of the federal context in which they occur.

DEFINING FEDERALISM

Despite their constant use by Canadians, and their frequent use in other countries, the word "federal" and its various derivatives are not lacking in ambiguity. Their history has been long and complex, and their polemical use is neither a recent nor a uniquely Canadian phenomenon. Even those who are professionally concerned with the study of federalism have failed to agree on what it means, what is included, and what should be excluded. As we shall see, almost any possible definition presents problems.

Certain words used in political discourse, like "legislature," "bureaucracy," or "election" are quite easily defined, for the fairly narrow and concrete phenomena to which they refer are easily recognized. Other words, such as "democracy," "liberalism," or "socialism" pose greater problems because they are broader in scope and too intimately associated with past and present ideological controversies to be defined in a manner that satisfies everyone. Some would go so far as to argue that these words are no more than ideological symbols, devoid of real content and substance. Certainly their repeated use as ideological symbols has left them vulnerable to such accusations.

Only a few political thinkers—Pierre Elliott Trudeau would probably be one of them—have endowed the concept of federalism with this heavy load of symbolic attributes. It has thus seemed plausible to treat federalism as a concrete, easily defined, and value-free concept. Yet somehow the effort to treat it thus never entirely succeeds. The concept of federalism seems to be a hybrid with some qualities from both categories of political concept.

In searching for definitions, the reader of the *Oxford English Dictionary* will find "federal" to mean "of or pertaining to a convenant, compact or treaty" but with the cautionary note that this definition is obsolete. Persevering, one finds a further definition: "of or pertaining to or of the nature of that form of government in which two or more states constitute a political unity while remaining more or less independent with regard to their internal affairs." Apart from the question-begging "more or less," which neatly evades the essence of the problem, this definition is notable chiefly for the fact that it establishes federalism as a form of *decentralized* government.

Even this apparent precision, however, vanishes when one seeks in the same dictionary the meaning of "federation," for this is said to mean "the formation of a political unity out of a number of separate states, provinces or colonies, so that each retains the management of its internal affairs." In this definition a new and different basis of distinction appears, for it is explicitly stated that the components of the federation, whether state, provinces, or colonies, previously enjoyed a separate existence.

Defining federalism in this way would seem to have the advantage that federal countries could be easily identified, but there are ambiguities here as well. The three Prairie provinces in Canada and a majority of the fifty states in the United States had no separate existence prior to the federal union; they were formed subsequently out of territories which the central government had acquired by purchase or conquest. Since it would be absurd to exclude Canada or the United States from any definition of federalism, the definition must be modified to specify that only some of the subnational units need to have enjoyed a previously separate existence.

So far we have been preoccupied mainly with distinguishing a federation from a non-federal or unitary state. However, a definition of federalism must also serve the purpose, which is even more essential in Canada's present circumstances, of distinguishing federalism from other forms of *decentralized* government. The European Community, for example, is not a federation because the powers of the Commission at Brussels and of the other community institutions are too insignificant in relation to the governments of the member countries. As was noted earlier the use of the term "federal" with reference to a "covenant, compact or treaty" is now considered obsolete, although at one time the word was so used. The "sovereignty-association" proposed by the Parti Québécois, as well as other hypothetical arrangements that would drastically reduce the powers of the central government in Canada, must be excluded from any useful definition of federalism, not because they are undesirable (although the author happens to be of this opinion) but because to include them in a category that also includes the United States and the Federal Republic of Germany would make the category too heterogeneous to have any analytic usefulness.

This brings us to another problem of semantics, namely the distinction between a *federation* and a *confederation*. These closely related words were not at first clearly distinguished, and in Canada are still not, but in the rest of the world they have gradually acquired distinct meanings. Outside of

Canada, "confederation" is a word used mainly by historians, most often in reference to various arrangements among sovereign states (usually for the purposes of mutual defence) that fall short of establishing a new state or a central government with meaningful power and authority. Perhaps the European Community, the North Atlantic Treaty Organization (NATO), and other such institutions are the closest contemporary equivalents of these early "confederations."

The earliest confederation in the English-speaking world was the New England Confederation, which lasted from 1643 to 1648, a period for much of which England was too distracted by its own bourgeois revolution to provide much protection for its North American colonies. Threatened by the Indian tribes and the nearby colonies of other European powers, the New Englanders formed an alliance and established a commission of eight delegates, four from each colonial government, to decide collectively on questions of defence and external relations. Since these delegates had no authority apart from that of the colonial governments that appointed them, and since in practice it soon appeared that any one government could veto a decision by the commissioners, this confederation was more like a modern international organization than a modern federal state.

In 1778, two years after the Declaration of Independence, the thirteen colonies formed a military alliance with rudimentary common institutions somewhat similar to those of the earlier New England Confederation. The agreement which brought this new arrangement into force was known as the Articles of Confederation, an appellation that would lead subsequent generations of Americans to associate the word "confederation" with loose alliances of this type, while reserving the word "federal" for their present, more centralized constitution. However, the Americans of the eighteenth century had not yet made this distinction. Instead, the word "federal" seems to have been used in the sense in which the *Oxford English Dictionary* now regards as obsolete, to refer to the Articles of Confederation themselves. At the Philadelphia Convention of 1787, where the present constitution of the United States was drafted, supporters of the Virginia Plan, on which that constitution is based, used the term "federal" in that same sense, and argued that a "merely federal" union, such as then existed, was inadequate to secure the objectives of "common defence, security of liberty, and general welfare." In its place they proposed to establish what they called a "national" government, which would have authority to impose its will on the states.

A delegate from New York, where opposition to the latter idea seems to have been exceptionally strong, protested that the Virginia Plan was unacceptable:

He was decidedly of the opinion that the power of the Convention was restrained to amendments of a Federal nature, and having for their basis the confederacy in being. . . . New York would never have concurred in sending Deputies to the Convention, if she had supposed the deliberations were to turn on a consolidation of the states, and a National Government.

In response to such sentiments, the nationalists who wanted "a consolidation of the States" began to use the reassuring and familiar word "federal" with reference to their own plans, although they did not abandon its use with reference to the Articles of Confederation.

This deliberate attempt to blur what was in fact a fundamental distinction can best be seen in the series of anonymous essays by which Alexander Hamilton, John Jay, and James Madison attempted to persuade the voters of New York to ratify the proposed new constitution. These essays, which still rank among the classics of political science, are themselves known as the Federalist Papers, although their purpose was to argue the inadequacy of "federalism" in its original sense. Once the union was achieved, the word "Federalist" was adopted as the name of the political party representing the mercantile and financial interests who wanted a strong central government and subordinate states. In fact Hamilton, the first leader of the Federalist Party, had presented at the Philadelphia Convention a plan for a constitution even more centralized than the one that was finally adopted. Some of Hamilton's ideas, although rejected by his own countrymen, were later to be incorporated in the British North America Act of 1867.

As a result of these developments, the word "federal" and its derivatives became associated with a considerable degree of centralization, at least in the United States. The Swiss Confederation, which until 1848 was little more than a loose alliance of sovereign states, and the German Confederation, an even more nebulous organization established by the Congress of Vienna in 1815, helped to perpetuate the view that "confederation" referred to a compact that fell short of establishing a new central government. The Swiss, however, somewhat confused the issue by continuing to use the word "confederation" even after they had adopted a constitution that was "federal" in the new American sense.

As far as Canada is concerned, one constitutional historian has speculated that the use of the term "confederation" to describe the proposed union of the British North American colonies had exactly the same purpose as the adoption of the word "federal" by proponents of the Virginia Plan after 1787. In both cases, according to this view, a word normally associated with the absence of a strong central government was deliberately misused by those who in fact intended to create one in an effort to confuse those who might find such a project alarming. John A. Macdonald was certainly using an idiosyncratic definition in 1861 when he stated that "the true principle of a Confederation" means a system in which all the powers not specifically assigned to the provinces were given to the central government, unlike the American constitution whose tenth amendment, adopted in 1791, said precisely the reverse. A.A. Dorion, the leading French Canadian opponent of Macdonald's "Confederation," was more correct, or at least more conventional, a few years later when he defined "a real confederation" as "giving the largest powers to the local governments and merely a delegated authority to the general government." However, Macdonald won and Dorion lost, so that Macdonald's usage of the term has acquired semiofficial status in Canada, however bizarre it may seem to Americans. Dorion's definition may be historically justified but has become somewhat irrelevant, since none of the "confederations" that Dorion had in mind are still in existence, nor have any new ones under that name been established. Both Canada and Switzerland, however, use the word "confederation" for what is actually a federal union in the modern American sense.

Although it is relatively easy to determine what federalism is not, the many writers on the subject have failed to agree on a satisfactory definition of what it is, even though almost every one of them has attempted to produce a definition. The most frequently used definitions, such as those used by K.C. Wheare, Danial Elazar, W.H. Riker, and Geoffrey Sawer, emphasize institutional and legal criteria: two levels of government, each independent of the other; a written constitution specifying the jurisdiction of each; judicial review of legislation as a means of maintaining the jurisdictional boundaries; the requirement that each level of government have a direct relationship with the people; and so forth. Political scientists like Elazar and Riker tend to interpret these criteria rather broadly, while lawyers like Wheare and Sawer are most inclined to exclude doubtful cases. Wheare, although born in Australia and teaching in England, included as federal constitutions only those which closely resembled the constitution of the United States, with the result that only Australia and Switzerland passed the test. He admitted, however, that Canada was a federal state in practice, even though certain features of the British North America Act departed from the federal norm.

Apart from the fact that they tell us little about how political systems really operate, these formal criteria are so restrictive that their applicability to even those considered the most federal of states can be questioned. Federal legislation in Switzerland is not subject to judicial review; provincial statutes in Canada can be disallowed; and the West German federal government is not completely independent of the *land* governments since the *länder* control the upper house of the federal parliament. One political scientist, Michael Reagan, has even questioned whether the United States qualifies as a federation by these criteria, since he considers that in practice there is no field reserved to the states in which Congress is unable to legislate.

In reaction against the rigidity and formality of these traditional criteria, writers on federalism began in the 1950s to explore alternative approaches to its definition. W.S. Livingston abandoned institutional criteria almost entirely and developed the concept of a "federal society," which he defined as any society in which economic, religious, racial, or historical diversities are territorially grouped. A formally unitary state in which political practices and conventions protected such diversities, such as the United Kingdom, should be considered to have some federal characteristics. Rufus Davis went a step further, questioning whether any "federal principle" could really be developed to distinguish federal from non-federal states; the difference was merely one of degree. Carl Friedrich defined federalism not as a static situation but as a process by which a number of separate political communities were gradually integrated.

While political scientists shifted their attention from formal institutions to political processes and behaviour, economists took an entirely different approach to defining federalism. Wallace Oates, in his book entitled *Fiscal Federalism*, wrote that federalism existed in any state where the public sector was decentralized, so that some decisions about taxing and spending were made by smaller territorial subdivisions in response to demands originating within themselves. From an economist's perspective it matters little whether such decentralization is protected by constitutional guarantees or whether it can be unilaterally revoked by the central government. At least in the short term, the economic consequences are the same in either case. While useful for its purpose, this definition is so broad that hardly any state, at least in the industrialized world, could avoid being classified as federal.

It is probably rash to attempt yet another definition of federalism when so many authorities have failed to agree on one that is totally satisfactory. Possibly no single definition of so elusive and controversial a concept could be satisfactory for all purposes. Nonetheless, the following definition is offered in the belief that it meets three essential criteria for a definition of federalism: (1) the definition should not be unduly restrictive; (2) it should serve to distinguish a federal state both from a unitary state and from looser forms of association; and (3) it should emphasize the political aspects of federalism.

With these criteria in mind, federalism will be defined as follows. It is a political system in which most or all of the structural elements of the state (executive, legislative, bureaucratic, judiciary, army or police, and machinery for levying taxation) are duplicated at two levels, with both sets of structures exercising effective control over the same territory and population. Furthermore, neither set of structures (or level of government) should be able to abolish the other's jurisdiction over this territory or population. As a corollary of this, relations between the two levels of government will tend to be characterized by bargaining, since neither level can fully impose its will on the other.

The condition that neither level of government should be able to abolish the other's jurisdiction effectively distinguishes federalism both from a unitary state and from looser forms of association. In a unitary state there may be some decentralization for administrative and even legislative purposes, but the central government can take back the power it has delegated to the lower levels of government or can even abolish them, as the British Parliament abolished the Parliament of Northern Ireland. In an alliance, league, or common market, on the other hand, the member states can withdraw or secede, an action which clearly prevents the central institutions from exercising any jurisdiction over their territories or populations. If the definition is a valid one, it follows that in a true federation the provinces or states have no right to secede. If such a right existed before, they surrendered it when they entered the federal union.

A somewhat legalistic way of expressing these characteristics of federalism is to say that the provinces or states are not sovereign entities, but at the same time the central government does not possess full and complete sovereignty either, since it lacks the power to abolish the other level of government. These facts may be represented symbolically by a written constitution, judicial review, elaborate procedures for amendment, and statements to the effect that sovereignty resides in "the people" (as in the United States) or "the Crown" (as in Canada). These symbolic aspects of federalism are not unimportant, but their importance exists only because they metaphorically represent, and may provide ideological justification for, real facts concerning the distribution of political power.

As to which countries are federal by this (or any other) definition, opinions will vary. Any effort to classify a particular country should be based on observation of how its political institutions actually operate. In some countries military coups and other changes of regime have occurred so frequently that one cannot say what is their "normal" or usual pattern of political activity. Others have simply not been studied enough for reliable data to be available. There is no doubt, however, that the few countries which are invariably included on any list of federations—and Canada is unquestionably one of these—would qualify as federations under this definition. On the other hand, countries such as the United Kingdom, which may have characteristics in common with at least some of the federations, would not.

FEDERALISM ON OTHER CONTINENTS

The origins of American federalism have been discussed already, while those of Canadian federalism will be considered in more detail in the next chapter. It would be unduly parochial, however, not to make a few comments about the origins of Swiss and German federalism.

Although they differ in many respects, an important similarity is the fact that in both cases a looser, non-federal association between sovereign states was transformed into a true federation as a result of war. In Switzerland the conservative Catholic cantons launched the Sonderbund War of 1847 to protect themselves against the emerging threat of bourgeois liberalism. Their defeat enabled the more progressive cantons to impose a federal constitution following the American model and establish a modern liberal state in place of the outmoded "confederation." In the German case, the defeat of Austria by Prussia in the war of 1866 led to the dissolution of the loose "confederation" which had been established in 1815 as the successor to the old Holy Roman Empire. With Austria now excluded from further involvement in German affairs, a Prussian-dominated federation was established in northern Germany in 1867. The southern states entered it voluntarily in 1870, at the end of which year it adopted the title of "German Empire." Some form of German federalism has existed ever since, except during Hitler's dictatorship and for a few years after his defeat.

In the twentieth century federal unions have been formed in Australia (1901), the USSR (1924), Malaya (1948), Rhodesia and Nyasaland (1953), the West Indies (1958), and Cameroun (1961). In four of these six cases the federating units were colonies of the British Empire, although in the Australian case the initiative for federation was taken entirely by the Australians themselves. Soviet federalism permitted the new Russian republic to reunite with most of the outlying territories of the old empire, which had been temporarily detached from Russia during its civil war. The Federal Republic of Cameroun united two territories which had been held under United nations trusteeship by Britain and France, respectively. In the early 1960s Malaya changed its name to Malaysia when it absorbed a number of other British colonies. The Rhodesia and Nyasaland and West Indian federations disintegrated at about the same time, with some of their components becoming independent and others remaining under British rule.

A number of other countries are frequently referred to as federations, although it cannot be said, at least without serious qualification, that they resulted from a union of previously separate entities. Argentina, Brazil,

Mexico, and Venezuela all adopted "federal" constitutions in the nineteenth century, possibly in imitation of the United States. Most external observers, however, are sceptical about Latin American federalism, on the grounds that the component states do not retain any meaningful degree of autonomy.

Outside of North America and central Europe, federalism has had its greatest influence on the Indian sub-continent, where one-fifth of the world's population lives. The British ruled most of India, including the present Pakistan and Bangladesh, as a unitary colony from 1857 until 1935. In the latter year the Government of India Act established provincial legislatures, and thus a sort of quasi-federalism similar to what John A. Macdonald intended for Canada. In 1947 the British handed over their authority to two new states, India and Pakistan, which between them soon absorbed the various princely states that had never been under direct British rule. Both successor states have adopted constitutions that divide legislative powers between two levels of government, and the subnational governments, at least in India, enjoy considerable autonomy. However, the central government in India was able to "reorganize" the boundaries of the component states soon after independence, an event that would surely be unthinkable in such genuinely federal countries as Canada, Switzerland, or the United States. It is also interesting that the Supreme Court of India, in an important case upholding the central government's power to expropriate mineral resources belonging to the states, declared flatly that India was a decentralized unitary state rather than a federal one.

The case of Nigeria is very similar. Although they had previously ruled it as a unitary state, the British endowed it with the dubious blessing of a federal constitution of 1954. It remained a federation after gaining its independence in 1960, but the federal constitution was suspended by the military regime during the ultimately successful civil war against the separatists in the southeastern province, who attempted with some foreign assistance to establish an independent "Biafra." Postwar Nigeria, however, has re-established subnational state governments, even though the boundaries of the new states bear no relation to the old.

Three European cases remain to be considered. Austria adopted a federal constitution in 1922, Yugoslavia in 1946, and Czechoslovakia in 1968. The Yugoslavian constitution of 1946 has since been replaced by a new one of almost unbelievable complexity, but its federal features have if anything been enhanced. All three countries are in a sense the successors of the Habsburg Empire which dissolved in 1918, and they share the common characteristic that their internal boundaries and component units have a longer history as distinct entities than have the countries themselves. On these grounds, and in terms of the real autonomy enjoyed by the subnational governments, Austria and Yugoslavia have at least as good a claim to be considered "federal" as India and Pakistan, even though they are not really unions of previously independent entities. The case of Czechoslovakia is more dubious.

EXPLANATIONS FOR FEDERALISM

An explanation for federalism which is particularly relevant to the central and eastern European experience was offered by Rudolf Schlesinger in a book published in 1945. Schlesinger suggested that federalism arose in situations where national consciousness was focussed on a collectivity which did not coincide with the traditional boundaries of dynastic states. In Germany the national community included a number of dynastic states, while in the Austrian and Russian empires the dynastic state included a number of national communities. In either case federalism developed, with one level of government corresponding to the rising forces of nationalism, industrialism, and the bourgeoisie. In Western Europe, where the new communities and the old units tended to coincide, there was no need for federalism, and unitary states have been the general rule.

Many students of federalism, however, refuse to recognize as a federation any state that did not result from a union of previously separate entities which retained their identities after union. As a result, efforts to generalize about the reasons why federations come into existence tend to ignore the ambiguous cases or those in which the subnational governments were established by devolutions of power from the centre. K.C. Wheare lists the conditions leading to federal union as follows: the need for common defence, desire for independence from foreign powers, desire to gain economic benefits, some previous political association, similar political institutions, geographical closeness, similar social conditions, and the existence of political elites interested in unification. No previous or subsequent writer on federalism has really added anything to this list.

Despite its completeness, or perhaps because of it, Wheare's list of conditions is not very informative. The first two conditions are almost indistinguishable, the last would seem to be present by definition, and several of the others are so vague as to be almost useless. Wheare does not present anything that can be called a theory of federal unification.

The most interesting theoretical question about the origins of federal unions is whether military insecurity or anticipated economic benefits is the more important motive, or whether in fact both must be present. It is also conceivable that a security motive might be more important in some cases and an economic motive in others.

The case for the pre-eminence of economic motives was made most memorably by Charles Beard in his classic study, *An Economic Interpreta-*

tion of the Constitution of the United States. Beard suggested that the move of the Americans to adopt their present constitution was led by merchant capitalists and that the constitution itself was carefully drafted to protect their economic interests. For Beard, American politics after the Revolutionary War were dominated by the conflict between his class and the more numerous but less influential farmers who, in his view, mainly opposed the constitution. The merchants wanted a strong central government to repress further revolutionary outbreaks by agrarian radicals (such as Massachusetts had experienced in 1786-87), to prevent the repudiation of debts and the printing of paper money, and to protect their commerce on the high seas. The adoption of the constitution marked the swing of the revolutionary pendulum back to the right and the restoration of "order."

Not all economic interpretations of federalism emphasize class conflict, as Beard's does. The kind of economic motives that Wheare seems to have had in mind are those emphasized by more conventional American historians and their Canadian and Australian counterparts: larger markets, the removal of tariff barriers, penetration of the western hinterlands, and so forth. Marxist historians, of course, would view even these types of motives as reflecting the interests of ruling classes, and perhaps as leading to conflict with other classes that opposed them. Even where there was such opposition, however, the establishment of a federal state might not be necessary to achieve these objectives. Western European capitalists seem to be achieving quite similar objectives through the very limited integrative arrangements represented by the European Community, which falls far short of establishing federalism.

Security motives for federal union are emphasized by William H. Riker, who views federalism as a "bargain" by which political elites in the states or provinces agree to sacrifice some, but not all, of their autonomy in return for protection against an external threat or, more rarely, a share in the benefits of military expansion and conquest. The bargain is usually initiated by a relatively large and powerful entity (Virginia, the Province of Canada, or Bismarck's Prussia) and accepted by smaller states or provinces, which have both more to lose (because they will have relatively little influence within a larger union) and more to gain (because they could not hope to attain security, let alone expansion, by themselves).

Obvious external threats to security were certainly present at the time of union in some federations, such as Switzerland, Bismarck's Germany, the USSR, and Pakistan. The importance of a security motive in the Canadian case will be discussed in the next chapter. Security motives are somewhat harder to discern, though not entirely absent, in other cases, such as those of Australia, postwar West Germany, and Cameroun.

It may be that no single factor can explain every instance of the formation of a federal union, and even in a particular case a variety of factors may contribute. The author of a recent book on federalism, R.D. Dikshit, adopts both of these assumptions. Dikshit's purpose is to explain not only why federal unions evolve, but also why they differ in the extent of the powers conferred on the central government, and why some federal unions are more durable and successful than others. Dikshit distinguishes factors leading to union from factors leading to the retention of some degree of regional autonomy. A preponderance of the first will lead to the formation of a unitary state, while a preponderance of the second will prevent any union from taking place. Only a balance between the two will lead to federalism, and only if the balance is maintained will federalism survive.

Dikshit's factors leading to union are essentially the same as K.C. Wheare's, although he differs from Wheare in including a common language, culture, and religion as one of his conditions. His factors conducive to the maintainance of regional autonomy are essentially the reverse of the factors leading to union, for example, regionally grouped cultural diversity rather than cultural homogeneity, competitive economies with conflicting interests rather than the expectation of economic benefits from union, and so forth. Federal union does not demand that all of the factors in either category be present, for there are several possible combinations that will bring it about, although the precise nature of the new federal state will vary accordingly. West Germany is a very centralized federation, according to Dikshit, because most of the factors leading to union were present in 1949, while the factors conducive to maintaining regional autonomy were virtually absent. Only the absence of a military threat (since the country was effectively protected by the United States) prevented a centralized unitary state from emerging instead of a federation. On the other hand, Pakistan at the time of its formation had practically all of the conditions which lead to the maintenance of regional autonomy, while the military threat from India was the only factor that contributed to union. The result was a weak federation that could not prevent the secession of its largest unit in the civil war of 1971.

EVALUATING FEDERALISM

For a Canadian audience it is perhaps necessary to explain that evaluating federalism means evaluating the consequences of having two distinct levels of government, rather than a national government only. Since most Canadians find it impossible to imagine Canada as a unitary state, few have considered it worthwhile to discuss and evaluate the relative merits of federal and unitary institutions. Some such discussion took place prior to

1867, but since then the vast majority of Canadians outside of Quebec have simply taken federalism for granted. In Quebec, admittedly, there has been controversy over federalism, but what is really being debated there is whether or not Quebec should be independent, not the advantages and disadvantages of federal institutions as such. No one in Quebec contemplates abolishing the provincial level of government.

In other parts of the world, by contrast, the respective merits of federal and unitary government have been lengthily, although inconclusively, debated. Among the more strikingly unfavourable assessments was that of former Nigerian Prime Minister Sir Abubaker Balewa, who at his last meeting with Harold Wilson said to him: "You are fortunate. One thing only I wish for you, that you never have to become Prime Minister of a federal and divided country."

Since he was assassinated four days after making this remark, and since his death proved to be the opening of the Nigerian civil war, Balewa's pessimism was probably justified. Others have expressed, although in less memorable circumstances, his view that federations are characterized by disorder, conflict, and political bickering, which may be the less attractive side of the intergovernmental bargaining that is, by our definition, an almost inevitable aspect of federal politics. Defenders of federalism, on the other hand, would argue that regional and cultural conflicts are obviously not caused by federalism, since they exist in unitary states like Ethiopia, Spain, or the United Kingdom.

A classic argument against federalism was presented by A.V. Dicey, a late nineteenth-century writer on British constitutional law, who maintained that federalism produced weak and ineffective government, conservatism, and legalism. Dicey's views, and especially his assertion that "federal government means weak government," may have some relevance for Canada today, almost a century after they were expressed. Federalism was weak, according to Dicey, because energy was wasted in conflicts between the two levels of government, because the central government had to respond to regional demands, or appear to do so, at the expense of efficiency and effectiveness, and because the power of either level to act was constrained by a rigid constitution. It was conservative because the existence of a rigid written constitution produced a "superstitious reverence" for existing principles and institutions. It was legalistic because lawyers and judges were inevitably called upon to interpret the constitution and define the respective powers of the two levels of government.

While much of Dicey's analysis is plausible, it is far from evident, with hindsight, that the unitary British system of government which he so admired avoided any of the defects which he associated with federalism. Nor is the untrammeled authority of the legislature invariably a blessing, as

Dicey complacently assumed in the salad days of Victorian liberalism. Finally, the connection asserted between conservatism and legalism may be questioned. Particularly in the United States, the judiciary has often been more liberal and enlightened than either the executive or legislative branches of government.

In Dicey's defence it may be argued that the United States, Canada, and Australia, all of which are federations, have lagged behind the unitary states of northern and western Europe in their provisions for social welfare, income security, full employment, and public ownership and control of the economy. Possibly the inefficacy of federalism, and the restrictions which it places on the power of the central government, are partly to blame.

The admirers of federalism have not lacked arguments of their own since the middle of the eighteenth century, when Montesquieu published his *De l'esprit des lois*. It is not entirely clear what Montesquieu meant by federalism, and no state that we would call federal existed in his lifetime, but his views greatly influenced the creators of the American constitution. As well as having originated the notion of "the separation of powers," Montesquieu argued that a federal republic was a means of combining the freedom possible in a small state with the security against external threats that was only possible in a large one.

Since in the thermonuclear era it is doubtful whether any state can guarantee security, a modern variation on Montesquieu's view might be that federalism combines the economic advantages of large size with the possibilities for self-government that exist in a smaller political community. A non-federalist could argue that neither part of this proposition is fully supported by experience. The prosperity of Norway, Switzerland, Singapore, and Kuwait suggests that size is not a prerequisite to economic success. On the other hand, the reputed benefits of grass-roots democracy and freedom in a "small" subnational political system may really exist in the Swiss canton of Appenzell-Inner-Rhodes but bear no discernible relation to the facts of political life in Quebec, Ontario, New York, or California, all of which are larger than many nation-states.

Another argument sometimes heard in support of federalism is really the converse of Dicey's argument against it. According to this view, a "weak" state whose power is divided between two sets of authorities and restrained by legal restrictions is safer than a "strong" and vigorous state, because it is less likely to be oppressive. Dispersed and divided power is less dangerous than concentrated power, and the cumbersome decision-making procedures in a federal state make it less likely that unpredictable eruptions of popular sentiment will be reflected in public policy. Even if government at one level tries to be oppressive, government at the other level, as well as the judiciary, will prevent it from doing too much harm.

This is essentially Madison's argument in the celebrated number ten of the Federalist Papers, and it recurs in several of the other papers as well. It was also a favourite argument of American conservatives during Franklin Roosevelt's New Deal and of Australian conservatives during the Labor Government of Gough Whitlam. When subjected to critical examination, this argument for federalism looks remarkably like an ideological facade for vested economic interests.

A somewhat different but related argument for federalism is that it protects minorities and enables cultural, linguistic, religious, and ideological diversity to flourish. A prominent supporter of this perspective is Pierre Elliott Trudeau, whose well-known but often misunderstood hostility to "nationalism" is really no more than the view that the state should not be intolerant of diversity and should not be identified with any ethnic or cultural group. In a federal state, he would argue, this is less likely to happen.

Several examples can be cited of diversities protected by federalism. Multilingualism in Switzerland provides an obvious example. West German states and Canadian provinces have adopted a variety of solutions to the difficult problem of the relationship between Roman Catholic and public education. Socialists in prewar Vienna and the CCF-NDP in Saskatchewan achieved important reforms that would not have been possible at the national level. The more progressive American and Australian states extended the vote to women and abolished capital punishment long before there was nation-wide support for these innovations.

Nonetheless, in certain respects this optimistic view of federalism is not fully supported by experience. Federalism may protect those minorities which happen to make up a majority within one of the provinces or states, but it protects them precisely by allowing them to act as majorities, which means that they in turn can oppress the sub-minorities under their jurisdiction. Federalism has ensured the survival of the French language in Canada, but it has been of no benefit to Chinese in British Columbia, Hutterites in Alberta, or Jehovah's Witnesses in Quebec. All of these groups were unpopular at various times, and the provincial governments were more responsive to the hostile sentiments directed against these minorities than was the more remote central government. Had Canada been a unitary state, these groups might have benefited. The history of blacks in the American South and of Australian aborigines in the state of Queensland supports a similar conclusion.

One is tempted to conclude that both the arguments against federalism and the arguments in its favour can be as easily refuted as supported. Franz Neumann, in his essay "On the Theory of the Federal State," concluded that federalism might be good, bad, or indifferent, depending on the circumstances, and that it was impossible to evaluate federalism in general. W.H. Riker, in his book on federalism, stated that each particular case of federalism had to be examined separately to determine the balance sheet of costs and benefits. Attempting to perform this exercise himself, although in a rather superficial manner, he decided that federalism had benefited francophones in Canada, white racists in the United States, and business interests in Australia. In a later essay, however, he concluded rather inconsistently that federalism really made no difference in terms of policy outcomes, a statement which he attempted to support by arguing that federal Australia was little different from unitary New Zealand. From this he reached the further conclusion, which readers of this volume may be unhappy to hear, that the study of federalism was a waste of time! While it is hoped that Riker was incorrect in this conclusion, his earlier view that each case of federalism should be examined individually on its own merits is one with which the present writer would concur. . . .

23   Consociational Democracy

The argument that pluralist state-society relations encourage stability, legitimacy, and democratic practices seems to be a compelling one, at least when it is applied to such political systems as the United States and Britain. These political cultures can be described as relatively homogeneous, so there is a reasonable expectation that majorities will be fluid, and that no single group in society will consistently lose in important political battles of the day. By the same token, it is not at all clear that overlapping pluralism is the only formula for political stability, legitimacy, and democratic practice. As Arend Lijphart points out in the following essay, democracy, political stability, and legitimacy are also found in societies that are fragmented and deeply divided along linguistic, regional, and religious lines. Lijphart, a Dutch political scientist now teaching at the University of California, San Diego, argues that fragmented societies can achieve stability, legitimacy, and democracy by different means, by what he calls consociational devices. Much of Lijphart's analysis draws upon the experiences of the Netherlands, Belgium, and Austria, but the consociational model has also been applied to other national settings, including Canada. Lijphart's reading, "Consociational Democracy," appears in its entirety in Kenneth McRae's *Consociational Democracy: Political Accommodation in Segmented Societies.*

● ● ● ● ● ● ● ● ● ●

TYPES OF WESTERN DEMOCRATIC SYSTEMS

In Gabriel A. Almond's famous typology of political systems, first expounded in 1956, he distinguishes three types of Western democratic systems: Anglo-American political systems (exemplified by Britain and the United States), Continental European political systems (France, Germany, and Italy), and a third category consisting of the Scandinavian and Low Countries. The third type is not given a distinct label and is not described in detail; Almond merely states that the countries belonging to this type "combine some of the features of the Continental European and the Anglo-American" political systems, and "stand somewhere in between the Continental pattern and the Anglo-American." Almond's threefold typology has been highly influential in the comparative analysis of democratic politics, although, like any provocative and insightful idea, it has also been criticized. This research note will discuss the concept of "consociational democracy" in a constructive attempt to refine and elaborate Almond's typology of democracies.

The typology derives its theoretical significance from the relationship it establishes between political culture and social structure on the one hand and political stability on the other hand. The Anglo-American systems have a "homogeneous, secular political culture" and a "highly differentiated" role structure, in which governmental agencies, parties, interest groups, and the communication media have specialized functions and are autonomous, although interdependent. In contrast, the Continental European democracies are characterized by a "fragmentation of political culture" with separate "political sub-cultures." Their roles "are embedded in the sub-cultures and tend to constitute separate sub-systems of rôles." The terms "Anglo-American" and "Continental European" are used for convenience only and do not imply that geographical location is an additional criterion distinguishing the two types of democratic systems. . . .

Political culture and social structure are empirically related to political stability. The Anglo-American democracies display a high degree of stability and effectiveness. The Continental European systems, on the other hand, tend to be unstable; they are characterized by political immobilism, which is "a consequence of the [fragmented] condition of the political culture." Furthermore, there is the "ever-present threat of what is often called the 'Caesaristic' breakthrough" and even the danger of a lapse into totalitarianism as a result of this immobilism.

The theoretical basis of Almond's typology is the "overlapping memberships" proposition formulated by the group theorists Arthur F. Bentley and David B. Truman and the very similar "crosscutting cleavages" proposition of Seymour Martin Lipset. These propositions state that the psychological cross-pressures resulting from membership in different groups with diverse interests and outlooks lead to moderate attitudes. These groups may be formally organized groups or merely unorganized, categoric, and, in Truman's terminology, "potential" groups. Cross-pressures operate not only at the mass but also at the elite level: the leaders of social groups with heterogeneous and overlapping memberships will tend to find it necessary to adopt moderate positions. When, on the other hand, a society is divided by sharp cleavages with no or very few overlapping memberships and loyalties—in other words, when the political culture is deeply fragmented—the pressures toward moderate middle-of-the-road attitudes are absent. Political stability depends on moderation and, therefore, also on overlapping memberships. Truman states this proposition as follows: "In the long run a complex society may experience revolution, degeneration, and decay. If it maintains its stability, however, it may do so in large

measure because of the fact of multiple memberships." Bentley calls compromise "the very process itself of the criss-cross groups in action." And
Lipset argues that "the chances for stable democracy are enhanced to the
extent that groups and individuals have a number of crosscutting, politically relevant affiliations." Sometimes Almond himself explicitly adopts
the terminology of these propositions: for instance, he describes the French
Fourth Republic as being divided into "three main ideological families or
subcultures," which means that the people of France were "exposed to few
of the kinds of 'cross-pressures' that moderate [their] rigid political attitudes," while, on the other hand, he characterizes the United States and
Britain as having an "overlapping pattern" of membership.

In his later writings, Almond maintains both the threefold typology of
Western democracies and the criteria on which it is based, although the
terms that he uses vary considerably. In an article published in 1963, for
instance, he distinguishes between "stable democracies" and "immobilist
democracies." The latter are characterized by "fragmentation, both in a
cultural and structural sense" and by the absence of "consensus on governmental structure and process" (i.e. the Continental European systems). The
former group is divided into two sub-classes: one includes Great Britain, the
United States, and the Old Commonwealth democracies (i.e. the Anglo-
American systems), and the other "the stable multi-party democracies of
the European continent—the Scandinavian and Low Countries and
Switzerland." And in *Comparative Politics: A Developmental Approach*,
published in 1966, a distinction is drawn between modern democratic
systems with "high subsystem autonomy" (the Anglo-American democracies) and those with "limited subsystem autonomy" and fragmentation
of political culture (the Continental European democracies). The third type
is not included in this classification.

In what respects are Switzerland, Scandinavia, and the Low Countries
"in between" the Anglo-American and Continental European democracies? Here, too, Almond consistently uses the two criteria of role structure
and political culture. A differentiated role structure (or a high degree of
subsystem autonomy) is related to the performance of the political aggregation function in a society. The best aggregators are parties in two-party
systems like the Anglo-American democracies, but the larger the number
and the smaller the size of the parties in a system, the less effectively the
aggregation function will be performed; in the Continental European
multi-party systems only a minimum of aggregation takes place. The
"working multi-party systems" of the Scandinavian and Low Countries
differ from the French-Italian "crisis" systems in that some, though not all,
of their parties are "broadly aggregative." Almond gives the Scandinavian
Socialist parties and the Belgian Catholic and Socialist parties as examples.

This criterion does not distinguish adequately between the two types of democracies, however: if one calls the Belgian Catholic party broadly aggregative, the Italian Christian Democrats surely also have to be regarded as such. On the other hand, none of the Dutch and Swiss parties can be called broadly aggregative.

Instead of using the extent of aggregation performed by political parties as the operational indicator of the degree of subsystem autonomy, it is more satisfactory to examine the system's role structure directly. Like the Anglo-American countries, the Scandinavian states have a high degree of subsystem autonomy. But one finds a severely limited subsystem autonomy and considerable interpenetration of parties, interest groups, and the media of communication in the Low Countries, Switzerland, and also in Austria. In fact, subsystem autonomy is at least as limited in these countries as in the Continental European systems. According to the criterion of role structure, therefore, one arrives at a dichotomous rather than a threefold typology: the Scandinavian states must be grouped with the Anglo-American systems, and the other "in-between" states with the Continental European systems.

The application of the second criterion—political culture—leads to a similar result. Almond writes that the political culture in the Scandinavian and Low Countries is "more homogeneous and fusional of secular and traditional elements" than that in the Continental European systems. This is clearly true for the Scandinavian countries, which are, in fact, quite homogeneous and do not differ significantly from the homogeneous Anglo-American systems. But again, the other "in-between" countries are at least as fragmented into political subcultures—the *familles spirituelles* of Belgium and Luxembourg, the *zuilen* of the Netherlands, and the *Lager* of Austria—as the Continental European states. Therefore, on the basis of the two criteria of political culture and role structure, the Western democracies can be satisfactorily classified into two broad but clearly bounded categories: (1) the Anglo-American, Old Commonwealth, and Scandinavian states; (2) the other European democracies, including France, Italy, Weimar Germany, the Low Countries, Austria, and Switzerland.

Fragmented but Stable Democracies

The second category of the above twofold typology is too broad, however, because it includes both highly stable systems (e.g., Switzerland and Holland) and highly unstable ones (e.g., Weimar Germany and the French Third and Fourth Republics). The political stability of a system can apparently not be predicted solely on the basis of the two variables of political culture and role structure. According to the theory of crosscutting cleavages, one would expect the Low Countries, Switzerland, and Austria, with subcultures divided from each other by mutually reinforcing cleavages, to exhibit great immobilism and instability. But they do not. These deviant cases of fragmented but stable democracies will be called "consociational democracies." In general, deviant case analysis can lead to the discovery of additional relevant variables, and in this particular instance, a third variable can account for the stability of the consociational democracies: the behavior of the political elites. The leaders of the rival subcultures may engage in competitive behavior and thus further aggravate mutual tensions and political instability, but they may also make *deliberate efforts to counteract the immobilizing and unstabilizing effects of cultural fragmentation*. As a result of such overarching cooperation at the elite level, a country can, as Claude Ake states, "achieve a degree of political stability quite out of proportion to its social homogeneity."

The clearest examples are the experiences of democratic Austria after the First World War and of pre-democratic Belgium in the early nineteenth century. The fragmented and unstable Austrian First Republic of the inter-war years was transformed into the still fragmented but stable Second Republic after the Second World War by means of a consociational solution. As Frederick C. Engelmann states, "the central socio-political fact in the life of post-1918 Austria [was that] the Republic had developed under conditions of cleavage so deep as to leave it with a high potential for—and a sporadic actuality of—civil war." The instability caused by the deep cleavage and antagonism between the Catholic and Socialist *Lager* (subcultures) spelled the end of democracy and the establishment of a dictatorship. The leaders of the rival subcultures were anxious not to repeat the sorry experience of the First Republic, and decided to join in a grand coalition after the Second World War. According to Engelmann, "critics and objective observers agree with Austria's leading politicians in the assessment that the coalition was a response to the civil-war tension of the First Republic." Otto Kirchheimer also attributes the consociational pattern of Austria's post-1945 politics (until early 1966) to "the republic's historical record of political frustration and abiding suspicion." Val R. Lorwin describes how the potential instability caused by subcultural cleavage was deliberately avoided at the time of the birth of independent Belgium: the Catholic and Liberal leaders had learned "the great lesson of mutual tolerance from the catastrophic experience of the Brabant Revolution of 1789, when the civil strife of their predecessors had so soon laid the country open to easy Habsburg reconquest. It was a remarkable and *self-conscious 'union of the oppositions'* that made the revolution of 1830, wrote the Constitution of 1831, and headed the government in its critical years."

The grand coalition cabinet is the most typical and obvious, but not the only possible, consociational solution for a fragmented system. The essential characteristic of consociational democracy is not so much any particular institutional arrangement as the deliberate joint effort by the elites to stabilize the system. Instead of the term "grand coalition" with its rather narrow connotation, one could speak of universal participation, or as Ralf Dahrendorf does, of a "cartel of elites." A grand coalition cabinet as in Austria represents the most comprehensive form of the cartel of elites, but one finds a variety of other devices in the other Western consociational democracies and, outside Western Europe, in the consociational politics of Lebanon, Uruguay (until early 1967), and Colombia. Even in Austria, not the cabinet itself but the small extra-constitutional "coalition committee," on which the top Socialist and Catholic leaders were equally represented, made the crucial decisions. In the Swiss system of government, which is a hybrid of the presidential and the parliamentary patterns, all four major parties are represented on the multi-member executive. In Uruguay's (now defunct) governmental system, fashioned after the Swiss model, there was *coparticipación* of the two parties on the executive. . . .

The desire to avoid political competition may be so strong that the cartel of elites may decide to extend the consociational principle to the electoral level in order to prevent the passions aroused by elections from upsetting the carefully constructed, and possibly fragile, system of cooperation. This may apply to a single election or to a number of successive elections. The *paridad* and *alternación* principles in Colombia entail a controlled democracy for a period of sixteen years, during which the efficacy of the right to vote is severely restricted. Another example is the Dutch parliamentary election of 1917, in which all of the parties agreed not to contest the seats held by incumbents in order to safeguard the passage of a set of crucial constitutional amendments; these amendments, negotiated by cartels of top party leaders, contained the terms of the settlement of the sensitive issues of universal suffrage and state aid to church schools. A parallel agreement on the suffrage was adopted in Belgium in 1919 without holding the constitutionally prescribed election at all.

Consociational democracy violates the principle of majority rule, but it does not deviate very much from normative democratic theory. Most democratic constitutions prescribe majority rule for the normal transaction of business when the stakes are not too high, but extraordinary majorities or several successive majorities for the most important decisions, such as changes in the constitution. In fragmented systems, many other decisions in addition to constituent ones are perceived as involving high stakes, and therefore require more than simple majority rule. Similarly, majority rule does not suffice in times of grave crisis in even the most homogeneous and consensual of democracies. Great Britain and Sweden, both highly homogeneous countries, resorted to grand coalition cabinets during the Second

World War. Julius Nyerere draws the correct lesson from the experience of the Western democracies, in which, he observes, "it is an accepted practice in times of emergency for opposition parties to sink their differences and join together in forming a national government." And just as the formation of a national unity government is the appropriate response to an external emergency, so the formation of a grand coalition cabinet or an alternative form of elite cartel is the appropriate response to the internal crisis of fragmentation into hostile subcultures.

Furthermore, the concept of consociational democracy is also in agreement with the empirical "size principle," formulated by William H. Riker. This principle, based on game-theoretic assumptions, states: "In social situations similar to n-person, zero-sum games with side-payments [private agreements about the division of the payoff], participants create coalitions just as large as they believe will ensure winning and no larger." The tendency will be toward a "minimum winning coalition," which in a democracy will be a coalition with bare majority support—but only under the conditions specified in the size principle. The most important condition is the zero-sum assumption: "only the direct conflicts among participants are included and common advantages are ignored." Common advantages will be completely ignored only in two diametrically opposite kinds of situations: (1) when the participants in the "game" do not perceive any common advantages, and when, consequently, they are likely to engage in unlimited warfare; and (2) when they are in such firm agreement on their common advantages that they can take them for granted. In the latter case, politics literally becomes a game. In other words, the zero-sum condition and the size principle apply only to societies with completely homogeneous political cultures and to societies with completely fragmented cultures. To the extent that political cultures deviate from these two extreme conditions, pressures will exist to fashion coalitions and other forms of cooperation that are more inclusive than the bare "minimum winning coalition" and that may be all-inclusive grand coalitions.

Almond aptly uses the metaphor of the game in characterizing the Anglo-American systems: "Because the political culture tends to be homogeneous and pragmatic, [the political process] takes on some of the atmosphere of a game. A game is a good game when the outcome is in doubt and when the stakes are not too high. When the stakes are too high, the tone changes from excitement to anxiety." Political contests in severely fragmented societies are indeed not likely to be "good games." But the anxieties and hostilities attending the political process may be countered by removing its competitive features as much as possible. In consociational democracies, politics is treated not as a game but as a serious business.

Factors Conducive to Consociational Democracy

Consociational democracy means government by elite cartel designed to turn a democracy with a fragmented political culture into a stable democracy. Efforts at consociationalism are not necessarily successful, of course: consociational designs failed in Cyprus and Nigeria, and Uruguay abandoned its Swiss-style consociational system. Successful consociational democracy requires: (1) That the elites have the ability to accommodate the divergent interests and demands of the subcultures. (2) This requires that they have the ability to transcend cleavages and to join in a common effort with the elites of rival subcultures. (3) This in turn depends on their commitment to the maintenance of the system and to the improvement of its cohesion and stability. (4) Finally, all of the above requirements are based on the assumption that the elites understand the perils of political fragmentation. These four requirements are logically implied by the concept of consociational democracy as defined in this paper. Under what conditions are they likely to be fulfilled? An examination of the successful consociational democracies . . . suggests a number of conditions favorable to the establishment and the persistence of this type of democracy. These have to do with inter-subcultural relations at the elite level, inter-subcultural relations at the mass level, and elite-mass relations within each of the subcultures.

Relations among the elites of the subcultures

It is easier to assess the probability of continued success of an already established consociational democracy than to predict the chance of success that a fragmented system would have if it were to attempt consociationalism. In an existing consociational democracy, an investigation of the institutional arrangements and the operational code of inter-elite accommodation can throw light on the question of how thorough a commitment to cooperation they represent and how effective they have been in solving the problems caused by fragmentation. *The length of time a consociational democracy has been in operation* is also a factor of importance. As inter-elite cooperation becomes habitual and does not represent a deliberate departure from competitive responses to political challenges, consociational norms become more firmly established. And, as Gerhard Lehmbruch states, these norms may become an important part of "the political socialization of elites and thus acquire a strong degree of persistence through time."

There are three factors that appear to be strongly conducive to the establishment or maintenance of cooperation among elites in a fragmented system. The most striking of these is the existence of *external threats* to the country. In all of the consociational democracies, the cartel of elites was either initiated or greatly strengthened during periods of international crisis, especially the First and Second World Wars. During the First World War, the comprehensive settlement of the conflict among Holland's political subcultures firmly established the pattern of consociational democracy. "Unionism"—i.e., Catholic-Liberal grand coalitions—began during Belgium's struggle for independence in the early nineteenth century, but lapsed when the country appeared to be out of danger. As a result of the First World War, unionism was resumed and the Socialist leaders were soon admitted to the governing cartel. . . .

A second factor favorable to consociational democracy, in the sense that it helps the elites to recognize the necessity of cooperation, is a *multiple balance of power among the subcultures* instead of either a dual balance of power or a clear hegemony by one subculture. When one group is in the majority, its leaders may attempt to dominate rather than cooperate with the rival minority. Similarly, in a society with two evenly matched subcultures, the leaders of both may hope to achieve their aims by domination rather than cooperation, if they expect to win a majority at the polls. Robert Dahl argues that for this reason it is doubtful that the consociational arrangements in Colombia will last, because "the temptation to shift from coalition to competition is bound to be very great." When political parties in a fragmented society are the organized manifestations of political subcultures, a multiparty system is more conducive to consociational democracy and therefore to stability than a two-party system. This proposition is at odds with the generally high esteem accorded to two-party systems. In an already homogeneous system, two-party systems may be more effective, but a moderate multiparty system, in which no party is close to a majority, appears preferable in a consociational democracy. The Netherlands, Switzerland, and Lebanon have the advantage that their subcultures are all minority groups. In the Austrian two-party system, consociational politics did work, but with considerable strain. Lehmbruch states: "Austrian political parties are strongly integrated social communities . . . and the bipolar structure of the coalition reinforced their antagonisms." The internal balance of power in Belgium has complicated the country's consociational politics in two ways. The Catholic, Socialist, and Liberal subcultures are minorities, but the Catholics are close to majority status. The Catholic party actually won a legislative majority in 1950, and attempted to settle the sensitive royal question by majority rule. This led to a short civil war, followed by a return to consociational government. Moreover, the Belgian situation is complicated as a result of the linguistic cleavage, which cuts across the three spiritual families. The linguistic balance of power is a dual balance in which the Walloons fear the numerical majority of the Flemings, while the Flemings resent the economic and social superiority of the Walloons.

Consociational democracy presupposes not only a willingness on the part of elites to cooperate but also a capability to solve the political problems of their countries. Fragmented societies have a tendency to immobilism, which consociational politics is designed to avoid. Nevertheless, decision-making that entails accommodation among all subcultures is a difficult process, and consociational democracies are always threatened by a degree of immobilism. Consequently, a third favorable fact to inter-elite cooperation is a *relatively low total load on the decision-making apparatus.* . . . In general, the size factor is important in this respect: the political burdens that large states have to shoulder tend to be disproportionately heavier than those of small countries. Ernest S. Griffith argues that "democracy is more likely to survive, other things being equal, in small states. Such states are more manageable. . . ." In particular, small states are more likely to escape the onerous burdens entailed by an active foreign policy. . . .

Inter-subcultural relations at the mass level

The political cultures of the countries belonging to Almond's Continental European type and to the consociational type are all fragmented, but the consociational countries have even clearer boundaries among their subcultures. Such *distinct lines of cleavage* appear to be conducive to consociational democracy and political stability. The explanation is that subcultures with widely divergent outlooks and interests may coexist without necessarily being in conflict; conflict arises only when they are in contact with each other. As Quincy Wright states: "Ideologies accepted by different groups within a society may be inconsistent without creating tension; but if . . . the groups with inconsistent ideologies are in close contact . . . the tension will be great." David Easton also endorses the thesis that good social fences may make good political neighbors, when he suggests a kind of voluntary *apartheid* policy as the best solution for a divided society: "Greater success may be attained through steps that conduce to the development of a deeper sense of mutual awareness and responsiveness among *encapsulated cultural units.*" This is "the major hope of avoiding stress." And Sidney Verba follows the same line of reasoning when he argues that political and economic modernization in Africa is bringing "differing subcultures into contact with each other and *hence* into conflict."

This argument appears to be a direct refutation of the overlapping-memberships proposition, but by adding two amendments to this proposition the discrepancy can be resolved. In the first place, the basic explanatory element in the concept of consociational democracy is that political elites may take joint actions to counter the effects of cultural fragmentation. This means that the overlapping-memberships proposition may become a self-denying hypothesis under certain conditions. Secondly, the view that any severe discontinuity in overlapping patterns of membership and allegiance is a danger to political stability needs to be restated in more refined form. A distinction has to be made between essentially homogeneous political cultures, where increased contacts are likely to lead to an increase in mutual understanding and further homogenization, and essentially heterogeneous cultures, where close contacts are likely to lead to strain and hostility. This is the distinction that Walker Connor makes when he argues that "increased contacts help to dissolve regional cultural distinctions within a state such as the United States. Yet, if one is dealing not with minor variations of the same culture, but with two quite distinct and self-differentiating cultures, are not increased contacts between the two apt to increase antagonism?" This proposition can be refined further by stating both the degree of homogeneity and the extent of mutual contacts in terms of continua rather than dichotomies. In order to safeguard political stability, the volume and intensity of contacts must not exceed the commensurate degree of homogeneity. Karl W. Deutsch states that stability depends on a "balance between transaction and integration" because "the number of opportunities for possible violent conflict will increase with the volume and range of mutual transactions." Hence, it may be desirable to keep transactions among antagonistic subcultures in a divided society—or, similarly, among different nationalities in a multinational state—to a minimum.

Elite-mass relations within the subcultures

Distinct lines of cleavage among the subcultures are also conducive to consociational democracy because they are likely to be concomitant with a high degree of *internal political cohesion of the subcultures*. This is vital to the success of consociational democracy. The elites have to cooperate and compromise with each other without losing the allegiance and support of their own rank and file. When the subcultures are cohesive political blocs, such support is more likely to be forthcoming. As Hans Daalder states, what is important is not only "the extent to which party leaders are more tolerant than their followers" but also the extent to which they "are yet able to carry them along."

A second way in which distinct cleavages have a favorable effect on elite-mass relations in a consociational democracy is that they make it more likely that the parties and interest groups will be the organized representatives of the political subcultures. If this is the case, the political parties may not be the best aggregators, but there is at least an *adequate articulation of the interests of the subcultures*. Aggregation of the clearly articulated interests can then be performed by the cartel of elites. In Belgium, the three principal parties represent the Catholic, Socialist, and Liberal spiritual families, but the linguistic cleavage does not coincide with the cleavages dividing the spiritual families, and all three parties have both Flemings and Walloons among their followers. . . . The religious and class issues have been effectively articulated by the political parties and have by and large been resolved, but the linguistic issue has not been clearly articulated and remains intractable. In Switzerland, the parties also represent the religious-ideological groups rather than the linguistic communities, but much of the country's decentralized political life takes place at the cantonal level, and most of the cantons are linguistically homogeneous.

A final factor which favors consociational democracy is *widespread approval of the principle of government by elite cartel.* This is a very obvious factor, but it is of considerable importance and deserves to be mentioned briefly. For example, Switzerland has a long and strong tradition of grand coalition executives, and this has immeasurably strengthened Swiss consociational democracy. On the other hand, the grand coalition in Austria was under constant attack by critics who alleged that the absence of a British-style opposition made Austrian politics "undemocratic." This attests to the strength of the British system as a normative model even in fragmented political systems, where the model is inappropriate and undermines the attempt to achieve political stability by consociational means.

Centripetal and Centrifugal Democracies

An examination of the other two types of the threefold typology of democracies in the light of the distinguishing characteristics of consociational democracy can contribute to the clarification and refinement of all three types and their prerequisites. In order to avoid any unintended geographical connotation, we shall refer to the homogeneous and stable democracies as the *centripetal* (instead of the Anglo-American) democracies, and to the fragmented and unstable ones as the *centrifugal* (instead of the Continental European) democracies. The centrifugal democracies include the French Third and Fourth Republics, Italy, Weimar Germany, the Austrian First Republic, and the short-lived Spanish Republic of the early 1930's. The major examples of centripetal democracy are Great Britain, the Old Commonwealth countries, the United States, Ireland, the Scandinavian states, and the postwar Bonn Republic in Germany. . . . To turn a centrifugal into a consociational democracy, true statesmanship is required. Moreover, it is incorrect to assume that, because the elites were not divided by irreconcilable ideological differences, mass politics was not ideologically fragmented either.

The second criticism of the cultural fragmentation thesis alleges, on the basis of independent evidence, that not only at the elite level but also at the mass level, ideology played a negligible role in France. Philip E. Converse and Georges Dupeux demonstrate that the French electorate was not highly politicized and felt little allegiance to the political parties. But the lack of stable partisan attachments does not necessarily indicate that the political culture was not fragmented. Duncan MacRae argues persuasively that political divisions did extend to the electorate as a whole in spite of the apparent "lack of involvement of the average voter." Even though political allegiances were diffuse, there were "relatively fixed and non-overlapping *social* groupings" to which "separate leaders and separate media of communication had access." The combination of fragmentation into subcultures and low politicization can in turn be explained by the negative French attitude toward authority. Stanley Hoffmann speaks of "potential insurrection against authority," and Michel Crozier observes that this attitude makes it "impossible for an individual of the group to become its leader." Strong cohesion within the subcultures was mentioned earlier as a factor conducive to consociational democracy; the lack of it in France can explain both that the French people were fragmented but at the same time not politically involved, and that the political elites did not have the advantage of strong support from the rank and file for constructive cooperation.

On the other hand, the example of France also serves to make clear that the lack of problem-solving ability as a cause of political instability must not be overstated. After all, as Maurice Duverger points out, in spite of all of the Fourth Republic's flaws and weaknesses, it "would have continued to exist if it had not been for the Algerian war." The critical factor was the too-heavy burden of an essentially external problem on the political system. Similarly, the fragmented Weimar Republic might have survived, too, if it had not been for the unusually difficult problems it was faced with.

Germany's experience with democracy also appears to throw some doubt on our threefold typology and the theory on which it is based. Weimar Germany was a centrifugal democracy but the Bonn Republic can be grouped with the centripetal democracies. In explaining this extraordinary shift, we have to keep in mind that cultural fragmentation must be measured on a continuum rather than as a dichotomy, as we have done so far. The degree of homogeneity of a political culture can change, although great changes at a rapid pace can normally not be expected. Three reasons can plausibly account for the change from the fragmented political culture of the unstable Weimar Republic to the much more homogeneous culture of the Bonn Republic: (1) the traumatic experiences of totalitarianism, war, defeat, and occupation; (2) "conscious manipulative change of fundamental political attitudes," which, as Verba states, added up to a "remaking of political culture"; (3) the loss of the eastern territories, which meant that, as

Lipset argues, "the greater homogeneity of western Germany now became a national homogeneity."

The degree of competitive or cooperative behavior by elites must also be seen as a continuum. Among the consociational democracies, some are more consociational than others; and many centripetal democracies have some consociational features. The phenomenon of wartime grand coalition cabinets has already been mentioned. The temporary Christian Democratic-Socialist grand coalition under Chancellor Kiesinger falls in the same category. In fact, the stability of the centripetal democracies depends not only on their essentially homogeneous political cultures but also on consociational devices, to the extent that a certain degree of heterogeneity exists. The alternation of English-speaking and French-speaking leaders of the Liberal party in Canada may be compared with the Colombian device of *alternación*. In the United States, where, as Dahl states, "the South has for nearly two centuries formed a distinctive regional subculture," cultural fragmentation led to succession and civil war. After the Civil War, a consociational arrangement developed that gave to the South a high degree of autonomy and to the Southern leaders—by such means as chairmanships of key Congressional committees and the filibuster—a crucial position in federal decision-making. This example also shows that, while consociational solutions may increase political cohesion, they also have a definite tendency to lead to a certain degree of immobilism. . . .

Part IV
The Political Process

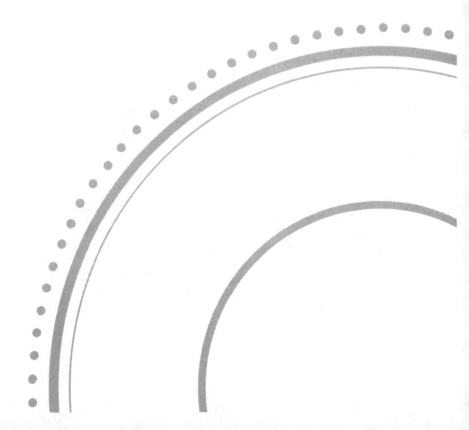

Introduction

In Part III we suggested that one of the more difficult problems facing all societies is organizing political authority. In Part IV we take another step in analyzing government and politics by examining the process that goes on within those structures. The readings in this section discuss the various aspects of the dynamic interaction that occurs among the individuals, institutions, and agencies that are involved in public decision making for societies.

Politics is a systematic process in which political inputs (demands and supports) are converted into political outputs (laws and policies). The process is influenced by a variety of factors: political culture, interest groups, political parties, the communications media, elections, an executive, a bureaucracy, the legislature, and the courts. The interaction of all these components produces public decisions for society. In practical terms, politics becomes the means for hammering out public policies on issues such as defence, health care, the environment, regional disparities, energy shortages, unemployment, welfare, and capital punishment. G. Bruce Doern and Peter Aucoin have described this policy-making process as

> a plurality of processes which are closely interlocked. More particularly, one might visualize a series of interlocking circles of activity, each encompassing different but usually related values, instruments of governing, and forms of contact between the executive-bureaucratic arena and the other arenas of Canadian politics.

The process of politics has cultural as well as structural dimensions. The structural dimension is obvious; it involves interest groups, legislatures, the courts, and so on. The cultural dimension is less obvious; it involves attitudes, beliefs, and values that provide an orientation to politics and the political process. Political culture is an important component because it is assumed to influence how individuals behave in politics. In Reading 24, Walter A. Rosenbaum delineates the various meanings of the concept of political culture. He also outlines some of the problems involved in researching political culture.

Interest groups are another integral part of the political process. Mancur Olson's reading on interest groups suggests that it is problematic to talk of group behaviour or more specifically, the behaviour of individuals within interest groups.

Reading 26 deals with political parties, a second informal institution in the process of politics. As most Western nation-states moved to universal adult suffrage, the political party emerged as a key instrument for organizing mass participation in politics. Theoretically, political parties provided a vital link between the rulers and the ruled, individuals with a means for contacting political leaders, and political leaders with a means for keeping their finger on the pulse of society. In practice, however, not all analysts feel political parties have lived up to their democratic expectations. The parties have come under fire for not fulfilling their role as the link between the people and their governors. John Meisel, in an interesting assessment of this problem, notes some of the primary reasons for the declining role of political parties.

Elections are the subject of Reading 27. In theory, elections are a constitutional device by which individual voters have some control over who will govern in society. Elected officials are held responsible to public opinion and are thought to be responsive to the ever-changing needs of society. Richard Rose offers an excellent discussion of some of the myths and realities of the electoral process.

The interaction of institutions in politics involves not only the informal activities of interest groups, political parties, and the communications media but also the formal, constitutional activities of legislatures, executives, the bureaucracy, and the courts. It is impossible at this point to delve into all the different arguments about these institutions and their activities. The following selections, however, highlight significant positions found in the literature today.

K.C. Wheare in Reading 28 outlines one argument that applies to most modern democratic legislatures: the idealized view that the representative assembly is the most important institution in the legislative process. In reality, however, as governments begin to play a larger role in society, the impetus for legislative proposals and the control of the legislative process become functions more of the executive than of the legislature. This leads to claims of the eclipse of power of representative assemblies and the rise of the paramount position of the executive. Wheare reviews the grounds for this argument and notes that more is involved than a simple shift in power. Rather, a shift in government responsibilities necessitates a change in the role of the executive *and* the legislature. Indeed, the basic functions of both institutions remain intact, but serious problems arise with policy formation and policy enactment as governments expand their responsibilities.

Many analysts now agree that the prime minister and the cabinet do indeed hold a position of dominance in the legislative process. The argument is based on the fact that cabinets, utilizing the extensive resources of the bureaucracy, initiate most legislative proposals, and apply party discipline in herding proposals past formidable barriers in a session of parliament. Through this command of the process, the cabinet is in a position to manage the vast household of government. The cabinet, then, becomes the focus of power for the legislative machinery.

It is rare indeed that an insider would discuss the role of minister, prime minister, or cabinet, in the policy-making process. But this is exactly what Richard Crossman does in Reading 29. The selection is a candid insider's view of the relationships between the prime minister, other ministers, and the civil service. Crossman offers a personal interpretation of the role of cabinet committees in initiating policy proposals, the predominant role of the prime minister in the cabinet process, and the complex relationship between the minister and the department for which he or she is responsible.

Invariably, bureaucracies pose a problem in modern democracies. Even though they are supposed to be "professional" organizations, standing above politics and administering without favour, they are one of the most powerful institutions in the political process. They have an agenda of their own, and without strong elected ministers to control their actions, they can become the dominant force in the political process. In Reading 30, Max Weber offers a classic analysis of the nature of bureaucracies in modern governments, indicating problems inherent in that organization.

The final selection, Reading 31, discusses the role of the courts in the political process in Canada after adoption of the Charter of Rights and Freedoms. Before the Charter, Canadian courts were not considered "activist," that is, they did not take an active role in challenging the law-making function of Parliament. In the past, the position of the courts was dictated by the principle of parliamentary supremacy and by the fact that no *written* charter limited the powers of Parliament. Once the Charter was passed, many critics and analysts speculated that the powers of Parliament would be trimmed, and that we were in for a period of judicial supremacy. Using court decisions since 1982, F.L. Morton assesses the impact of the Charter on the roles of the courts and Parliament. He suggests that compared to pre-Charter numbers, the courts are exercising judicial review more frequently.

24 Political Culture

The study of government and politics consists of two dimensions: the cultural and the structural. Familiar examples of political structures are interest groups and political parties, or the executive, legislature, and judiciary. Political culture is the "psychological" dimension of politics, reflecting an individual's orientation to the political world.

Political culture consists of the attitudes, beliefs, and values one holds regarding the political process and one's place in that process. Political culture can influence individual political behaviour by affecting one's choice of a candidate or political party in an election. Political culture can also influence the interaction of institutions in the political process. For example, the way freedom is valued in a society may well influence the relationship between interest groups and the executive or the administration.

Another important aspect of political culture is how it is transmitted to individuals in society. Political socialization is the process whereby political attitudes and values are transmitted from generation to generation. A number of institutions in society serve as the vehicles for the transmission process: the family, schools, peer groups, the work place, and government itself.

This section by Professor Walter A. Rosenbaum from the University of Florida provides a good description of the concept of political culture. He outlines numerous facets of the concept, and suggests some of the difficulties in researching political cultures. It is an abridged version of "The Meaning of Political Culture," which appears in his book *Political Culture*.

● ● ● ● ● ● ● ● ●

A fragmentation grenade explodes inside a crowded Catholic pub in Northern Ireland, shredding the air with shrapnel, killing four people, and adding another vicious episode to a civil war between Protestants and Catholics that has already claimed more than a thousand victims in that violence-racked land. Far away, a Montreal housewife removes from a supermarket shelf a ketchup bottle with a unique label, a modest symbol of crisis averted. Found only in Canada, the label bears French and English wording of equal size proclaiming "ketchup" and "ketchup aux tomates"; repealing the law requiring such bilingual labels would produce a parliamentary crisis. To

Canada's south, an opinion poll declares that the American public, apparently shaken by continuing revelations of scandal within the executive branch, is losing confidence in the Presidency—a scant 19 per cent of the public express strong faith in that institution. Still, the American people do not seem moved to demand any radical alterations in their political system.

Such provocative items, chosen from one day's news, are likely to prompt the question "Why?" Why cannot Catholics and Protestants in Northern Ireland reach a political accommodation without civil war? Why is language a politically explosive issue in Canada? Why do Americans express low confidence in their Chief Executive yet remain curiously undemonstrative in the sort of situation that has provoked political violence in other nations? Here—in our effort to understand both the commonplace and the extraordinary in political life—the study of *political culture* properly begins. The concept of political culture offers a potentially powerful, and almost always useful, approach to daily political events by identifying the underlying psychological forces that shape much of civic life.

Political culture can be defined in two ways, depending upon the level at which we want to study political life. If we concentrate on the individual, political culture has a basically psychological focus. It entails all the important ways in which a person is subjectively oriented toward the essential elements in his political system. We want to know what he feels and thinks about the symbols, institutions, and rules that constitute the fundamental political order of his society and how he responds to them. In effect, we are probing the psychological dimension of a person's civic life, we ask what bonds exist between him and the essentials of his political system and how these affect his behavior.

The second definition of political culture refers to the collective orientation of people toward the basic elements in their political system. This is a "system level" approach. We are interested in how large masses of citizens evaluate their political institutions and officials. To say, for example, that a nation's political culture is largely "integrated" means that most people within the system have similar, or compatible, political culture orientations which are congenial to the political institutions within which they live. When political culture is discussed, it usually refers to these mass political orientations across the whole political system.

Before sharpening this definition, I can briefly illustrate how an awareness of political culture enhances our understanding of the political events we described above. Northern Ireland's violence, for example, flows in part from the widespread conviction among the Catholic minority that the government is illegitimate and in part from the profound distrust of each other's religious communities that permeates the Catholic and Protestant factions alike, frustrating political accommodation and moderation. In short, one must know something about public attitudes toward government and toward other political factions before explaining the civil war. In a similar vein, Canada's official bilingualism is comprehensible only when we note the importance that the large French minority attaches to its language and culture; its conviction that it is struggling for cultural survival against the English majority, and its determination, forces official governmental recognition of its cultural demands, even to the level of ketchup bottles. Finally, Americans have traditionally held their Constitution in high esteem, believing that the government it designed is legitimate and proper; moreover, there is broad public conviction that political change should be orderly and peaceful, following the customary means ordained by the Constitution. Undoubtedly, this sentiment keeps most citizens loyal to their basic governmental system and wary of radical or violent change. They may have been disillusioned with President Nixon but not disposed to demand major refashioning of the Presidency; they may criticize Congress or the Court, but they are not yet prepared to redesign either institution. There are, to be sure, no simple, all-inclusive explanations for complex political events; political culture never explains all. Still, a sensitivity to the perspective it provides on political life adds depth and richness to our appreciation of political events.

THE ESSENTIALS OF POLITICAL CULTURE

To say that political culture involves the important ways in which people are subjectively oriented toward the basic elements of their political system is an accurate but not yet satisfactory definition. One needs a firmer notion of what "subjective orientations" this involves and, consequently, we need to spell out, clearly and concretely, the distinctive elements of thought, feeling, and behavior that concern us. At this point a nettlesome issue arises. Scholars themselves have never reached a consensus on the proper components of political culture; so many different formulations have been offered (twenty-five by one count) that one might think he was grappling with the riddle of the Sphinx. At one extreme, some analysts include in political culture "all politically relevant orientations either of a cognitive, evaluative or expressive sort"—so unbounded a definition that an investigator would have to spend an interminable time compiling an elephantine list of orientations to be sure nothing *politically relevant* escaped notice. At the other extreme, certain analysts attempt to make the list manageable by limiting political culture to orientations toward national political institutions, a good beginning except that it may omit other dimensions of political life very instrumental in shaping the fundamental political order of a society. Fortunately, this profusion of definitions need not mean intellectual anarchy, for one can distill from them a set of common items most scholars would agree belong among the essentials; we shall call these the "core components" of political culture.

The Core Components

What the core elements appear to share is a fundamental importance in shaping a nation's political order. Whenever analysts offer such a list they are, in effect, using a rule of thumb: Those dimensions of an individual's thoughts, feelings, or behaviors that are linked to the creation and maintenance of a society's fundamental political order belong under the label "political culture." Thus, insists one observer, political culture must be limited to the "attitudes, beliefs and sentiments that give order and meaning to the political process and provide the underlying assumptions and rules that govern behavior."

It is helpful to think of these core components as orientations toward different elements in the political order. Such a list commonly includes the following particulars:

1. *Orientations Toward Governmental Structures*
   a. *Regime Orientation*—How an individual evaluates and responds to the basic governmental institutions of his society, its symbols, officials, and norms (collectively, the "regime"); this may include a more detailed investigation of orientations toward specific institutions and offices or an investigation of preferences for alternative governmental structures.
   b. *Orientations Toward Governmental Inputs and Outputs*—How individuals feel and respond toward various demands for public policy ("inputs") and policy decisions made by government ("outputs"); this may include an inventory of a person's knowledge concerning how these processes operate, what demands he may make upon government, and how effective he believes governmental policy to be.
2. *Orientations Toward Others in the Political System*
   a. *Political Identifications*—The political unit (nation, state, town, region), geographic areas, and groups to which one feels he belongs, that are in some significant subjective sense a part of his own social identity; in particular, these include those units and groups to which he feels a strong loyalty, obligation, or duty.
   b. *Political Trust*—The extent to which one feels an open, cooperative, or tolerant attitude in working with others in civic life; essentially, political trust expresses the intensity of a person's conviction that other individuals or groups mean him well (or ill) in political life.

   c. *"Rules of the Game"*—An individual's conception of what rules
      should be followed in civic life; these subjective preferences may
      or may not be consistent with prevailing law and other norms
      supposed to govern civic conduct.
3. *Orientations Toward One's Own Political Activity*
   a. *Political Competence*—How often, and in what manner, a person
      participates in civil life, the frequency with which he uses the
      political resources available to him in civic affairs; this may
      include some evaluation of his knowledge of his political
      resources.
   b. *Political Efficacy*—"The feeling that individual political action
      does have, or can have, an impact on the political process"; this
      includes a belief that political change is possible and that one can
      accomplish change through civic action—individuals are cus-
      tomarily ranked on a scale according to whether their "sense of
      political efficacy" is "high" or "low."

When an investigator turns his attention to the political culture of any
society, he is likely to concentrate upon those political culture orientations
that are *widely shared*, on the assumption that they are most likely to
influence the political process because they affect the behavior of large
masses. For instance, if an examination of American political culture concentrates upon political trust and reveals that a very small portion of the
population exhibits a political paranoia toward Catholics, an investigator
would probably consider this sentiment less important for the operation of
the political system than a finding that most Americans are generally
trustful, or at least tolerant, toward the political motives of other religious
groups. (Of course it would be important to examine the political orientations of the anti-Catholic minority in order to understand their own political behavior.) Moreover, many of these political culture orientations are
implicit, and often unconscious, in an individual's life—so basic that he hardly
reflects upon them. In this sense, many are "primitive" orientations because they are "so implicit and taken for granted that each individual holds
them and believes that all others hold them"; they become "unstated
assumptions, or postulates, about politics." Though held unconsciously,
these beliefs and attitudes govern civic behavior, help shape the governmental order, and, for many people, define political reality. We should also
note (because emphasizing a concept often seems to make it larger than life)
that there is nothing metaphysical or otherwise superhuman about the
operation of political culture. Political culture *expresses itself in the daily
thinking and activity of people* going about the business of civic life just as
their other beliefs and feelings are expressed in other aspects of the social

TABLE 1.1
Some Operational Definitions of Political Culture Orientations

Orientation	Operational Definition
Political Identification	Nation of citizenship Political units and groups toward which one feels positively or negatively Political units and groups with which one is most often involved
Political Trust	Willingness to collaborate with various groups in different types of social action Group memberships Rating of groups in terms of trustworthiness, political motives, type of membership, etc.
Regime Orientations	Belief in the legitimacy of the regime Feelings toward, and evaluations of, major political offices and regime symbols Involvement in political activity supporting or opposing the regime
"Rules of the Game"	How one feels political opinions should be expressed Concepts of political obligations for oneself and others Concepts of how political decisions should be made by government Attitudes toward political deviation and dissent
Political Efficacy	Belief that government is responsive to one's opinions Belief in importance of civic activism and participation Belief in possibilities of political change
Political Competence	Frequency of voting and other types of political activity Knowledge of political events and their influence on oneself Interest in political affairs

Orientation	Operational Definition
Input-Output Orientation	Satisfaction with governmental policy
	Knowledge of how political demands are made on government
	Belief in effectiveness of policy inputs and outputs

world. Many beliefs and feelings embraced in the term "political culture" can be considered normal, commonplace, even dull—but extremely important precisely because they are so frequently commonplace; they define what is often the basic political order, the "given" in civic behavior for a society. To study political culture is, in many respects, to hold up a mirror to ourselves. We (individually and collectively) are the carriers of the culture, who not only observe it in others but also express it in our own behavior. In short, "political culture" is a conceptual shorthand for feelings, thoughts, and behaviors we note, or infer, from watching men living out their civic daily lives. . . .

A Growing Interest

Long before modern scholars minted the term "political culture" much of what it now includes was studied under such names as political ideology, national character, and political psychology; still, in the past several decades, political analysts have approached the topic with a greater sense of urgency and greater investments of time and resources than ever before, so that the study has reached an unprecedented intensity within the last decade. Behind this surge of interest lie several explanations. More than anything else, the pervasive political violence in the modern world, the problems of nation building in the postcolonial countries, and the recent availability of survey research methods that offer an especially useful device for enlarging our understanding of the field have stimulated a renewed interest in political culture.

Political instability is now a global commonplace. Since 1945, there have been successful coups in eighteen of twenty Latin American countries, in seven Central African nations, and in six Middle Eastern and West African nations. Even the older Western European and North American nations have endured political upheavals; the boundaries and regimes of European countries have been redesigned with sometimes startling rapidity, and internal turmoil is chronic in many countries. Since World War II the Greeks, for instance, have experienced five years of civil war, several general elections involving fifty political parties, three dozen governments, three successful coups, the fall of a constitutional monarchy, three referenda, and assorted bloody political riots. In addition, the post-World War II period has spawned a host of new African and Asian nations struggling, and often failing, to create and maintain national governments in the aftermath of their colonial experience. These struggles, in particular, have forcefully raised the problems of nation building in a major concern among both scholars and statesmen involved in the quest for global peace.

These developments were especially congenial to a renewed interest in political culture, for it became apparent that explanations of political stability and nation growth, if they could be found, must go beyond an examination of different governmental forms or constitutions, or other formalities; rather, some deep probing seemed imperative to understand how emotional and attitudinal linkages are formed between members of a political community and their government and to describe how different patterns of linkage encouraged or inhibited national development and order. Moreover, such issues could not be resolved without some cross-national comparisons of political cultures; the study of political culture had to be global in its sweep. At this point, an additional incentive appeared in the development of survey research methodology, which seemed to make the empirical study of political culture especially practical by providing scholars with a technique for interviewing large numbers of individuals and obtaining detailed information about their political culture. Although the survey research technique is only one method for studying political culture (we shall shortly examine many others) it has been widely used and has undoubtedly contributed to the growing interest in the field.

The *survey research* methodology used in political culture study is an adaptation of public-opinion study techniques that have already been tested and proven in the United States and most other Western countries. Survey research enables scholars to carefully probe the civic orientations of many individuals in a multitude of national settings, to collect and process the data with great rapidity, and to apply very sophisticated techniques of interpreting the results. This means, among other things, that scholars can now go "into the field" to study national populations directly, can obtain wholly new types of information, and can tabulate results with new versatility and precision. With such new methods, not only could new questions be asked and new data collected, but there appeared the promise that for the first time a truly solid, diversified, empirical base could be provided for generalizing about patterns of political culture and their consequences.

Beyond this, interest in political culture has been stimulated by the problem of bridging the gap between the "macro" and "micro" levels of political life. As survey research and other techniques provide a growing abundance of information about how individuals feel and respond to civic life, the problem arises of relating these "micro" studies of individual political behavior to the performance of whole political systems or major subunits—the "macro" level of analysis. The concept of political culture seems to offer an intellectual link between individual behavior and the survival and performance of political systems, because it relates the general to the particular. Many analysts reason that the essential components of political culture, that is, the individual orientations, must ultimately have a powerful influence upon the performance of whole political systems, so that these individual attitudes can be related to the political order in which they evolve.

The bond between system performances and mass political orientations is not a fact but, rather, a working hypothesis that spurs investigators to test its validity; the incentive is that the results, should they show a strong link between political culture and political system performance, would provide an enormous "pay-off" in the form of a greater understanding of the foundations of political order and chaos.

VARIATION AND CHANGE IN POLITICAL CULTURE

One essential, and intriguing, question about political culture is, How does it develop and change? This issue arises in different ways. Looking at a nation which has experienced more than a century of general political order and great continuity in its political institutions, a researcher suspects that there must be considerable stability within its political culture and seeks to discover how this is maintained. Another researcher, observing a once stable system degenerating into political violence, wonders if one explanation may be a sudden disruption in the traditional political culture and looks for the source. Yet another researcher, studying a newly developing nation, traces many of its difficulties in reaching a consensus on the form of its government to different patterns of political culture within the system; he wants to know why differing cultural patterns persist. In such ways, it becomes apparent that any understanding of political culture must, at some point, explain the origin, development, and change of the particular system under consideration. Let us examine several formative influences upon political culture generally believed to be important.

Political Socialization

To many analysts, the study of political culture begins with the maxim "political behavior is learned behavior." They assert that a person's political orientations are powerfully shaped by the individuals and institutions that influence him early in life, particularly by home, school, and friends. In general, political socialization refers to the "process whereby the individual learns his political values, attitudes, beliefs and behaviors." In the perspective of political socialization, an individual is born, psychologically, the citizen of no land; he does not know what government is "his," is ignorant of the officials, symbols, rituals, and values he is supposed to honor or despise, and must be taught his political identity. In his earliest years, therefore, a person is likely to be taught the most fundamental political orientations he is expected to have—that is, he first acquires the rudiments of political culture under the powerful molding force of institutions to which he is deeply attached and from which he is especially open to influence. Of course, individuals "learn" about politics throughout their lives and, in varying degrees, alter political perspectives; virtually no one enters adulthood with an immutable political orientation. In many political systems, apparently, persons who become members of the political elite are socialized into the values, behaviors, and attitudes considered appropriate to their position at a much later time in life than they acquire their basic orientations toward the political order. Generally, it appears that the nature and extent of one's political socialization in a society may depend upon the population group to which one belongs and what political role one will play in it. Still, analysts place great emphasis upon early learning because they believe it is particularly influential and resistant to later change. In fact, one scholar asserts that the major point of early socialization is "induction into the political culture."

When study moves to political socialization, attention centers upon two questions: (1) which institutions are most active in socializing individuals into a political system? and (2) what is the content of the political information communicated to individuals? As one compares political systems, it is apparent that the political socialization of the young will often be the responsibility of very different institutions, and that the nature of the material taught will vary enormously. In the United States, most Western European nations, and Great Britain, most early socialization is handled by family and school; in Communist countries, however, a child may be exposed early and continually to socialization through organizations representing the Communist Party and may, indeed, be taken out of the family for long periods of time and given intensive experience in Party-inspired work and recreation programs. In some nations, religious denominations attempt to shape the political perceptions of growing children. It is impossible to list all the religious, political, ethnic, or vocational groups that might play a part in socializing children into political life, for it is always a matter to be determined on a country-by-country basis.

In the same manner, the content of political socialization varies enormously between nations. In the United States, for example, the schools largely confine socialization to teaching "good citizenship," which usually means inculcating a respect for government and community, teaching the basic rituals of the political system (voting, for example), and instilling interest and pride in civic history. In other systems, by way of contrast, children may be taught early to have strong attachments to particular leaders, ideologies, and parties, and to have equally strong hostility to current enemies of the state or party; the spectacle of kindergarten children in the People's Republic of China playing games involving guerilla wars against "capitalist aggressors" is a graphic illustration of how far ideological war can be carried into the basic socialization scheme of a nation. Again, it is less important at this point to identify national patterns of socialization than to develop a sensitivity to the range and variety of socializing agents and the political messages they convey.

In political systems with considerable continuity of governmental institutions and stable civic processes, political socialization is most likely to be a conservative process, initiating new generations into the political values and behaviors of the ongoing system or inducing relatively modest change. Indeed, many analysts assert that the continuing stability of a political system depends, in good measure, upon the ability of the socialization process to perform this conservative function. It is understandable, then, why newly established regimes advocating changed ideologies and governmental structures are likely to place such enormous emphasis upon controlling the education system and on managing other institutions which educate the young. New modes of socialization are used to bring coming generations under the banner of the new movement.

Despite the plausibility of these assertions about the impact of political socialization on political culture, most of them have yet to be proven. It is known that there is some carry-over of political values, attitudes, and behaviors from childhood education into adulthood—in most European nations and the United States, for example, adult party preference and attitudes toward major policy problems seem to be moderately correlated with childhood learning. At the same time, there are: no conclusive evidence that most adults largely reproduce political orientations learned in childhood, no firm evidence about which institutions are likely to be most effective in childhood political learning, and few empirical studies closely following changes in political orientation through the lifetime of a sample of individuals. In many respects, this lack of information arises from the difficulty of obtaining reliable information about childhood socialization from adults and from obstacles to isolating a set of individuals for study through the life cycle. But an important additional problem is the inability of researchers to get access to populations in non-Western societies (particularly Communist systems) and the consequent poverty of data available for making generalizations on a truly cross-cultural basis. Thus, the most reasonable conclusion seems to be that far more empirical studies are needed before the role of political socialization in political culture development can be accurately assessed.

Historical Experience

Another very broad category of factors that affect individual orientations toward political systems are those events and experiences encountered through the life cycle after childhood socialization is past. Because political learning is a lifelong process and political orientations are, to some degree, susceptible to change in most people, we naturally expect an adult's political views and behaviors to respond, in some manner, to the historical events that form part of his own life. . . .

The events most likely to affect a nation's political culture are those affecting great masses of people directly, profoundly, and tangibly—wars, depressions, and other crises. Such events throw the capacities of government into sharp relief, causing people to become deeply involved in political life and, often, testing and examining their basic feelings, beliefs, and assumptions about it. Major social crises often leave profound impressions upon mass political orientations. In Germany and Japan, the disastrous management of World War II, leading to the desolation of both nations, left the existing regimes and their ideologies badly discredited among large segments of the population; this situation made the task of reconstructing the governments of West Germany and Japan along more democratic lines considerably easier. Deep aversion to the prewar forms of government has remained in both nations. The United States Government's role in Vietnam, together with the administrations' failure to maintain public support for continued involvement, left large masses of Americans, especially the young, alienated from the system (at least temporarily). The civil wars in Northern Ireland, the Congo, and Algeria made establishment of national governments by consensus extremely difficult, since the violence spawned deep political distrust among major religions and social factions in those nations. It is not only dramatic events, however, which cause mass political orientations to develop and change significantly; like water on the rock a slow but steady succession of occurrences may gradually wear away old values and replace them with new ones. It is important to recognize that political learning is lifelong and that basic political orientations often alter with the passage of time and circumstance.

Socio-economic Variables

A common discovery in political culture studies is that political orientations are often strongly associated with the socio-economic characteristics of populations. This means that variations among socio-economic groups within a polity tend to include significantly different patterns of political culture. This is one reason for the well-known fact that in virtually no society is there a political culture pattern typical of almost all individuals or social groups; group political orientations strongly deviant from the predominant one in a society are called "sub-cultures." Evidence of socio-economic influence on political orientations abounds. In the United States, studies reveal that trust in government and confidence in the effectiveness of political action through traditional forms is diminished among blacks, Indians, and other minorities who feel the force of discrimination; in African nations, where regional and tribal loyalties are often very strong, the political groups or governmental units to which an individual feels most strongly attached may depend upon his tribal lineage, place of residence, or family background. One of the major tasks in political culture research is to identify these socio-economic variations in a society and to describe them. Almost any socio-economic characteristics may be associated with variations in political orientation within a society; the ones most frequently noted are race, occupation, family or caste, education, and income.

There are several reasons why social factors are so often associated with variations in political orientation. Frequently, political status within a society is determined by social status; since political rights, obligations, and benefits may be tied to social position, it is quite likely that individuals with different social backgrounds will have quite divergent views of political life. Social groups privileged with easy access to government, considerable material rewards from the system, and other indulgences may understandably feel more attached to the dominant institutions and values of civic life than those who are, in various ways, deprived or discriminated against. Moreover, it often happens that social status within societies is tied to education; those within the middle and upper levels of the social hierarchy, having received better education than those in lower social classes, may feel more confident of their political skills, better informed about civic life, and more aware and interested in political life, and may demonstrate many other political orientations that differ from those of less educated individuals. Finally, differing social characteristics may lead to very different expectations about what government should do: Landowners and laborers, creditors and debtors, professionals and nonprofessionals are not likely to seek the same ends from civic life nor receive the same satisfactions; social cleavages within societies are almost always rich in potential clashes of political interest and in varying assessments of how well the system operates or should operate.

Political Variables

Any list of the factors shaping and modifying political culture would be incomplete without attention to government itself and to political parties. No group has a greater stake in the development and change of political culture than does a nation's governmental elite, for their continued existence and effectiveness may depend, in the long run, upon how the mass of people are oriented toward them and toward the political institutions they manage. All governments place heavy emphasis upon controlling the major institutions of political socialization (especially the educational system) and on prescribing, in varying degrees, what shall be taught; the intent is to produce a mass political culture compatible with the regime and, once this is achieved, to preserve it. In cases where a major change in regime may occur within a society—a "modernizing" elite taking the reins of government from a traditional one or a Communist regime succeeding a non-Communist one—the new government often places a high priority upon the reshaping of the political culture through the re-education of children and adults into the new allegiances and values they are expected to have with the change of political order. In these instances, no longer rare, the regime becomes the most powerful agent in remolding a political culture.

In many polities, political parties play a major role in shaping mass political orientations. This may be in collaboration with, or opposition to, the dominant regime. In totalitarian countries, it is common for the single dominant party to be an organ of the regime and to penetrate all major social, occupational, cultural, and political aspects of life, taking the lead in teaching and rewarding whatever political orientations are desired by the regime. In many societies, however, political parties are part of the regime's opposition (and, in some cases, may be prohibited from overt activity); they may submit members to intensive indoctrination with political values, loyalties, and attitudes quite hostile to the dominant regime or some of the other political parties—the common situation, for instance, when Marxist parties operate in non-Marxist systems. The impact of party indoctrination will vary, of course, among political systems. In the United States, Great Britain, and most other Western European countries the dominant parties share a basic agreement on the nature of the constitutional order and the proper political processes for the nation; pronounced differences in party programs show up with respect to policy rather than regime norms. Thus, as a rule, party members are not likely to possess sharply different political culture attributes by virtue of belonging to different parties. By contrast, parties which represent regional, social, religious, or other interests sharply at variance with the dominant regime may well be socializing members into a very different cultural orientation from those found in other parties.

This by no means exhausts the number of factors which may be important in shaping or transforming a political culture. Nor should one treat what has been said about the shaping of political culture as some unalterable truth. In reality, all the factors we have suggested as important in shaping political culture, and all the ways in which they seem to affect that culture, should be considered as working hypotheses—the best approximation to the truth we can make with the information now available to us. Our view of political culture is largely shaped by the methods and data at hand; as new methods of inquiry become available and new sources of information open up, our understanding of the forces shaping political culture is bound to change. In one sense, this is frustrating to both researcher and reader. It is far more satisfying to be told "the truth" about political culture than to be told what "seems" to be the truth. In another sense, however, the tentativeness of our conclusions leaves us open to new information and new arguments. This keeps the imagination flexible and guards against dogmatism. Moreover, it underscores how dependent we are on our techniques of study for the conclusions we reach. Indeed, it is not possible to judge the adequacy of our understanding of political culture unless we know how the information is gathered and what strengths or weaknesses lie in our methods. Thus, it is both logical and necessary to examine, briefly, how our conclusions about political culture are formed. This means turning to the techniques for the study of political culture.

25 Interest Groups

A prominent assumption of liberal democratic pluralist political systems is that although individuals, on their own, may have little influence on the outcome of political decisions, they are nonetheless free to join with others in society to pursue common objectives. That right, usually, is guaranteed by the freedom to associate. Understanding how interest groups work, consequently, has been an important project for political scientists, and a number of classic studies, including Arthur Bentley's *The Process of Government* (1908) and David Truman's *The Governmental Process* (1953), represent scholarly landmarks in this tradition. In the following selection, Mancur Olson summarizes some of the central ideas behind a recent classic, *The Logic of Collective Action*, which has heavily influenced contemporary thinking about interest groups. Olson argues that interest groups work in a political marketplace, and that in order to understand why individuals join groups and why some groups are more effective than others, we should apply market thinking to politics. The key questions inspired by this line of thinking are: What are the costs and benefits of joining a group? Do groups provide selective benefits? Or can individuals free ride? Does the size of a group affect its ability to provide collective goods? Olson's thesis, originally developed in *The Logic of Collective Action*, has been modified in some important respects, but the line of reasoning applied to explain individual-group behaviour remains intact.

Mancur Olson is a Distinguished Professor of Economics at the University of Maryland. Selection 25 is taken from his book *The Rise and Decline of Nations: Economic Growth, Stagflation, and Social Rigidities.*

●●●●●●●●●●

I

The argument of this book begins with a paradox in the behavior of groups. It has often been taken for granted that if everyone in a group of individuals or firms had some interest in common, then there would be a tendency for the group to seek to further this interest. Thus many students of politics in the United States for a long time supposed that citizens with a common political interest would organize and lobby to serve that interest. Each individual in the population would be in one or more groups and the vector of pressures of these competing groups explained the outcomes of the political process. Similarly, it was often supposed that if workers, farmers, or consumers faced monopolies harmful to their interests, they would eventually attain countervailing power through organizations such as labor unions or farm organizations that obtained market power and protective government action. On a larger scale, huge social classes are often expected to act in the interest of their members; the unalloyed form of this belief is, of course, the Marxian contention that in capitalist societies the bourgeois class runs the government to serve its own interests, and that once the exploitation of the proletariat goes far enough and "false consciousness" has disappeared, the working class will in its own interest revolt and establish a dictatorship of the proletariat. In general, if the individuals in some category or class had a sufficient degree of self-interest and if they all agreed on some common interest, then the group would to some extent also act in a self-interested or group-interested manner.

If we ponder the logic of the familiar assumption described in the preceding paragraph, we can see that it is fundamentally and indisputably faulty. Consider those consumers who agree that they pay higher prices for a product because of some objectionable monopoly or tariff, or those workers who agree that their skill deserves a higher wage. Let us now ask what would be the expedient course of action for an individual consumer who would like to see a boycott to combat a monopoly or a lobby to repeal the tariff, or for an individual worker who would like a strike threat or a minimum wage law that could bring higher wages. If the consumer or worker contributes a few days and a few dollars to organize a boycott or a union or to lobby for favorable legislation, he or she will have sacrificed time and money. What will this sacrifice obtain? The individual will at best succeed in advancing the cause to a small (often imperceptible) degree. In any case he will get only a minute share of the gain from his action. The very fact that the objective or interest is common to or shared by the group entails that the gain from any sacrifice an individual makes to serve this common purpose is shared with everyone in the group. The successful boycott or strike or lobbying action will bring the better price or wage for everyone in the relevant category, so the individual in any large group with a common interest will reap only a minute share of the gains from whatever sacrifices the individual makes to achieve this common interest. Since any gain goes to everyone in the group, those who contribute nothing to the effort will get just as much as those who made a contribution. It pays to "let George do it," but George has little or no incentive to do anything in the group interest either, so (in the absence of factors that are completely left out of the conceptions mentioned in the first paragraph) there will be little, if any, group action. The paradox, then, is that (in the absence of special arrangements or circumstances to which we shall turn later) large groups, at least if they are composed of rational individuals, will *not* act in their group interest. . . .

II

One finding in *The Logic* is that the services of associations like labor unions, professional associations, farm organizations, cartels, lobbies (and even collusive groups without formal organization) resemble the basic services of the state in one utterly fundamental respect. The services of such associations, like the elemental services or "public goods" provided by governments, if provided to anyone, go to everyone in some category or group. Just as the law and order, defense, or pollution abatement brought about by government accrue to everyone in some country or geographic area, so the tariff obtained by a farm organization's lobbying effort raises the price to all producers of the relevant commodity. Similarly, as I argued earlier, the higher wage won by a union applies to all employees in the pertinent category. More generally, every lobby obtaining a general change in legislation or regulation thereby obtains a public or collective good for everyone who benefits from that change, and every combination—that is, every "cartel"—using market or industrial action to get a higher price or wage must, when it restricts the quantity supplied, raise the price for every seller, thereby creating a collective good for all sellers.

If governments, on the one hand, and combinations exploiting their political or market power, on the other, produce public or collective goods that inevitably go to everyone in some group or category, then both are subject to the paradoxical logic set out above: that is, the individuals and firms they serve have in general no incentive voluntarily to contribute to their support. It follows that if there is only voluntary and rational individual behavior, then for the most part neither governments nor lobbies and cartels will exist, unless individuals support them for some reason *other* than the collective goods they provide. Of course, governments exist virtually everywhere and often there are lobbies and cartelistic organizations as well. If the argument so far is right, it follows that something *other* than the collective goods that governments and other organizations provide accounts for their existence.

In the case of governments, the answer was explained before *The Logic of Collective Action* was written; governments are obviously supported by compulsory taxation. Sometimes there is little objection to this compulsion, presumably because many people intuitively understand that public goods cannot be sold in the marketplace or financed by any voluntary mechanism; as I have already argued, each individual would get only a minute share of any governmental services he or she paid for and would get whatever level of services was provided by others in any event.

In the case of organizations that provide collective goods to their client groups through political or market action, the answer has not been obvious, but it is no less clear-cut. Organizations of this kind, at least when they represent large groups, are again not supported because of the collective goods they provide, but rather because they have been fortunate enough to find what I have called *selective incentives*. A selective incentive is one that applies selectively to the individuals depending on whether they do or do not contribute to the provision of the collective good.

A selective incentive can be either negative or positive; it can, for example, be a loss or punishment imposed only on those who do *not* help provide the collective good. Tax payments are, of course, obtained with the help of negative selective incentives, since those who are found not to have paid their taxes must then suffer both taxes and penalties. The best-known type of organized interest group in modern democratic societies, the labor union, is also usually supported, in part, through negative selective incentives. Most of the dues in strong unions are obtained through union shop, closed shop, or agency shop arrangements which make dues paying more or less compulsory and automatic. There are often also informal arrangements with the same effect; David McDonald, former president of the United Steel Workers of America, describes one of these arrangements used in the early history of that union. It was, he writes, a technique

> which we called . . . visual education, which was a high-sounding label for a practice much more accurately described as dues picketing. It worked very simply. A group of dues-paying members, selected by the district director (usually more for their size than their tact) would stand at the plant gate with pick handles or baseball bats in hand and confront each worker as he arrived for his shift.

As McDonald's "dues picketing" analogy suggests, picketing during strikes is another negative selective incentive that unions sometimes need; although picketing in industries with established and stable unions is usually peaceful, this is because the union's capacity to close down an enterprise against which it has called a strike is clear to all; the early phase of unionization often involves a great deal of violence on the part of both unions and anti-union employers and scabs.

Some opponents of labor unions argue that, since many of the members of labor unions join only through the processes McDonald described or through legally enforced union-shop arrangments, most of the relevant workers do not want to be unionized. The Taft-Hartley Act provided that impartial governmentally administered elections should be held to determine whether workers did in fact want to belong to unions. As the collective-good logic set out here suggests, the same workers who had to be coerced to pay union dues voted for the unions with compulsory dues (and normally by overwhelming margins), so that this feature of the Taft-Hartley Act was soon abandoned as pointless. The workers who as individuals tried to avoid paying union dues at the same time that they voted to force themselves all to pay dues are no different from taxpayers who vote, in effect, for high levels of taxation, yet try to arrange their private affairs in ways that avoid taxes. Because of the same logic, many professional associations also get members through covert or overt coercion (for example, lawyers in those states with a "closed bar"). So do lobbies and cartels of several other types; some of the contributions by corporate officials, for instance, to politicians useful to the corporation are also the result of subtle forms of coercion. . . .

III

Small groups, or occasionally large "federal" groups that are made up of many small groups of socially interactive members, have an additional source of both negative and positive selective incentives. Clearly most people value the companionship and respect of those with whom they interact. In modern societies solitary confinement is, apart from the rare death penalty, the harshest legal punishment. The censure or even ostracism of those who fail to bear a share of the burdens of collective action can sometimes be an important selective incentive. An extreme example of this occurs when British unionists refuse to speak to uncooperative colleagues, that is, "send them to Coventry." Similarly, those in a socially interactive group seeking a collective good can give special respect or honor to those who distinguish themselves by their sacrifices in the interest of the group and thereby offer them a positive selective incentive. Since most people apparently prefer relatively likeminded or agreeable and respectable company, and often prefer to associate with those whom they especially admire, they may find it costless to shun those who shirk the collective action and to favor those who oversubscribe.

Social selective incentives can be powerful and inexpensive, but they are available only in certain situations. As I have already indicated, they have little applicability to large groups, except in those cases in which the large groups can be federations of small groups that are capable of social interaction. It also is not possible to organize most large groups in need of a collective good into small, socially interactive subgroups, since most individuals do not have the time needed to maintain a huge number of friends and acquaintances. . . .

All the arguments showing the difficulty of collective action mentioned so far in this chapter hold even when there is perfect consensus about the collective good that is desired, the amount that is wanted, and the best way to obtain the good. But if anything, such as social heterogeneity, reduces consensus, collective action can become still less likely. . . .

Consensus is especially difficult where collective goods are concerned because the defining characteristic of collective goods—that they go to everyone in some group or category if they are provided at all—also entails that everyone in the relevant group gets more or less of the collective good together, and that they all have to accept whatever level and type of public good is provided. A country can have only one foreign and defense policy. . . .

In short, the political entrepreneurs who attempt to organize collective action will accordingly be more likely to succeed if they strive to organize relatively homogeneous groups. The political managers whose task it is to maintain organized or collusive action similarly will be motivated to use indoctrination and selective recruitment to increase the homogeneity of their client groups. This is true in part because social selective incentives are more likely to be available to the more nearly homogeneous groups, and in part because homogeneity will help achieve consensus.

IV

Information and calculation about a collective good is often itself a collective good. Consider a typical member of a large organization who is deciding how much time to devote to studying the policies or leadership of the organization. The more time the member devotes to this matter, the greater the likelihood that his or her voting and advocacy will favor effective policies and leadership for the organization. This typical member will, however, get only a small share of the gain from the more effective policies and leadership: in the aggregate, the other members will get almost all the gains, so that the individual member does not have an incentive to devote nearly as much time to fact-finding and thinking about the organization as would be in the group interest. Each of the members of the group would be better off if they all could be coerced into spending more time finding out how to vote to make the organization best further their interests. This is dramatically evident in the case of the typical voter in a national election in a large country. The gain to such a voter from studying issues and candidates until it is clear what vote is truly in his or her interest is given by the difference in the value to the individual of the "right" election outcome as compared with the "wrong" outcome, *multiplied by the probability a change in the individual's vote will alter the outcome of the election.* Since the probability that a typical voter will change the outcome of the election is vanishingly small, the typical citizen is usually "rationally ignorant" about public affairs. Often, information about public affairs is so interesting or entertaining that it pays to acquire it for these reasons alone—

this appears to be the single most important source of exceptions to the generalization that *typical* citizens are rationally ignorant about public affairs. . . .

The limited knowledge of public affairs is in turn necessary to explain the effectiveness of lobbying. If all citizens had obtained and digested all pertinent information, they could not then be swayed by advertising or other persuasion. With perfectly informed citizens, elected officials would not be subject to the blandishments of lobbyists, since the constituents would then know if their interests were betrayed and defeat the unfaithful representative at the next election. Just as lobbies provide collective goods to special-interest groups, so their effectiveness is explained by the imperfect knowledge of citizens, and this in turn is due mainly to the fact that information and calculation about collective goods is also a collective good. . . .

This argument also helps us to understand certain apparent inconsistencies in the behavior of modern democracies. The arrangement of the income-tax brackets in all the major developed democracies is distinctly progressive, whereas the loopholes are more often tilted toward a minority of more prosperous taxpayers. Since both are the results of the same democratic institutions, why do they not have the same incidence? As I see it, the progression of the income tax is a matter of such salience and political controversy that much of the electorate knows about it, so populist and majoritarian considerations dictate a considerable degree of progression. The details of tax laws are far less widely known, and they often reflect the interests of small numbers of organized and usually more prosperous taxpayers. Several of the developed democracies similarly have adopted programs such as Medicare and Medicaid that are obviously inspired by the concerns about the cost of medical care to those with low or middle incomes, yet implemented or administered these programs in ways that resulted in large increases in income for prosperous physicians and other providers of medical care. Again, these diverse consequences seem to be explained by the fact that conspicuous and controversial choices of overall policies become known to the majorities who consume health care, whereas the many smaller choices needed to implement these programs are influenced primarily by a minority of organized providers of health care.

The fact that the typical individual does not have an incentive to spend much time studying many of his choices concerning collective goods also helps to explain some otherwise inexplicable individual contributions toward the provision of collective goods. The logic of collective action that has been described in this chapter is not immediately apparent to those who have never studied it; if it were, there would be nothing paradoxical in the argument with which this chapter opened, and students to whom the argument is explained would not react with initial skepticism. No doubt the practical implications of this logic for the individual's own choices were often discerned before the logic was ever set out in print, but this does not mean that they were always understood even at the intuitive and practical level. In particular, when the costs of individual contributions to collective action are very small, the individual has little incentive to investigate whether or not to make a contribution or even to exercise intuition. If the individual knows the costs of a contribution to collective action in the interest of a group of which he is a part are trivially small, he may rationally not take the trouble to consider whether the gains are smaller still. This is particularly the case since the size of these gains and the policies that would maximize them are matters about which it is usually not rational for him to investigate. . . .

V

Even when contributions are costly enough to elicit rational calculation, there is still one set of circumstances in which collective action can occur without selective incentives. This set of circumstances becomes evident the moment we think of situations in which there are only a few individuals or firms that would benefit from collective action. Suppose there are two firms of equal size in an industry and no other firms can enter the industry. It still will be the case that a higher price for the industry's product will benefit both firms and that legislation favorable to the industry will help both firms. The higher price and the favorable legislation are then collective goods to this "oligopolistic" industry, even though there are only two in the group that benefit from the collective goods. Obviously, each of the oligopolists is in a situation in which if it restricts output to raise the industry price, or lobbies for favorable legislation for the industry, it will tend to get half of the benefit. And the cost-benefit ratio of action in the common interest easily could be so favorable that, even though a firm bears the whole cost of its action and gets only half the benefit of this action, it could still profit from acting in the common interest. Thus if the group that would benefit from collective action is sufficiently small and the cost-benefit ratio of collective action for the group sufficiently favorable, there may well be calculated action in the collective interest even without selective incentives.

When there are only a few members in the group, there is also the possibility that they will bargain with one another and agree on collective action—then the action of each can have a perceptible effect on the interests and the expedient courses of action of others, so that each has an incentive to act strategically, that is, in ways that take into account the effect of the individual's choices on the choices of others. This interdependence of individual firms or persons in the group can give them an incentive to bargain with one another for their mutual advantage. . . . The upshot of all this, as I explain elsewhere, is that "small" groups can often engage in collective action without selective incentives. In certain small groups ("privileged groups") there is actually a presumption that some of the collective good will be provided. Nonetheless, even in the best of circumstances collective action is problematic and the outcomes in particular cases are indeterminate. . . .

Obviously, when we get to large groups measured in millions or even thousands, the incentive for group-oriented behavior in the absence of selective incentives becomes insignificant and even imperceptible. . . .

Other things being equal, *the larger the number of individuals or firms that would benefit from a collective good, the smaller the share of the gains from action in the group interest that will accrue to the individual or firm that undertakes the action. Thus, in the absence of selective incentives, the incentive for group action diminishes as group size increases, so that large groups are less able to act in their common interest than small ones.* If an additional individual or firm that would value the collective good enters the scene, then the share of the gains from group-oriented action that anyone already in the group might take must diminish. This holds true whatever the relative sizes or valuations of the collective goods in the group. . . .

The significance of the logic that has just been set out can best be seen by comparing groups that would have the same net gain from collective action, if they could engage in it, but that vary in size. Suppose there are a million individuals who would gain a thousand dollars each, or a billion in the aggregate, if they were to organize effectively and engage in collective action that had a total cost of a hundred million. If the logic set out above is right, they could not organize or engage in effective collective action without selective incentives. Now suppose that, although the total gain of a billion dollars from collective action and the aggregate cost of a hundred million remain the same, the group is composed instead of five big corporations or five organized municipalities, each of which would gain two hundred million. Collective action is not an absolute certainty even in this case, since each of the five could conceivably expect others to put up the hundred million and hope to gain the collective good worth two hundred million at no cost at all. Yet collective action, perhaps after some delays due to bargaining, seems very likely indeed. In this case any one of the five would gain a hundred million from providing the collective good even if it had to pay the whole cost itself; and the costs of bargaining among five would not be great, so they would sooner or later probably work out an agreement providing for the collective action. The numbers in this example are arbitrary, but roughly similar situations occur often in reality, and the

314 The Political Process

contrast between "small" and "large" groups could be illustrated with an infinite number of diverse examples.

The significance of this argument shows up in a second way if one compares the operations of lobbies or cartels within jurisdictions of vastly different scale, such as a modest municipality on the one hand and a big country on the other. Within the town, the major or city council may be influenced by, say, a score of petitioners or a lobbying budget of a thousand dollars. A particular line of business may be in the hands of only a few firms, and if the town is distant enough from other markets only these few would need to agree to create a cartel. In a big country, the resources needed to influence the national government are likely to be much more substantial, and unless the firms are (as they sometimes are) gigantic, many of them would have to cooperate to create an effective cartel. Now suppose that the million individuals in our large group in the previous paragraph were spread out over a hundred thousand towns or jurisdictions, so that each jurisdiction had ten of them, along with the same proportion of citizens in other categories as before. Suppose also that the cost-benefit ratios remained the same, so that there was still a billion dollars to gain across all jurisdictions or ten thousand in each, and that it would still cost a hundred million dollars across all jurisdictions or a thousand in each. It no longer seems out of the question that in many jurisdictions the groups of ten, or subsets of them, would put up the thousand-dollar total needed to get the thousand for each individual. Thus we see that, if all else were equal, small jurisdictions would have more collective action per capita than large ones.

Differences in intensities of preference generate a third type of illustration of the logic at issue. A small number of zealots anxious for a particular collective good are more likely to act collectively to obtain that good than a larger number with the same aggregate willingness to pay. Suppose there are twenty-five individuals, each of whom finds a given collective good worth a thousand dollars in one case, whereas in another there are five thousand, each of whom finds the collective good worth five dollars. Obviously, the argument indicates that there would be a greater likelihood of collective action in the former case than in the latter, even though the aggregate demand for the collective good is the same in both. The great historical significance of small groups of fanatics no doubt owes something to this consideration.

VI

The argument in this chapter predicts that those groups that have access to selective incentives will be more likely to act collectively to obtain collective goods than those that do not, and that smaller groups will have a greater likelihood of engaging in collective action than larger ones. The empirical portions of *The Logic* show that this prediction has been correct for the United States. More study will be needed before we can be utterly certain that the argument also holds for other countries, but the more prominent features of the organizational landscape of other countries certainly do fit the theory. In no major country are large groups without access to selective incentives generally organized—the masses of consumers are not in consumers' organizations, the millions of taxpayers are not in taxpayers' organizations, the vast number of those with relatively low incomes are not in organizations for the poor, and the sometimes substantial numbers of unemployed have no organized voice. These groups are so dispersed that it is not feasible for any nongovernmental organization to coerce them; in this they differ dramatically from those, like workers in large factories or mines, who are susceptible to coercion through picketing. Neither does there appear to be any source of the positive selective incentives that might give individuals in these categories an incentive to cooperate with the many others with whom they share common interests. By contrast, almost everywhere the social prestige of the learned professions and the limited numbers of practitioners of each profession in each community has helped them to organize. The professions have also been helped to organize by the distinctive susceptibility of the public to the assertion that a professional organization, with the backing of government, ought to be able to determine who is "qualified" to practice the profession, and thereby to control a decisive selective incentive. The small groups of (often large) firms in industry after industry, in country after country, are similarly often organized in trade associations or organizations or collusions of one kind or another. So, frequently, are the small groups of (usually smaller) businesses in particular towns or communities. . . .

26　　　　Political Parties

In Western liberal democracies, political parties evolved with the extension of the franchise. As universal adult suffrage was achieved, political parties became a fundamental institution associated with democracy. Providing a critical link between society and government, the rulers and the ruled, they were facilitators of modern participatory politics.

Political analysts have theorized that political parties were vital in making democracies work. Parties were said to perform many important roles in the political process—acting as an outlet for public involvement in politics, providing representation and recruitment, and serving to integrate a variety of interests in society.

While political parties are highly visible and active at time of elections, they have not been crucial players between elections in the policy-making process. In fact, other institutions in the political process such as the executive and the bureaucracy have become the central focus in organizing the public policy agenda. This shift in responsibility from political parties to the political executive has led to hypotheses about the "decline of political parties." John Meisel's article addresses this issue by reviewing the traditional roles of political parties, and explaining why some of these roles have been assumed by other organizations in the governmental process.

John Meisel is Sir Edward Peacock Professor of Political Science at Queen's University, Kingston, Ontario. He has written a number of books and articles on elections, political parties, and politics in Canada. He is a former chairman of the Canadian Radio-television and Telecommunications Commission; has served on numerous royal commissions, task forces, and inquiries; and is a past president of the Canadian Political Science Association. The reading, "The Decline of Party in Canada," appears in *Party Politics in Canada*.

● ● ● ● ● ● ● ● ● ●

Anthony King, in a searching paper analyzing the role of parties in liberal democracies, summarizes much of the relevant literature by listing six usually cited functions of parties: (1) structuring the vote; (2) integration and mobilization of the mass public; (3) recruitment of political leaders; (4) organization of government; (5) formation of public policy; and (6) aggregation of interests. He notes that there is a good deal of imprecision in the manner in which political scientists deal with the roles of parties and that the importance of their functions tends to be exaggerated. Nevertheless, he concludes, parties are critical components of the political process and they need to be studied, albeit with greater precision than is often the case.

This article shares King's view and, although it focuses on the relative decline of political parties in Canada, it should not be interpreted as arguing that the parties and the party system are insignificant. Parties clearly still influence critical aspects of politics and, most notably, they influence who occupies the government benches in parliament and who heads the various departments and ministries. The emphasis in this article is on federal politics, although many of the observations also apply to the provincial arena.

Parties still perform the first function listed: they structure the vote in most elections, except at the municipal level. They, to some measure, present options to the electorate about current issues and so can be said to organize mass opinion, although one is often tempted to conclude that they disorganize it. As for the related role of mobilizing the public, a remarkably high proportion of Canadians participate in elections in one way or another, and by no means just by voting. The preparation of electoral lists, staffing the polling booths, and organizing the campaigns on a polling-division by polling-division basis all takes a great deal of effort, most of which is provided by volunteer activists. This not only enables the electoral process to function, it increases the public's knowledge of political questions and facts. It is well-established that a greater sense of partisan attachment is associated with a greater knowledge of politics.

Nevertheless, an increasing number of Canadians have sought to participate in politics and public life outside the framework of parties—in tenants' or neighbourhood organizations or through voluntary associations, from unions to environmental or anti-nuclear groups. There was an upsurge of such "unconventional" politics in the sixties in the United States and to a lesser extent in Canada, but there is some uncertainty about the degree to which non-partisan politics has continued to flourish in North America in the seventies. Although the situation in Canada is a little ambiguous, there is no doubt that the proportion of people in the United States who identify with political parties in the sense that they think of themselves as Democrats or Republicans is steadily declining.

Parties also recruit politicians, although many question whether, in general, politics attracts a sufficiently high calibre of individuals. Data are unavailable on this point but some speculate that other careers appeal to the ablest Canadians and they conclude that we could do with a good deal more talent in the parties. This question raises another, also imperfectly understood puzzle: what characteristics make for a good politician? Indeed, what is a good politician?

By deciding which partisan team forms the government and who is in opposition, parties do organize government in an important way. But there is little doubt that a great many decisions about what is placed on the public agenda and at what time, are forced on political parties by events, non-political decision-makers and very often the preferences of powerful civil servants, whose reponsibility to the politicians is increasingly more formal than real. Even the organization of the government—the way in which legislation is drafted and considered by the cabinet and its committees, the extent to which outside interests are consulted, the manner in which policies are administered—is more likely to reflect the wills of a small number of senior civil servants than the decision of senior party officials, including the ministers. It is indeed questionable whether the government party leader—the prime minister—continues to function as a party person after accession to power or whether the party role and influence are maintained as a successful administration becomes accustomed to power and develops close relationships with senior civil servants.

In short, one must ask whether the parties really play the central role liberal democratic theory ascribes to them in organizing government and in the formation of public policy. And, given the changes in communication and the importance of voluntary associations and interest groups, one wonders about the relative unimportance of parties in the processes which aggregate the interests of various individuals and groups into satisfactory policies.

In seeking to identify the main manifestations of, and reasons for, the decline of party, relative to other political factors, this essay distinguishes between long-run factors, most of which are universal in liberal democracies and appear to a greater or lesser extent in most highly industrialized and post-industrial societies, and those which are of more recent origin and uniquely Canadian.

LONG-RUN REASONS FOR PARTY DECLINE

Rise of the Bureaucratic State
Modern political parties evolved from small cliques of power-wielders when the extension of the franchise necessitated the organization of mass electorates. The greater participation of the public in political life led, in conjunction with other factors, to the emergence of the positive state—one which increasingly participated in virtually every aspect of the human experience. But the "ancestors" of our political institutions and the political parties serving them evolved at a time when governments were dealing

with a limited range of problems, and when only a small minority of the population was politically active. Under these conditions parties were able to act as suitable links between the small electorate and the even smaller number of political decision-makers.

The continuous expansion of governmental activities has created mounting problems for the legislative and representative system. Up until the First World War, the Canadian parliament dealt with only a small number of issues, met seldom and required little specialized and technical knowledge to operate. Now the number and complexity of the areas in which the federal government operates are so vast that it is quite impossible for MPs to be abreast of what is going on. At best, each can become reasonably well-informed about one or two areas.

The expansion of government activities and the increasingly complicated nature of government decisions have reduced the capacity of elected officials to deal with many important public issues and necessitated the restructuring of many governmental institutions. Thus MPs and even cabinet ministers are often incapable of fully understanding the problems and options confronting them, and the normal structure of ministries is being supplemented by a large number of quasi-independent administrative, regulatory and judicial boards and commissions not directly responsible to the elected representatives of the public or to party politicians. In short, an important shift has occurred in the locus of power of liberal democracies, from elected politicians to appointed civil servants, whose links to political parties are indirect and increasingly tenuous. This means that parties, supposedly in control of the political process and responsible to the public for its performance, are often little more than impotent observers of processes they cannot control and the results of which they can only rubber stamp.

A good illustration is the case of irregularities in the sale of reactors by Atomic Energy of Canada Ltd., a crown corporation, to Argentina and Korea. There were strong suspicions that bribes had been paid and that the foreign exchange regulations of some countries had been violated. Enormous commissions were also allegedly paid to shadowy foreign agents. One of the reactors was sold at a loss of over 100 million dollars. The Public Accounts Committee of the House of Commons held extensive hearings and questioned closely Mr. J.L. Gray, president of Atomic Energy of Canada at the time of the sales. His stonewalling of the issue, and that by everyone else connected with the matter, was so effective that the House of Commons committee failed to shed light on the sales and finally had to let the case rest.

Pluralism and the Rise of Interest Group Politics
Before the expansion of governmental activities and the increase in their complexity, the usual pattern of lawmaking was relatively simple. Ministers or the whole cabinet, with or without prompting by their civil servants, decided on the broad outlines of what needed to be done. Civil servants, drawing on expert knowledge and advice, prepared the necessary background papers and draft proposals. These were discussed by the ministers, in the absence of their civil servant advisors, and ultimately presented to parliament for enactment. The basic decisions were essentially those of politicians and their officials. More recently, a more involved process of legislation has evolved, partly because of the need to deal with problems having enormous ramifications, partly in an effort to make government more participatory, and partly in response to the claims of a market-oriented, pluralist society in which political parties depend on the financial support of powerful economic interests or of unions. Before any law or important administrative decision is decided upon, an intense consultation between officials and representatives of various vested interests takes place. There has been a striking increase in lobbying by interest groups who have the resources and capacity to do so. Many important decisions are arrived at through private consultations between civil servants and spokesmen for various vested interests, during which politicians play no role. By the time ministers enter the decision-making process, the die is cast and only minor changes, if any, can be made. The *general* interest, therefore, as aggregated by political parties, tends to receive scant attention and parties are left with little choice but to approve what has already been decided by others. The process of consultation is for the most part totally non-partisan and most ministers engaged in it act as governmental decision-makers, far removed from their party personas. For the government party caucus to disown government policies already decided on after considerable negotiations would be politically harmful and is hardly ever heard of. Convincing testimony of the relative impotence of parties is found in Robert Presthus's study of Canadian interest groups, which shows that the latter spend considerably more time and effort lobbying bureaucrats than members of parliament. Furthermore, it is clear that having recourse to pressure group participation in policy-making is not a feared or temporary phenomenon. The Canadian government, like many others, has institutionalized the practice by appointing large numbers of advisory committees and other bodies designed to ensure the pressure of interested parties in the policy process.

Incipient Corporatism

A related phenomenon received wide attention during the ill-fated, mid-1970s anti-inflation program of the federal government. Although the case is derived from Canadian experience, the phenomenon is not unique to this country. Efforts to control prices and wages required the cooperation of both management and labor. The idea was that federal economic policy would emerge from regular consultations between the government and representatives of labor, industry and business and that a group comprised of these interests would become institutionalized as a permanent consultative body. In the end, this structure was never established. It is difficult to see how this kind of change in the governmental process could have been made without undermining the power of parliament and hence of political parties. Compromises delicately wrought by a tripartite council would not likely be upset by the House of Commons even if members of the majority party wished to repudiate the deals made by their leadership.

Recourse to the tripartite consultative process reflects a tendency toward a new form of corporatism—a process of arriving at collective decisions through the efforts of representatives of the main "functional" interests in the country rather than of its territorial delegates. Because corporatism is usually associated with fascism, it is viewed with suspicion; but there is nothing inevitably authoritarian in it. There are corporatist elements in the usually high regarded Swedish politico-economic system. But whatever its general merits, corporatist institutions supplement legislatures and reduce the importance of political parties. . . .

Federal-Provincial Diplomacy

Another and increasingly threatening cause of the decline in the importance of parties lies in the changing nature of Canadian federalism. Accommodation between the various regions of the country (and to some extent, between special interests which happen to be in part regionally based) is taking place more and more through two mechanisms which are largely unrelated to party politics. The first of these is the federal-provincial prime ministerial conference, where Ottawa and the provinces hammer out compromises touching virtually every aspect of human experience. Most of these are the result of delicate bargaining on the part of eleven governments which sometimes cannot help but take positions imposed by other negotiators and which therefore cannot be anticipated by legislative caucuses, let alone by party supporters.

The second procedure through which policies are agreed upon by the federal and provincial governments is the regular meeting and consultation among federal and provincial officials. There are now thousands of such encounters annually and hundreds of formally established committees, task forces and work groups in which decisions are made which bind the participating governments. As with prime ministerial meetings, these encounters reach decisions which can be reversed or altered only at great cost—one not likely to be risked by rank-and-file members of political parties.

It can be argued that governments, at the ministerial level, are composed of leading party politicians and that their actions are in a sense those of political parties. This is technically correct, but the infrequent and unfocused expression of party opinion and the almost nonexistent party activity between elections deprive elected officials of any viable contact with their party organisms. There is, in contrast, a striking frequency and intensity of contacts between office-holding politicians and civil servants and spokesmen for vested interests. It is no exaggeration to argue that although ministers, and through them, the officials who serve under them, formally reflect party interests, they do not do so in any meaningful way. Between elections, except for occasional and exceedingly rare party gatherings, the cabinet *is* the party, insofar as the government side of the equation is concerned. Thus, such major policy changes as the introduction of wage control in the 'seventies and Trudeau's 1983 resolve to play a mediating role between the superpowers were introduced without any party involvement of any sort.

The Rise of Electronic Media

Until the advent of radio and particularly of television, politicians were the most effective means through which the public learnt about political events. In many communities across the country the political meeting was not only an important means of communication but also prime entertainment. Political issues were personalized by politicians who, in addition to adding colour to the consideration of matters of public policy, lent the political process a gladiatorial dimension that heightened its public appeal.

Television has, to a great extent, changed all that. The average Canadian spends several hours a day watching all manner of programs among which political material plays a relatively minor role. The entertainment value of face-to-face politics has declined since there are so many other exciting things to watch. And the public perception of the political process and of political issues that remains is derived from television treatment of the news and of political personalities. Public taste and public opinion on almost everything is being shaped by television programs and television advertising. Politics and politicians are filtered by a medium in which the primary concern is often not enlightenment, knowledge or consciousness-raising but maximal audiences and profits. This has meant that even major political events like the choosing of national party leaders are dominated by the requirements of television. The organization and scheduling of meetings are arranged so that the most appealing events occur during prime time, when they are broadcast, and all other aspects, even the quality of discussion and the time spent on critical issues, are made subservient to the demands of the electronic media.

Television has to some extent wrested the limelight from party politicians; but, on the other hand, it provides a matchless opportunity for the public to witness the party game. Its coverage of the most colourful political events — leadership conventions, elections, and so-called debates between party leaders — furnishes unprecedented opportunities for parties to be seen in action. The problem is, of course, that the exposure is chosen by the media largely for entertainment value, rather than as a continuous in-depth exploration of the dominant political issues and partisan strategies. The focus tends to be on the people who report and comment on political news rather than on the political actors themselves. One result of this tendency is that public opinion on political matters is shaped as much by media intermediaries as it is by the protagonists representing the various parties. Furthermore, the key role of television is changing the character of political leadership. It is now virtually impossible for anyone who is not "telegenic" to be chosen as party chief. His or her presence and style on television can make or break a politician; yet, these are only some (and not the most important) attributes of an effective political and governmental figure.

Investigative Journalism
Although television has come to occupy a key position in the manner in which the public perceives political and party life, it has not eclipsed the more traditional ways of reporting and analyzing news and of entertaining the public. Newspapers and periodicals still receive considerable attention, particularly among the politically most active members of the public. Partly, no doubt, in response to the competition provided by TV and partly because of the intense rivalry among some of the major printed media, newspapers and magazines have recently resorted to numerous ploys designed to attract attention and a wider audience. Among these, investigative journalism — a return of sorts to the old muckraking days — has been particularly important. Many of the major papers and some of the periodicals have sought to discover governmental lapses and to reveal wrongdoing on the part of local, provincial and federal authorities. These efforts at exposing flaws and shortcomings, errors, dishonesty and inefficiency perpetrated by governments have often led to the establishment of judicial and quasi-judicial inquiries and to the corroboration of the sins unearthed by the sleuthing journalists. The watch-dog function of the print and electronic media is important to the present argument because it can be

seen as an encroachment upon, or at least a complement to, the role of opposition parties. They, of course, are the agents par excellence, according to conventional theory, for keeping governments on their toes and for publicizing their misdeeds.

Although opposition politicians and investigative journalists no doubt derive mutual benefit from one another's activities, the recent increase in the role of the media as agents unearthing governmental malfeasance, regardless of how beneficial it may be, detracts from one of the most essential roles of opposition parties—that of criticizing the government. This is not to say the activities of the journalists inhibit or hamper opposition politicians; on the contrary, the latter exploit them; but the relative importance of government debate is reduced when much of the combat occurs outside the party arena—on the printed page or the television screen. One of the questions presented by the new or perhaps revived emphasis in the media on tracking down governmental errors of commission or omission is in fact whether the often vigorous reportorial initiative of the media does not reflect a decline in the energy and resourcefulness of opposition parties. Like many of the arguments presented above, this is a question requiring systematic research.

Whatever the reasons, a considerable challenge of, and check on, governments today originate outside the realm of political parties and tend to reduce the effectiveness of the party system. The media may be able to report governmental failings, but they cannot provide alternative governments—one of the functions of opposition parties. By sharing with others the task of exposing and criticizing official actions (and by often being outdone by them), opposition parties lose some of their credibility as alternatives to the current power-holders.

Opinion Polling

Increasingly widespread use of opinion polls by the small groups of officials and cronies working with the party leader has diminished the need to rely on the knowledge of public attitudes by local militants and elected politicians. The vast, sensitive network of contacts, reciprocal favours, and exchanges of information which characterized the relationship between party leaders and their followers has to some extent been attenuated by the use of scientific sampling, sophisticated interviewing techniques and subtle statistical analyses. While the results are in some respects more reliable, there is also a decided loss: the interplay between public opinion and the leadership exercised by politically informed and concerned activists is substantially reduced. There is likely less debate and argument, since local party people are no longer encouraged to take the pulse of their "parishioners" and to mediate between the grass roots and the leadership.

Public opinion, as defined by pollsters, guides political decisions more and political decision-makers are less involved in forming public opinion. Two consequences, at least, are relevant for our purposes: the character of political leadership and of political styles has changed and the party organization is no longer needed as an essential information network.

The Domination of Economic Interests

There is little agreement among scholars about the exact role of economic factors in the sociopolitical realm. Are the forces and relations of production basic causes of all other aspects of social organization or can social organization be manipulated through political means? Whatever one's judgment, one does not need to be an economic determinist to acknowledge that governments have frequently found it difficult to resist certain kinds of economic pressures or to work against certain economic realities. This vulnerability is enhanced by the greatly increased number and power of multinational corporations. These vast, globe-girdling enterprises are rarely dependent on their operations in any one political jurisdiction and are adept at playing one interest against another. The behaviour of the oil companies before, during and after the oil crisis of the seventies is a case in point. Even those who doubt that Canadian industry and business can withstand governmental pressure cannot ignore the fact that the multinationals, recognizing no loyalties other than to their balance sheets, can obviate, ignore, influence and even dominate Canadian governments. A striking example came to light in the autumn of 1977 when Inco, a Canadian-based multinational, which has benefited from lavish tax and other concessions, announced that it would lay off 3,000 employees in Canada. Against arguments to the effect that the company was at the same time using funds provided by Canadian taxpayers to expand productivity capacity overseas, a senior vice-president indicated that "fears of government takeover and other economic recriminations in Indonesia and Guatemala forced Inco . . . to cut back production in Canada where massive layoffs could be made with little prospect of serious political interference." This episode provides an illuminating vignette illustrating the impotence of the Canadian government and of Canadian political parties, in the face of economic pressure from industry. This subservice of the political realm to the economic is related to the prevailing value system and dominant ideologies: when parties and governments buckle under economic pressure, they do so because they do not believe in interfering with private enterprise.

One-Party Dominance

Finally, among the long-run, general factors leading in the decline of party in Canada is the very nature of the Canadian party system. Its chief feature during this century has been that it is a one-party dominant system, in which the important alternation is not between different parties in office but between majority and minority Liberal governments. Increasingly, the line between the government and the Liberal party has become tenuous, leading Liberals have become ministerial politicians and the opposition parties have been out of office for so long that they are seldom perceived as being capable of governing, sometimes (according to one scholar) even by themselves.

Canada has long been in a situation in which there has been a serious loss of confidence in the government and in the government party and at the same time no corresponding or compensating sense that the opposition might do better. The latter was perceived as inexperienced, fragmented and disposed to attack on principle everything and everyone who had anything to do with the government. Public opinion polls taken after the 1975 Conservative leadership convention showed a major decline in Liberal support and a corresponding upsurge in Conservative fortunes, but the election of a Parti Québécois government in November 1976 reminded Canadians of the woefully weak position of the Conservatives in Québec and of the fact that, in the past, only the Liberals (among the major parties) have tried to find a satisfactory accommodation between French and English Canada. The fear of national disintegration drove many voters back towards the Liberals, albeit with very little enthusiasm. Despite extensive doubt about the Liberal's capacity to provide adequate government (particularly west of the Ottawa River), the Conservatives were able, after the 1979 election, to form only a minority government which was toppled a few months after coming to power by the combined vote of the Liberals and NDP.

This reinforced the already strong sense, among most leading Liberals, that they are indispensable and (since the Canadian public seems to recurrently favour them), nearly infallible in dealing with Canadian problems. The sense of self-assurance—an increasingly important element in the party's physiognomy—has itself contributed a great deal to the decline of party in Canada.

Among the many other consequences of one-party dominance, one requires special notice in the present context. The less favoured parties (unless they are essentially doctrinaire organizations which attract ideologues regardless of electoral opportunities) experience great difficulty in attracting candidates of top quality. Highly successful and ambitious individuals do not, for the most part, wish to forsake promising careers in exchange for a difficult electoral campaign and, at best, an almost permanent seat on the opposition benches. In a system in which parties in power alternate, able deputies know that part of their career is likely to be spent in the cabinet and they may therefore be attracted to a political career even if their preferred party does not, in the short run, seem to stand a good chance of election.

SHORT-RUN CAUSES: THE LIBERAL STYLE

Disdain of Parliament

Prime Minister Trudeau is not, as has often been noted, a House of Commons man. He seems to hold parliament in low esteem and is on record as questioning the intelligence of his opponents. He seldom uses parliament as the platform for important pronouncements, preferring to deliver policy statements or general reflections on the state of the country in public speeches, television interviews or press conferences. Having entered politics relatively late in life, and having been strongly critical of the Liberals, Pierre Trudeau's personal circle appears to be outside the ranks of the party he now leads, and outside of parliament. The two intimate colleagues who entered politics with him, Jean Marchand and Gérard Pelletier, were also not at home in the House of Commons milieu and have retired from it.

A significant decision of Mr. Trudeau, in the present context, was his move in 1968 to establish regional desks within the privy council office, which were designed to keep abreast of developments and ideas in the regions. A more party-oriented prime minister would have relied on his party contacts and on colleagues in the House of Commons rather than on civil servants, and there was much criticism of the prime minister's move in the House of Commons and privately, among Liberal backbenchers. The desks as such have been abandoned but the government continues to bypass the House of Commons on some critical issues. . . .

Confusing the Public

A certain amount of sophistry is indigenous to politics when it comes to governments justifying their failure or unanticipated changes in their policies and strategy. But the public is not likely to maintain respect for either its government or the whole political system when it is confronted by an administration which, after an election, completely repudiates a major policy stand or when it welcomes into its ranks a former opposition member who has been a vociferous leader against one of its most important pieces of legislation. The Liberal party has done both, thereby weakening confidence in the integrity of our political parties and of their practitioners.

One of the principal differences in the platforms of the Liberal and Conservative parties in the 1974 election was the question of how to combat inflation. The Conservatives advocated a temporary price and wage freeze (pending the development of a permanent policy), for which the Liberals excoriated them, arguing that the public would never accept such controls. Having done much to undermine confidence in officially sanctioned constraints, and having given the impression that Canadians could not be trusted to cooperate in such a program, the government in 1975 introduced its own anti-inflation program, which froze wages and tried (unsuccessfully) to control prices. Not surprisingly, the government that campaigned on a vigorous anti-controls platform encountered considerable opposition when it tried to apply them.

The general language policy of the Official Languages Act of 1969 is one of the most important Liberal government attempts to promote national unity. Robert Stanfield, then Conservative leader, succeeded in persuading his party to follow him in supporting the language bill, but he was challenged and about twenty of his followers broke party ranks. None of them was more implacably opposed to efforts designed to assure that both French and English speaking Canadians could deal with the federal government in their own language than Jack Horner, the member for the Crowfoot constituency in Alberta. Mr. Horner had consistently been one of the most savage opponents of efforts to protect the French language and to create in Canada an ambience agreeable to francophones. However, after unsuccessfully contesting the Tory leadership, Mr. Horner became disillusioned with the leadership of his successful rival, crossed the floor of the House, and ultimately became a Liberal cabinet minister.

It is not always easy to distinguish between our two old parties but some basic diverging orientations do in fact divide them. One is the attitude they adopt towards French Canada. Although the official leadership of the Conservative party has, under Robert Stanfield, Joe Clark and Brian Mulroney, been sympathetic to the aspirations of French Canada, the party has always been plagued by a bigoted wing of members who lacked comprehension of and sympathy for Quebec. Mr. Horner, as a leading member of this group, was a strange bedfellow for the Liberal MPs, the former targets of his venom. While this move gave the Liberals a much needed prairie seat and Mr. Horner a cabinet post long before he might otherwise have received one (if ever), it made a mockery of what our political parties allegedly stand for.

Decline in Ministerial Responsibility
It has been a cardinal principle of the cabinet system of government that individual ministers are responsible for anything that is done by the ministries and departments for which they are responsible. The civil service is supposed to be an anonymous body without political views, obediently carrying out the commands of its masters, the politicians. This has always been something of a fiction, of course, since senior civil servants must

provide useful advice and so there is no point in their totally ignoring the partisan and political constraints impinging on the ministers. The tendency for ministers and deputy ministers to see the world in like fashion is particularly pronounced in a one-party dominant system in which the collaboration between a minister and his or her deputy may continue for many years. All this notwithstanding, the principle of ministerial responsibility has had a long and respected tradition in Canada, at least in the sense that ministers, as politicians, have assumed complete responsibility for the actions of their civil servants and their departments. The political party in office has thus been the beneficiary of all the popular things done by the public service and the victim of its failings.

Recent developments have altered the once well-established principle of ministerial responsibility. First, there is a rapid turnover in the various ministries. The result is that few ministers have a chance to master the complex business of their ministry before they are assigned a new portfolio. While an alert and hard-working minister can be briefed fairly quickly by his new subordinates, it takes a prodigious amount of work and insight, and a great deal of time, to be able to become the effective head of a department and to lead it. Until this happens—and many ministers of course never gain the upper hand—the politicians are in a sense the captives of their officials. Ministers may, under these conditions, take formal responsibility for what is done in their name but the real power lies elsewhere. . . .

Plebiscitary Tendencies

All of the short-run causes for the decline of party mentioned so far were laid at the doorstep of the Liberals. While that party has been an important cause of the process of party attenuation, it should not, of course, be assumed that it is the sole culprit. The opposition parties have been unable to present an acceptable alternative and have failed to convince the public that they could remove some of the ills currently afflicting the country. Nor can party politicians of any stripe be held responsible for the fact that much of the political decision-making has shifted from the conventional sites to federal-provincial negotiations, where parties do not fit neatly.

A recent factor that might possibly further impair the viability of parties is also not of the Liberals' making, although Mr. Trudeau's reaction to it might exacerbate its effect on the place of parties in our system. The Parti Québécois' insertion of the referendum into our political process takes away from the monopoly enjoyed by parties in deciding certain issues. The PQ is of course not the first to introduce direct consultation of the public to Canadians. W.L. Mackenzie King had recourse to this device during the conscription crisis in the Second World War, and two referenda were held before Newfoundland became part of Canada. But the commitment of the

PQ government to conduct a referendum to decide whether Quebecers wish to break or redefine their relationship with the rest of the country has brought forth an indication that Ottawa might itself conduct a similar vote.

Referenda normally ignore political parties and emphasize policy options, thereby diminishing the importance of parties in the political process. If they are held very infrequently, and only with respect to such fundamental issues as the nature of the country and its constitution, then they are unlikely to do much damage to the role of parties. But once they are used in one case, it may be impossible to prevent them from being applied to other issues—for example, the reintroduction of capital punishment, or language legislation—and they might slowly usurp some of the functions performed by parties. Any federal recourse to referenda is therefore seen by some opposition members as a potential further encroachment on the traditional role of parties.

CONCLUSION

The above catalogue of factors and developments reducing the relative importance of parties touches only some of the highlights; it is a partial and superficial look at a very complex phenomenon. This article's emphasis on federal politics has, for instance, led it to neglect the all-important provincial sphere and the interaction between federal and provincial party organizations. And our skimming of the high points has led to a neglect of some serious questions posed by these developments. We might have asked, for instance, whether the reason for the Liberal party's role in reducing the importance of parties is to be found in the fact that it is a quasi-permanent government party or in some special characteristics associated with Canadian Liberalism at the federal level. Does the Ontario Conservative party play a similar role in the decline of party in that province?

Our purpose here is not to answer these kinds of questions, important though they are, but to indicate that significant changes are occurring which alter the role played by political parties. If a series of limited advantages is allowed to reduce the overall effectiveness of a major mechanism for decision-making without producing at least an equally useful alternative, then the cost to society may be unexpectedly high. One is reminded in this connection of one of R.K. Merton's celebrated "theories of the middle range:"

> Any attempt to eliminate an existing social structure without providing adequate alternative structures for fulfilling the functions previously fulfilled by the abolished organization is doomed to failure.

Now it is true that no one is consciously trying to eliminate Canadian parties or even to reduce their importance, and that Merton was thinking of the return or rebirth of a structure whose function was needed. But the parties' sphere of influence and effectiveness is being reduced, by design or not. It may be to the country's advantage to reassign the functions of parties if they are being neglected: society might find other ways of performing these needed functions. There is a danger, however, that the alternatives may be less satisfactory and in other respects—in the field of individual freedom, for instance—potentially very harmful.

The Canadian party system is far from being perfect, but the world is full of examples showing how appalling some of the alternatives can be. That considerable reform is needed is clear. We can benefit from some of the changes occurring now and from ones which could be instituted. Students of Canadian parties need to decide which features deserve preservation and which require change. And before they are in a position to do that, they must undertake more extensive study of the issues raised here.

27 Elections

Elections are still the cornerstone of liberal democracies. Even though we take them for granted, and many individuals choose not to vote, elections remain the crucial institution in our governmental process. It is trite but true that elections legitimize governmental powers. The fact that citizens of a polity can, on a regular basis, choose who will govern remains one basic reason for our consent in the process. The fact that we go to the polls to vote people into office, or to throw them out, reinforces the limited character of our government.

In Reading 27, Richard Rose points out the significance of elections for individual voters as well as for the political system as a whole. He then briefly examines some of the ways in which we have tried to explain the act of voting. While voting studies may be a science, precise reasons for exercising individual volition are almost inexplicable.

The fact remains that at election time the people are sovereign. Yet, as Rose notes, beyond elections that sovereignty is "limited and short lived." A government's mandate is secure as long as it maintains confidence in the House. But elections constitute only one means by which individuals in a polity can participate in the political process. Between elections interest groups, political parties, and individual actions may place a great deal of pressure on governments. If governors want to be re-elected, they must heed at least some of the pressure. That elections always loom on the horizon is highly consequential for the system as whole.

Richard Rose is a professor and director of the Centre for the Study of Public Policy at the University of Strathclyde, Scotland. He has extensive publications in British and American politics, and political parties and voting studies. This selection is from his book *The Problem of Party Government.*

● ● ● ● ● ● ● ● ● ●

The liberal philosophy of politics pervasive in Britain assigns a particularly important role to elections. The demands of individuals are meant to cause the governing party to respond by producing benefits satisfying the majority of the electorate: individuals will then modify their demands and party preferences in a continuing feedback of views, in which the voters are the prime movers of the system. Alternatively, the prime mover in politics can be seen as the governing party, making demands upon the individual to pay taxes, obey laws, provide military service, etc. Citizens immediately respond by complying with or ignoring government injunctions (cf. Rose, 1973, p. 467). In Britain, they can also respond with their votes; in countries without free competitive elections, their only form of protest may be subversive action. . . .

THE POSSIBLE CONSEQUENCES

The literature of politics contains many assertions about the possible significance of elections for individual voters and for the political system generally. The two perspectives are related, but it is useful to distinguish between a citizen's view, and the much wider perspective of the political scientist.

The potential significance of an election for individual voters may include the following factors:

First, voting involves individual *choice* of governors or major governmental policies. Joseph Schumpeter (1952, chapters 21-3) and Robert T. McKenzie (1963, chapter 11) emphasize the voter's task as nothing more and nothing less than that of choosing between teams of competing leaders at general elections. In America, the use of primary elections to choose candidates gives a much greater measure of choice than is present in duopolistic competition, or in simple-plurality general election contests. Referenda and balloting on constitutional amendments afford voters the opportunity to choose or reject specific policies, but this device is now everywhere of limited political importance. A number of writers have argued that voters also choose between policy alternatives in national elections. But few academic analysts would go so far as to assert that voters can mandate their representatives at an election, although the word "mandate" is still prevalent in the discourse of politicians.

Second, voting permits individuals to participate in a reciprocal and continuing exchange of influence with office-holders and candidates. The need for election or re-election may lead incumbents and candidates to alter their policies in order to retain or gain office. This approach is dynamic, because it considers how alternatives for choice are derived, and what the elected do. Carl Friedrich (1937, p. 203ff.) has described the exchange of influence between elections as arising from "a law of anticipated reactions" in which politicians continuously adjust policy decisions on the basis of assumptions about future as well as past voter preferences. Voters can also influence the selection of candidates, even in the absence of primary elections, if party leaders are sensitive to popular preferences. For example, the anticipated electoral unpopularity of Sir Alec Douglas-Home led to his resignation as leader of the Conservative party in 1965.

334 The Political Process

Third, voting can encourage or help maintain individual allegiance to the existing constitutional régime. A voter may feel that he owes voluntary acceptance of the authority of a popularly elected régime whether or not his preferred party wins, or even in the absence of a choice of parties. The government of the elect gains a populist rather than a Calvinist meaning; *vox populi* replaces *vox dei*. In an essay on the politics of Afro-Asian nations, Edward Shils (1962, p. 38) has gone so far as to argue:

> The granting of universal suffrage without property or literacy qualifications is perhaps the single factor leading to the formation of a political society. . . . The drawing of the whole adult population periodically into contact with the symbols of the center of national political life must, in the course of time, have immeasurable consequences by stirring people up and giving them a sense of their own potential significance, and attaching their sentiments to symbols which comprehend the entire nation. The importance of electoral participation as a means of reinforcing allegiance can be seen in arguments for compulsory voting. In the late nineteenth century, these arguments had liberal connotations. In the past four decades, compulsory voting has often been associated with Communist and Fascist regimes.

Fourth, voting can contribute to an individual's disaffection from the existing constitutional régime. Disaffection may be induced by the result of a specific election, or it may have non-electoral antecedents and simply be reinforced by an election in which an individual does not wish to endorse any of the alternatives. A modicum of involuntary non-voting is always to be expected on grounds of health and travel. Organized boycotts of ballots are infrequent and difficult to organize. The tactic is sometimes invoked in Ireland. Sinn Fein campaigned in the 1973 Northern Ireland Assembly elections with the slogan, "Vote early and spoil your ballot early." Their efforts met with little success. The fear of disaffection arising from an election result with many spoiled ballots or votes for extremist parties has led some authors to produce arguments "In Defence of Apathy."

Fifth, voting has emotional significance for individuals, The epigraph to this chapter by R.B. McCallum (1955, p. 509), the founder of the Nuffield series of election studies, illustrates this doctrine. W.J.M. Mackenzie (1954, 1957) suggests that the ritual function of voting may, at its highest, be comparable to a coronation service. The frequent use of sporting or military metaphors to describe elections suggests that for some persons election contests provide emotional satisfaction akin to watching athletic events or old war films, with the behaviour of individual contestants more important than the result. At a low level of intensity, the emotional significance of voting may be compared to that derived from "being done good to" by listening to a sermon, or fulfilling a minor social duty.

Sixth, voting may be functionless, devoid of any emotional or politically significant consequences for individuals. This extreme form of apathy is not likely to be found among many people who personally record their votes. But very high turnout figures for non-competitive elections suggest that substantial numbers of subjects may have had votes recorded in their name, while they had no personal awareness of voting.

The potential significance of elections for the political system as a whole can be described as follows:

First, elections are a recognized means of providing succession in leadership. The problem of political succession is common to all systems, for even a lifetime dictator will eventually need replacement. At a minimum, an election, even if a plebiscite with only one individual seeking endorsement, provides a legal means for validating a claim to govern. In the Western world, elections are expected to involve competition between two or more possible claimants to succeed to office, and the presence or absence of competition is a basic characteristic distinguishing "free" elections. In Britain, elections are said to decide who governs. This is not an inevitable consequence, for the electoral system does no more than provide Members of Parliament. It is the party system that converts the results of a parliamentary election into a government. Only five of the fifteen men who have become Prime Minister in this century first entered Downing Street as the immediate consequence of a general election victory.

Second, elections can be used to control the policy decisions of government. Nowhere in England are voters allowed to determine by referendum what policies shall prevail. In Scotland and Wales citizens are allowed to vote on laws licensing the sale of drink, and in Northern Ireland a referendum was held in 1973 on the maintenance of Ulster as part of the United Kingdom. American states have shown much greater enthusiasm for balloting on legislation, whether to enact or repeal it. In many states, Americans can also vote on tax rates or the issuance of local authority bonds to finance capital expenditure.

Third, elections can influence the policy decisions of government. In post-war Britain, the electoral calendar has a significant influence upon the government's economic policy. In the months preceding a general election, the governing party will seek to manipulate economic conditions to maximize a sense of prosperity. Often, the post-election consequence is the adoption of deflationary policies to compensate for the artificially induced boom created in a pre-election period.

Fourth, elections can help to legitimate a régime or to maintain its legitimacy. In countries where constitutional authority is relatively recent, citizen allegiance cannot be taken for granted. Moreover, the Constitution itself may vest ultimate authority in the people. In such circumstances, only by popular election (whether competitive or not) can governors claim formal legitimacy for their actions. In Britain, authority is derived from the Crown. In the nineteenth century, the gradual expansion of the franchise allowed a slowly increasing portion of subjects to participate as citizens in choosing men who would advise and exercise this authority. Today, elections provide a justification for the authority of governors who must take decisions with which many will disagree. The ultimate argument for obeying a law is that it is made by people elected to be law-makers.

Fifth, in extreme cases, elections may lead to the repudiation of a régime because of the intensity of conflict among groups competing for office. Repudiation may take the form of a refusal of a government to leave office following its apparent defeat, the revolt of losers (e.g. the response of Southern states in America to the election of Abraham Lincoln in 1860) or the abolition of the existing régime by a newly elected government. For example, the election of an African government in Northern Rhodesia made maintenance of a Federation in Central Africa impossible; in the blunt words of Kenneth Kaunda to his opponents, "My friend has lost—and lost forever" (Mulford, 1964, p. 186). The only occasion on which a British election led to the repudiation of authority occurred in Ireland. In 1918 Sinn Fein, the pro-independence party, won an overwhelming majority of seats in twenty-six counties of Southern Ireland. While the contingency may be very remote, it is interesting to speculate what the reaction would be at Westminster if Scotland or Wales returned a majority of Nationalists at a British general election.

Sixth, to describe an election as functionless is to state that it has no observable, verifiable consequences for the political system. It would be possible to hypothesize that in many new nations where elections are unfamiliar, communications poor and administration primitive, elections may tend toward this. But an election which has no observable impact upon control of office is not necessarily functionless, for an uncontested election can be a slack resource which citizens invoke in case of political controversy. In urban and rural districts councillors may be returned year after year without contest until an issue, such as a motorway or a new housing estate, causes controversy and a contested election within a previously undivided community.

While elections have nearly the same mechanical features everywhere, they do not have the same functions. *The World Handbook of Political and Social Indicators* (Taylor and Hudson, 1972, Table 2.9) reports that among

136 nations, 112 regularly have events meeting conventional definitions of elections. Insufficient evidence is available for another sixteen countries, primarily in Africa. Only eight nations (of which Spain is the only European example) do not regularly hold elections.

Elections usually involve the participation of a majority of a country's adult population. The average turnout for elections in a hundred countries for which this could be calculated is 79.5 per cent. As of 1970, Britain ranks seventy-sixth for voter participation—but still ahead of the United States, where the 1972 Presidential election turnout of 55.7 per cent was ninety-second. While the statistics from some countries reporting high voter turnout are suspect, Britain also lags far behind most Western nations in voting participation. Of the nine member nations in the European Economic Community, Britain, along with Ireland, consistently ranks lowest in the proportion participating in national elections.

The significance of an election for a political system can be crudely indicated by noting whether countries have free, competitive elections, and whether the majority of the electorate is literate. As these two conditions vary, the potential significance of an election is likely to vary. According to *World Handbook* figures, thirty-eight countries have free elections and at least half their electorate is literate. In these countries elections can provide for the peaceful succession of office-holders, and also influence policy. Several nations have competitive elections, but a predominantly illiterate electorate; India is the only one to have had free elections endure for any significant period of time. It is doubtful whether the electorate can consciously affect policy, because of the limitations upon the feedback of political information imposed by illiteracy.

In societies without free competitive elections, the chief significance of a ballot is likely to be legitimating a régime or encouraging disaffection if results go wrong. This is most likely in those sixteen societies, mostly Communist, which have a majority of literate adults, while lacking competitive elections. The act of voting for an approved state is likely to have meaning whether it signifies identification with governors, passive acceptance of the powers that be, or the indignities of coerced "choice." In the thirty-six primarily Afro-Asian nations that lack competitive elections and have a majority of illiterate voters, elections are most likely to be functionless, an act undertaken in conformity to alien custom, lacking even the significance of native rites. . . .

THE USES OF ELECTIONS
Voting has a much greater significance for the political scientist or the candidate than it has for the voter. For individuals, a chief function of voting is emotional or allegiance-maintaining. Englishmen regard it as their duty

to vote, and this view is supported by strong social pressures. When an election is held, from 60 to 80 per cent of persons will vote, even if they can see no difference between the parties, think the election result will have no effect on themselves, do not care who will win the election and do not identify with any of the parties (Butler and Stokes, 1964; see also Campbell *et al.*, 1960, pp. 97-105).

Theories that describe elections as occasions of choice or political influence usually include assumptions about the presumed rationality of voters. The term rationality is one for which there is no standardized meaning. Rationality in voting might require individuals to have a high degree of political information and powers of logical reasoning. Yet Anthony Downs (1957) has shown that logically it is irrational for a voter to meet the criteria of rationality outlined above. The authors of *The American Voter* have estimated that only about one-seventh of the electorate can give a reasonably detailed and consistent explanation of their party preferences (Campbell *et al.*, 1960, chapter 10). A similar proportion would hold true for Britain. That fraction of the electorate positively concerned about the election outcome is not making a choice between Conservative, Labour and Liberal candidates, but rather, affirming an identification with one of these parties. An election is not only an occasion for a voter to confirm his allegiance to government, but also to confirm loyalty to a party with which he has long identified, on social and psychological motives, or, as in February 1974, to reject an identification.

The full significance of the formally political act of voting is best understood if one allows through the full implications of the social psychologist's dictum, "Our approach is in the main dependent on the point of view of the actor" (Campbell *et al.*, 1960, pp. 27ff.). The language of political science unfortunately leads us to narrow our attention from the multiplicity of roles that an individual has, by defining him in terms of one relatively minor and intermittent role, that of voter. The word voter refers to an abstraction, just as much as does the term economic man. The chief social roles of an individual are those of spouse, parent, relative, wage-earner, friend, etc. For most individuals the role of citizen or subject is likely to be of little significance; the act of voting exhausts his commitment to political activity. It would thus be much more accurate and only a little cumbersome if, instead of writing about voting behaviour, we wrote about the behaviour of ordinary individuals in electoral situations.

This argument does not mean that politics is relatively less important for an individual than participation in other more or less voluntary social organizations. Only a minority of Englishmen are regularly active in trade unions, churches or other major institutions of English life. The level of participation is not different in kind when one compares party politics, trade unions and organized religion. In religion and in trade unionism, the great majority of individuals have a group identification, as is the case in politics; yet there, too, only a small minority go beyond identification and regularly participate in activities of the groups with which they identify. The great bulk of individuals are much more concerned with primary group relationships among family and friends than they are with the goals of relatively remote national institutions.

The failure of the literature of voting behaviour to cope properly with this phenomenon is partly methodological. In a situation in which each adult is eligible to vote, studying voters by means of a national cross-section sample is logical, even though the great majority interviewed will be answering questions of far more interest to the interviewers than to the surveyed. Confronted by an interviewer asking questions about politics, a substantial number of individuals may give a long series of don't know answers or answers of low intensity, consistency or durability. . . .

Any judgement about the meaning of elections is determined by the standards adopted for evaluation. Understandably, politicians and students of politics tend to forget that most citizens do not have the time or inclination to follow political events as closely as they do. Reciprocally, politicians may know less about gardening, sports, industry or trade union work than those who specialize in non-political affairs. Approaching an election from the point of view of the voter leads one to consider what it is reasonable for him to do. An inability to show great knowledge of politics is not proof that an individual votes unreasonably.

John Plamenatz (1958, p. 9) has argued, "A choice is reasonable, not because the chooser, when challenged, can give a satisfactory explanation of why he made it, but because if he could give an explanation, it would be satisfactory." Studies of voting behaviour find that the great majority of voters cannot give a satisfactory explanation of their own volition. Yet a careful reading of any set of life-history interviews makes it clear that intellectually satisfactory justifications of choice can be elucidated for many inarticulate voters, whether elderly spinsters, embittered miners or bus conductors, prosperous young married couples, or middle-aged shop-keepers. Instead of discussing politics in terms of explicit ideologies and relating these to issues in Parliament, such individuals usually view politics in terms of simpler, more persisting distinctions concerning group interests, or the nature of the times, voting for the government in good times and against it in bad. If such criteria are accepted as reasonable for the ordinary individual to apply, then, instead of one-seventh of the electorate being considered reasonable, that is, having a detailed, coherent political outlook, more than three-quarters of the British electorate can be classified as reasonable voters (cf. Campbell *et al.*, 1960, chapter 10).

The functions of elections cannot be seen in isolation from other elements of the political process. Collectively, voters are sovereign one day in every four or five years. This sovereignty is limited and short lived. Voters can choose who governs, but not how they are governed. An individual gains a very small amount of influence by the act of voting. Yet without the familiar mechanisms of elections, Britain could not be governed as we know it today. Inheritance, co-option, a *coup d'état* or violence—devices used elsewhere to constitute governments—would be invoked.

If an individual wishes to be more than a mere voter, he must seek additional means to express his views. He can act through the market place, voting with his feet about economic policies by changing jobs, altering his consumer spending, increasing his effort at work, or emigrating. The extreme sensitivity of British government to fluctuations in economic conditions makes such actions prompt and important constraints upon the government of any party. A person wishing to go beyond the minimal influence of a voter can also join a political party, using organization to strengthen his individual voice in the politics of collective choice.

28   Legislatures

Contrary to popular belief, legislatures do not govern. In fact, the executive, or the cabinet, governs. This is especially true in the parliamentary system where the assembly has little autonomy because of political party discipline. The cabinet, if it has a majority in the house, can do almost what it chooses as long as the backbenchers' support is maintained in parliament. In a presidential system, however, the separation of powers and the absence of party discipline nurture a more autonomous assembly, which can come closer to governing.

In this reading, K.C. Wheare addresses the question of whether legislatures are declining in terms of their power or efficiency. The answer is both yes and no. Legislative assemblies still perform important roles such as representation, and legislative committees sharpen legislation. And one of the most important functions of a legislature is to exercise its powers of "oversight," for example, its power to hold the executive and the bureaucracy accountable. But according to Wheare, legislatures do not exist to govern. We should not expect the legislative assembly to be all things to all people. Rather, the object is for the legislature to be as efficient as possible in performing its particular roles in the legislative process.

Sir Kenneth Wheare has had a distinguished academic career as Gladstone professor of government and public administration at Oxford University. He served as rector of Exeter College and vice Chancellor at Oxford. His publications include *Government by Committee: An Essay on the British Constitution* (1955), *The Constitutional Structure of the Commonwealth* (1960), *Federal Government,* 4th ed. (1963), and *Modern Constitutions,* 2nd ed. (1966). This selection is from the second edition of his book *Legislatures.*

● ● ● ● ● ● ● ● ● ●

I

When Lord Bryce was putting together some general conclusions and observations about legislatures in his enormous book *Modern Democracies,* he entitled one chapter "The Decline of Legislatures." And he followed it with a chapter called "The Pathology of Legislatures." Both chapters really deal with the same question: What are the ills to which legislatures are subject and which cause them to go into decline? A careful study of what Bryce wrote shows that he did not find it possible to give a straight or simple answer to this very general question. It is sometimes assumed, however, by those whose reading may perhaps have gone no further than the chapter headings, that Bryce believed in a general decline of legislatures. . . .

It is helpful in discussing whether or not legislatures have declined to ask in what respect it is asserted that they have or have not declined. Is it a decline in power? Or is it a decline in efficiency? The two do not necessarily go together. A legislature may be doing too much, it may be keeping control of too wide a range of functions and as a result may not have the time or the capacity to perform them effectively. If it declined in power, it might increase in efficiency. Again, is it a decline in public esteem that is alleged? It could be argued with some force that the French legislature did not decline in power under the Third and Fourth Republics, but none the less it did decline in public esteem. Or it may be that a decline in public interest is suggested. Public esteem and public interest do not necessarily go together. The activities of a legislature may provide a great deal of news: legislatures may often be in the public eye: their proceedings may be notorious. But they may stand low in public esteem. Or, finally, in some discussions of the decline of legislatures it would seem that it is a decline in manners, in standards of behaviour which is being asserted.

It is necessary, also if a sound judgement on the subject is to be reached, to be clear by which standard the alleged decline is being measured. Is it being alleged that legislatures have declined in powers or in efficiency or in public esteem or in public interest in relation to their own former position, or is it that, in relation to other political or social institutions, particularly the executive or party organizations or the trade unions or employers' organizations or the radio and television, the decline has occurred? Legislatures may have retained their own powers or efficiency or prestige or indeed have increased them, but they may none the less have declined in these respects relatively to other institutions which have increased their powers and improved their position.

If a general survey is made of the position and working of legislatures in the present century, it is apparent that, with a few important and striking exceptions, legislatures have declined in certain important respects and particularly in powers in relation to the executive government. A feature of the development of political institutions in this period has been the great growth of executive power as a result largely of the demands made by two world wars, economic crises, the adoption of collective or socialist or welfare policies, and the persistence of international tension. Governments now do a great deal that they did not do formerly, but most of what they do was not done by anybody before. In particular it was not done by the legislature. The increase of powers by the executive has not been the result of taking away from the legislature things which it did before. Legislatures, indeed, do more than they did and legislators work longer hours and interest themselves in a wider range of subjects. Absolutely their powers have increased. Relatively to the executive government, however, they have, in almost all cases, declined.

In one sphere, perhaps, it looks as if the executive has taken away a part of the legislature's functions, and that is in the matter of making the laws. The exercise by the executive of law-making powers, particularly by the growth of delegated legislation, has meant that the legislature no longer makes all the laws or even all the important laws. Even if we put aside as exceptional and perhaps ephemeral the taking away from the legislature by the executive in France of a large part of the law-making power by the provisions of the Constitution of the Fifth Republic, there remains the fact that in most countries, though the legislature retains the power to make all the laws, it has in fact delegated to the executive the exercise of this power over a wild field. It is true that this delegation can be withdrawn and its exercise controlled, but none the less in practice it is clear that the executive makes part of the laws.

It can be argued, of course, that the legislature itself nowadays spends as much time on law making as ever it did or indeed more time than it did. It deals with important principles, and debates policies which are embodied in statutes. It could not find the time to deal effectively with the mass of rules which are made by the executive under delegated powers. This is true in many countries and to this extent it is permissible to say that the executive is not taking away from the legislature something which it has done or could do. In terms of time devoted to law making and the quantity of its legislative output the legislature may not have declined absolutely; it is only in relation to the executive that it can be said to have declined.

II

Against the background of a decline of legislatures in relation to the executive, there stand out one or two interesting exceptions. In the first place there are examples of legislatures whose position can hardly be said to have declined even relatively as against the executive. One example is the Congress of the United States, whether it be considered as a bicameral legislature or its two chambers be considered separately. It is true that the executive in the United States has increased considerably in its powers in this century, particularly since the inauguration of President Franklin D. Roosevelt. But a strong case can be made for the view that Congress has actually increased its power in the political system and that its position in relation to the executive is at least as strong as it was. There have been times when, as at the beginning of President Franklin Roosevelt's first term, Congress was willing to accept presidential leadership, but quite soon it asserted its independence, and the task of managing Congress has been as complex and difficult since that period as it was before. It may be that the presidency has overshadowed Congress in public interest, and it is natural that the doings of one man should be easier to visualize and to praise or condemn than the complicated workings of groups of representatives and Senators. But congressional committees of inquiry, and individual Senators and Congressmen have rivalled and at times overshadowed the doings of the President. It is, of course, impossible to prove that Congress has or has not declined in relation to the executive. These judgements are matters of impression and opinion. A careful study of the American political system in operation, however, seems to support the judgement that Congress still holds its own with the executive.

A similar judgement may be offered about the position of the French legislature under the Third and Fourth Republics. Indeed it is possible that some students of French politics might interpret the history of the two Republican constitutions as an illustration of the decline not of the legislature but of the executive. What is certain is that the French legislature maintained its position as the maker and destroyer of cabinets throughout the period, and in this respect it suffered no decline, absolute or relative. Its history raises the question: Is decline necessarily a bad thing? Might it not have been a better thing for France if there had been a decline in the power of the legislature? A stronger cabinet, with some measure of control over the legislature, might have improved the efficiency of the legislature itself, in particular in the making of laws. A judgement on this question involves an opinion upon what are the proper functions of a legislature. If one function is to produce and support a government, the French legislature was inefficient, but its inefficiency did not arise from a decline in its power. . . .

III

In discussing the relative decline of legislatures it is natural to think first of the effect of the growth in power and importance of the executive. But there are other political and social institutions whose existence and growth have affected the position of the legislature. One important function of a legislature is to be "a congress of opinions" (in John Stuart Mill's phrase), a forum of debate and discussion on political and social questions. Walter Bagehot in his *English Constitution* described it, in speaking of the British House of Commons, as the "expressive" function and the "teaching" function. These functions legislatures have shared with the press for a long period. But the invention of sound radio and television has produced a formidable rival in this sphere. Citizens can now hear and see speakers and debates and discussions on political and social questions which may seem to them to be more interesting and persuasive, less concerned with the arid controversies of party welfare, than what is provided by the speeches of legislators, inside or outside their chambers. The legislature has to take its place as one only and that not always the most impressive of the forums in which public questions are discussed. Public opinion is influenced by these speeches and discussions on the air and legislators find themselves under pressure by their constituents who are less ready to accept the customary explanations. Some legislatures, indeed, have resented the discussion on the radio and television of issues which are being or are about to be discussed by the legislature itself, and have attempted to control this outside discussion. This attitude may be easy to understand, but it is difficult to justify. A wider and freer discussion of public questions may reduce the relative importance of the legislature as a forum of debate, but if it arouses a wider interest in such questions and produces a better informed electorate, it is a good thing.

Some legislatures—Australia and New Zealand are examples—have in fact seized the opportunity provided by radio to broadcast their proceedings or parts of their proceedings. In this way their debates have become better known; a greater number of citizens has an opportunity to hear and to see what goes on in the legislature. Such arrangments could produce an increase in the public interest in the legislature, if not inevitably in the public esteem. There is indeed some dispute about whether legislators behave better or worse when they know that they are being heard or seen by their fellow citizens. It can hardly be doubted that they would behave differently. It is clear, however, that although radio and television may have affected the position of the legislatures as a forum of debate by providing rival forums, they have also provided an instrument by which the work of the legislature may be made known to a far wider public than was ever possible when reliance was placed almost entirely on the press and the public meeting.

There is a further important function of a legislature which it has come to share with other institutions, and that is its function as a committee of grievances, as a body whose members individually and collectively have the task of bringing to the notice of the government and of the public the complaints of the citizens. Here again there is no question of an absolute decline. The amount of work which legislators do in attending to the complaints or requests of their constituents is greater, not less, than it was fifty years ago. These duties, more perhaps than any others, have converted the post of legislator from a part-time to a full-time job in Britain and in many other countries. At the same time, however, other institutions have taken up some part of the task and do much that would probably remain undone if legislators alone were expected to do it. The great extension of governmental power and services has brought the citizen into contact with the administration to a much greater extent than ever before and the task of dealing with the complaints and difficulties which arise is more than members of the legislature alone can cope with. This is one reason why the institution of the Ombudsman, as developed in Scandinavia, has aroused interest in other countries. New Zealand appointed an Ombudsman in 1962, and Britain did so in 1967.

Perhaps the principal development which has led to the redress of grievances becoming no longer the exclusive function of the legislature, however, is the growth of trade and professional associations, one of whose chief functions is the promotion and protection of the interests of their members. These organizations cover almost the whole economic and social field, and they are powerful enough and expert enough to be able to take up directly with the administration, and at the appropriate level, any complaints or grievances which their members may have. They do not need to work through members of the legislature, though there may be occasions when they find it better to do so. In a wide range of matters, however, it will be more expeditious and more satisfactory both to them and to the executive if they act direct with the department behind the scenes.

Departments on their side, too, have begun to develop a policy and a technique for dealing with the difficulties and complaints of citizens and to encourage them to come direct to the office with their grievances. The appointment of public relations officers is one example of the methods which the administration uses to deal with complaints and remove misunderstandings. These matters are no longer left exclusively to the minister's explanations in reply to criticisms and questions in the legislature.

IV

A discussion of the powers and influence of trade and professional associations and other interest groups leads to a consideration of a further respect in which it is sometimes alleged that legislatures have declined. It is said that they are nowadays much less independent than they were, because so much of importance is decided outside by negotiations between the government and the organized interests concerned, and the task of the legislature is no more than that of applying a rubber stamp. There is certainly some truth in this assertion; what is more difficult to know is the extent of it, whether it has increased, and whether legislatures are, in this respect, roughly where they always were, or have declined in power or independence. It is difficult to avoid the impression that there has been a decline, and that the British House of Commons provides a good example of it. It is also difficult to know what can be done about it. It is not to be expected that the varied interests of a country can be completely and accurately represented in a legislature elected on party lines in territorial constituencies. On the other hand, it would not be thought desirable to have a legislature consisting almost entirely of the representatives of vested interests, however respectable these interests might be. But there must be some machinery through which consultation with interested and affected parties can be carried out, and there exists, therefore, in a country like Britain, a whole system of regularly constituted consultative councils and advisory committees whose opinions are available to departments.

There is nothing wrong in this. But the danger is that when things have been worked out very carefully in a department in consultation with these outside bodies, they tend to be presented to the legislature rather as *faits accomplis*. If members criticize them and seek to modify them, they are told, as likely as not, that as these proposals have been worked out carefully, taking into account the views of all those who have been consulted, it is not possible to alter them. It is natural that this should produce a feeling of frustration among legislators, whether on the government or on the opposition side. They feel all the more frustrated, perhaps, because they know that if, at an earlier stage, they had asked for information on the government's intentions and had suggested a debate, they would have been told that, as discussions were still going on, a debate was inadvisable, that no information could be disclosed at this stage, and that negotiations might be put in jeopardy by reason of what might be said in open debate.

In this respect the legislature's function as a forum of debate is affected and not merely its function as a maker of laws. This is a serious situation. It is indeed common in the British parliament to hear it said, when members wish to talk about a subject, that the time is not ripe. Something is being said or done behind the scenes which makes it inappropriate to discuss the matter in public just now. In international affairs it is often possible to see the force of this argument, but not perhaps quite so often as it is put forward. In home affairs it is usually harder to accept. There is indeed a difficult dilemma here. On the one hand there is the situation where legislators talk too soon—and the United States Congress has provided examples of this; on the other there is the situation of which the British House of Commons is an example, where, when a member may talk, he may talk too late.

V

Much of the discussion of the decline of legislatures is based on the assumption that decline was possible. There is a myth of a golden age of legislatures when wisdom and oratory and gentlemanly behaviour and public spirit all seemed somehow to flourish and to flourish together. It is difficult to know when this could have been. Bryce himself believed that in some countries there had been no decline, for the standard had not been high enough to admit of the possibility of decline. His choice of examples — Australia and Canada — cannot have pleased everybody; some might have expected him to find examples more readily in Central and South America.

Evidence for the existence of the golden age is not easy to weigh. There were great orators in the British House of Commons in the nineteenth century, but the voice of Churchill in the twentieth was as great as the voice of Gladstone in the nineteenth. And is oratory to be preferred to a simple conversational style? Were the speeches of members of parliament in the nineteenth century more interesting to their hearers than those in the twentieth century? Were there not bores who specialized in economics and foreign relations in those days as in these? If we are to speak of a decline in manners, it is proper to remark that there has never occurred in the House of Commons since 1919 disorder of the kind or degree which was a feature of the 1880s when the Irish members were at their liveliest, or in the years between 1909 and 1914 when Lloyd George's budget, the reform of the House of Lords, and Irish Home Rule were under discussion. It is not too much to assert that the House of Commons is better behaved since 1919 than in the century before that date. It is hard to escape the conclusion that the golden age recedes as we approach it.

The fact is that the decline of legislatures may be an interesting question to discuss in general terms, but it is difficult if not impossible to decide. If we try to make the question more precise, we may confine ourselves to a discussion of decline in efficiency. We must then ask ourselves: What are legislatures for? What functions ought they to perform? The answer will not be the same in all cases. For one thing, the question of size intrudes itself once more. There are some things a legislature of 100 members or less can do which a legislature of 600 or more cannot do. But one or two assertions of general validity can be made. It is not the function of a legislature to be the sole forum of debate or the sole committee of grievances in its country's political system; these functions must and should be shared with other bodies. It is not the function of a legislature to govern. These are truisms, yet it is the unwillingness of legislatures to give up the claim and the attempt to be and to do all these things that has resulted, in many countries, in decline not in powers but in efficiency. To do less and, perhaps thereby, to do it better, may often prove to be the safeguard against the decline of legislatures.

29   Cabinets

It is rare indeed to have anyone talk about the inner workings of a cabinet, especially a former minister. The cabinet process and all its interchange is about the most secretive part of the governmental process. Most ministers are very guarded about their work in cabinet because it is very personal. Richard Crossman, however, a former Cabinet minister in the Labour party in Great Britain, has written a revealing piece about the inner struggles that go on among the people trying to run a government.

He discusses the role of cabinet committees and how collective ministerial responsibility came into being. Also, he indicates clearly that the prime minister dominates the cabinet. With the different powers accumulated over the years, there is no doubt that the prime minister is far more than ''first among equals.''

He also describes in some detail the power struggle between ministers and civil servants. By now all of us should realize that the legislative process is not simply a parliament passing laws that are in the best interest of society. The legislative process is a power struggle between individuals and groups, all of whom have their own agenda about what laws and policies should be enacted. Crossman's revelation about the minister and civil servants is a classic reading about that struggle. It demonstrates how a powerful department in the bureaucracy attempts to manipulate the minister, raising the old question, ''do civil servants rule or serve?''

Richard Crossman, a prominent member of the Labour party, was a cabinet minister in Harold Wilson's government from 1964 to 1969. Before and after, he was also a professor of politics at Oxford University. The reading is excerpted from lectures that he delivered to an American audience at Harvard University in 1970 and that appear in his book *The Myths of Cabinet Government*.

●●●●●●●●●

We saw last night that Cabinet proceedings are recorded by the Cabinet Secretariat. They do not take down in shorthand what was actually said because they prefer to record [what] should have been said. They are Platonists, not Aristotelians. If you record what a Minister did say it might not turn out to be a precise instruction. There might be a little fuzziness, a little confusion. We can't afford to have confusion when the Civil Service is being given its marching orders.

Cabinet Minutes started in 1916 in World War I, under Lloyd George's Cabinet and with Maurice Hankey in charge. The sytem was then developed very rapidly; we already had by the end of World War I a system of decision-taking by the Cabinet, decisions which then became the marching orders for the Civil Service.

THE POWER OF CABINET COMMITTEES

The next stage of this was to extend it from Cabinet to Cabinet committees. Now, as a matter of fact, in 1903 a Committee of Imperial Defence had been founded with Arthur Balfour, the Prime Minister, in the Chair, and with the Chiefs of Staff present. Still today the only Cabinet committee at which officials are present, other than Secretaries, the people who record it, is the Defence Committee. The Chiefs of Staff are present and can take part. I must say, having been there for some years, it is disappointing how rarely they do take part. But they are there and they can. We still have the traditional Defence Committee and the Prime Minister in the Chair, and it still goes on much as it was before.

By the end of World War I there were not only Cabinet Minutes but there were minutes being recorded of 165 committees. You see how they multiplied and grew in war-time. But at the end of the war we returned to normalcy in Britain, as you did in America, and, therefore, we ended many Cabinet committees, and got back to pre-war routine. Indeed, it was not until the Second World War that we started the full committee system again. Then they were rapidly evolved under Winston Churchill, and in the 1945 Labour Government Clement Attlee, who was a formidable man in terms of Cabinet management, retained and developed the whole committee system, not merely as a war-time expedient but as a permanent part of Cabinet Government. These committees are divided into those which the Prime Minister chairs, and those which are chaired by Ministers selected by the Prime Minister, Ministers usually without departmental responsibility, such as the Lord President, Lord Privy Seal, or Minister without Portfolio.

Now, in our doctrine, each Cabinet committee is a microcosm of the Cabinet. May I remind you again that a Cabinet decision is formulated by the Prime Minister and follows his elucidation of the consensus which has been achieved. Now, what happens in the Cabinet also happens in each of the multifarious committees below Cabinet level. Each Chairman has the same responsibility of recording the conclusions and the decision; and the moment that any Cabinet committee's decision is recorded, it has the same validity as a Cabinet decision—unless it has been challenged in committee and the issue accepted by the Prime Minister as one to be decided by Cabinet.

So notice that this really means not only that the committee is a microcosm of the Cabinet but that it can exert within its terms of reference the power of the Cabinet. Six or seven Cabinet Ministers meet together and whatever decision they record is binding with the same binding force as though it had been made by the whole Cabinet in Cabinet session. This is a convenient method of reducing the number of Cabinet meetings and ensuring that decisions are taken in reasonable time.

Notice that I said each of these committees is enunciating marching orders to Whitehall with all the bindingness of a Cabinet decision, unless the minutes record that a Cabinet Minister or his representative present dissented from the decision and wished to have it raised in Cabinet. I should perhaps add that in our Wilson Cabinet (but each PM arranges such things as he wants) a Minister can only appeal from the Cabinet committee to Cabinet with the consent of the *Chairman* of the committee. That is a great limitation on the power of the Cabinet Minister, the fact that he has got to get the consent of the Chairman, who, of course, has been selected by the Prime Minister. He and the PM have ways of seeing that a Minister can't get to the Cabinet even if he wants to. I should personally like to see that changed.

Now you may be interested as to what subjects are discussed in a Cabinet committee. First of all, all legislation must be processed through a Cabinet committee. For example, I have been dealing with pensions. My proposals for the reform of the whole of Social Security are put to the Cabinet committee appointed for this purpose, section by section, not just as a bill, but as policy papers, and discussed at length by this committee. Provided I can get agreement in the committee, I can get the pension plan presented as a draft White Paper and cleared at a single Cabinet discussion. Then it is binding on all members of the Cabinet equally even though they have not been present at the detailed discussions. After that, the Bill must go through the Legislation Committee.

Secondly, though this sounds very generalised, anything is raised or discussed in a Cabinet committee for which a Minister feels he will need the support of his colleagues. Weak Ministers will be constantly putting things to Cabinet committees to get backing from their colleagues, and proud and strong Ministers won't bother their colleagues because they hope to drag them along without discussing it with them. It is always a nice question about your colleagues, whether they will be happier if you bother them with insignificant and secondary issues and insist they turn up on committees and give you their approval, or whether they prefer just to read it in the

Times, and say, "Well, he's done it again and it's a little bit late to object now."

Ministers differ in their views of how to handle their colleagues. That is why the only definition of what goes to a Cabinet Committee is what a Minister thinks he can't safely get away with without a Cabinet committee. Unless the Prime Minister settles it himself, anything goes to full Cabinet which is deadlocked at a lower level, and this, of course, is owing to the doctrine of collective Cabinet responsibility.

THE LEGEND OF MINISTERIAL RESPONSIBILITY TO PARLIAMENT

You will remember that in Bagehot's time a Minister still had individual ministerial responsibility to the House of Commons. The House could censure and ultimately sack Ministers for failings in their Departments. This has long since disappeared. I mean, it is still there as a legend. But now, very often, the worse a Minister manages his Ministry, the more difficult it is to get him removed because it would be an injury to the prestige of the Government. So the more the House of Commons bellows against the Minister, the stronger usually is the Prime Minister's determination to protect him in order to strengthen the hold of the Government on the House of Commons.

So the old theory that the House of Commons could demand the dismissal of the Minister and he would then be dismissed is largely antiquated. Every Minister is covered by full collective Cabinet responsibility and, of course, that means every Government Department is covered in the same way, in the sense that the bigger the fiasco in the Department, the more tempting it is to cover it up. This is collective responsibility in its modern sense.

Of course, if incompetence is too obvious or too damaging, the Prime Minister, in due course, will have a shuffle, but he will very rarely have it on the ground that a Minister has failed and must be moved. Maybe he will have to be promoted to the House of Lords for greater responsibilities, or to a post in the colonies overseas. In some cases, the Minister will refuse to be kicked upstairs and will voluntarily retire to the back benches. But the reason given will seldom be because he was incompetent or because there was a failure in his Ministry.

Such things occurred frequently in the nineteenth century. We don't let it happen now because we have a collective Cabinet responsibility for the actions of individual Ministers. So a Minister has to make up his mind when faced with a departmental catastrophe whether colleagues ought to be forewarned, or whether it is best to present them with a fait accompli in the Press and tell them they had better damn well see him through. It is a matter of taste how to handle colleagues in that particular contingency.

POWERS OF THE OPPOSITION: "THE USUAL CHANNELS"

Every Cabinet meeting starts with a discussion of next week's business and parliamentary matters. This may be what differentiates us from the Americans. All members of the Cabinet are members of the Commons (or Lords) and are constantly aware of the troubles we are having over the road in the Palace of Westminster, and discussing how they should be handled, and what will be the next cause of trouble.

This is a constant preoccupation of a British Cabinet—its sensitivity to the House of Commons. But, may I remind you, that does not mean its troubles come primarily from the official Opposition. You can't please the Opposition. They can never win, since you can always vote them down. Their views are not important from this point of view. What matters is the view of your own people whose votes you require to maintain your majority.

Having said this, let me add that there is one area where the power of the men who sit on the Opposition front bench is real and can be decisive. That area is the allocation of Parliamentary time, the sessional, weekly, and daily timetables arranged largely by verbal agreements—"through the usual channels." This relationship between the Opposition Chief Whip and the Government Chief Whip is so vital to the working of our Parliamentary system and such a characteristic example of what Bagehot would call "an efficient secret" that I must spend a little time on it.

I have talked as though the Cabinet had effectively destroyed the independent power of Parliament at one fell swoop. Actually the process began, largely by accident, in the 1880s as the result of the skilful work of the Irish Nationalists at sabotaging the working of Parliament. The old procedure had given almost unlimited licence to private members to bring forward the business they desired. Government could only get its business through because of the bi-partisan consensus which restrained the private members from insisting too far on their rights. Since the Irish had no such scruples, the Liberal Government was forced to introduce procedural limitations on private members' rights, including not only the timetabling of particular Bills by means of the guillotine but also Government control of the sessional timetable.

This transfer of power from Parliament to the Cabinet was only possible because both the big English parties wanted to defeat the Irish filibuster. The transfer, in fact, took place with the consent and connivance of the official Opposition, which now emerged as the "Shadow" Cabinet, ready to replace the real Cabinet whenever it got the chance, but equally ready to concede the time the Government required to get its legislation through provided only that the Shadow Cabinet was given a fair chance too. The method of achieving this was to allocate to the official Opposition all the so-called Supply Days which had been previously used by Parliament in order to control public expenditure. Traditionally the House of Commons has always claimed the right to investigate the working of the Executive before approving the funds it needs. Under the new arrangement evolved between 1880 and 1905 Parliamentary control of the Executive largely disappeared. Instead Parliamentary time was divided into three parts: (1) the time the Government requires to get its business, including its legislation, through the House; (2) the time which must be conceded to the Opposition for criticising the Government and stating its case; (3) the time left over, which is allocated to private members.

It is this control of the timetable which enables the Government to dominate Parliament. You will see that it came about not because the six hundred members who make up Parliament suddenly surrendered their rights to the Cabinet, but owing to an understanding between two big Party machines, which decided to handle management jointly by leaving the management of the timetable to the two Chief Whips. Time-tabling (which works in the Lords as well as in the Commons) depends on the tiny group of apparently humdrum Civil Servants through whose continuous day and night mediation the two Chief Whips conduct their negotiations. The Cabinet is naturally content to accept the co-operation of the Shadow Cabinet in getting its business through. As for the Shadow Cabinet, since its main desire is to become the real Cabinet as soon as possible, it has a strong common interest with the Government in preserving a system under which it shares four fifths of its parliamentary time with the Government— thereby reducing to a minimum the time available to private members and rebel groups in either of the two big parties. Thus Cabinet control of Parliament is exerted—at a price. It must obtain the active connivance of the Official Opposition by sharing with it the planning of the timetable, and the responsibility for keeping the debates within the time limits they have agreed upon. This requires the continuous and intimate cooperation of the Government and Opposition Chief Whips "through the usual channels."

There is, however, one very important proviso. In the last resort, even today, the Government remains at the mercy of the Opposition. At any moment, if the Opposition feels driven to do so, it can withdraw its co-operation and bring Parliament to a standstill. The powers which prevent a repetition of the Irish filibuster are genuinely powerful. Even so, if the Opposition gets really nasty, it can soon make life impossible for the Government, which needs to keep a stream of formal business, administrative orders and approvals moving through Parliament in order to prevent a complete paralysis setting in. Thus there does remain an ultimate sanction; and even the most compliant Opposition leadership can be forced to use it if the Government is really outraging Parliament and public opinion outside. There are times in the life of each Parliament when Opposition back benchers have recourse to filibuster and obstruction. But normally the operation of the usual channels keeps business proceeding according to timetable despite these outbursts.

It was, for instance, the operation of the usual channels which assured the Labour Government of the passage of the Kenya Asian Bill, which in the U.S.A. would, I guess, have been ruled unconstitutional by the Supreme Court. On the other hand, it was the withdrawal of co-operation through the usual channels which forced the Labour Government to jettison its Parliament Bill reforming the Lords.

POWERS OF THE PRIME MINISTER

Now I want to explain why I think that Cabinet government has been developing into Prime Ministerial government. Here is my list of the six powers the Prime Minister wields.

1. First of all, remember each Minister fighting in the Cabinet for his Department can be sacked by the Prime Minister any day. We must be constantly aware our tenure of office depends on his personal decision. I remarked last time that he is not a "free" man in the sense that he can, for example, sack all the undisputed incompetents in his team—without upsetting his own position. But even though he is balancing forces in the Cabinet rather than ordering them, he has, in my view, tremendous power—something which any Cabinet Minister is aware of every day of his life. I am aware I am there at the Prime Minister's discretion. The Prime Minister can withdraw that discretion on any day he likes without stating a reason. And there's nothing much I can do about it—except succeed—and so build up my own strength.

2. The second of the powers of the Prime Minister is that he decides the agenda of the Cabinet. Say that I think something is terribly important: I must get it through and I've had a row in the Cabinet committee. I register my dissent and ask for it to go to Cabinet. Somehow it does not occur on the agenda week after week. I fume—but the PM has the last word. The agenda is fixed in Number 10; and the two men who fix the agenda—the Prime Minister and the Secretary to the Cabinet—decide what issues shall be fought out, what shall not.

3. Thirdly, the Prime Minister decides the organisation of the Cabinet committees. What committees exist, how they are manned—above all, who are the Chairmen—all this is entirely a matter for the Prime Minister. As I

mentioned in the last lecture, there is one committee where there are only one or two members, and that's the committee which decides the contents of the Budget—nearly always the Chancellor in consultation with the PM. After that, twenty-four hours before the Budget Speech, the Cabinet, as a matter of form, have the proposals presented to them for comment.

But there are many other issues, awkward issues where it is up to the Prime Minister to decide what kind of Cabinet committee the issue is put to. Shall it contain ten Departmental Ministers; shall it be limited to junior Ministers; or shall it be only three Senior Ministers? He's absolutely free in adjudicating to which members of the Cabinet or of the Government the issue shall be put in committee. He can in fact virtually decide whether the proposition is buried without ever coming to Cabinet, or whether it comes with certain amendments, or whether it is given top priority and pushed through intact.

Of course, all this has a tremendous effect on the doctrine of collective responsibility. This is a doctrine which many people in America regard as the distinguishing characteristic of British Cabinet Government, but I am not so sure they all understand how it works today. In Bagehot's time collective responsibility used to mean that every member of the Cabinet had the right to take part in the Cabinet discussion; but after the discussion was over, he was bound by the decision which had been reached. That was the original notion. That's what you find in Bagehot.

Collective responsibility now means something totally different. It means that everybody who is in the Government must accept and publicly support every "Cabinet decision," even if he was not present at the discussion or, frequently, was completely unaware the decision had been taken. As we have seen, collective decision-taking is now fragmented, and many major decisions may be taken by two, three, four, or five Ministers. But the moment they have been taken, *and minuted*, they have the force of a decision taken by the whole Cabinet, and are binding on a hundred-odd members of the Government.

This is an interesting transformation of the old notion of collective responsibility which enormously increases Prime Ministerial power. There is all the difference in the world between a Prime Minister who has to carry twenty colleagues with him when anything of importance is being decided, and a new-style Prime Minister who has appointed one hundred colleagues as his agents, each of them with a specific job to do, and only permitted to hear after the event nine tenths of the decisions for which he shares collective responsibility. It is by this transformation that Cabinet Government, in my view, has been evolved into what I call "Prime Ministerial Government."

4. But that does not conclude the powers of the Prime Minister. To an American audience I need not stress the significance of the fact that he has almost a monopoly of patronage. He personally controls the "Honours List." He has an unchallenged free hand in selecting new members of the House of Lords. This latter gives him a useful device for retiring ageing or incompetent Ministers without disgrace—purging his Government by promotion into the Upper Chamber, which really deserves the nickname of "the best club in the world."

As for other appointments, paid and unpaid, there are many, many thousands which departmental Ministers make. All the important ones have to be approved, however, by Number 10 Downing Street. A Prime Minister at the centre of our centralised Party Oligarchy wields far more effective personal control in the field of patronage than an American President.

5. Even more important than the control of patronage is the control of the Civil Service which a Prime Minister has exercised—again since the period of Lloyd George. During World War I, and up until 1919, the heads of the various Departments in Whitehall were mostly selected from inside the Department; and it was the Minister who made the decision.

Then Lord Rhondda, who was wartime Minister of Food, made a decision rather like Caligula, who, as you remember, decided to make his horse Consul. He made his Private Secretary the Permanent Secretary—the Head of the Department. This so shocked Lloyd George that he sent out a minute which said that in the future all heads of Departments would be appointed by the Permanent Secretary of the Treasury, in consultation with the Prime Minister.

Today all number twos as well as all Number Ones are made by the Prime Minister and the Head of the Civil Service, who, by the way, is now different from the Head of the Treasury. There is now a trinity of power in Whitehall: (1) the Permanent Secretary of the Treasury, who is a very powerful man in his own right because of the unique power exercised by his department; (2) the Head of the Civil Service, who is the Permanent Secretary of the new Civil Service Department; (3) the Secretary of the Cabinet. These are men, I would say, of equal status and power, and this trinity under the Prime Minister controls promotion to the top jobs in the Civil Service.

The change which began in 1919 completely transformed not only the nature of the promotions in Civil Service but also the power of the Prime Minister. Before this, you were appointed Head of the Department because you knew something about it. This idea that in order to be a good Permanent Secretary of Education you must know about education is long since defunct. The Permanent Secretaries now are professional administrators with minds so trained that they can move from Department to Department, and within a week administer any Department equally skilfully. This is what we call our "Mandarin System."

As I told you, I did Greek at Oxford, and a study of Greek philosophy is an almost perfect training for a Mandarin. It means you know nothing in particular about what you are actually doing but you have a "perfectly trained mind." We have evolved the requirement that if men want to rise to the top, they must mark themselves out as they rise, for example, through the Ministry of Education as being able to run Transport just as well. Non-expertise is the mark of a man who is going to get on in the British Civil Service.

There is one other mark that he requires. He requires a period in the Treasury. This is the "Hallmark," if I may say so, of a man doomed to success. A period in the Cabinet Secretariat is pretty useful for promotion prospects, but a period in the Treasury counts for a lot more because ex-Treasury Civil Servants make up an open conspiracy. Everybody who has once been in the Treasury always belongs to it in spirit and can be reckoned on to tell the Treasury most of what it wants to know about any Department in which he serves.

I very early discovered as a Minister that my Department could not keep a secret from the Treasury. Long before I was ready, my plans would be disclosed to the Treasury by my loyal Permanent Secretary on the ground that one must really consider the national good and not be parochial about Housing. That is why the Treasury nearly always wins the battle against a Department.

But let's get back to the Trinity of Power. You can now see why I claim that the Prime Minister has a peculiar and unique power, apart from the Cabinet altogether. He is the only politician to whom these three all-powerful Civil Servants look as their political master.

6. His final power is his personal control of Government publicity. I have told how Government policy is promulgated in Whitehall as Cabinet Minutes. The Government's Press relations are conducted by the Number 10 press department at its daily press conferences. That means we have a daily, coherent, central explanation of what the Government is doing—an explanation naturally in terms the Prime Minister thinks right.

Anyway, the media of mass publicity tend to personalise politics; and as our politics centre on Number 10, and as much of the news is released from Number 10, you can see how natural it is for the Press to be fed with the Prime Minister's interpretation of Government Policy, and to present him as the Champion and spokesman of the whole Cabinet in the battle against the "shadow" enemy on the other side.

Now I have listed his powers, do you see what I meant by Prime Ministerial government? It does not mean that he is a dictator; it does not mean he can tell his Ministers what to do in their Departments. But it does mean that in this discussion and argument and battle of Whitehall this man in the centre, this Chairman, this man without a Department, without apparent power, can exert, when he is successful, a dominating personal control. This explains why a British Cabinet is always called a "Wilson Cabinet" or a "Macmillan Cabinet." It is because every Cabinet takes its tone from the Prime Minister. The way the Prime Minister conducts it and administers it will give it its particular character. Usually it is dominated by his personality, and, if it is not, this is because he prefers to exert his control in less obvious ways. Attlee, I gather, pretended not to run the Cabinet. Actually, he was a quite ruthless little man, and fairly often he was savage and cruel and even unjust. There are various ways of exercising power and getting your way as Premier, some more dramatic and theatrical than others. All I am saying is that the way a Cabinet works, the way it functions, is determined by its Prime Minister. . . .

MINISTERS AND CIVIL SERVANTS

The greatest danger of a Labour Cabinet is that its members will be corrupted from being a team of Socialists carrying out a collective Cabinet Strategy into a collection of individual departmental Ministers. The greatest temptation is that I should be too interested in the praise of the Department and too pleased at being told how well I am doing: "Wonderful Minister, you're putting all this Party thing behind you, and really working for the Department—that's so fine of you." And before I know what, I am beginning to lose interest in the causes for which I was sent to fight in Parliament.

Therefore, the battle is really for the soul of the Minister. Is he to remain a foreign body in the Department, inserting into the departments things they don't like, a political dynamo, sparking off things they don't want, things he wants and the Party wants? Or is he to become *their* Minister, content to speak for them? There is nothing easier than being a departmental success. Nothing easier at all. The Private Office sees to that.

That's one danger—that Ministers may become departmental spokesmen. The other danger we face is that the Departments get together and dictate to the politicians behind the scenes at Whitehall. I have said something about Cabinet committees. I have not revealed to you that parallel to each Cabinet committee is an official committee. Say you have a Cabinet committee consisting of seven Cabinet Ministers to discuss a problem which affects five Departments. There will be an official committee consisting of officials from those five Departments, who will seek, as far as possible, to achieve an official solution which they can recommend to their Ministers, rather than have the risk of the Ministers fighting it out with five conflicting departmental briefs and coming to a collective political decision on their own. Whitehall likes to reach an official compromise at official level first, so that the Ministers are all briefed the same way.

The emergence of these official committees is something which has been going on for the last fifteen years, and I will give you an example of how it works from my own life. At one time I was Minister of Housing, and I was very keen to substitute local income tax for local rates as the main basis of our local taxation. So I made a speech or two about this before I squared my officials. What happened? An official committee was established which did a tremendous lot of work in order to prove that rates were the only practical form of local taxation. And so before I could get to my colleagues and argue the case for the local income tax, every one of my colleagues had been briefed by his officials that there was no alternative to the rates. So that was that! If Whitehall gangs up on you it is very difficult to get your policy through, or even to get a fair hearing for a new idea.

Let me sum up this part of my argument. The effective Minister is the man who wins the support of his Department without becoming its cherished mascot. To do so he has to strike a balance. He needs the acquiescence, at least, of the Department in what he is up to, and for this he needs to be a success in the Department's eye. So he's got to appease them by winning a number of their battles for them in the Whitehall war.

Simultaneously, he must hold his own in the paper war. Every Department wages a paper war against its Minister. They try to drown him in paper so that he can't be a nuisance. Every night, as you know, we receive our red boxes. When I get home to my house in London about ten or eleven at night from the House of Commons, there are one, two, three, four, or even five boxes, which include not only the papers for next day's meeting but the decisions which I have to take that night before reaching the Ministry the next day. The first job you have to do is to prevent yourself becoming a slave of the red box.

By the way, it's no good thinking you can evade this by use of the telephone. At one time I was very irate; I thought, I won't sign this damn stuff, I'll do it all by phone. That has no effect on the British Civil Service. What they care about is the written word. Even the word "yes" or "no" written on paper is enough. So I awake at six and I work until half past eight or nine, working through the boxes so that every decision is taken and sent back to them duly minuted and initialled.

You must never let them defeat you. You must never fail to give a decision back in writing. If you do that, and if you do it having clearly read the documents — and that's important too — then you have some chance of asserting your authority.

Having asserted your authority, the next thing is to select a very few causes and fight for them. The greatest danger of a Radical Minister is to get too much going in his Department. Because, you see, Departments are resistant. Departments know that they last and you don't. Departments know that any day you may be moved somewhere else and they can forget you. It does not pay you to order them to change their minds on everything. For one thing, they can't. There's a limit to the quantity of change they can digest.

Select a few, a very few issues, and on those issues be bloody and blunt because, of course, you get no change except by fighting. I know there are people who believe you can achieve things in Whitehall without a battle with your Department. Well, it hasn't been my experience, and a very good thing too. If I want to change something and they have got their own departmental policy, they are bound to say, "Look, before we are going to change our departmental mind for a temporary Minister, he must show that he really means it. First of all, he must be able to answer all our arguments; secondly, his will power must be sufficient so that when we refuse to do anything week after week he must notice it, he must send for us, he must bully us." There might be a fight and a triumph. It's like a man with a woman in a Victorian novel, if you know what I mean. They are females to our males. They aren't prepared to give way without a good fight before it happens. But you can't afford to have fights on many things. You must have them on one or two or three issues.

In all this, as I have said, it's no good being brilliant or successful unless you have powerful allies. Your officials know whether you are on good terms with the Prime Minister or not. They know whether the Chancellor is willing to give you the money or not long before you do because their information is better than yours. They have an unrivalled grapevine in Whitehall. They brief each other.

Therefore, it's no good being heroic unless you have one or two good big guns on your side, and this explains why Ministers are inclined not to back too many causes in the Cabinet. Why wasn't I fighting for the Right on X or Y or Z? Because I couldn't afford to make too many enemies by espousing causes I wasn't vitally concerned in, when I needed the support of these colleagues in my own departmental affairs. The need to have allies in your own field limits your altruistic activity in other fields. I won't go further than that. I think you will see what I mean.

TASKS OF A RADICAL PRIME MINISTER

. . . I fancy a Prime Minister could well calculate that the amount of time a strong man can be in a Department and go on fighting is not much more than three years. After that symbiosis occurs of the most dangerous character. He actually starts getting on with the Department too well. For about three years he remains an active foreign body and there can be a creative friction—a battle out of which something comes. But sooner or later a point is reached where he gets too close to the Department. I would know and care too much about Health after three more years, and then I might be a dangerous person because I might align myself with these Health people against the Cabinet.

This explains this continuous shuffling of a British Cabinet. They are shuffled because the PM did not select his Cabinet Ministers as experts on Health and Defence and so forth, but rather as members of a political team elected to do a definitive collective job. And each is to be inserted into the huge rigid structure of a Department in order to get things moving inside the way the Government wants.

So the PM's task is to keep a watch on his Ministers to see that they aren't getting too respectable, too Department-minded, that they are not developing a Ministry-based independence of the Cabinet.

Secondly, he must be concerned with the machinery of the Government. The Prime Minister has an absolute control here. He can create new Departments; he can chop Departments in half. This constant threat is a wholesome way of keeping the Civil Service on their toes.

Thirdly, he supervises reforms of the Civil Service. We are now doing a major reform with the abolition of the class system in the Civil Service. These are things where the Prime Minister is personally responsible.

I end this second lecture with one question. If the Labour Government has made mistakes and suffered failures, would I attribute these failures and mistakes to the Civil Service? My answer is "no." I am absolutely clear that the chance you have as a Government or as a Minister of changing things in Britain is enormous; provided that the Government is a team; provided the Ministers are capable of keeping their political drive while helping the Department and working eighteen hours a day. Provided they have these qualities, they have an instrument which is trained to accept change. I said "accept change"—of course, they often fight it. Of course they do, but that's part of their job. But the point is they only fight to the point where you have licked them, and that's all you can ask.

So, when we are looking at the record of a Government, I wouldn't attribute its failings to the British Civil Service. I would say that normally when a Government fails it is not because the Civil Service blocks it, but because the Government team has not had a clear enough sense of direction. A Government which really knows where it is going, a Government which has a series of measures ready, prepared, well thought out, has to hand in Britain an instrument which will enable it to carry out all it wants.

30 Bureaucracy

Growth of modern government administration (known also as the civil service or bureaucracy) has paralleled the growth of modern governmental functions. As governments took on more societal responsibilities, more people and organizations were needed for example, to administer agricultural programs, to build roads, to run the public school system, or to dispense unemployment benefits. This is not to say large bureaucracies are found only in modern governments. Indeed, two thousand years ago Chinese "Mandarins" were an integral part of the administration of Chinese empires. However, according to Max Weber, a number of distinctive characteristics accompany the development of modern bureaucracies.

Administrative officials, as opposed to elected officials, represent the large reservoir of resource people on whom public policy-makers depend for technical expertise. These bureaucracies have to become "professional" organizations in that they provide a vocation for the qualified. In theory, they are detached from the political world, and operate in an impersonal and impartial way. Employment in the organization must be by competitive examination to avoid accusation of political patronage and nepotism. At the same time, professional bureaucratic organizations must follow institutionalized procedures for administration that are established to avoid situations of privilege or favour.

While one can, theoretically, construct a large, professionalized bureaucracy that does administer fairly, there is an inherent problem with modern bureaucracies. Because elected officials depend on the expertise and information of bureaucrats, those bureaucrats and their organizations become very powerful in the policy-making process; and yet they are not responsible to the voters.

In the reading that follows, Max Weber provides an analysis of modern bureaucracies and indicates the problems inherent in that organization. Weber (1864-1920) is generally considered the most important sociologist of the twentieth century. The excerpts on bureaucracy printed here are from his masterwork *Wirtschaft und Gesellschaft*, translated by H.H. Gerth and C. Wright Mills in *From Max Weber: Essays in Sociology*.

● ● ● ● ● ● ● ● ●

1: CHARACTERISTICS OF BUREAUCRACY

Modern officialdom functions in the following specific manner:

I. There is the principle of fixed and official jurisdictional areas, which are generally ordered by rules, that is, by laws or administrative regulations.

1. The regular activities required for the purposes of the bureaucratically governed structure are distributed in a fixed way as official duties.

2. The authority to give the commands required for the discharge of these duties is distributed in a stable way and is strictly delimited by rules concerning the coercive means, physical, sacerdotal, or otherwise, which may be placed at the disposal of officials.

3. Methodical provision is made for the regular and continuous fulfilment of these duties and for the execution of the corresponding rights; only persons who have the generally regulated qualifications to serve are employed.

In public and lawful government these three elements constitute 'bureaucratic authority.' In private economic domination, they constitute bureaucratic 'management.' Bureaucracy, thus understood, is fully developed in political and ecclesiastical communities only in the modern state, and, in the private economy, only in the most advanced institutions of capitalism. Permanent and public office authority, with fixed jurisdiction, is not the historical rule but rather the exception. This is so even in large political structures such as those of the ancient Orient, the Germanic and Mongolian empires of conquest, or of many feudal structures of state. In all these cases, the ruler executes the most important measures through personal trustees, table-companions, or court-servants. Their commissions and authority are not precisely delimited and are temporarily called into being for each case.

II. The principles of office hierarchy and of levels of graded authority mean a firmly ordered system of super- and subordination in which there is a supervision of the lower offices by the higher ones. Such a system offers the governed the possibility of appealing the decision of a lower office to its higher authority, in a definitely regulated manner. With the full development of the bureaucratic type, the office hierarchy is monocratically organized. The principle of hierarchical office authority is found in all bureaucratic structures: in state and ecclesiastical structures as well as in large party organizations and private enterprises. It does not matter for the character of bureaucracy whether its authority is called 'private' or 'public.'

When the principle of jurisdictional 'competency' is fully carried through, hierarchical subordination—at least in public office—does not mean that the 'higher' authority is simply authorized to take over the business of the 'lower.' Indeed, the opposite is the rule. Once established and having fulfilled its task, an office tends to continue in existence and be held by another incumbent.

III. The management of the modern office is based upon written documents ('the files'), which are preserved in their original or draught form. There is, therefore, a staff of subaltern officials and scribes of all sorts. The body of officials actively engaged in a 'public' office, along with the respective apparatus of material implements and the files, make up a 'bureau.' In private enterprise, 'the bureau' is often called 'the office.'

In principle, the modern organization of the civil service separates the bureau from the private domicile of the official, and, in general, bureaucracy segregates official activity as something distinct from the sphere of private life. Public monies and equipment are divorced from the private property of the official. This condition is everywhere the product of a long development. Nowadays, it is found in public as well as in private enterprises; in the latter, the principle extends even to the leading entrepreneur. In principle, the executive office is separated from the household, business from private correspondence, and business assets from private fortunes. The more consistently the modern type of business management has been carried through the more are these separations the case. The beginnings of this process are to be found as early as the Middle Ages. . . .

IV. Office management, at least all specialized office management—and such management is distinctly modern—usually presupposes thorough and expert training. This increasingly holds for the modern executive and employee of private enterprises, in the same manner as it holds for the state official.

V. When the office is fully developed, official activity demands the full working capacity of the official, irrespective of the fact that his obligatory time in the bureau may be firmly delimited. In the normal case, this is only the product of a long development, in the public as well as in the private office. Formerly, in all cases, the normal state of affairs was reversed: official business was discharged as a secondary activity.

VI. The management of the office follows general rules, which are more or less stable, more or less exhaustive, and which can be learned. Knowledge of these rules represents a special technical learning which the officials possess. It involves jurisprudence, or administrative or business management.

The reduction of modern office management to rules is deeply embedded in its very nature. The theory of modern public administration, for instance, assumes that the authority to order certain matters by decree—which has been legally granted to public authorities—does not entitle the bureau to regulate the matter by commands given for each case, but only to regulate the matter abstractly. This stands in extreme contrast to the regulation of all relationships through individual privileges and bestowals of favor, which is absolutely dominant in patrimonialism, at least in so far as such relationships are not fixed by sacred tradition.

2: THE POSITION OF THE OFFICIAL

All this results in the following for the internal and external positions of the official:

I. Office holding is a 'vocation.' This is shown, first, in the requirement of a firmly prescribed course of training, which demands the entire capacity for work for a long period of time, and in the generally prescribed and special examinations which are prerequisites of employment. Furthermore, the position of the official is in the nature of a duty. This determines the internal structure of his relations, in the following manner: Legally and actually, office holding is not considered a source to be exploited for rents or emoluments, as was normally the case during the Middle Ages and frequently up to the threshold of recent times. Nor is office holding considered a usual exchange of services for equivalents, as is the case with free labor contracts. Entrance into an office, including one in the private economy, is considered an acceptance of a specific obligation of faithful management in return for a secure existence. It is decisive for the specific nature of modern loyalty to an office that, in the pure type, it does not establish a relationship to a *person*, like the vassal's or disciple's faith in feudal or in patrimonial relations of authority. Modern loyalty is devoted to impersonal and functional purposes. Behind the functional purposes, of course, 'ideas of culture-values' usually stand. These are *ersatz* for the earthly or supramundane personal master: ideas such as 'state,' 'church,' 'community,' 'party,' or 'enterprise' are thought of as being realized in a community; they provide an ideological halo for the master.

The political official—at least in the fully developed modern state—is not considered the personal servant of a ruler. Today, the bishop, the priest, and the preacher are in fact no longer, as in early Christian times, holders of purely personal charisma. The supra-mundane and sacred values which they offer are given to everybody who seems to be worthy of them and who asks for them. In former times, such leaders acted upon the personal command of their master; in principle, they were responsible only to him. Nowadays, in spite of the partial survival of the old theory, such religious leaders are officials in the service of a functional purpose, which in the present-day 'church' has become routinized and, in turn, ideologically hallowed.

II. The personal position of the official is patterned in the following way:

1. Whether he is in a private office or a public bureau, the modern official always strives and usually enjoys a distinct *social esteem* as compared with the governed. His social position is guaranteed by the prescriptive rules of rank order and, for the political official, by special definitions of the criminal code against 'insults of officials' and 'contempt' of state and church authorities. . . .

2. The pure type of bureaucratic official is *appointed* by a superior authority. An official elected by the governed is not a purely bureaucratic figure. Of course, the formal existence of an election does not by itself mean that no appointment hides behind the election—in the state, especially, appointment by party chiefs. Whether or not this is the case does not depend upon legal statutes but upon the way in which the party mechanism functions. Once firmly organized, the parties can turn a formally free election into the mere acclamation of a candidate designated by the party chief. As a rule, however, a formally free election is turned into a fight, conducted according to definite rules, for votes in favor of one of two designated candidates. . . .

3. Normally, the position of the official is held for life, at least in public bureaucracies; and this is increasingly the case for all similar structures. As a factual rule, *tenure for life* is presupposed, even where the giving of notice or periodic reappointment occurs. In contrast to the worker in a private enterprise, the official normally holds tenure. Legal or actual life-tenure, however, is not recognized as the official's right to the possession of office, as was the case with many structures of authority in the past. Where legal guarantees against arbitrary dismissal or transfer are developed, they merely serve to guarantee a strictly objective discharge of specific office duties free from all personal considerations. In Germany, this is the case for all juridical and, increasingly, for all administrative officials. . . .

4. The official receives the regular *pecuniary* compensation of a normally fixed *salary* and the old age security provided by a pension. The salary is not measured like a wage in terms of work done, but according to 'status,' that is, according to the kind of function (the 'rank') and, in addition, possibly, according to the length of service. The relatively great security of the official's income, as well as the rewards of social esteem, make the office a sought-after position, especially in countries which no longer provide opportunities for colonial profits. In such countries, this situation permits relatively low salaries for officials.

5. The official is set for a '*career*' within the hierarchical order of the public service. He moves from the lower, less important, and lower paid to

the higher positions. The average official naturally desires a mechanical fixing of the conditions of promotion: if not of the offices, at least of the salary levels. He wants these conditions fixed in terms of 'seniority,' or possibly according to grades achieved in a developed system of expert examinations. Here and there, such examinations actually form a character *indelebilis* of the official and have lifelong effects on his career. To this is joined the desire to qualify the right to office and the increasing tendency toward status group closure and economic security. All of this makes for a tendency to consider the offices as 'prebends' of those who are qualified by educational certificates. The necessity of taking general personal and intellectual qualifications into consideration, irrespective of the often subaltern character of the educational certificate, has led to a condition in which the highest political offices, especially the positions of 'ministers,' are principally filled without reference to such certificates. . . .

6: TECHNICAL ADVANTAGES OF BUREAUCRATIC ORGANIZATION

The decisive reason for the advance of bureaucratic organization has always been its purely technical superiority over any other form of organization. The fully developed bureaucratic mechanism compares with other organizations exactly as does the machine with the non-mechanical modes of production.

Precision, speed, unambiguity, knowledge of the files, continuity, discretion, unity, strict subordination, reduction of friction and of material and personal costs—these are raised to the optimum point in the strictly bureaucratic administration, and especially in its monocratic form. As compared with all collegiate, honorific, and avocational forms of administration, trained bureaucracy is superior on all these points. And as far as complicated tasks are concerned, paid bureaucratic work is not only more precise but, in the last analysis, it is often cheaper than even formally unremunerated honorific service.

Honorific arrangements make administrative work an avocation and, for this reason alone, honorific service normally functions more slowly; being less bound to schemata and being more formless. Hence it is less precise and less unified than bureaucratic work because it is less dependent upon superiors and because the establishment and exploitation of the apparatus of subordinate officials and filing services are almost unavoidably less economical. Honorific service is less continuous than bureaucratic and frequently quite expensive. This is especially the case if one thinks not only of the money costs to the public treasury—costs which bureaucratic administration, in comparison with administration by notables, usually substantially increases—but also of the frequent economic losses of the governed caused by delays and lack of precision. The possibility of administration by notables normally and permanently exists only where official management can be satisfactorily discharged as an avocation. With the qualitative increase of tasks the administration has to face, administration by notables reaches its limits—today, even in England. Work organized by collegiate bodies causes friction and delay and requires compromises between colliding interests and views. The administration, therefore, runs less precisely and is more independent of superiors; hence, it is less unified and slower. All advances of the Prussian administrative organization have been and will in the future be advances of the bureaucratic, and especially of the monocratic, principle.

Today, it is primarily the capitalist market economy which demands that the official business of the administration be discharged precisely, unambiguously, continuously, and with as much speed as possible. Normally, the very large, modern capitalist enterprises are themselves unequalled models of strict bureaucratic organization. Business management throughout rests on increasing precision, steadiness, and, above all, the speed of operations. This, in turn, is determined by the peculiar nature of the modern means of communication, including, among other things, the news service of the press. The extraordinary increase in the speed by which public announcements, as well as economic and political facts, are transmitted exerts a steady and sharp pressure in the direction of speeding up the tempo of administrative reaction towards various situations. The optimum of such reaction time is normally attained only by a strictly bureaucratic organization.

Bureaucratization offers above all the optimum possibility for carrying through the principle of specializing administrative functions according to purely objective considerations. Individual performances are allocated to functionaries who have specialized training and who by constant practice learn more and more. The 'objective' discharge of business primarily means a discharge of business according to *calculable rules* and 'without regard for persons.'

'Without regard for persons' is also the watchword of the 'market' and, in general, of all pursuits of naked economic interests. A consistent execution of bureaucratic domination means the leveling of status 'honor.' Hence, if the principle of the free-market is not at the same time restricted, it means the universal domination of the 'class situation.' That this consequence of bureaucratic domination has not set in everywhere, parallel to the extent of bureaucratization, is due to the differences among possible principles by which polities may meet their demands.

The second element mentioned, 'calculable rules,' also is of paramount importance for modern bureaucracy. The peculiarity of modern culture, and specifically of its technical and economic basis, demands this very 'calculability' of results. When fully developed, bureaucracy also stands, in a specific sense, under the principle of *sine ira ac studio* [impartiality]. Its specific nature, which is welcomed by capitalism, develops the more perfectly the more the bureaucracy is 'dehumanized,' the more completely it succeeds in eliminating from official business love, hatred, and all purely personal, irrational, and emotional elements which escape calculation. This is the specific nature of bureaucracy and it is appraised as its special virtue.

The more complicated and specialized modern culture becomes, the more its external supporting apparatus demands the personally detached and strictly 'objective' *expert*, in lieu of the master of older social structures, who was moved by personal sympathy and favor, by grace and gratitude. Bureaucracy offers the attitudes demanded by the external apparatus of modern culture in the most favorable combination. As a rule, only bureaucracy has established the foundation for the administration of a rational law conceptually systematized on the basis of such enactments as the latter Roman imperial period first created with a high degree of technical perfection. During the Middle Ages, this law was received along with the bureaucratization of legal administration, that is to say, with the displacement of the old trial procedure which was bound to tradition or to irrational presuppositions, by the rationally trained and specialized expert. . . .

9: THE LEVELING OF SOCIAL DIFFERENCES

Bureaucratic organization has usually come into power on the basis of a leveling of economic and social differences. This leveling has been at least relative, and has concerned the significance of social and economic differences for the assumption of administrative functions.

Bureaucracy inevitably accompanies modern *mass democracy* in contrast to the democratic self-government of small homogeneous units. This results from the characteristic principle of bureaucracy: the abstract regularity of the execution of authority, which is a result of the demand for 'equality before the law' in the personal and functional sense—hence, of the horror of 'privilege,' and the principled rejection of doing business 'from case to case.' Such regularity also follows from the social preconditions of the origin of bureaucracies. The non-bureaucratic administration of any large social structure rests in some way upon the fact that existing social, material, or honorific preferences and ranks are connected with administrative functions and duties. This usually means that a direct or indirect economic exploitation or a 'social' exploitation of position, which every sort of administrative activity gives to its bearers, is equivalent to the assumption of administrative functions. . . .

10: THE PERMANENT CHARACTER OF THE BUREAUCRATIC MACHINE

Once it is fully established, bureaucracy is among those social structures which are the hardest to destroy. Bureaucracy is *the* means of carrying 'community action' over into rationally ordered 'societal action.' Therefore, as an instrument for 'societalizing' relations of power, bureaucracy has been and is a power instrument of the first order—for the one who controls the bureaucratic apparatus.

Under otherwise equal conditions, a 'societal action,' which is methodically ordered and led, is superior to every resistance of 'mass' or even of 'communal action.' And where the bureaucratization of administration has been completely carried through, a form of power relation is established that is practically unshatterable.

The individual bureaucrat cannot squirm out of the apparatus in which he is harnessed. In contrast to the honorific or avocational 'notable,' the professional bureaucrat is chained to his activity by his entire material and ideal existence. In the great majority of cases, he is only a single cog in an ever-moving mechanism which prescribes to him an essentially fixed route of march. The official is entrusted with specialized tasks and normally the mechanism cannot be put into motion or arrested by him, but only from the very top. The individual bureaucrat is thus forged to the community of all the functionaries who are integrated into the mechanism. They have a common interest in seeing that the mechanism continues its functions and that the societally exercised authority carries on.

The ruled, for their part, cannot dispense with or replace the bureaucratic apparatus of authority once it exists. For this bureaucracy rests upon expert training, a functional specialization of work, and an attitude set for habitual and virtuoso-like mastery of single yet methodically integrated functions. If the official stops working, or if his work is forcefully interrupted, chaos results, and it is difficult to improvise replacements from among the governed who are fit to master such chaos. This holds for public administration as well as for private economic management. More and more the material fate of the masses depends upon the steady and correct functioning of the increasingly bureaucratic organizations of private capitalism. The idea of eliminating these organizations becomes more and more utopian. . . .

Under normal conditions, the power position of a fully developed bureaucracy is always overtowering. the 'political master' finds himself in the position of the 'dilettante' who stands opposite the 'expert,' facing the trained official who stands within the management of administration. This holds whether the 'master' whom the bureaucracy serves is a 'people,' equipped with the weapons of 'legislative initiative,' the 'referendum,' and the right to remove officials, or a parliament, elected on a more aristocratic or more 'democratic' basis and equipped with the right to vote a lack of confidence, or with the actual authority to vote it. It holds whether the master is an aristocratic, collegiate body, legally or actually based on self-recruitment, or whether he is a popularly elected president, a hereditary and 'absolute' or a 'constitutional' monarch. . . .

14: THE 'RATIONALIZATION' OF EDUCATION AND TRAINING

We cannot here analyze the far-reaching and general cultural effects that the advance of the rational bureaucratic structure of domination, as such, develops quite independently of the areas in which it takes hold. Naturally, bureaucracy promotes a 'rationalist' way of life, but the concept of rationalism allows for widely differing contents. Quite generally, one can only say that the bureaucratization of all domination very strongly furthers the development of 'rational matter-of-factness' and the personality type of the professional expert. This has far-reaching ramifications, but only one important element of the process can be briefly indicated here: its effect upon the nature of training and education.

Educational institutions on the European continent, especially the institutions of higher learning—the universities, as well as technical academies, business colleges, gymnasiums, and other middle schools—are dominated and influenced by the need for the kind of 'education' that produces a system of special examinations and the trained expertness that is increasingly indispensable for modern bureaucracy.

The 'special examination,' in the present sense, was and is found also outside of bureaucratic structures proper; thus, today it is found in the 'free' professions of medicine and law and in the guild-organized trades. Expert examinations are neither indispensable to nor concomitant phenomena of bureaucratization. The French, English, and American bureaucracies have for a long time foregone such examinations entirely or to a large extent, for training and service in party organizations have made up for them. . . .

Social prestige based upon the advantage of special education and training as such is by no means specific to bureaucracy. On the contrary! But educational prestige in other structures of domination rests upon substantially different foundations.

Expressed in slogan-like fashion, the 'cultivated man,' rather than the 'specialist,' has been the end sought by education and has formed the basis of social esteem in such various systems as the feudal, theocratic, and patrimonial structures of dominion: in the English notable administration, in the old Chinese patrimonial bureaucracy, as well as under the rule of demagogues in the so-called Hellenic democracy.

The term 'cultivated man' is used here in a completely value-neutral sense; it is understood to mean solely that the goal of education consists in the quality of a man's bearing in life which was *considered* 'cultivated,' rather than in a specialized training for expertness. The 'cultivated' personality formed the educational ideal, which was stamped by the structure of domination and by the social condition for membership in the ruling stratum. Such education aimed at a chivalrous or an ascetic type; or, at a literary type, as in China; a gymnastic-humanist type, as in Hellas; or it aimed at a conventional type, as in the case of the Anglo-Saxon gentleman. The qualification of the ruling stratum as such rested upon the possession of 'more' cultural quality (in the absolutely changeable, value-neutral sense in which we use the term here), rather than upon 'more' expert knowledge. Special military, theological, and juridical ability was of course intensely practiced; but the point of gravity in Hellenic, in medieval, as well as in Chinese education, has rested upon educational elements that were entirely different from what was 'useful' in one's specialty.

Behind all the present discussions of the foundations of the educational system, the struggle of the 'specialist type of man' against the older type of 'cultivated man' is hidden at some decisive point. This fight is determined by the irresistibly expanding bureaucratization of all public and private relations of authority and by the ever-increasing importance of expert and specialized knowledge. This fight intrudes into all intimate cultural questions. . . .

31   Courts

Judicial review is an integral part of any federal system of government. Judicial review can be defined as the ruling by the courts on the constitutionality of legislation or executive action. In Canada, the practice of judicial review changed considerably with the adoption of the Charter of Rights and Freedoms in 1982.

Prior to 1982, the courts generally exercised a narrow interpretation of the power of judicial review. The British doctrine of parliamentary supremacy prevailed, and the courts rarely intervened to strike down a law of Parliament, for example, ruling it unconstitutional and thus null and void. However, the courts would rule on whether federal or provincial legislation was indeed a federal or provincial responsibility. Sections 91 (federal powers) and 92 and 93 (provincial powers) of the Constitution Act (1867) were used as the basis for decisions. If the courts, for example, decided a federal act was *ultra vires*, unconstitutional in the sense that it was outside the jurisdiction of the federal government, then obviously it was a provincial responsibility. And the same applied to provincial responsibilities; if those acts were *ultra vires*, then they were a federal responsibility. Thus, this form of judicial review was compatible with parliamentary supremacy; one level of government, federal or provincial, was always "supreme."

With the adoption of the Charter of Rights and Freedoms, however, judicial review has come to raise another issue—the supremacy of the constitution—because the constitutional rights of individuals are enumerated in the Charter. If individuals feel their Charter rights are violated by either level of government, they can take the dispute to the courts. Courts are now asked, in effect, to place the disputed legislation of federal or provincial parliaments alongside the Charter.

F.L. Morton reviews the decisions of the Supreme Court of Canada since passage of the Charter. He suggests that the Court has become more of an "activist" Supreme Court in that it is ruling more frequently on the constitutionality of federal and provincial legislation. This selection is a revised and updated version of the essay which appeared in the second edition of this book. F.L. Morton is a professor of political science at the University of Calgary.

● ● ● ● ● ● ● ● ● ●

INTRODUCTION
When the Charter of Rights and Freedoms was proclaimed in 1982, it had both critics and boosters. The latter held "Charter Day" celebrations and enthusiastically predicted the bold beginnings of a more just society in which individual and minority rights would be "guaranteed" by the courts. Critics gloomily predicted that the Charter would replace parliamentary supremacy with judicial supremacy, and thus mark an end to "responsible government" in Canada. With the benefit of eight years experience under the Charter, we can now see that both these claims were exaggerated. The impact of the Charter on Canadian society has been mixed, with both positive and negative developments. This article describes some of the more important Charter decisions and impacts since 1982, and then assesses their effect on Canadian politics.

I. CONTINUITY AND CHANGE
The Charter introduced three principal changes into the Canadian political system. First, it replaced (or at least qualified) parliamentary supremacy with constitutional supremacy. Second, it explicitly recognized the practice of judicial review—the role of the courts to interpret and enforce the Charter, and to refuse to enforce any statute that conflicts with the Charter. Third, unlike the 1960 Bill of Rights, the restrictions spelled out by the Charter apply to both levels of government, the provinces as well as the federal government.

Under parliamentary supremacy, final authority for all public policy matters—including the protection of civil liberties—rests with Parliament. Under a system of constitutional supremacy, the powers of both the legislature and the executive are restricted by written limitations, which are interpreted and enforced by the courts. Under the latter system a court may overrule the legislature and nullify a law, if it is found to violate a right protected in the constitution. This is not possible in a system of parliamentary supremacy.

The differences between parliamentary supremacy and constitutional supremacy are not as great as they first appear. Neither is nor ever was absolute. Just as parliamentary supremacy was limited by the norms of the "unwritten constitution," the charter's efficacy ultimately depends upon public opinion. The American experience with racial segregation until 1954—despite the constitutional guarantee of "equal protection of the laws"—tragically demonstrates that the existence of a Bill or Charter of Rights is no "guarantee" that rights will be respected. Under the Charter, as before, the ultimate protection of justice in Canadian society is still in the ethical quality of public opinion—the collective commitment of all Canadians to fair play and tolerance of diversity.

Notwithstanding the ultimate power of public opinion, the enhanced status of the Charter does have important practical consequences. Unlike the 1960 Bill of Rights, which was only a federal statute, the Charter is part of Canada's written constitution. The constitutional status of the Charter, combined with the explicit authorization of judicial interpretation and enforcement in section 24, meant that the Canadian courts would play a much more active and influential role in defining the meaning of the enumerated rights. The 1960 Bill of Rights did not explicitly authorize judicial review, and as a result Canadian judges proved to be very self restrained in its interpretation. No such ambiguity restrains Charter interpretation.

II. THE CHARTER AS A CATALYST FOR A NEW JUDICIAL ACTIVISM

One of the simplest measures of the Charter's impact is to compare the pre- and post-Charter decisions of the Supreme Court of Canada in civil liberties cases. The outcome of these decisions can be interpreted as tending toward judicial self-restraint or judicial activism. Judicial activism denotes a disposition of judges to broadly interpret rights and a corollary willingness to strike down statutes or exclude evidence in criminal cases. Judicial self-restraint denotes the opposite tendency: to interpret rights in a manner that avoids conflict with legislative decisions or interference with pre-trial police investigations. An activist court uses the power of judicial review to intervene and to influence the making and enforcement of laws. A self-restrained court tends to avoid such intervention.

By November, 1989, the Supreme Court had decided its first one hundred Charter cases. In 35 cases the individual litigant won; in 61 cases the Crown won; and there were 4 cases with no clear winner. This success ratio of 35 percent compares to a comparable ratio of only 15 percent (5 out of 34) under the 1960 Bill of Rights (1960-82). In its Charter decisions the Supreme Court has already declared invalid portions of 19 statutes, compared to just one such instance of judicial nullification under the Bill of Rights. The Supreme Court has also overruled several of its own Bill of Rights decisions in order to rule in favour of Charter litigants in similar cases. Together, the higher success rate, the larger number of nullifications, and the overruling of pre-Charter precedents are all indicators of a new era of judicial activism ushered in by the Charter.

III. IMPACT OF THE CHARTER ON PUBLIC POLICY

Judicial interpretation of the Charter is also changing various areas of public policy. The area most affected has been the Criminal Code and criminal law enforcement. The Supreme Court has given a broad interpretation to the legal rights enumerated in section 7-14 of the Charter, in effect creating a new code of acceptable police conduct. For example, the Supreme Court's interpretation of section 10(b)—the right to counsel—has had a major impact on policing. It has been interpreted to require police to immediately inform anyone they detain or arrest that they have the right to the assistance of counsel and the right not to speak until they obtain such assistance. Police have been told that they cannot persist in questioning suspects if they have asked for a lawyer, nor use tricks such as placing undercover agents in jail cells. If suspects are too intoxicated to understand the utility of the right to counsel, police must cease questioning until they sober up. If arrested persons say they want a lawyer but cannot afford one, the Court has said that section 10(b) requires the police to provide one. The cumulative effect of these decisions is to greatly decrease the likelihood of voluntary confessions or incriminating statements, since the first thing a lawyer tells a client is to say nothing to the police.

In a sharp reversal of pre-Charter practice, the Court has established a policy of excluding evidence from a trial if the police do not follow any of the new rules outlined above, no matter how good the evidence may be. This new "exclusionary rule" has forced the Crown to discontinue prosecution in thousands of criminal cases because of lack of sufficient evidence. The net effect of the Court's activism in this area has been to substantially enhance the procedural defenses of those accused of crimes—a result applauded by civil libertarians and defense lawyers. The cost has been a proportional decrease in the efficiency of law enforcement and crime control, a trend that worries others.

The Charter decision with the greatest policy impact to date has been the 1988 *Morgentaler* abortion decision. By a margin of 5-2, the Court ruled that the abortion law violated section 7 of the Charter, thus forcing the Mulroney government to deal with the politically charged abortion issue. The government struggled for more than two years to frame a new abortion policy. In June, 1990, after several failed attempts, the House of Commons in a free vote adopted Bill C-43, a compromise measure that leaves abortion in the Criminal code but allows therapeutic abortions when a pregnancy threatens the life or health of the mother. Bill C-43 abolishes the old requirement of committee approvals, and now leaves the determination of the threat to health to a woman and her doctor. In this respect, it closely follows the Dickson judgement in the *Morgentaler* decision.

A lesser known Charter case but one with a major policy impact was the 1985 *Singh* decision. *Singh* struck down the procedures for hearing applications for refugee status under the Immigration Act. It forced the government to provide a mandatory oral hearing for refugee applicants. This decision had the unintended consequences of creating a backlog of 124,000 refugee claimants; an amnesty for 15,000 claimants already in Canada; $179 million dollars in additional costs; and a new refugee law that some critics say is more unfair than the original one. The new refugee law took effect January 1, 1989. Eighteen months later, the government announced that the "new" Immigration and Refugee Board would quadruple its capacity to keep up with applications. This would allow the Board to hire an additional 280 public servants (to add to the present 496) at an additional cost of $20 million. This increase brings the annual budget of the new Board to $80 million.

Another major policy impact of the Charter has been in the area of Sunday-closing legislation. Directly overruling its own Bill of Rights precedent from 1962, the Supreme Court ruled in *Big M Drug Mart* (1985) that the federal Lord's Day Act enforced in Alberta violated the freedom of religion provision of the Charter. Two years later in its *Edwards Books* decision, the court upheld an Ontario Sunday-closing statute enacted for the explicitly secular purpose of a common day of rest. A majority of the Court rejected the argument that its effect was to violate the freedom of religion of non-Sunday sabbatarians whose religious beliefs required them to close on Saturday.

Despite the fact that its law was upheld, the Ontario government repealed the Sunday-closing provisions of its *Retail Holiday Act*, and substituted a local option for municipalities. In Alberta, the Lougheed government was reluctant to deal with what it regarded as an emotional, no win issue, and also left the problem to municipalities to handle on a local option basis. Critics say that while the local option policy sounds good in theory, it does not work in practice. When one community forces its merchants to close while a neighbouring community allows its retail stores to remain open, the retailers in the first community lose potential sales. Research suggests that the resulting economic pressure creates a "domino effect" that forces all municipalities to open, especially in urban corridors such as Oshawa-Toronto-Hamilton and Edmonton-Red Deer-Calgary. The result has been increasingly wide-open Sunday shopping in both provinces.

Another important area of public policy directly affected by a Charter decision was the conduct of federal elections. The Canada Elections Act placed strict limitations on independent "political action committee" expenditures in federal elections. Just prior to the 1984 national elections, the National Citizens' Coalition, a conservative public interest group, successfully challenged these provisions as a violation of the "freedom of expression" provision of the charter. While the demise of the law had little effect in the 1984 elections, the subsequently elected Conservative government never acted to plug the hole created by the decision. This became important during the November 1988 elections, which turned into a one-issue referendum on the Free Trade Agreement with the United States. The absence of any legal restrictions on non-party spending allowed pro-free-trade groups to spend millions of dollars on political advertising in the closing weeks of the campaign. This advertising blitz helped to reverse an eleventh-hour surge of anti-FTA sentiment and to re-elect Prime Minister Mulroney and his Tories. Thus a 1984 Court of Queen's Bench judge's interpretation of the Charter right to freedom of expression may have influenced the fate of the 1988 Free Trade Agreement, one of the most important decisions ever made by Canadians.

IV. IMPACT OF THE CHARTER ON INTEREST GROUP BEHAVIOUR

The most enduring impact of the Charter may be on the political process through the creation of a new forum for interest group activity. Historically Canadian interest groups have concentrated their lobbying activities at the cabinet and senior levels of the bureaucracy. Unlike their American counterparts, they avoid lobbying parliamentary committees and have rarely used litigation as a political tactic. This pattern of Canadian interest group activity is explained by the closed character of the Canadian policy-making process. Unlike the American separation of powers, in the parliamentary system there is very little opportunity to influence public policy in either parliamentary committees or in the courts. The tradition of parliamentary supremacy relegates the courts to a secondary political role and a more legalistic exercise of the judicial function. Interest groups accordingly concentrate their efforts at this single access point of the policy process. The adoption of the Charter of Rights has changed this situation by creating a new access point. Interest groups which fail to achieve their policy objectives through the traditional political party and bureaucratic channels can now turn to the courts.

Good examples of interest group success can be found in the area of minority language rights. English groups within Quebec and Francophones outside of Quebec have both used section 23 of the Charter to gain more favourable education policies from their respective provincial governments. As soon as the Charter was adopted, the Quebec Protestant School Board challenged the education provisions of Bill 101 in Quebec. Known as the "Charter of the French Language," the impugned sections of Bill 101 severely restricted access to English-language education in Quebec.

This policy was ruled an unconstitutional violation of section 23 by the Supreme Court. In its 1990 *Mahé* decision, the Supreme Court also ruled that section 23 entitled Francophones in Edmonton, Alberta, not just to separate French-language schools but also to administrative control over the instruction, curriculum, and buildings. The impact of the *Mahé* decision will extend far beyond Alberta because there are similar section 23 suits pending in most other English-speaking provinces that will now have to follow the *Mahé* precedent.

The most publicized instances of interest group use of the Charter have been the pro-choice and pro-life challenges to Canada's abortion law. Pro-choice groups spent over half a million dollars in legal fees to finance Dr. Henry Morgentaler's successful challenge, discussed above. Pro-life groups spent almost as much to support the Charter challenge of Joe Borowski, the tenacious ex-NDP cabinet minister from Winnipeg. Borowski argued that the existing abortion law was too permissive and violated the unborn child's right to life, as protected by section 7 of the Charter. Unfortunately for Borowski, his case arrived at the Supreme Court just nine months after the Court had struck down the abortion law in the Morgentaler case. The Court ruled that because there was no longer an abortion law to challenge, the Borowski case had become moot, and declined to answer the question of the rights of the unborn under the Charter.

The best organized interest group use of the Charter has been mounted by Canadian feminists. Feminists gained a headstart on other interest groups by successfully lobbying Parliament for favourable wording of the section 15 equality rights provisions while the Charter was still in draft stage. Soon after, the Canadian Advisory Council on the Status of Women commissioned a study that concluded with the adoption of the Charter, "we find ourselves at the opportune moment to stress litigation as a vehicle for social change." The study recommended the creation of a single, nationwide "legal action fund" to coordinate and pay for a policy for "systematic litigation" of strategic "test cases." On April 13, 1985, only days before the equality rights section of the Charter came into effect, the Women's Legal and Education Action Fund (LEAF) was launched. Its purpose is "to assist women with important test cases and to ensure that equality rights litigation for women is undertaken in a planned, responsible, and expert manner."

Since its inception, LEAF has raised more than a quarter of a million dollars from private sources and has received a million-dollar grant from the government of Ontario. It has also received funding from the federal Court Challenges Program. LEAF has participated in numerous Charter cases both as litigants and as interveners. It intervened successfully in both the *Borowski* and *Daigle* abortion cases. It also experienced success in cases involving a "boys only" hockey league in Ontario, the use of original surnames by married women, and the eligibility of natural fathers for "maternity" leave. Perhaps LEAF's most important achievement came in the Supreme Court's first major equality rights decision, *Andrews*, in which the Court adopted an interpretation of section 15 that favours "disadvantaged groups," precisely what LEAF had argued for. More than any other interest group, Canadian feminists have done their homework and are now poised to use Charter litigation to advance their policy objectives.

Interest group use of Charter litigation was encouraged by the Court Challenges Program announced in September 1985 by the federal government. The government allocated nine million dollars over five years to fund litigation arising under the equality rights, language rights, and multiculturalism provisions of the Charter. Applications for financial support are screened according to the criteria of "setting of social justice priorities . . . legal merit . . . [and] consequences for a number of people," in other words, for maximum policy impact. Selected cases are eligible for $35,000 at each stage of litigation—trial, provincial appeal court, and the Supreme Court of Canada. During its first five-year mandate, the Court Challenges Program funded 150 equality rights cases and 50 language rights cases, including the *Mahé* and *Quebec Protestant School Board* cases discussed above. In 1990 Parliament renewed the Court Challenges Program for another five years with funding in excess of $13 million dollars.

V. IMPACT OF THE CHARTER ON FEDERALISM
A second important impact of the Charter is its centralizing effect on Canadian federalism. Decisions about policy issues that were previously made by provincial governments sensitive to different regional particularities must now meet minimum national standards imposed by the Supreme Court's Charter decisions. Restrictions on Sunday shopping, on who can practice law in a province, and on the level of minority language education services are all areas that have been affected in this manner. This trend is likely to increase. The Charter is grounded in a universalistic logic—the idea that all people should enjoy equal rights regardless of where they live—and this discounts the value of local or regional difference. The trend toward homogenization is reinforced by the fact that the final meaning of the Charter is provided by a national supreme court that is much less responsive to local public opinion than are the ten provincial legislatures.

The Supreme Court struck down eleven provincial statutes and eight federal statutes in its first one hundred Charter decisions. While the quantitative impact of the Charter on the two levels of government has been roughly equal, there are some interesting qualitative differences. Seven of the eight nullifications of federal statutes were procedural in character; and with the important exception of abortion, the federal legislation overturned by the Court has not involved major policy concerns. By contrast, nine of the eleven nullifications of provincial statutes were substantive in character, and seven of them were based directly or indirectly on French-English minority language and education issues—a perennial source of conflict in Canadian politics.

Five provinces have lost legislation to Charter challenges: Quebec, British Columbia, Alberta, Saskatchewan, and Manitoba. Of the five, Quebec has been most affected. At the time the Charter was adopted, René Lévesque bitterly denounced section 23, which was clearly intended to strike down the education policy embedded in Bill 101. "No self-respecting Quebec government," he declared, "could ever abandon the smallest fraction of this fundamental right to protect the only French island in the English-speaking sea of the North American continent." Because section 23 is excluded from the scope of the section 33 legislative override, Quebec had no alternative but to accept the Court's decision.

Three years after the Protestant School Board case, the Supreme Court struck down another section of Bill 101—the "French only" requirement for public signs. Quebec Anglophones, especially the 650,000 living in Montreal, considered it oppressive and humiliating, and challenged it as a violation of the Charter right to freedom of expression. Quebec nationalists considered the "French only" rule essential to preserving the "French face" of Quebec, and harshly denounced the Supreme Court's decision. The Liberal government of Robert Bourassa—contrary to promises it had made to Anglophone voters in the 1985 election—gave in to nationalist sentiment and invoked the section 33 legislative override to reinstate the "French only" public signs policy. This override of the Supreme Court's decision infuriated many people in English Canada, and this negative reaction contributed to the subsequent defeat of the Meech Lake Accord.

In one sense, Quebec presents the clearest example of the counter-majoritarian character of judicial review, where the Court uses the Charter to protect the rights of a local minority against the local majority. From a different perspective, however, the same decisions, particularly in conjunction with the language-rights cases from Alberta, Manitoba, and Saskatchewan, show how the Charter, through the Supreme Court, can serve as a vehicle for imposing majority rule rather than restricting it. The catch is that what is being imposed is the will of a *national* political majority against what is deemed to be the perverse and unacceptable behaviour of regional majorities in Quebec or the West.

VI. EVALUATING THE CHARTER'S IMPACT

The judicial decisions and events described above are without precedent in Canadian politics, and would be virtually unthinkable without the advent of the Charter. Nor is there any doubt that this trend will continue. The volume of Charter litigation has swelled to over five hundred reported cases annually. In only eight years the Supreme Court decided one hundred Charter cases, almost triple the total number of Bill of Rights cases— 35—that it heard between 1960 and 1982. Charter decisions now account for approximately 25 percent of the Supreme Court's annual caseload and show no sign of decreasing. Equally important, this new style of Charter politics has the support of important elites, including the media, intellectuals, lawyers and the law schools, feminists, and other human rights groups. There can be no turning back the clock.

At the time of its adoption, Peter Russell described the principal impact of the Charter not so much as the creation of new rights, but rather a new way of making decisions about rights, in which the courts play a much more authoritative role. Decisions about public policy that were made by elected legislators and civil servants are now often reviewed and revised by judges. Russell described this change as the "judicialization of politics." The preceding sections have shown what the "judicialization of politics" has meant in practice. Now it is time to evaluate these changes.

Critiques of judicial policy-making through the exercise of judicial review can be conveniently classified under two headings. First there is the problem of institutional legitimacy: Should judges be allowed to overrule legislative policy decisions? The second is the problem of institutional capacity: Can judges make good policy? The question of the legitimacy of judicial review is an old one. People have long debated how in a democracy, in which legitimate authority is based on the consent of the governed, unelected, tenured-until-retirement judges can be allowed to overrule the policy decisions of elected, accountable legislatures and executives. The concern with institutional capacity is more recent. Conceding that judicial review makes some judicial policy-making inevitable, it focuses on the practical question of whether courts have the necessary equipment to make competent policy choices.

While the Charter was clearly intended to empower the Court to strike down offending statutes, it did not spell out the precise rules which should govern the judicial exercise of this awesome new power. Under what circumstances should unelected, unaccountable judges overrule the policy judgements of the democratically elected Parliament and provincial legislatures? There is an easy answer to this question: whenever Parliament or a provincial legislature makes a clear mistake and enacts a law that obviously violates the Charter. The problem is that the case of the "clear mistake–

obvious violation" is rare. Neither level of Canadian government is likely to enact laws that violate the core meaning of Charter rights, for which there is general consensus and support. Nor are individuals or groups likely to waste their money going to court to challenge statutes that clearly do not violate the core meaning of a right. The example of the "clear mistake" allows us to justify the judicial veto in theory but is rare in actual practice.

More common is the case which contests the peripheral meaning or outer limits of a Charter right. The Morgentaler and Borowski cases are both typical examples. No fair person can reasonably claim that the right to abortion for the mother or the right to life for the foetus/unborn is *clearly* included in section 7 of the Charter. The text, its legislative history, and past practice all dictate otherwise. But at the same time, no one can reasonably deny that such meanings might be implied by the broadly worded rights to "life, liberty and security of the person." That is, it is plausible to interpret section 7 as including either of these specific rights as falling within its outer limits.

To say that Morgentaler's or Borowski's Charter claims are plausible, however, is not to say that a judge should accept them and declare the abortion law invalid. It is a matter of personal opinion, an issue over which reasonable people can reasonably disagree. But if it is essentially a matter of opinion and not a "clear mistake," why should the opinion of several unelected judges take precedence over the collective judgement of democratically elected representatives of the people? To do so risks placing the Court above Parliament and undermining Canadian democracy.

The anti-democratic character of judicial review under the Charter can be minimized or maximized by two factors. The first is the way in which judges exercise their new power. Do they limit their use of the judicial veto to cases in which there is a "clear mistake-obvious violation"? If they do, it is hard to pin the "anti-democratic" label on the decision. They are merely enforcing the clear mandate of the constitution. Those who do not like the decision can direct their criticism at the constitution, not the court.

Another way in which the courts can minimize the anti-democratic character of judicial review is by basing a decision to strike down a law on the narrowest possible reasoning. The Supreme Court's abortion decisions—or non-decisions—are again a good example of this. In the *Morgentaler* decisions, all the judges except Justice Wilson avoided dealing with the claim that the Charter creates any new rights to abortion. The two dissenters said the Charter did not—and therefore the Court should not—even address the abortion issue. But the other four judges in the majority, while they struck down the law, did so for relatively narrow, procedural reasons, thereby leaving Parliament a great deal of room to craft a new abortion policy. When Mr. Borowski arrived nine months later, the Court invoked the mootness doctrine to avoid addressing the question of the unborn child's right to life under the Charter, thereby leaving Parliament free to take the first step on this issue.

Interest group use of litigation as a political tactic is the other obvious threat to Canadian democracy posed by the Charter. If interest groups which lose in the traditional arenas of electoral and legislative politics can run to the courts, invoke the Charter, and have their political defeats turned into victories by the courts—in the absence of a "clear mistake–obvious violation"—the integrity of Canadian democracy would clearly be eroded.

Whether this occurs depends in part on the zeal and skill with which interest groups use the Charter, but ultimately on how the Supreme Court exercises its discretion. To date, the Supreme Court has by and large rebuffed invitations to overturn—or preempt—the policy outcomes of the normal political-legislative process. It has sidestepped the principal Charter claims of both sides of the abortion issue. It has refused invitations by labour unions to constitutionalize the "right to strike." On the other hand, the Court has accepted interest group invitations to intervene in the Sunday shopping controversy and even more so in the area of minority language rights. Also in *Andrews*, its only major equality rights decision, the Court gave a very expansive definition of equality that has encouraged groups like LEAF to think that they can win policy change through litigation.

The other major concern with judicial policy-making under the Charter concerns the ability of courts to make policy choices. The judicial process, with its strict rules against hearsay evidence and preference for sworn testimony, is not organized to deal with public input and political accommodation. Nor do courts have the authority to follow up policy decisions or revise them if necessary. The judicial process tends to have a narrow focus. It is preoccupied with the rights and duties of the litigants, and often misses the interconnectedness of social problems and policy. A change in one area of social relationships is likely to cause unintended changes in related areas. These unintended consequences may create new problems worse than the original. These are all familiar problems for students of public policy, but are hardly typical judicial considerations.

A good example of the potential downside of judicial policy-making can be found in some of the Supreme Court's legal rights decisions. As outlined above, the Court has used this section of the Charter to write a new code of police conduct in the pre-trial stages of the criminal process. While these decisions have been applauded by some for expanding the rights of the accused, there is no doubt that cumulatively they have made the investigative and evidence-gathering work of the police less efficient. From a policy-maker's perspective, the advantages should be weighed against the disadvantages, but the judicial preoccupation with "rights" makes these concerns secondary.

Another example of the pitfalls of judicial policy-making can be found in the Court's approach to the Sunday-shopping controversy. The Court has insisted on treating this controversy as a freedom of religion issue, when religion is clearly only one—and perhaps not the most important—issue at stake. The corporate character of the litigants strongly suggests that commercial interests are also very much in play. Outside the courtroom, the secular character of the Sunday-closing dispute is reflected in the political coalitions that have formed in both Alberta and Ontario to contest the issue. While church groups are part of the pro-Sunday-closing coalition, its real political strength comes from organized labour and smaller, family-owned businesses. Likewise, shopping mall owners and chain stores, not non-Christian merchants, are the most powerful supporters of the wide-open Sunday shopping.

The broader evidence suggests that the principal dispute is not over a freedom of religion issue but a socio-economic or "quality of life" issue. Do the economic advantages of a seven-day retail shopping week outweigh the social advantages of a uniform day of rest where all members of a family—especially in an era of two-income and single-parent families—can be together? What about the freedom of religion of employees and families who own stores in malls? How—and who—is to balance their freedom of religion against that of management?

While there are plausible arguments both for and against Sunday-closing laws, the issue is not simply a question of freedom of religion. Yet this is how the Court has treated it, a predictable consequence of the narrow rights-oriented focus of the judicial process and the ability of litigants to successfully exploit the "tunnel vision" character of the judicial process.

The *Singh* decision is a good example of the unintended consequences of judicial policy-making and of the Court's inability to do anything about them. In requiring the government to add an oral hearing to the refugee determination process, the Court thought that it was improving the plight of applicants. Instead, under the revised law, while there is now a right to a hearing, it is much more difficult for potential refugees to get into Canada to exercise this right. In addition, the hearing provision has required hiring hundreds of new civil servants at a cost of several hundred million dollars. Policy-makers other than judges would have anticipated these costs and weighed them against the putative advantage of adding an oral hearing to the process.

VII. CONSTITUTIONAL SUPREMACY WITHOUT JUDICIAL SUPREMACY

The Charter of Rights has proven to be a mixed blessing, with both positive and negative political impact. The negatives associated with the judicialization of politics should not be allowed to obscure the positive potential of the Charter as a readily available check on police excesses and abuses, heavy-handed government bureaucrats, and overzealous or malevolent political majorities.

Nor are the dangers inherent in the judicialization of politics inevitable consequences of the Charter. As the examples illustrate, they result from judicial fallibility. In some cases judges will be perceived as striking a statesmanlike balance between private interest and public interest, and in some they will fail. The Supreme Court of Canada can exercise its final appellate jurisdiction to correct the Charter "mistakes" of lower courts. But what if the Supreme Court makes a Charter decision that is clearly deleterious to the public interest? A Chief Justice of the American Supreme Court once said that his court was "not final because it was infallible, but infallible because it was final." Is the same now true of the Supreme Court of Canada?

Happily, the answer is no. Constitutional supremacy is not the same as judicial supremacy. While primary responsibility for Charter interpretation is vested in the courts, this does not mean that the courts should or do have the final say on all questions of constitutional policy. While the rule of law obliges the other branches of government to comply with the decision of the Supreme Court in any particular case, democratic principles prohibit nine, non-elected, tenured judges from setting permanent constitutional policy, especially where the Charter meaning is ambiguous and the public policy impact is undesirable.

Section 33 of the Charter provides a potential remedy for judicial fallibility of this magnitude. If a court rules that a statute is void because it violates the Charter, section 33 allows Parliament or a provincial legislature to re-enact the statute by inserting an additional clause stating that it shall take effect "notwithstanding" the relevant section of the Charter. Section 33 is commonly referred to as the "legislative override" power, because it allows a government to override a judicial interpretation of the Charter that it thinks is too harmful to the public interest.

Section 33 has been used sparingly to date. The Alberta government threatened to use it to protect the anti-strike clause of its public employees act, but never had to, as the courts subsequently upheld the act. The Saskatchewan government attached the notwithstanding clause to a back-to-work law in order to protect it from an earlier Court of Appeal precedent. This precedent was subsequently overturned by the Supreme Court, rendering Saskatchewan's use of the override unnecessary. Quebec, however, has used the section 33 power to shield itself from the impact of the Charter. To protest the adoption of the Charter without its consent, the Parti Québécois government of René Lévesque routinely attached a "notwithstanding" clause to all Quebec laws, past and present. This practice was discontinued in 1986 by the new Liberal government of Robert Bourassa. However, the Bourassa government used section 33 to reinstate the "French only" Public Signs law in 1988 after it had been declared invalid by the Supreme Court. Bourassa's use of the override was very popular among French Quebeckers, but strongly condemned by most English-speaking Canadians.

Civil libertarian enthusiasts and the media have portrayed section 33 in a very negative light, as undermining or "gutting" the Charter. This criticism is overstated, as it rests on two false assumptions: that judges are infallible and that the meaning of Charter rights is self-evident and widely agreed upon. The infallibility of judges need hardly be commented on. As to the second proposition, it suffices to say that almost no Charter cases involve clear conflicts between rights and wrongs, but rather questions of where to draw the outer limits on the application of traditional rights in new contexts. Section 33 is more accurately described as a form of "legislative review of judicial review." Just as judicial review serves as a check on a certain kind of legislative mistake, so legislative review serves as a check on judicial error. Also, when used by a provincial government as in the Quebec Public Signs Case, section 33 can be used to protect provincial rights against the centralist tendency of the Charter.

What the critics of section 33 are trying to say is that it is open to abuse, which is certainly true. But what they ignore is that a government that abuses its section 33 power to violate clearly defined and widely recognized rights must face the ultimate check in a democracy—the judgement of the voters. In this light, section 33 can be seen as avoiding the American dilemma of allowing constitutional supremacy to degenerate into judicial supremacy. Rather it places responsibility for observing constitutional rights on legislatures as well as the courts, thus creating a legislative-judicial partnership, the final outcome of which the people shall judge.

Acknowledgments

Peter Bachrach and Morton S. Baratz, "Two Faces of Power" in Henry S. Kariel ed., *Frontiers of Democratic Theory*. (New York: Random House, 1970). Originally published in the *American Political Science Review* 56 (Dec. 1962): 947-52 (abridged). Reprinted by permission of the authors.

Stephen F. Cohen, from "Gorbachev and the Soviet Reformation" in Stephen F. Cohen and Katrina vanden Heuvel, *Voices of Glasnost: Interviews with Gorbachev's Reformers*. (New York: W.W. Norton & Company, 1989), pp. 13-32. Reprinted by permission of W.W. Norton & Company, Inc. Copyright © 1989 by Stephen F. Cohen and Katrina vanden Heuvel.

Bernard Crick, from "Politics" in *In Defence of Politics*, second edition. (Chicago: University of Chicago Press, 1972), pp. 15-34 (abridged). Reprinted by permission of the University of Chicago Press and George Weidenfeld & Nicolson Limited.

Richard Crossman, from *Myths in Cabinet Government*. (Cambridge, Mass.: Harvard University Press, 1972), pp. 41-69 (abridged). Reprinted by permission of the publishers.

Roger Gibbins and Neil Nevitte, from "Canadian Political Ideology: A Comparative Analysis" in *Canadian Journal of Political Science* 18 (1985): 577-98.

Thomas Hill Green, from "Lecture on Liberal Legislation and Freedom of Contract," in *The Works of Thomas Hill Green*, ed., R.L. Nettleship. (London, 1885-88), vol. 3, pp. 365-386.

Thomas Hobbes, from *Leviathan*, printed in *The English Works of Thomas Hobbes*, ed., Sir William Molesworth. (London, 1839), chapter 17. Orthography modernized following *Hobbes Selections*, ed. Frederick J.E. Woodbridge (New York: Charles Scribner's Sons, 1930), pp. 335-340.

Gad Horowitz, from "Conservatism, Liberalism and Socialism in Canada: An Interpretation," *Canadian Journal of Economics and Political Science* 32 (1966): 143-170. Reprinted by permission of the author.

Arend Lijphart, from "Consociational Democracy" in Kenneth McCrae ed., *Consociational Democracy: Political Accommodation in Segmented Societies*.

(Toronto: McClelland and Stewart, 1974), pp. 70-97. Originally published in *World Politics* 21 (1969): 207-55. Reprinted by permission of the author.

Juan J. Linz, from "An Authoritarian Regime: Spain" in *Mass Politics: Studies in Political Sociology*, eds., Erik Allardt and Stein Rokkan (New York: Free Press, 1970), pp. 251-71 (abridged). Reprinted from *Cleavages, Ideologies and Party Systems*, eds., Erik Allardt and Yrjo Littunen (Helsinki: The Westermarck Society, 1964). Reprinted by permission of Erik Allardt.

Karl Marx and Friedrich Engels, *Manifesto of the Communist Party*, trans. Samuel Moore. (London, 1888), section 1.

John Meisel, from "The Decline of Party in Canada" in Hugh Thorburn ed., *Party Politics in Canada*, 5th ed. (Scarborough, Ont.: Prentice-Hall, Canada, 1979), pp. 98-114 (abridged). Reprinted by permission of the publishers.

John Stuart Mill, from *On Liberty* as reprinted in *Utilitarianism and Other Writings*. (Cleveland: Meridian Books, 1962), pp. 135-38, 205-207.

Hans J. Morgenthau, from "Realism" in *Politics Among Nations: The Struggle for Power and Peace*, 4th edition, 3-14 (abridged). Copyright 1948, 1954, © 1960, 1967 by Alfred A. Knopf, Inc. Reprinted by permission of the publisher.

Benito Mussolini, from *Enciclopedia Italiana* 14 (1932), and translated in Ion S. Munro, *Through Fascism to World Power: A History of the Revolution in Italy*. (Freeport, N.Y.: Books for Libraries Press, 1971; reprint of 1933 edition), pp. 302-309.

Neil Nevitte, Herman Bakvis, and Roger Gibbins, from "The Ideological Contours of 'New Politics' in Canada: Policy, Mobilization and Partisan Support" in the *Canadian Journal of Political Science* 17 (1989): 475-503.

Michael Oakeshott, from "On Being Conservative," in *Rationalism in Politics* (London: Methuen, 1962), pp. 168-196 (abridged). Reprinted by permission of the author's estate.

Mancur Olson, from "The Logic" in *The Rise and Decline of Nations: Economic Growth, Stagflation, and Social Rigidities*. (New Haven, Conn.: Yale University Press, 1982), pp. 17-35 (abridged). Reprinted by permission of the publishers.

Justice Ivan Rand, from *Roncarelli v. Duplessis* (1954), 16 D.L.R., second edition, 696-709 (abridged).

Ernest Renan, from "What is a Nation?" in *Poetry of the Celtic Races and Other Essays*. (New York: Kennikut Press, 1896), pp. 61-83 (abridged).

Richard Rose, from *The Problem of Party Government*, Pelican edition. (Middlesex, England: Penguin Books, 1976), pp. 90-108 (abridged). Reprinted by permission of Macmillan, London and Basingstoke.

Walter A. Rosenbaum, from "The Meaning of Political Culture," in *Political Culture*. (New York: Praeger Publishers, 1975), pp. 3-33. Reprinted by permission of Greenwood Publishing Group, Inc., Westport, CT.

Garth Stevenson, from *Unfulfilled Union: Canadian Federalism and National Unity*, 3rd ed. (Agincourt: Gage Publishing, 1989), pp. 1-19 (abridged). Copyright © Gage Educational Publishing Company. Used by permission of the author and publisher.

Leonard Tivey, from the Introduction to *The Nation-State: The Formation of Modern Politics*. Published by Martin Robertson, 1981, pp. 1-9 (abridged). Reprinted by permission of Basil Blackwell Ltd and the author.

Douglas Verney, from *Analysis of Political Systems*. (London: Routledge and Kegan Paul, 1959; New York: The Free Press of Glencoe, 1959), pp. 17-56 (abridged). Reprinted by permission of the publishers.

Max Weber, from *Wirtschaft and Gesellschaft*, H.H. Gerth and G. Wright, trans., in *From Max Weber: Essays in Sociology* (New York: Oxford University Press, 1958), pp. 196-244 (abridged). Reprinted by permission of the publisher.

K.C. Wheare, from *Legislatures*, 2nd ed. (New York: Oxford University Press, 1968), pp. 147-57 (abridged). Reprinted by permission of Oxford University Press.